Paul J. Hallinan

First Archbishop of Atlanta

Paul J. Hallinan

First Archbishop of Atlanta

by

Thomas J. Shelley

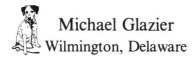 Michael Glazier
Wilmington, Delaware

About the Author

Rev. Thomas J. Shelley holds a doctorate in Church History from Catholic University and is on the staff of St. Joseph's Seminary in Dunwoodie, N.Y.

First published in 1989 by Michael Glazier, Inc., 1935 West Fourth Street, Wilmington, Delaware 19805.

Library of Congress Cataloging-in-Publication Data

Shelley, Thomas J.
    The life of Archbishop Paul Hallinan/ by Thomas J. Shelley.
       p.   cm.
    Bibliography: p.
    Includes index.
    ISBN 0-89453-768-7
    1. Hallinan, Paul J. 2. Catholic Church—United States—Bishops—
Biography.   I. Title.
BX4705.H236S53   1989
282′ .092′4—dc19
[B]   89-30674
                               CIP

Typography by Phyllis Boyd LeVane   B
Printed in the United States of America

UT DILIGATIS INVICEM

Contents

Foreword

"The first lesson of Newman's life is that of a great effort to recover the full Christian truth and to present it in all its primitive attractiveness."[1] *Mutatis mutandis,* these words of Charles Stephen Dessain can be fittingly applied to the life of Paul Hallinan. From his boyhood days in Painesville, Ohio, to his death in Atlanta, Georgia, at the relatively early age of fifty-seven, the mind of this highly articulate and active man seemed to be focused on drawing the maximum number of human beings whom he met along life's journey to an acceptance of Christian truth, so that they might benefit, as he had, from that source of inspiration and support. His natural verve and enthusiasm in that regard were deepened and enlivened with his appointment in 1946 as chaplain of the Newman Club of Cleveland College. Throughout the remainder of his life John Henry Newman continued to be a prime influence in shaping Paul Hallinan's thought and conduct.

My initial contact with the subject of this biography came in March, 1955, when a letter arrived containing the question, "May I take the liberty of asking your help in a matter relating to American history?"[2] From that time on to within a few months before he died our exchange of correspondence was frequent with occasional meetings along the way. If at the outset a mutual interest in American Catholic history was the bond that drew us together, the relationship expanded beyond professional interests as I came to admire increasingly the future archbishop's extraordinary combination of gifts—his dedication to the true and to the real in life, his openness to every new approach that his critical mind found of sound quality while remaining loyal to all that was of enduring value in the old, his sharp intelligence, and his engaging sense of humor with a marked ability to laugh at himself.

In a word, here was a finely balanced life that showed unfailingly a courageous and critical attitude toward the unworthy, the shoddy, and the tasteless, yet remained singularly free from revealing toward others a meanness of spirit, condescension, or a self-serving purpose. That same balance prevented Paul Hallinan from lending comfort to extremists of any variety as, for example, when in 1967 he told his Georgia Catholics:

> Those who nostalgically look back at a church whose note was immobility, whose language was obscure, whose altars were ornaments are not on the right path. Those who carelessly seek the new, without regard to the sacred tradition that was so dear to the man they call their patron, Pope John XIII, will not find a refreshed, revitalized faith.[3]

If the lives of the common run of humankind seldom rise above that of routine, such was surely not the case with this lively man. Scarcely had he become accustomed to one form of activity than another of a quite different character opened before him. Thus with studies at the University of Notre Dame and Saint Mary's Seminary in Cleveland behind him, the young priest's five years in the parochial ministry gave way to service as an army chaplain in the Pacific during World War II. There then followed a decade or more as chaplain to Catholic students in secular colleges until 1958 when he was named Bishop of Charleston and after four years in South Carolina there came the appointment as first Archbishop of Atlanta. In no one of these varied tasks was he other than successful, a statement that I will let stand without further elaboration, for I am conscious of how much he disliked flattery, a sentiment shared by his biographer.

The success that marked Hallinan's career was due in no small measure to his open and cheerful approach. As he told an audience at Notre Dame in 1962, "Only a man who is devoid of Christian hope can look at the world today and throw up his hands. Only a philosophy that is drained of all meaning can find expression today in a shudder or worse, a tired yawn."[4] That same buoyant spirit carried him through every challenge he encountered, as it did when this northern-born churchman took over his new post in the deep South at a time when the ideal of racial justice was far from being universally accepted and observed. That was evident in the forthright affirmation spoken on the day of his installation as Archbishop of

Atlanta when he declared:

> Small in numbers but great in loyalty, our Catholic people are trying to reflect the unity of Christ's Mystical Body as they move toward the reality of full racial justice, with prudence, with courage, with determination.[5]

If those words sound relatively mild today they were not so in that time and place. One might say they were the measure of the man, for the same courage and determination characterized his outstanding contribution to the heated debates on the liturgy during Vatican Council II, to his furtherance of Christian education of all levels, in fact, to every undertaking on which he set his heart and mind.

These and other salient features of Paul Hallinan's career are described in detail by Father Shelley in this engaging biography, a work that embodies the results of thorough archival research, a command of the printed sources, and a series of personal interviews with friends and acquaintances of the archbishop. If the gradual unfolding of Hallinan's life brought to Thomas Shelley a deepening appreciation of his moral and intellectual stature and his notable qualities of leadership, that appreciation was not permitted to exlude mention of certain weaknesses, such as the archbishop's occasional impetuous judgments or a tendency now and then to believe that matters were as good as he thought they were, or as he hoped they would turn out to be. The Paul Hallinan I knew well would have asked for nothing less than this critical and realistic appraisal. Moreover, he would have been gratified by his biographer's clarity of expression, a quality he sought and achieved in his own writings, an added attraction of this thoroughly readable work.

The constant stream of biographies of Americans of every walk of life—statesmen, artists, literary figures, business executives, and educators—bears impressive witness to the reading public's taste for history in this form. The same can be said for notable leaders in the world of religion where biography not only informs but often offers inspiration as well for the things of the spirit. Paul Hallinan's life span embraced an era of radical, even revolutionary, change in both Church and State, and his intense interest in all that was going on around him thrust him into the swirling currents of his time. That uncommon zest for life on the move, so to speak, almost invariably produced positive results, for even the involvement in secular under-takings did not seriously detract from his priestly character, nor did that involvement cause lasting embarrassment in either the civic or the ecclesiastical realm where he meant to serve.

Archbishop Hallinan had a profound respect for the past without having succumbed to the temptation of the antiquarian who may be said to venerate the past for its own sake. He studied history at John Carroll University and Western Reserve University, earning a doctorate at the latter while carrying out the duties of an active archbishop, an achievement unprecedented either before or since in the nearly two centuries since the founding of an episcopal hierarchy in this country. Both in his role as an historian and as a churchman he fulfilled the ideal once expressed by the famous English historian, David Knowles, when he pictured the historian in these words:

> As he watches, he looks to see whether a man, by and large during his life, shows any evidence of acting according to a divine or moral law outside himself, whether he ever sacrifices his own profit or pleasure for the sake of a person or a principle; whether he shows evidence of loving other men, where by love we understand the classical definition of wishing them well and doing well to them; whether he puts justice before expediency; whether he is sincere and truthful.[6]

John Tracy Ellis
Professorial Lecturer in Church History
The Catholic University of America

Acknowledgements

History has not been kind to Paul Hallinan. His reputation faded quickly after his death, and few American Catholics today would recognize his name or be able to identify any contribution which he made to American Catholicism. This author has not been able to find a single reference to him in the Catholic press in the past eighteen years. Part of the neglect is understandable, since many of the issues with which he was identified have ceased to be issues: the liturgical changes have been implemented; ecumenism is a recognized part of Catholic life; the civil rights movement has largely achieved its goals; and the Vietnam war is only a memory. However, it still seems odd that someone who figured so prominently in defining a Catholic position on these issues should be so completely forgotten today.

There was nothing in Hallinan's early life to indicate that he would become one of the most progressive figures in the American hierarchy. As a young priest he shared the intellectual narrowness and rigidity of most of his clerical contemporaries, but he had an open and inquiring mind. Under the impact of Newman work, his graduate studies at Western Reserve University, and especially, the Second Vatican Council, he developed and refined his views on many points, and he gave a warm welcome to the *aggiornamento* announced by Pope John XXIII. As a bishop he was generally regarded as a liberal, but he could with equal justice be regarded as a moderate conservative, for he was essentially a centrist, with an instinctive aversion for extremists on both the right and the left.

I am grateful to Monsignor John Tracy Ellis, for suggesting this topic to me in the first place and for his generous help and encouragement at every stage of research and writing. I also wish to thank Fathers Gerald P. Fogarty, S.J., and Robert Trisco for the benefit of their comments. I owe a special debt to my bishop, John Cardinal O'Connor, whose interest in church history made it possible for me to study at the Catholic University of America and to have the necessary time to write this book.

Many people gave me invaluable assistance in the course of my research. Joseph Cardinal Bernardin allowed me to use Archbishop Hallinan's diaries and other papers in his possession, and he clarified many aspects of Hallinan's life for me in a lengthy interview. Father Theodore Marszal, the adminstrator of the Cathedral of St. John the Evangelist in Cleveland, Ohio, gave me complete access to his extensive collection of Hallinan Papers and, on several occasions, offered me the hospitality of his rectory. Bishop Anthony M. Pilla of Cleveland, Bishop Ernest L. Unterkoefler of Charleston and Archbishop Thomas A. Donnellan of Atlanta permitted me to use their respective diocesan archives. Monsignor Frederick R. McManus gave me the benefit of his firsthand knowledge of Hallinan's work on the liturgy; John Cardinal Krol and John Cardinal Dearden shared with me their personal recollections of the archbishop; Mrs. Clare McIvor and Miss Agnes Lynch, first cousins of Archbishop Hallinan, gave me detailed information about his parents and family background.

Several archivists went well beyond the call of duty or courtesy in helping me to locate important materials; I am particularly grateful to Ms. Christine Krosel, Director of Archives of the Diocese of Cleveland; Dr. Anthony Zito, Archivist of the Catholic University of America; Dr. Warren Willis, Archivist of the United States Catholic Conference; and Mr. Richard Boylan of the National Archives of the United States.

I also wish to thank Mr. Peter J. Lysy, Assistant Archivist of the University of Notre Dame; Father Theodore Marszal, administrator of St. John's Cathedral, Cleveland; Sister Marguerita Smith, O.P., Archivist of the Archdiocese of New York; Sister Mary Laurent Duggan, C.S.J., Chancery Administrator of the Diocese of Savannah; Ms. Nora Lee Pollard, Archivist of the Diocese of Baton Rouge; Father William C. Burn, Archivist of the Diocese of

Charleston; Monsignor Charles H. Rowland, Chancellor of the Diocese of Charleston; Monsignor Thomas R. Duffy, Vicar General of the Diocese of Charleston; Monsignor Noel Burtenshaw, Director of Communications of the Archdiocese of Atlanta; Mrs. Sally K. Grubbs, former secretary to Archbishop Hallinan; Mr. and Mrs.John Maloney of Rocky River, Ohio; Monsignor Daniel F. Hoye, General Secretary of the United States Catholic Conference; Father John Gurrieri, Executive Secretary of the Bishops' Committee on the Liturgy; Mr. John Page, Executive Secretary of the International Commission on English in the Liturgy; Ms. Elayne Browne, Director of Medical Records, St. Joseph's Hospital, Atlanta, Georgia; Mr. John Wilson, United States Army Center of Military History, Washington, D.C.; Dr. William C. Baldwin, Historical Division, Office of the Chief of Engineers, United States Army, Fort Belvoir, Virginia; Monsignor Ralph Wiatrowski, Chancellor of the Diocese of Cleveland; Father Peter M. Mihalic, St. Mary Our Lady of the Lake Seminary, Cleveland, Ohio; Sister Ellen Gaffney, R.D.C., Archbishop Corrigan Memorial Library, St. Joseph's Seminary, Dunwoodie, Yonkers, New York; Monsignor Edwin F. O'Brien, Rector of St. Joseph's Seminary, Dunwoodie, Yonkers, New York; and Father John T. Monaghan, Cardinal Spellman High School, Bronx, New York.

Last but not least, I deeply appreciate the assistance of Mr. Joseph G.E. Hopkins, a stellar member of that dwindling fraternity of competent and dedicated editors, who read the entire manuscript. His eagle eye and unfailing good judgment saved me from many blunders.

Thomas J. Shelley
June 8, 1988

1

Painesville

John Gunther once described Ohio as "a giant carpet of agriculture studded by great cities."[1] Paul Hallinan spent most of his adult life in the largest of these cities as a priest of the Diocese of Cleveland, but his roots went back to one of the prettiest parts of Ohio's agricultural carpet, to the little community of Painesville, located in the heart of picturesque Lake County. Although Painesville is only thirty miles east of Cleveland, at the turn of the century it was the smallest city in the smallest county in the state, and, when Paul was born there on April 8, 1911, it was still only a "city" of some 5,500 people.[2]

To this day the rural charm of Painesville presents a striking contrast to the urban sprawl of Cleveland. Painesville resembles nothing so much as a New England village which Yankee ingenuity has somehow transplanted to the shores of Lake Erie. In fact, that is precisely what happened. Painesville is located in the former Western Reserve of Connecticut, which once stretched for 150 miles along the southern shore of Lake Erie in a belt fifty miles wide, the portion of the old Northwest Territory which Connecticut retained when it ceded the rest of its Western land claims to the federal government in 1786. Settlement began ten years later under the auspices of the Connecticut Land Company, which persuaded many New Englanders to seek their fortune in the West. One of them was General Edward Paine, who arrived in the Western Reserve in 1800 and established a settlement on the banks of the Grand River near the present site of the city that bears his name.[3]

Growth was slow but steady, and in 1832 Painesville became an incorporated town. In 1840 it was selected as the county seat of the newly formed Lake County, and in 1902 Painesville unexpectedly became a city, when the state legislature passed a law automatically conferring the status on any municipality of more than 5,000 people. (In the 1900 census Painesville reported 5,024 people.)[4]

Throughout the nineteenth century northeastern Ohio retained strong traces of its New England heritage. A native son, James A. Garfield, said in 1873: "There are townships on this Western Reserve which are more thoroughly New England in character and spirit than most of the towns of the New England of today."[5] Seventy years later the supervisor of the Ohio Writers Project of the WPA noticed the same phenomenon. "Through all the years of change," he said, "in perhaps a more unqualified way ... than other counties in Northeastern Ohio, Lake County [has] kept the New England character that shaped its early life."[6]

The visitor to the older towns notices at once the physical resemblance with New England. Many of the communities were laid out around a village green or public square, flanked by a high-steepled Congregational church on one side and a Greek-revival city hall or court house on the other side. Such is downtown Painesville today. After the Civil War, when the inevitable monuments to the Union Army began to appear on every village green, Painesville outdid most of its neighbors with a huge granite column commemorating the role of the volunteers from Lake County in several important engagements, including the battle of Atlanta. Concern with education was another New England legacy. Oberlin was consciously patterned after a New England college town, and Painesville had its own girls' academy as early as 1859, the Lake Erie Female Seminary (later Lake Erie College), inspired by Mary Lyon's experiment in women's education at Mt. Holyoke College.[7]

In politics the New England influence was also apparent. The Western Reserve was a hotbed, first for Whigs, then for Free Soilers, abolitionists, and radical Republicans; and, long after the Civil War, attachment to the Republican Party remained strong in Painesville and environs. The *enfant terrible* of Reconstruction politics, Senator Ben Wade, made his home in neighboring Ashtabula County. William McKinley was born in 1843 in Niles, forty-five miles southwest of Painesville. The farm from which Garfield ran his Presidential campaign of 1880 was (and is) located in Mentor, a few miles west of

Painesville. Not until the early decades of the twentieth century did Republican strength begin to wane when industrialization and immigration brought many newcomers to the Western Reserve. In Fairport Harbor, a few miles above Painesville, the population was eighty-five percent foreign born by 1940, and most of them were staunch Democrats.[8] The nineteenth Congressional District, once represented by Garfield and considered one of the safest Republican seats in the country, never elected a Republican to Congress between 1934 and 1976.[9]

Painesville, however, remained largely untouched by the economic development that transformed sleepy Fairport Harbor and other towns into busy industrial and commercial centers. Even the advent of the electric interurban in 1896, which provided easy and inexpensive access to Cleveland, failed to change the character of Painesville. It remained a small, neat, prosperous community, deriving its income mainly from the dairy industry and truck farms, the orchards and nurseries of Lake County. The largest industry in the city was the Coe Company, manufacturers of veneer-making machinery, and in the 1920's the total payroll of the company did not exceed fifty workers. The population for the most part consisted of middle-class home-owners, overwhelmingly native-born (86.8% in 1922), predominantly Protestant and Republican, and intensely conservative, so much so that the large Cleveland banks had to conduct educational campaigns to convince people of the soundness of home mortgages.[10]

This was the Painesville where Paul Hallinan was born in 1911, a community of tree-lined streets, manicured lawns and comfortable homes, where the Painesville band gave free weekly concerts during the summer at the music pavillion in the public square. It was the embodiment of self-reliant, small-town America in the confident years before the First World War. "Painesville: The Prettiest Little City in the United States" was the motto which the *Telegraph-Republican* carried under its masthead for some months in 1914.

Three "steam" railroads and an interurban line connected Painesville with the rest of the world, and a trolley car ran from the New York Central depot to the court house on the public square. Within the city limits there were six churches, five public schools, two hotels, two banks, St. Mary's parochial school, Lake Erie College, a Salvation Army post, and a YMCA building which made the clever claim that it had "the most floor space and the best equipment in proportion to the population of any city in the world."[11] A local booster waxed lyrical about the prospects of the area in an illustrated history of the county published in the year after Paul's birth. "Of the twelve counties in the state comprising the Western Reserve," he said, "Lake is the smallest in area, the fairest to look upon, and the richest in resources."

> Here are meadows, moors, groves, plains, graceful knolls, rugged ridges, ravines, gorges, bold hills and gentle slopes. There are gushing springs of sparkling water and murmuring brooks, placid pools, rushing rivers, and in the distance, the vast blue waters of Lake Erie breaking against the sanded and scalloped shores.[12]

Although the Catholic community in Painesville was small, it was well established by the year of young Hallinan's birth. In the 1830's Irish immigrants had come to Ohio to dig the canals and build the railroads. A few of them settled in Painesville, a village of 1200 inhabitants in 1837. In the 1840's it was customary for a priest to come from Cleveland three or four times a year to say Mass for the Catholics in private homes. One of the them, Father Peter McLaughlin, usually traveled by boat and in 1842 he found six or seven Catholic families in Painesville. In 1850 Painesville received its first resident pastor, Father Peter Peudeprat, whose parish included all of Lake, Geauga, and Ashtabula Counties. In 1857 his successor, another Frenchman and native of Bishop Amadeus Rappe's home diocese, Father Charles Coquerelle, erected St. Mary's Church and added a parochial school in 1863.[13]

Paul's mother, Rose Jane Laracy, was a native of Painesville, born there in 1876. Her family had settled there well before St. Mary's Church was built. Rose Jane's maternal grandparents, James Morgan (1797-1868) and Bridget Murphy (1795-1880) were both natives of County Armagh, Ireland. They had married in Ireland, raised a family there and emigrated to the United States in a sailing vessel at an unknown date. In Painesville they lived in a substantial house at 218 Elm Street. Three of their children remained in Ireland; seven others either traveled with them to the United States or were born here. Their eldest daughter, Ellen Morgan, born in 1844, married Michael Laracy, a native of County Louth, Ireland, in St.

John's Cathedral in Cleveland on November 20, 1867. The young couple made their home in Cleveland, where their first child was born, but they moved to Painesville around 1869, took up residence in the Morgan home on Elm Street and remained there for the rest of their lives. Apparently several of Ellen Morgan Laracy's unmarried sisters also lived with them in the same house.

Michael Laracy and Ellen Morgan Laracy (Paul's maternal grandparents) had eight children, seven daughters and a son who died in infancy. One daughter, Anna Laracy, entered the Sisters of the Holy Humility of Mary. Three others, Mary, Catherine and Julia, did not marry and for many years ran a dry goods store on Main Street. The youngest of the three married daughters was Rose Jane Laracy, Paul's mother, who married Clarence Cornelius Hallinan (1875-1955) in St. Mary's Church, Painesville, in 1907.[14]

Paul's father was a native of Erie, Pennsylvania. His grandfather, James A. Hallinan, was born in Ennis, County Clare, Ireland, in 1838; he emigrated to the United States at an unknown date, and worked as a landscape gardener in the Hudson Valley. In 1867 he married Margaret E. McNierney (1848-1914) of Kingston, New York, moved to Erie, Pennsylvania, and raised a family of eight children, five boys and three girls. Paul's father, Clarence, moved to Detroit in the 1890's and worked for several years in the printing business before moving to Painesville, where he worked as a florist for the Storrs and Harrison Nurseries. There he met Paul's mother, a graduate of the Spencerian Business College in Cleveland, who was employed by the same firm as a bookkeeper.[15]

Paul's parents bought a home at 545 East Erie Street which still stands, a two-story white frame house, where they lived until the death of Paul's mother in 1952. Their first child, Robert James, died in infancy in 1909. Paul was born on April 8, 1911, and a second son, Arthur, was born in December 1916.

Paul was a frail and delicate child until he was about two years old. He had another serious bout with illness in the seventh grade, when he came down with pleurisy. Aside from these two illnesses, he had a happy and contented childhood growing up in Painesville. As the first boy of his generation in the family, he was the object of everyone's attention—his parents, grandparents, and especially his three maiden aunts. Even customers at their store noted how they doted on their young nephew.[16]

This attention did not spoil young Hallinan. He was a good student at St. Mary's School, where he skipped the eighth grade. He also learned to play the piano, a skill which he put to good use on many occasions in the future. He received First Communion at St. Mary's Church on May 12, 1918, and was confirmed there on May 28th of the same year. St. Mary's also brought Paul into contact with Father William J. Gallena, who came to Painesville as pastor in 1913 and remained until his death fifty-one years later. A graduate of the North American College in Rome and a man of scholarly tastes and strong views, "Doc" Gallena had a great influence on young Paul and became his lifelong friend and mentor. Another priest who was to become a close personal friend was Father John F. Dearden, the future cardinal, who was a curate in the parish from 1935 until 1937, when Hallinan was a student at St. Mary's Seminary.

Paul once said that he could not remember a time when he did not want to be a priest, but that, if he had not become a priest, he would have become a journalist.[17] For the rest of his life, wherever he was, he was either writing for a newspaper or starting one himself. The habit began in Painesville when, as a youngster, he and his brother Arthur circulated a newsletter among their family's friends and neighbors. Paul found a more serious outlet for his talent in 1927 when he obtained a summer job with the Painesville *Telegraph*, the local daily newspaper. He did so well that he was invited back every year and worked on the paper for a full ten summers before his ordination. Usually he wrote copy for the sports page, but he received other assignments as well. On one occasion, when he was sent to cover a wedding, he displayed a Hallinan characteristic which became more pronounced as he got older: a willingness to try a new approach to an old problem. Instead of following the usual journalistic practice of lavishing attention on the bride, Paul practically ignored the bride and focused his story on the groom. Like some of his later innovations, it was not well received by everyone, and it was the last time that he covered a wedding.[18]

Between the First World War and the beginning of the Great Depression, the population of Painesville doubled, reflecting the general prosperity of the area. There was still little heavy industry, except for the Diamond Alkali Company, which opened a chemical plant in Fairport Harbor in 1912. Such enterprises were the exception in Lake County, however, and economic development was due mainly to an industry which enhanced rather than blighted the beauty of the landscape, horticulture, or more precisely, large commercial nurseries. The first person to recognize the natural advantages of Lake County's soil and climate for this business was Jesse Storrs, a native of the Finger Lakes region of New York, who started a small nursery in Painesville in 1854. By the 1920's it was a giant firm, Storrs and Harrison Company, spread over 1,200 acres with forty-five greenhouses, claiming to be the largest "departmental" nursery in the United States.[19] As Storrs and Harrison prospered, others successfully imitated them. By 1927 there were over 20 nurseries in the county with 4,000 acres under cultivation, and earnings reached two million dollars a year. Some were small family operations; others like the Cole Nursery covered 600 acres. One firm, run by the six Kallay Brothers, distributed every year 50,000 catalogues printed in Hungarian, a practice which they continued until 1950. Six of the largest nurseries in the state were located within five miles of Painesville, and the Lake County nursery belt, six to ten miles deep, extended for twenty miles along the shore of Lake Erie with Painesville almost exactly in the center.[20]

A ride along Route 2 in the summertime was a delightful experience, as one writer described it in 1935:

> All the way from the Eastern boundary of Lake County at Madison through Painesville and Mentor to Willoughby on the Western boundary, the road is lined with gardens . . . [and] is in continuous bloom from early spring until the first frosts come.[21]

Many Painesville men served an apprenticeship at Storrs and Harrison, and then went into business for themselves. That is what Paul's father did. In 1917 Clarence Hallinan left Storrs and Harrison and opened a florist shop in downtown Painesville. A short time later, he built a greenhouse and office next to his home on East Erie Street and went into the nursery business. He attracted a loyal clientele and eventually bought an additional twenty-three acres to provide stock for his expanding trade. He was never rich, but he was able to provide a comfortable living for his family even during the Depression. He was a pewholder at St. Mary's Church until Father Gallena abolished the practice in 1926, and Hallinan donated the substantial sum of $350 to the building of the new St. Mary's School in 1921.[22] He was also able to send his two sons to the nearest Catholic high school, Cathedral Latin School in Cleveland.

The only unpleasant shadow over Paul's early years was the appearance of the Ku Klux Klan in Ohio in the early 1920's. For a few years the Klan was a powerful force in state politics, mustering 200,000 members, second in size only to the notorious Indiana Klan. Columbus and Akron both elected mayors friendly to the Klan. In Niles on November 1, 1924, the National Guard was called out to prevent violence between Klan and anti-Klan demonstrators.[23] Closer to home, Chagrin Falls and Mentor were both centers of Klan activity. In one Painesville bank a sign appeared in the window; "Help Wanted: No Negroes or Catholics."[24] One Sunday morning at Mass Father Gallena accused the Painesville *Telegraph* of fostering, or at least condoning anti-Catholic bigotry, and he issued an order to his parishioners from the pulpit of St. Mary's to cancel their subscriptions to the paper.[25]

The storm passed and left no lasting scars on Paul. When he went to work for the *Telegraph*, he was neither apologetic nor overly aggressive about his faith. One staffer said: "His greatest asset was the friendly smile that always covered his face."[26] No doubt his genial temperament helped, but what mattered most was that he did his job competently and fairly, winning the respect and confidence of the staff that had provoked Father Gallena's broadside. It was a good apprenticeship for him in more ways than one, and helped to prepare him for the day when he would be equally successful as bishop of two Southern dioceses with overwhelmingly Protestant populations.

Paul entered Cathedral Latin School in September 1924, commuting every day from Painesville on the "accommodation train," as generations of Americans once called the local train that made all the stops. The trip was easier than one might think. Paul's home was no more than a five-minute walk from the Painesville depot of the New York Central, and the old East 105th Street Station in Cleveland was only a few blocks from Cathedral Latin. The ride normally took no more than a half-hour.

At the time that Paul came to Cathedral Latin, it was acquiring a reputation as a school with excellent academic standards and a very popular football team. (In November 1938, 55,000 fans turned out to watch Cathedral Latin defeat West Tech at Municipal Stadium.) The first principal, Father Edward F. Mooney, who opened the school in

1916, later became the first Cardinal Archbishop of Detroit. Much to Mooney's chagrin, Bishop Joseph Schrembs, newly appointed to Cleveland in 1921, handed the school over to the Marianists (a religious order of teaching priests and brothers) a year later, and they retained control until the school closed in June 1979.

In addition to Paul, several other alumni went on to become distinguished members of the hierarchy. John Dearden, later Cardinal Archbishop of Detroit (in succession to Cardinal Mooney), graduated from Cathedral Latin a few years before Hallinan went there. John Krol, later Cardinal Archbishop of Philadelphia, came to Cathedral Latin two years before Paul. Floyd L. Begin, Bishop of Oakland, and Raymond J. Gallagher, Bishop of Lafayette, Indiana, were both alumni. So was John J. Meng, president of Hunter College in New York City, who graduated from Cathedral Latin the June before Paul entered the school. Another prominent alumnus was one of Paul's classmates, John F. Huth, later an editorial writer for the Cleveland *Plain Dealer*.

Despite the daily round trip from Painesville, Paul managed to make the honor roll every year at Cathedral Latin, a record matched by only a dozen other boys in a graduating class of almost 200. He also found the time to play the saxophone in the school orchestra and to participate in a wide variety of extra-curricular activities. In his senior year, he was editor-in-chief of the Yearbook, assistant editor of the school newspaper, chairman of the prom committee and the ring committee, and secretary of the sodality. The seniors elected him class president and described him in the Yearbook as "a great leader . . . and a friend of everyone." Another student quipped that he spent what spare time he had catching the train to Painesville and fending off jokes about his home town.[27]

The principal during Paul's four years was Father Joseph Tetzlaff, S.M., an old-fashioned pedagogue with a Teutonic love of law and order. Hallinan described him years later in carefully measured language which implied more than it said as "a fine priest, wise leader and more than adequate disciplinarian."[28] By the time that Paul graduated from Cathedral Latin, he had decided that he wanted to be a priest. However, Father Gallena dissuaded him from entering the seminary immediately and suggested that he apply instead for admission to the University of Notre Dame. Notre Dame accepted him, and in the fall of 1928 he went off to South Bend.

Notre Dame was still a relatively small school with 3,000 under-graduates, but it was already famous thanks to its football team. It became even more famous that fall when Knute Rockne used his "Win One for the Gipper" speech to beat a much stronger Army team. In the 1920's and 1930's the university built its reputation on football, not on scholarship. It did not have the financial resources of the Ivy League colleges or the great state universities of the Mid-West, and it was not a powerhouse of higher studies in any meaning-ful sense. (There were only fifty-nine graduate students in 1932.) However, its hardworked faculty, with little time or incentive for research or publishing, contained a number of dedicated and effective teachers who excelled in the classroom and offered their students a solid intellectual foundation.[29]

The President was Father Charles L. O'Donnell, C.S.C., who took advantage of Depression-era prices to embark on a building campaign and major expansion of the university, although the en-rollment actually declined by a third due to economic conditions. Almost every year that Paul was there, a new building went up: the Law Building in 1930; two residence halls and a new power plant in 1931; the Commerce Building and Engineering Building in 1932. To help pay the bill of nearly three million dollars, Notre Dame provided Knute Rockne with a new football stadium in 1930 with seats for 59,000 fans, three times the capacity of the old wooden grandstands.[30]

The ascetic regime under which the students lived differed little from that of a seminary. They were required to attend daily morning and evening prayer as well as Mass every Saturday and Sunday. After evening prayer, they were expected to be either in their rooms or in the study hall. Classwork consumed eighteen to twenty hours a week with at least as much time demanded of the students in private study. Permission was required to leave the campus, and movies and dances were limited to weekends.

The most prominent figure on campus, overshadowing even the President, was the redoubtable and ubiquitous Prefect of Religion, Father John F. O'Hara, C.S.C., later President of Notre Dame and Cardinal Archbishop of Philadelphia. Although he was ordained only twelve years in 1928, O'Hara was already a legend at Notre Dame, a tall, thin, chain-smoking man with a quick smile and an uncanny ability to remember the name of almost every student. He had the same gift that Paul later displayed as a curate and chaplain, that of winning the confidence of young people and communicating his own enthusiasm to them. As counsellor and confessor and tireless promoter of frequent Communion, O'Hara made an indelible impression on a whole generation of Notre Dame students who appreciated his total devotion to them.[31]

The spirituality fostered by O'Hara was intensely moralistic and individualistic. He encouraged a whole range of private devotions, such as the rosary, novenas, and visits to the Blessed Sacrament. He placed special emphasis on frequent confession and daily Communion, and he used every conceivable technique, such as Mother's Day, Father's Day, First Friday, the death of an alumnus or the illness of a student, to promote frequent reception of the sacraments. In addition to two early morning Masses, Holy Communion was available for the students in Sorin Hall every day from 5:15 A.M. until noon. Critics accused O'Hara of stressing daily Communion to such a degree that he actually neglected the central place of the Mass in Christian worship. He answered his critics by saying: "It is not daily Mass that brings daily Communion; it is daily Communion that fosters daily Mass."[32]

O'Hara was a lion for work, and he had a mania for statistics and for quantifying religious data that would make him the envy today of any researcher of the *Annales* school. When he introduced the practice of perpetual adoration of the Blessed Sacrament to the students in 1929, he calculated that "five hundred half-hours of adoration were necessary for the success of the enterprise."[33] On one occasion, during a student retreat, he posted this notice on a bulletin board:

> Figure it out for yourself. To repeat. Confessions are heard after supper every evening in the Church and in the basement chapel. Six priests can hear 250 confessions in the hour after supper.[34]

Every year after 1921, O'Hara made elaborate surveys of the religious practices of the students and published the results in an annual *Religious Bulletin* which quickly became famous on Catholic campuses across the country. To accompany the *Religious Bulletin* for 1928, he drew up a graphic chart (which looks rather like a map of the South Pole) illustrating the daily variations in the reception of

Holy Communion, and he concluded that total Communions for the academic year 1927-1928 were 311, 226![35]

There was also a strong Puritan streak in O'Hara which led him to ban the *American Mercury* and the writings of Ernest Hemingway from the library. He was ever on the alert to protect his boys from the influence of German psychologists, French novelists, modern sociologists, American jazz, and the local girls whom they might meet on weekends in the dance halls of South Bend.[36]

Students who absented themselves from chapel or resisted O'Hara's invitations to see him were likely to receive a postcard, "an open card," he called it, "which practically broadcasts their delinquency." One favorite which O'Hara liked to send before vacations carried this lugubrious message:

> Danger lurks in every road.
> Death knows no distinction.
> Insurance against both:
> Receive the sacraments before going home.
> Sorin Chapel—anytime.[37]

O'Hara's efforts at character-building might easily have backfired and turned students away from what they perceived to be a morbid and mechanical kind of piety. In fact, O'Hara's own zeal and sincerity prevented that from happening. "John Faithful," they called him in recognition of his single-minded dedication to them, and he sent off thousands of them from Notre Dame as devoted alumni and committed Catholic laymen.

It is difficult to assess the influence of O'Hara on Hallinan. Paul must have come into contact with him frequently. No one on campus could avoid him. Some of the methods which Paul used as a curate working with young people, especially his efforts to promote frequent Communion, resemble closely the techniques used by O'Hara. And Father Theodore Marszal has discovered in the archives of the Archdiocese of Atlanta many of O'Hara's daily *Religious Bulletins*, which Paul carefully annotated in his own hand and kept to the day of his death.[38]

On the other hand, there are also indications that Paul took with a generous grain of salt O'Hara's fulminations against modern literature. On his bookshelf he had the works of Willa Cather, George

Meredith, John Galsworthy, Dorothy Parker, the humorists Frank Sullivan and Robert Benchley, and Ogden Nash. More significantly he was a frequent contributor to the *Juggler*, the campus comic magazine, which O'Hara had criticized more than once for its "unedifying" humor.

In later years Paul's friends often assumed that he had majored in English or journalism at Notre Dame. In fact, his major was philosophy, but he found plenty of opportunity to develop his literary talents on campus. There were four principal undergraduate publications, and Paul involved himself with all of them. He spent four years on the staff of the *Scholastic*, the Notre Dame newspaper, the last year as editor-in-chief. His big moment on the paper came on March 31, 1931, when, as assistant editor, he rushed through the presses an extra four-page edition announcing the news of Knute Rockne's death before the local South Bend newspaper broke the story.

In his junior year Paul won the coveted post of editor-in-chief of the *Dome*, the Notre Dame yearbook. The results so impressed the Knights of Columbus that, in the following year, they asked him to edit *Santa Maria*, the publication of the Notre Dame Council of the Knights. Paul also contributed to *Scrip*, a literary quarterly, but he seemed to have a special predilection for the *Juggler* in whose pages he tried his hand at imitating Robert Benchley and Ogden Nash. In essays like "The Collegiate Handbook of Etiquette," he poked fun at campus customs and the foibles of his fellow students. The humor was good-natured and courteous, but it was not particularly funny, and it had little of Benchley's zest and bite. Nor did his imitations of Ogden Nash come close to duplicating the character of the original.[39]

Paul graduated from Notre Dame on June 5, 1937, *magna cum laude*, thirty-first in a class of 534. He also received the Dockweiler Medal for the best philosophy essay submitted by any senior.

Three months later he entered the Cleveland diocesan seminary, Our Lady of the Lake, on Ansel Road. The building was only eight years old, a handsome brick structure with a splendid chapel and library, built in the Spanish style around two inner courtyards, overlooking Rockefeller Park and only a short distance from the Cleveland Art Museum and Severance Hall. The proximity of the seminary to the cultural centers of Cleveland was more theoretical than real, however, for the seminary routine allowed the students little opportunity to take advantage of them. Ordinarily the seminary course was six years long: two years of philosophy and four years of theology. Since Paul had completed his college education at Notre Dame, however, he was allowed to skip the first year of philosophy. One of his classmates was John Krol, who had entered the seminary system two years after his graduation from Cathedral Latin.

The curriculum was the standard one in use in most seminaries in the United States. Paul had no difficulty meeting the Latin or philosophy requirements. He received a smattering of Greek and Hebrew and much heavier doses of church history, Scripture, canon law, and dogmatic and moral theology. He did very well academically, rarely receiving a grade of less than ninety percent in any course, and the daily schedule of meditation, Mass, spiritual devotions and study was not very different from that at Notre Dame.

The rector, Monsignor James M. McDonough, was not a trained scholar, but most of the fourteen priests on the resident faculty possessed advanced degrees in the subjects which they taught. Father Michael J. Hynes, professor of church history, had a doctorate in historical science from the University of Louvain as well as a licentiate in theology from the University of St. Thomas Aquinas (the Angelicum) in Rome. Oddly enough, in view of Hallinan's later interest in history, he does not seem to have been particularly close to Hynes. Rather, the professor who made the deepest impression on him was Father William Newton, professor of Sacred Scripture and one of the first American diocesan priests to earn a doctorate at the Pontifical Biblical Institute.

The only seminary notebooks which Hallinan kept in later life were those from his Scripture courses with Newton. It is understandable why he did so; both men had the same kind of inquiring mind and wide range of pastoral interests. Years later, one former student remembered especially one of Newton's favorite aphorisms; when new data challenged time-honored theories of biblical interpretation, said Newton, "it was time to look again at what we previously thought to be true." Such attitudes were hardly common (and hardly possible) among Catholic Scripture professors in the years before *Divino Afflante Spiritu*, the encyclical of Pope Pius XII in 1943, which revolutionized Catholic biblical studies. Newton later taught for a brief period at the Catholic University of America, and he helped to establish the Catholic Biblical Association and the *Catholic*

Biblical Quarterly. During Hallinan's years at the seminary, Newton was diocesan director of Newman Clubs, and later as a pastor in Elyria, he organized the first parish council in the diocese, joined the local Council of Churches, and was honored by the Catholic Interracial Council for his work on behalf of racial justice in the 1960's— at a time when his former student was winning similar praise as Archbishop of Atlanta.[40]

The ethnic diversity of the student body reflected the character of Cleveland Catholicism. In Hallinan's deacon class of twenty seminarians, there were Germans, Irish, Poles, Slovaks, a Lithuanian, a Slovene and a Czech. One of the things which impressed John Krol was Hallinan's ability and willingness to relate well to seminarians of every nationality. "He was thoroughly catholic in his outlook," said the future cardinal, without a trace of prejudice or snobbery toward any ethnic group.[41]

The school year always included at least one week-long retreat. Thirty years later Hallinan still recalled one of those retreats which he made in his second year at Our Lady of the Lake. He could not remember the name of the retreat master, but what he did remember was

> the relentless examination of conscience I gave myself as I walked miles and miles in a circle, silent, thinking, deciding what kind of priest I would be.[42]

Summers were still free, and every year he returned to Painesville to live at home and to work on the *Telegraph.* In his last summer on the paper, he had the pleasure of being acting editor for two days, in full charge of turning out two issues. Ordination day was February 20, 1937, when Bishop Joseph Schrembs ordained Paul and nineteen other classmates to the priesthood in St. John's Cathedral in Cleveland.

The next day he celebrated his first solemn Mass in St. Mary's, Painesville. Several hundred people jammed the church, including a delegation of fifty workers from the *Telegraph,* who also printed a special edition of the paper that day in his honor. It was the only Sunday edition in the newspaper's 115-year history. Actually it was the Saturday paper with a special front page; the headline read: "Rev. Fr. Paul Hallinan Celebrates His First Mass," and the rest of the page was filled with tributes from his former colleagues, most of them non-Catholics, expressing a bit awkwardly but with obvious sincerity their best wishes to Paul. One of them wrote:

> His old newspaper friends are all for him, one and all. They are proud of him, are glad for him and will be pulling for him to become Pope someday.

More realistically and more prophetically, another person used a printer's slang expression for the last line of copy to say: "A sincere hope that it is not '30' for his splendid newspaper technique and his ability to master the pen."[43]

2

St. Aloysius

On March 12, 1937, Father Hallinan was notified of his first assignment: St. Aloysius Church in the Glenville area of Cleveland.[1] On the following Friday afternoon a very somber and apprehensive Father Hallinan appeared at the rectory of St. Aloysius at 10932 St. Clair Avenue. The first assistant at the parish, Father Francis G. Zwilling, saw him walk up the front steps and ring the doorbell. It was the only time in his life that he ever saw Paul look so serious.

His apprehension was understandable. For the Catholic Church in this country it was the golden age of the large urban parishes, a world which has now vanished as completely as the Painesville of the 1920's. Big city parishes were then prized assignments for pastors, conferring status and prestige on their incumbents who enjoyed lifetime tenure and little accountability to anyone except God and themselves, provided that they did not run the parish onto the rocks financially. Their parishioners, often first and second-generation Americans with lively memories of anti-Catholic bigotry, were extraordinarily docile and tolerant of even the most autocratic pastors who could lay claim to a lifestyle unmatched by their contemporaries in any walk of life, except perhaps Chinese warlords in the more remote provinces.

The pastor whom young Father Hallinan was about to meet was Monsignor James T. Malloy, seventy-three years old and a native of County Mayo, Ireland. He had been in charge at St. Aloysius for thirty-four years. Revered by his parishioners, he was a man with a keen sense of his own authority, and he had the reputation among the younger clergy of Cleveland as a man who did not suffer fools gladly, especially when they happened to be his curates. Paul introduced himself to Malloy, and they disappeared into the pastor's rooms. When they emerged after a brief conversation, the new assistant was grinning from ear to ear. It was the beginning of five happy years for him at St. Aloysius.[2]

Cleveland was quite a different world from Painesville, with smokestacks and blast furnaces instead of nurseries and orchards. The youthful priest was hardly a stranger to it, however, after four years at Cathedral Latin School and five years at the major seminary on Ansel Road.

It was an interesting place for any newly-ordained priest to begin his ministry. In the 1930's Cleveland was the sixth largest city in the United States, with over 900,000 people. Only New York, Chicago, Philadelphia, Los Angeles and Detroit had larger populations. It was also one of the great workshops of the nation, fifth among American cities in the value of its manufactured products, the second biggest foundry center in the nation, and the leading Great Lakes port for the shipment of iron ore. The Terminal Tower complex had recently transformed the area around Public Square, relieving the city of its image as a grimy industrial center and allowing Clevelanders to boast for a few years that they had the tallest building in the country outside of New York City.

Along with Chicago, the city ranked as one of the great ethnic melting-pots of the nation. In 1930, a quarter of the population was foreign-born, and another forty percent were the children of foreign or mixed parents.[3] In 1937, the Catholic Church had fifty-three national parishes, representing twelve different nationalities, within the city limits. There were also several dozen Protestant churches with foreign-born congregations and a large Jewish community. World War I and the restrictive immigration laws of the 1920's put an end to this growth and accelerated the assimilation of the immigrants, but in the 1930's there were still many homogeneous ethnic neighborhoods and the city was blanketed with schools, social clubs, orphanages and other institutions founded by the many different nationalities who had made their home in Cleveland.[4]

Cleveland's dependence on heavy industry made the city especially vulnerable to the Depression, and it was estimated in 1938 that one out of every three Clevelanders had been on relief at some time during that era.[5] As a local newspaper reporter recalled:

> No one was untouched. Either he had lost his job or had his wages cut. He couldn't get his money out of the bank, or borrow on his frozen assets. He couldn't sell his house or the vacant lot he had invested in, for no one else had any cash either. If he was lucky, he dragged along from week to week or lived with better-fixed relatives. If he was unlucky, he went on relief and eventually wound up raking leaves in make-work projects.[6]

By the time that Paul was ordained in 1937, the worst of the Depression was over, and the social welfare programs of the New Deal were providing assistance to those who were still out of work. For those who could find work, wages in the large factories were five percent higher than in 1928, and the Internal Revenue Service reported a 100% increase in tax receipts over 1936.

On the other hand, economic conditions were still precarious for many Clevelanders. The mayor claimed that the city could not afford to pay a $6,000 raise voted by the City Council for municipal janitors and elevator operators. Hundreds of people were so desperate for work that they showed up at the Public Square Building in response to advertisements for jobs in war-ravaged Spain. A new element came into the city's life with widespread labor unrest and strikes, as the CIO tried to organize many of the big factories. In December 1936 a sit-down strike of 7,000 employees at the Fisher Body Company plant lasted into the new year. In July 1937 the Ohio National Guard was called out to protect non-strikers at three Cleveland plants of the Republic Steel Company. When the Greyhound Bus Company tried to break a strike in November 1937, a driver lay down between the front and rear wheels of a bus about to depart, bringing all operations in the terminal to a halt.[7]

Politically, Cleveland remained very conservative. Other big cities gave Al Smith large majorities in 1928, but Cleveland voted for Herbert Hoover despite its large Catholic immigrant population. Through most of the Depression it continued to elect Republican mayors and public assistance was among the most niggardly in the country: $3.48 a week for a family of four in 1932.[8] When Frank J. Lausche was elected mayor in 1941, it only proved that Clevelanders tended to vote conservative even when they elected Democrats.

In the clerical argot of the day, St. Aloysius was certainly a *bon ton* parish, one of the biggest and busiest on the East Side. It was located in a fine residential neighborhood only four miles from Public Square, but much of the development was of very recent vintage. When Monsignor Malloy came there in 1903, three years after the parish was established, much of Glenville consisted of empty lots and it was not even part of Cleveland but an independent city. There were scarcely 200 Catholics in the whole parish. Malloy saw enormous changes during his years there as more and more people moved from the older neighborhoods of Cleveland to find a better life for themselves and their children. The city followed them, annexing Glenville in 1905.

In 1910 the total population of the area included within the boundaries of the parish was approximately 11,236. By 1920 it tripled to 34,119, reached a peak of 47, 439 in 1930, and then leveled off under the combined impact of the Depression and the beginning of the flight to the suburbs. By 1940 it had declined slightly to 45,460.[9] Obviously not all of these people were Catholics. Indeed, one of the features which made St. Aloysius different from many other Cleveland parishes of that day was the religious and ethnic diversity of Glenville. Along the lakeshore the parish included most of the wealthy village of Bratenahl, the home of some of the leading business executives of Cleveland. To their great relief, Bratenahl was separated from the rest of the parish by the *cordon sanitaire* of the New York Central Railroad. In the western part of the parish, south of St. Clair Avenue, there was a large Jewish population which spilled over into adjacent neighborhoods to form one of the two largest Jewish communities in Cleveland with an estimated 32,000 people in 1932.[10] There was also a minuscule black population in the same part of the parish, approximately 270 in 1930 and 430 in 1940, the beginnings of the huge influx of blacks who would change St. Aloysius into a black inner-city parish by the 1960's.

Unlike many other cities, when Cleveland grew in the 1920's and 1930's, it grew horizontally, not vertically. In Glenville, for example, despite the huge increase in popuation, very few apartment houses were built. Almost half of the population (forty-six percent) lived in one-family homes in 1930, the rest almost exclusively as tenants in two or three-family homes. They were spacious well-built wooden houses, with big rooms, high ceilings and front porches, set close together on tree-lined streets running north and south of the St. Clair Avenue streetcar line, which carried commuters and shoppers to and from downtown in fifteen minutes.

About one-third of the total population was foreign-born, heavily Polish and Russian in the Jewish sections, mainly English, Scottish, Irish and German in the rest of the parish. Another third of the population were the children of foreign-born or mixed parents. The parishioners of St. Aloysius were overwhelmingly Irish and German, but both nationalities were thoroughly Americanized by 1937. Father Zwilling noted with amusement that the Germans were content to have a priest with a German name, even though he did not speak a word of the language. The Irish too were rapidly loosening their ties to the old country, unlike the Irish-Americans in some of the more cohesive West-Side parishes.[11]

One former parishioner described St. Aloysius many years later as "middle class, but working middle class." The census statistics confirm her recollections. Only four percent of the adults over twenty-five were college graduates. Approximately eighteen percent had completed four years of high school. In 1930, over 5,000 people worked in the construction industry, automobile manufacturing, the iron and steel industry, on railroads and streetcars, and in assorted other manufacturing businesses. Many of them were hard hit by the Depression. In 1940, when recovery was well under way, nine percent of the work force was either out of work or employed by the WPA or other emergency agencies. Perhaps the most amazing statistic of all was one which cut completely across religious and ethnic lines and did much to explain the social stability of Glenville: the number of divorced people was incredibly small by the standards of a later age. Roughly one percent of the adult population, or fewer than 500 people, listed themselves as divorced in 1930.

St. Aloysius claimed to have 1,700 families or 7,800 active parishioners, an enormous number for any parish, but still less than twenty-five percent of the total population.[12] The parish "plant" was entirely the work of Monsignor Malloy. There was a large rectory, a convent, two schools with over 850 students, and, the pride and joy of the parish, a magnificent Romanesque church seating 1,275 people, which was huge even by the generous standards of Cleveland's Catholic churches. Malloy built it in 1924 at the cost of over $400,000 and paid off the debt so rapidly that it was consecrated at the time of dedication.

the first time that that had ever happened in any Cleveland parish.[13]

Unlike the pastor, a curate in the 1930's led a curiously ambivalent existence in most parishes, very regimented in some ways, very free in other ways to develop his own talents. He was tied to a system of duty days and a well-defined sacramental ministry which included daily and Sunday Mass, confessions every Saturday afternoon and evening, Communion calls on First Fridays, baptisms on Sunday afternoons, and weddings, wakes and funerals at almost any time. These could be heavy obligations in a parish like St. Aloysius, where there were eight Sunday Masses (the first at 5:30 A.M.), three weekday Masses, and, in a typical year, 73 funerals, 88 weddings and 177 baptisms. The parish priests could expect to spend long hours in the confessional on the days before Christmas and Easter, when as many as 7,000 parishioners would receive Holy Communion. There were also three hospitals in the parish as well as several nursing homes and a large number of Communion calls.

Once these obligations were satisfied, however, a curate was usually left to his own devices (and the pastor's acquiescence) to find further outlets for his ministry. Much depended on the individual's own industry and creativity. Father Hallinan had an abundance of both, and soon after his arrival at St. Aloysius he singled out two areas of special concern: youth work and writing. James Malloy and his succesor, Monsignor James T. Daly, encouraged him to pursue both.

Father Robert E. Murphy, the second assistant in the parish, had started the Stalpian Club in 1936 for young adults twenty years and older. Paul established a similar club for those between the age of sixteen and twenty. He called it the Alcyon Club, an acronym for the St. Aloysius CYO Club. The two clubs complemented each other and worked together on many projects, and so did their moderators. The two priests made the parish a social and recreational center for hundreds of young people still feeling the effects of the Depression, who often had no jobs, little money and plenty of opportunity for mischief. It was perhaps the last decade when any parish could serve such a purpose, before teenage affluence brought competition from motion pictures, cars and television. Many parishes provided such programs for their young people in the 1930's, but St. Aloysius did it on a grand scale.

Father Murphy was a few years older than Paul, a rough-and-ready individual and former high school football player, who had a special interest in promoting athletics among the young adults of the parish. Paul did the same for his group, and the Alcyons soon had their full complement of teams in the local CYO leagues. But Hallinan also broadened the appeal of the club by offering the youngsters a wide variety of activities: boatrides, picnics, skating parties, hayrides, horse-back riding, dancing, bowling or just listening to the radio in the club room in the basement of the school, which was open every evening until 10:45 and on Sunday afternoons.

There were also debates on such topics as "The Pope and Modern Problems," and "Resolved: That the Labor Union is the Workingman's Best Friend for a Square Deal." There was a library committee which maintained a pamphlet rack in the Alcyon Club room and promoted such novels as Owen Francis Dudley's *The Masterful Monk* and Willa Cather's *Shadows on the Rock*. There was even a welfare committee responsible for visiting sick members of the club in the hospital and for hosting an annual Christmas party for the children at St. Joseph's Orphanage.

Paul put his own musical talent to work by producing an annual musical, which became so popular that he had to use Shaw Auditorium in the local public high school. He composed the music, wrote the lyrics and served as combination producer, director, business manager and publicity agent. He also involved hundreds of people in the pro-duction of the shows: the Mother's Club sold tickets; the Men's Club solicited advertisements for the program from the neighborhood mer-chants; the young people painted the scenery, constructed the sets and played in the orchestra; and 400 or 500 people came out each evening to see the performances.[14]

When judging the vitality of parish life in the 1930's it would be difficult to overestimate the importance of social events like the St. Aloysius Musicals, or the Parish Bazaar, or the annual Mother's Club Picnic, or a host of other organized activities. These gatherings were the counterpart to the stern moralizing that went on in the pulpit; they furnished the opportunity for parishioners to meet and mingle with one another and with their priests. Like the parish societies, they were a powerful means of fostering parish spirit and parish identity, and they demonstrated that it was possible to have a genuine Christian community (although that expression was hardly used) even in the midst of an anonymous urban neighborhood.

The Stalpians and Alcyons were so successful that they attracted young people from other parishes and even non-Catholics. Father Zwilling was delighted because they provided his convert classes with a constant supply of young recruits. Others accused Hallinan of being a matchmaker because of the number of weddings among former members of the club. The Stalpians and Alcyons also inspired a tremendous loyalty, so much so that fifty years later former members still spoke with pride and affection about the clubs and their moderators.[15]

Francis Zwilling thought that Hallinan was really the "sparkplug" behind the two clubs, and he attributed the latter's success to the fact that "for him religion was a happy experience and he had the faculty of communicating that enthusiasm to others." He was blessed with a naturally cheery disposition, and everyone who knew him at St. Aloysius seems to remember a smile that was hard to resist. He also liked to talk and sing and play the piano in the company of young people. But the members of the Alcyon Club noticed other things too. He was willing to listen as well as talk. When he greeted someone, his attention was total; there were no glances over their shoulder to see who was next in line. They also noticed that he avoided the mistakes of Father Murphy, whose attempts at chumminess often misfired, leaving the youngsters confused and him angry. For all his friendliness, Hallinan remained a stickler for propriety. He always wore his Roman collar and insisted on being addressed as "Father Hallinan."

Personality alone does not explain his success. He also showed a genuine flair for organization. When he started the Alcyon Club in January 1938, he had forty youngsters at the first meeting. He challenged them to double their numbers by the time of the next meeting in two weeks. They did so, and the Alcyons soon had over 200 members. Before long, the young priest gave them a written constitution, duly ratified by the members, which assigned well-defined roles to each of the officers and committees.

He gave the same attention to the Communion breakfast, held twice a month after the 11:15 Mass. A few days before each breakfast, every member got a postcard reminding him or her of the date. (Presumably the message was less alarming than Notre Dame's Father O'Hara would have made it.) A good touch was the special section roped off at the 11:15 Mass for members of the club. Even better was the appointment of Alcyon ushers with the enviable job of escorting away unwary adults who wandered into the reserved pews.

Paul usually spoke at the conclusion of each breakfast; on one occasion in 1939 when he did not, he may have regretted it, for the guest speaker took as his topic: "What's Wrong with the Boy of Today?" His conclusion was that "the boy of today is softer than the boy of yesterday."

Parishioners of St. Aloysius who knew young Father Hallinan fifty years ago are quick to point out that his popularity was not limited to any age group. He got on well with everyone, and he was as much at home with adults or the elderly as with the young people of the parish. One way that he reached this larger audience was through the Sunday bulletin. The years at St. Aloysius were one of the few periods in Paul's life when he did not have the opportunity to write for a newspaper, but he made the Sunday bulletin serve the same purpose. Each week Zwilling wrote the standard notices and announcements, and Hallinan used the rest of the bulletin for his own comments on topics of the day. His remarks were necessarily brief, but they give some fascinating and surprising glimpses of Hallinan's ideas and opinions at that time.

When he discussed theology in the bulletin, almost invariably it was moral theology, with a heavy emphasis on law and obligation couched in the most narrow and rigid terms. His harshness seems out of character for someone who was so jovial and optimistic and who later became a warm admirer of Father Bernard Häring, C.Ss.R., but he was simply reflecting the stern legalism which prevailed everywhere in the Catholic Church at that time. For example, before Lent each year, like every parish priest, he explained the Lenten regulations in excruciating detail, down to the fine points of the use of suet to season foods on days of abstinence. One summer he devoted a column to the obligation to attend Mass on vacation, and he announced that "unless you are 1¼ hours from a church, you are obliged to attend Mass every Sunday and Holyday of Obligation."[16]

Lateness at Mass was another topic which brought out the rigorist in him. One Sunday he simply reproduced an article from *Extension* magazine which calibrated with mathematical precision how many parts of the Mass one could miss without committing a mortal sin. Lest this casuistical *tour de force* be considered an invitation to laxity, however, the author added this sobering warning:

> In determining the gravity of the sin of missing parts of the
> Mass, attention must be paid to the degree of neglect in taking
> precautions to prevent being late. There rests upon those who have
> arrived tardy for Mass the obligation of supplying the parts missed
> by attendance at those parts of another Mass whenever possible. If
> the parts missed are supplied by attendance at another Mass, *the
> consecration and Communion must be parts of the same Mass.*[17]

In those days the niceties of liturgical observance occupied a place
somewhere between low priority and no priority at all in Paul's
calculations of what was important. An exception occurred, however,
over the use of the Wedding March from *Lohengrin* in Catholic
marriage ceremonies. The music was already banned from weddings
at St. Aloysius, and Hallinan defended the prohibition vigorously on
the grounds that *Lohengrin* was

> . . . typical of the great German composer's point of view. It begins
> with the suspicion of murder and ends with a broken vow. It is
> woven around black magic, the threat of war, a bitter domestic
> quarrel, and a complete absence of the loyal trust without which
> Christian marriage cannot exist.[18]

A less likely victim of Hallinan's wrath was the Scottish Catholic
novelist, A.J. Cronin, who won widespread acclaim in this country
with *The Keys of the Kingdom.* Hallinan, however, dismissed the
book's success as a "trend" which would lead Catholics to a "wishy-
washy surrender of Christ's truth." He objected strenuously to a passage in the book in which a priest assured a dying atheist that God
believed in him, even if he did not believe in God. Hallinan reacted
to the dialogue with outraged orthodoxy. "As a sample of Catholic
teaching," he said, "it is false. It is worse than false, it is sugar-coated
bunk." He thought that he had detected a whiff of indifferentism,
and he lectured Cronin sternly about his lack of theological expertise.

> Being in good faith isn't just being ignorant and not to blame for it.
> Being in good faith means using the grace that God grants to
> everyone that all might have the essentials. If, as many do, the
> dying man at some time rejected this Grace, he is to blame.[19]

Even at his most censorious, however, Hallinan could still be funny. He once wrote a playful criticism of the boys who waited outside the church every Sunday morning looking for the girls without ever venturing inside themselves. "The Street Corner Admirals," as he called them, were readily identifiable: "Clothes a bit on the gaudy side ... conversation a bit on the purple side ... intellect a bit on the lopside." Some of his best pieces for the bulletin were the non-polemical ones, simple essays explaining the origins of the Forty Hours Devotion, or the meaning of Christmas, or the papal election of 1939, or the work of the St. Vincent de Paul Society in the parish. As one might expect, the activities of the Stalpians and the Alcyons got frequent coverage, especially the annual musical. When ticket sales lagged one year, he published a "letter" from the doorman at the Shaw Auditorium, describing how much he enjoyed watching the rehearsals every evening.[20]

On rare occasions Hallinan used the bulletin to comment on social and economic issues. His column for Labor Day in 1939 was strongly populist in tone, excoriating employers who failed to pay their workers a decent wage. His vehemence may have been due to the bitter strike, just recently ended, at the Fisher Body Company plant on Coit Road which was the eastern bounday of the parish. On July 31, 1939, there had been serious violence at the plant between 3,000 pickets and 450 policemen, which left forty-one people seriously injured and another dozen in jail.[21]

Paul made no reference to the strike, but he made a plea for a living wage in language that was certainly inspired, directly or indirectly, by Father John A. Ryan, professor of moral theology at the Catholic University of America and one of the leading Catholic authorities on the subject.

> And what is a living wage? A man must receive a wage that will enable him to live in ordinary comfort; that will support his family in ordinary circumstances and enough to provide for his old age, for extraordinary expenses and to provide a little inheritance for his children. Very few of our employers are paying a "just" wage according to this definition. They absolutely refuse to allow the Christian principles of justice and rights to enter into their system of economics.[22]

Another occasion when he dropped his customary reticence about public events was the Japanese attack on Pearl Harbor, this time courageously resisting efforts to whip up empty-headed jingoism or hatred for the enemy. On the Sunday after Pearl Harbor, he printed in the bulletin St. Francis of Assisi's Prayer for Peace and the Prayer for Enemies from the Roman *Missal*. He regretted, he said, that he had heard so many people say "I hate" and "My country right or wrong." He warned his parishioners against adopting "an angry and senseless vocabulary" and said that all believers had three sacred duties to fulfill:

1. To defend their country, under its responsible leadership, even with their lives if necessary.

2. To study news carefully, to discuss war without personal prejudice, to keep their heads, not to hate.

3. To pray for peace, a just and lasting peace.[23]

He repeated the same message in a series of articles for the bulletin in January and February 1942. Lest anyone think that he did not feel the same emotions as everyone else, he mentioned that, as he wrote, he had on his desk a letter from a young ensign who had since been killed at Pearl Harbor. His principal concern was the mindless visceral response of so many people to the outbreak of the war. "Thoughts ... confused, half-formed thoughts! Thoughts which need thinking, much more thinking before we are worthy to call ourselves intelligent Americans." While he had no doubts about American objectives in the war, he was extremely suspicious of the motives of our Russian allies, and even of the British, wondering aloud if Churchill were as determined as Disraeli had been to preserve the British Empire. He was especially fearful that the world would be no better than it had been after World War I:

> God granting us a victory, will it be written off in the blood of 1918? Will the peace then be a surface peace, doomed to break open in time and give off hatred and war again?[24]

By the time that these words appeared in the bulletin, the 11:15 Mass was being offered every Sunday for the boys from St. Aloysius who were in the armed forces. Air raid drills for the children in the school had become a familiar routine. In the church vestibule on Sunday mornings, families lined up to register the names and addresses of boys who had joined the army, navy or marines. Even the annual musical showed the signs of war in 1942, with a special section of the auditorium reserved for the parents of servicemen. By the summer of that year, many of the Stalpians and Alcyons were in the armed forces, some of them already in Australia. It was not long before Father Hallinan followed them as an army chaplain, as did Father Murphy and Father Zwilling (who had left St. Aloysius in 1939).

Within a month of Pearl Harbor, Paul spoke to the vice-chancellor, Monsignor Vincent B. Balmat, saying that he would be willing to serve as an army chaplain, if the need should arise. During the next six months several factors led to his final decision to enter the service. For one thing, he met Father O'Hara of Notre Dame (now Bishop O'Hara of the Military Ordinariate) when he was in Cleveland, and O'Hara told him that the army needed several hundred Catholic chaplains immediately. Also he could not help but notice the call-up of so many young men from the parish, and many times he heard them and their parents say how much they would like to see more Catholic chaplains in the armed forces.

He made a retreat during the second week of June, 1942, and after much prayer and reflection, he came to the conclusion that he could be of much more service in the army than at St. Aloysius. He told the diocesan chancellor, auxiliary Bishop James A. McFadden: "Every boy who comes home on furlough strengthens that feeling for me." In an interview with his ordinary, Archbishop Joseph Schrembs, on August 8, 1942, he stressed the same points. On August 14, the Archbishop gave him permission to apply for admission to the Army Chaplain Corps, which he did immediately.[25] In his application he described himself as a Catholic priest and former newspaper reporter during the summers of 1927-1936. He was officially appointed a chaplain on September 9, with the rank of first lieutenant, and on the following day was ordered to report on September 30, to the Chaplains' Training School at Harvard University.[26]

St. Aloysius gave both Murphy and Hallinan a lavish sendoff with a parish reception on September 22 at the Glenville High School auditorium. Paul sent a gracious note to the parish bulletin, thanking the parishioners for their generous purse and for five happy years of parish work that "were never a burden" to him. He also wrote a farewell letter for the Alcyons' newspaper, and there he unburdened himself more candidly about his real feelings on leaving St. Aloysius:

> It isn't the statistics that seem important now, they've all been recorded. The things that stick now are the memories of good, clean-cut times ... hikes and boat rides and hay rides and parties ... laughter that was never forced, fun that was never vulgar.... You remember a crowded Communion rail, a letter from a boy who once got into trouble. You remember again that parade of faces, heads held high because the Alcyon Club was the best club in town and all of us knew it.[27]

Urban neighborhoods change rapidly in twentieth-century America, and Glenville today is part of Cleveland's sprawling black ghetto. St. Aloysius Church still dominates St. Clair Avenue—a bit grimier and shabbier than it was in Hallinan's day—but still an imposing landmark and a reminder of a remarkable chapter in American Catholic history. In parishes like St. Aloysius all across the country the Church organized an amazingly successful apostolate to large numbers of Catholic immigrants and their children who were just climbing the ladder of success and making their way into the lower middle class. At the critical point when these people entered the mainstream of American life, parishes like St. Aloysius strengthened their faith and solidified their attachment to the Catholic Church. So close was the connection that a whole generation of parochial school students grew up identifying the parish, rather than the neighborhood, as the place where they lived.

There was a darker side to this idyllic picture, however, and that was the isolation of Catholics from the intellectual and cultural currents around them. "To thousands of our fellow Americans," lamented Leonard Feeney, S.J., in the early 1940's, "we Catholics are known merely as the people who eat fish on Friday."[28] It was a rare individual in the Catholic community who took notice of such complaints. Certainly young Father Hallinan did not. Armed with the rigid theology and spirituality that he had acquired at Notre Dame and at the seminary, he was thoroughly at home in the comfortable little world of St. Aloysius parish. Some priests of his era never outgrew such experiences and spent the rest of their lives trying to recreate the atmosphere of the 1930's and 1940's in circumstances that were totally inappropriate. That was not so with Hallinan. When he went off to war in the spring of 1942, it was the first of several occasions on which he demonstrated an impressive capacity for growth and flexibility in the face of new challenges.

3

World War II

Throughout his life Paul Hallinan had a knack of being on the cutting edge of things. For a newly ordained priest in the 1930's, as he had soon discovered, there was no more exciting apostolate than running a parish youth program. After the war the same could be said of the Newman clubs (the Catholic student organization at secular colleges), which attracted some of the most articulate and dynamic young clergy in the country—among them Father Hallinan. Still later, during his ten years as bishop and archbishop, he readily involved himself in the major issues of the day: civil rights, liturgical reform, ecumenism, and the implementation of the Second Vatican Council.

Paul's army years were no exception to the rule. He spent only one month in training at Harvard before he received his first assignment on October 31, 1942, to Camp Edwards, Massachusetts, the headquarters of the Engineers Amphibian Command.[1] It was one of the newest and most innovative units in the United States Army, established after the fall of Singapore and the Japanese sweep through the islands of the southwest Pacific.

Experts from many services—the Army, Navy, Coast Guard, Coast and Geodetic Survey, the British Army and the Royal Navy—were gathered at Camp Edwards in 1942. Their task was to organize, train and equip amphibious units for the United States Army as quickly as possible. The staff searched through the records of 200,000 officers and three million enlisted men to obtain qualified recruits for these units. In the summer of 1942 they had gone to yacht clubs and boating organizations, giving direct commissions to 400 volunteers. Six brigades (each consisting of 3,667 men) were quickly organized through such methods.[2]

Hallinan stayed at Camp Edwards for only one week. He was preparing to leave with the Second Brigade for additional training in Florida, when an urgent request from General Douglas MacArthur in the Pacific led to an abrupt change of plans. The Second Brigade was ordered to proceed directly to Fort Ord, near Monterey, California, there to await transport to Australia.[3] Hallinan left Camp Edwards on November 9 in one of nine troop trains which moved the brigade to the west coast with daily stops along the way for exercise on the station platforms. To the soldiers' surprise, the cars were Pullman sleepers, and the new chaplain used one of the compartments to celebrate Mass each day of the trip.

At Fort Ord he got his first taste of life at a regular army post, offering Mass and hearing confessions, visiting the guardhouse and the base hospital, counseling and giving religious instructions. At this time he also received his permanent assignment: to the 542nd Engineer Amphibian Regiment (soon to be renamed the 542nd Engineer Boat and Shore Regiment). Almost half of his unit was Protestant, a third Catholic, three percent Jewish, and fifteen percent had no religion at all.[4]

The brigade expected to be at Fort Ord for only a few days; instead they stayed there two months because of the shortage of transports. The time was not wasted, since the troops continued their training exercises in Monterey Bay. Hallinan got ten days leave at the end of November. On Christmas Eve he was deacon at a Solemn High Mass offered by the brigade chaplain, Father Leonard A. LeClair, for over 3,000 men, the only time that the whole brigade was assembled for Mass. Finally on January 24, 1943, the troops began to embark at San Francisco for the long trip across the Pacific to Australia.[5] Their transports traveled alone, each one zig-zagging its way across the ocean to avoid Japanese submarines. On Paul's ship there were the usual complaints about boredom and inactivity. A favorite pastime for the troops was reading anything that they could get their hands on, especially the ship's newspaper. This was a mimeographed sheet called the *Goldbricker*, edited by the former reporter for the Painesville *Telegraph*. For the benefit of the folks back home, he later described a typical Sunday morning aboard ship:

> At 10 minutes to 11, the buglers sound "Church Call." The early
> morning routine of alerts, calisthenics, inspection is over: everybody
> is taking it easy . . . watching dolphins sliding by the ship, reading,
> waiting in lines for library, magazines, candy, coke . . . just plain old
> American boondoggling. . . .

Since he was the only chaplain on board, at eleven o'clock he conducted a General Service on the foredeck, consisting of hymns, Scripture readings, a sermon and blessing, for the Protestants. Then, as a
corporal prepared the altar and vestments, he heard confessions and
celebrated Mass for the Catholics in the same place at noon.[6]

The ship docked finally at Brisbane on the east coast of Australia.
"Docked" is not quite the right word: there was no gangplank; the
troops had to scramble down the ship's ladders to disembark. To the
disappointment of some, there were no aborigines riding kangaroos to
handle the luggage. Hallinan's main reaction was relief that the ocean
voyage was over: "How damned glad I was to get off the damned
transport," he said.[7]

After landing, the 542nd regiment had little time to enjoy Brisbane.
They were headed for Rockhampton, a city of 40,000 about 400 miles
to the north. Before they got there, one further travel adventure awaited
them: a two-day trip across the empty brown plains on the narrow-
gauge Queensland Railways. Australians used to warn American servicemen with a straight face that "lots of people have died of starvation
on the Queensland trains," but even they complained of the yellow
dust, soot, burrs and grasshoppers that were the normal accompani-
ment of any trip.[8] Hallinan agreed that a ride on the "rattler" was
unique and he could not believe that the cars they used were really
intended for passengers. The only pleasant feature was the pineapples
which he bought along the way.

They reached their destination, a camp just north of Rockhampton,
around six in the evening. The scene was one of feverish activity as the
soldiers went to work setting up tents and storing equipment. Mosquitos were everywhere, but Hallinan did not mind because the setting
reminded him so much of rural Ohio. The site had been selected,
according to General Eichelberger, Commander of the Eighth Army,
because of Queensland's semi-tropical climate. Nearby beaches, hills
and woods made it an ideal training area. The camp never got a
formal name. It was only a temporary facility for reassembling the

brigade as it arrived piecemeal in Australia throughout February and March at many different ports on the east coast. Everyone knew that they would soon be moving again "up north" or to "far shore," euphemisms for the war zone in New Guinea.

Hallinan was there for six months. In addition to the routine duties of any overseas chaplain, he had some special responsibilities because of local circumstances. One serious cause of friction between Australians and Americans was marriages between American servicemen and local girls. With 500,000 Australian men in the armed forces, it threatened to become a major problem; in fact over 10,000 such marriages occurred. Hallinan did his best to discourage them by emphasizing the problems that would inevitably arise after the war. He was happy to point out later that only five men from the 542nd married Australian girls and he noted drily that this was not a problem in New Guinea.

Australian hospitality left him with another and more pleasant problem: working with the Australian Red Cross and the Catholic Servicemen's Group to arrange weekend holidays in local homes for the enlisted men. He also continued to edit the regimental newspaper together with his chaplain's assistant, Corporal Thomas J. Farrell.

People who knew Hallinan after the war often referred to "the Hallinan touch," his characteristically gracious way of doing things. There was evidence of that already in Australia, such as his decision to print and distribute 1,800 Mother's Day cards for the men to send home.[9] He showed a particular sensitivity towards the Jewish men in his regiment, always arranging a Friday night service for them, or, whenever possible, transportation to a synagogue in Rockhampton. One Jewish soldier, who was a native of Cleveland and the brother of a rabbi, was so pleased that he wrote a letter home to his parents that wound up in the Cleveland *Plain Dealer*:

> As a Jew I want all Cleveland Jewry to know that Father Hallinan, who is from Cleveland, made it possible for us to hold our traditional Passover services here in this area under the most trying conditions.... This is only one of the things Father Hallinan has done for our small group.... I am writing these few lines on behalf of the men of the regiment. We want all Cleveland to know how we feel about Captain Paul J. Hallinan, who is God's messenger to us.[10]

The living conditions at Rockhampton were spartan and it was necessary to use a large recreation tent for Sunday Mass. Hallinan set out to remedy the situation by building a permanent chapel and he got enthusiastic support from the men of the regiment. They hardly needed coaching at reading blueprints and agreed to build a chapel for him from local stone and timber. For incidental expenses they were as generous with their money as with their time and labor. They also got considerable help from Australian civilians, one of whom donated the lumber. Paul decided to dedicate the chapel to St.Christopher on the grounds that he was the first "amphibian saint," and he noted optimistically that he had operated successfully "from near shore to far shore." The chapel was finished by the end of April with wooden seats and communion rail, a stone altar and pulpit and a rear office for the chaplain. Hallinan's pride was obvious in his description of the project in his monthly chaplain's report:

> With voluntary contributions from enlisted men and officers and hearty cooperation of the whole regiment, a chapel has been constructed in 5 weeks, seating approximately 180 and accommodating as many as 300....[11]

After the building was finished, the chaplain asked the local bishop, Romuald Hayes of Rockhampton, to pay a visit. The bishop was delighted with the building, tried out the pulpit for size, said it was "so American," and remarked that the rough-hewn timbers reminded him of the Tom Mix movies that he had seen. He offered to say Mass in the chapel and Hallinan invited him to come for Confirmation. A few days later he sent Hallinan a present, a copy of Robert Hugh Benson's novel, *By What Authority,* and Paul wondered if it were a subtle reminder that he had built the chapel without asking the bishop's permission.

Actually, Hallinan spent some of his most pleasant hours in Australia at the cathedral rectory in Rockhampton. He enjoyed the company of the priests there and soon acquired a tremendous admiration for Bishop Hayes. "I don't want to be a bishop at all," he wrote in 1943, "but if I had to be, I'd want to be like Bishop Hayes of Rockhampton." What impressed him most about Hayes was his ability to put everyone at ease. It was the result, he thought, of the bishop's gift for listening: "He was totally there while you were speaking; he had a complete absence of absent-mindedness." It was also at the cathedral rectory that, for the only time in his life, he borrowed a book which he did not return. It was a good choice: Alfred O'Rahilly's life of Father William Doyle, S.J., an Irish chaplain in the British army during the First World War.

After Bishop Hayes' Confirmation visit, he thought that it would be diplomatic to invite the local Protestant clergy to come and perhaps hold a Protestant service for the men of the regiment. He approached the Methodist minister who was the secretary of the local ministerial association, the Reverend Mr. Tainton, who reacted to the invitation with undisguised suspicion that it was some kind of Romish plot. When Hallinan mentioned that he would also provide food, Tainton became even more alarmed. Hallinan wondered if visions of the Borgias were flashing through his head. Tainton remarked that such an invitation was so unusual; it would never have come from the local Irish clergy. "They are so definitely opposed to anything English," he said. "Probably," Hallinan replied, "because for so many centuries the English were opposed to anything Irish." The visit was postponed, then cancelled.

The most unpleasant experience that Hallinan had in Australia occurred on his thirty-second birthday, April 8, 1943. By noon that day, he said that he had experienced the rage of a ten-year-old boy whose dog had just been chloroformed. He was on his way to visit the hospital in Rockhampton with his driver, Pvt. Leonard Morris, when he passed the car of Brigadier General William F. Heavey. Heavey had recently issued an order that no one should use a vehicle unless it had a full complement of men. When the general spotted two empty seats in Hallinan's jeep, he ordered him to stop, berated him for wasting gasoline, and ordered him to return to camp. His parting shot was: "Roll down those sleeves. Try to *look* like an officer."

Hallinan's first reaction was to write a letter of protest to the Chief of Chaplains in Washington. However, the brigade chaplain, Father Leonard LeClair, took the matter in hand and got assurances that there would be no interference with the work of the chaplains. "We won the fight," Hallinan said, "but I lost the chance to fight." By a curious coincidence, when he was promoted to captain eight days later, the order was signed by General Heavey, but it was the last promotion that he ever got.

It was not his only brush with military authority. He had no problems with his first commanding officer, Lieutenant Colonel Robert J. Kasper, for whom he had enormous respect. Kasper, however, was very young for combat command of a regiment, and in May 1943 he became executive officer of the 542nd, relinquishing command to an older man, Colonel Benjamin C. Fowlkes.

Fowlkes soon noticed that the General Services were not well attended and he attempted to find a direct military solution for the problem. First he asked Hallinan to take the services. He quite properly replied that he need not and would not do so as long as a Protestant chaplain was available. One week later the Protestant chaplain was sent "up north." Hallinan found himself obliged to conduct a General Service for the first time since the troopship days. The first Sunday all went well. The next week he was away on bivouac. He returned on Saturday night to discover that Fowlkes had issued orders that those going to chapel should march there in military formation and that the first sergeant should report to the chaplain the number of men present from each company. Fowlkes also told the officers that he would like them to be present as well.

Hallinan was furious when he discovered what had happened. He spent the following week speaking to each company individually, assuring them that attendance at services was voluntary and discussing several reasons for going or not going to chapel. Among the latter reasons that he mentioned was "desire to create an impression on someone." Hallinan said: "I think everybody understood." The following week Fowlkes rescinded his order.[12]

After six months as an army chaplain, Hallinan tried to sort out his experiences. Evening Mass was a new phenomenon for him. After some initial hesitation, he decided that he liked it very much and that it was absolutely necessary, if the Eucharist was to be made available to the troops. On Monday evenings he conducted the Novena of the Miraculous Medal. At St. Aloysius he had wise-cracked that the best novena was that of the fifty-two Sundays, but, when he saw the devotion of the men who came on Monday evening, he had to admit that "the common sense of the faithful must always be reckoned with." A Notre Dame practice which he imported to Australia were outdoor stations of the cross, fourteen small crosses nailed to trees around the chapel. After Mass each evening there was the rosary in common, which not only appealed to many of the men but served a very practical purpose for Hallinan as a substitute for the recitation of his Office. (If said alone, fifteen decades of the rosary were required.)

Hallinan was genuinely proud of the Catholic officers and enlisted men of the 542nd because he got the same cooperation from them that he had gotten from the youngsters at St. Aloysius. "After all," he told Monsignor James Daly, his former pastor there, "they're only Stalpians, Alcyons ... a little bit older, a little bit farther from home." It convinced him that a priest's work was basically the same wherever he might be.[13]

Relationships with non-Catholics were an area where he was still feeling his way. He was certainly no bigot, as is evident from his concern for the Jewish soldiers in the regiment. When a Mohammedan soldier from the Philippines complained about his dogtag, Hallinan had a machinist make him a special one with MOH stamped on it for his religion. Many of the men in the 542nd were Southern Baptists and Methodists, but that did not present the slightest problem to him on the personal level. "He had the whole regiment with him, Protestant as well as Catholic," said Colonel Kasper, who recalled one Christmas Midnight Mass in New Guinea when his choir consisted entirely of Protestants and Jews.[14]

On the other hand, he was extremely touchy about doing or saying anything which might suggest even tacit approval of indifferentism. Whenever someone would say to him (no matter how inoffensively), "I believe that one religion is as good as another," he would snap back, "I don't. If I did, I wouldn't waste my time as a priest for ten minutes." He was embarrassed by a letter from a Protestant minister to one of the men congratulating Hallinan for conducting the "Protestant" General Services. Thereafter, whenever he held these services, he refrained scrupulously from joining with the congregation in the alternative recitation of the Psalms.

He complained that at times he had to have the tenacity of an Aquinas and the tact of an Emily Post to balance the demands of doctrinal integrity against the equally compelling demands of Christian charity. It is doubtful if anyone realized the struggle that was going on inside him, behind the jolly facade. He had no doubt that objectively Protestants and Jews were both wrong: "Jews cling to a seed that was never allowed to germinate into its flower and tree; Protestants clutch broken branches that have become detached from the trunk." At the same time he could not deny the good faith of the non-Catholics, and he recognized that Christ's command to love, not hate, certainly applied to Protestants and Jews.

Part of the reason for his dilemma was the Catholic theology of the day. Often written by men who had never met a live Protestant in their lives, it inculcated a positive horror of worship with non-Catholics under threat of the direst canonical penalties. Even the most innocuous recognition of other religions was considered tantamount to a repudiation of the Catholic Church's own exclusive claims.

He was not the only one who was grappling with the difficulty of reconciling the theories in the theology manuals with the realities of American life. Back home, Archbishops Edward F. Mooney of Detroit and Samuel A. Stritch of Chicago, Father Wilfrid Parsons, S.J., and Father John Courtney Murray, S.J., were all groping towards a satisfactory solution to this same problem. However, at this stage in his life, Hallinan was much more in sympathy with the intransigent views of Fathers Francis J. Connell, C.Ss.R., and Joseph C. Fenton.[15] "I want no watery Faith for my diet," he said, "and I don't intend to feed it to anyone else."[16]

Before he left Australia he got a week's leave to make a retreat with the Redemptorists in Sydney. It also gave him an opportunity to do a little sightseeing. Like many Americans abroad for the first time, he tended to judge everything on the basis of how closely it resembled the United States. When he saw Brisbane for the second time, he disliked it even more than the first time, dismissing it as an "overworked version of a small town having a circus." Sydney was different and better. "Detroit without the Ford plant," he called it. He even liked the streetcars because they reminded him of the ones in Cleveland. The Redemptorists were gracious hosts and he was grateful to them for their material and spiritual hospitality:

> The second day I disappeared into the bush with my breviary.... There in a scraggling growth on a hillside, looking down at Sydney's Bay, I found the solitude I'd been searching for [for] a year. It was a chance not only to pray to God, but to converse with Him. To the echo of some startled birds, I actually chanted the Benedictus and the Magnificat when I came to them in the Office of the day.[17]

The Second Brigade left Australia in the same why that it came: piecemeal. During June and July, individual companies of the 542nd pulled out of Rockhampton for the "far shore." Hallinan disliked the dispersal of the regiment because he lost contact with so many of his friends, and it left him with little to do at Rockhampton. Finally the rest of the regiment received orders to depart also. They traveled by the "rattler" to the port of Gladstone and spent the night there trying to sleep on plywood strips in a huge warehouse. On Sunday, August 1, 1943, he said Mass on the dock at Gladstone, and that evening he left on a Liberty ship bound for New Guinea.[18]

He spent the next seventeen months at various places on the north coast of New Guinea and the offshore islands, as the American and Australian armies gradually pushed the Japanese back and opened the way for the recapture of the Philippines. The most direct way to dislodge the Japanese from their positions on New Guinea—an assault overland from Port Moresby—was impossible because of the rugged terrain. The mountains of the Owen Stanley range in the center of New Guinea rise to heights of 16,000 feet, and there were no railroads or paved roads anywhere on the island. The only alternative was a series of landings on the north coast carried out by the amphibious engineers, and it was in these operations that the new units demonstrated their effectiveness, eventually employing over 2,000 boats of various sizes and shapes.

Getting there was not half the fun. It took sixteen days for the Liberty ship to cover a four-day voyage. For twelve days they lay at anchor in Milne Bay at the southeastern tip of New Guinea, forbidden to go ashore because the area was saturated with malaria.[19] The official rate was 4,000 per 1,000 which meant that the average person would catch malaria four times a year. General Heavey described the place as "a pestilential hole." Finally they reached their destination, Oro Bay, which until recently had been a small native village surrounded by coconut trees.[20]

New Guinea was an exceptionally unpleasant place to wage war. The official United States Army history of the campaign gives a graphic description of the atrocious conditions under which the troops had to fight:

> The rainfall at many points . . . is torrential. It often runs as high as 150, 200 and even 300 inches per year, and during the rainy season, daily falls of 8 or 10 inches are not uncommon. The terrain, as varied as it is difficult, is a military nightmare. Towering saw-toothed mountains, densely covered by mountain forest and rain forest, alternate

> with flat, malarial coastal areas made up of matted jungle, reeking
> swamp, and broad patches of knife-edged kunai grass 4 to 7 feet
> high. The heat and humidity in the coastal areas are well nigh un-
> bearable.... Along the streams the fringes of the forest become
> interwoven from ground to treetop level with vines and creepers to
> form an almost solid mat of vegetation which has to be cut by the
> machete or bolo.... Leeches abound everywhere; and the trees are
> so overgrown with creepers and moss that the sunlight can scarcely
> filter through to the muddy tracks below.[21]

Like everyone else Hallinan had to depend on atabrine to ward off
malaria. Mosquitos, leeches, grubs and assorted insects were another
menace against which leggings and insect repellant were not always
effective. Surprisingly, snakes were not a big problem on New Guinea,
but as he said: "You'd almost welcome a snake you could see in
preference to ants that you only *know* are in your pants." Clothing was
constantly wet from rain and perspiration, resulting in many kinds of
fungus and skin diseases. Worst of all, perhaps, was the psychological
effect of such gruesome surroundings. Around the time that Hallinan
was landing at Oro Bay, the Third Australian Division, which was in
action farther up the coast, sent this report to headquarters:

> Such conditions of rain, mud, rottenness, stench, gloom, and above
> all the feeling of being shut in by the everlasting jungle and ever-
> ascending mountains, are sufficient to fray the strongest nerves. But
> add to them the tensions of the constant expectancy of death from
> behind the impenetrable screen of green, and nerves must be of the
> strongest, and morale of the highest, to live down these conditions.[22]

For a chaplain there were practical advantages to serving with an
engineers regiment, as Hallinan had discovered in Rockhampton when
they built a chapel for him. They built another one for him at Oro Bay
in three weeks, only this time it had a sand floor and thatched roof. It
was big enough to seat 200 men and was furnished with an altar,
communion rail, pulpit and even reredos of highly polished black
palm branches.[23] Yet he did not have much time to enjoy it. He kept
moving up the coast with the army. He was at Lae in November and
from late December 1943 to early April 1944 at Finschhafen, both
recently captured from the Japanese by the Australians with the help
of the Second Brigade. From Finschhafen he noted laconically in his

monthly reports that "combat conditions exist." What he did not mention was his own activities in combat.

MacArthur's strategy in New Guinea was not to advance overland step by step, but to gain ground rapidly by a series of surprise landings behind enemy lines along the coast. Hallinan took part in several of these missions. From Finschhafen he joined the troops who landed at Saidor on January 2, 1944. He joked about the fact that, on his first afternoon there, while he was saying the rosary with some of the men after Mass, a Japanese plane appeared overhead. At first the men continued to kneel and make the responses. When the shadows of the plane began to be annoying, they retired to their foxholes in some haste. "God helps those who help themselves," their chaplain said, "faith is not damn foolishness."[24] He was with the first troops who went ashore at Saidor, and the adjutant added this comment to his monthly chaplain's report: "Throughout the entire period the high morale of this unit was due in large measure to the untiring services of Chaplain Hallinan."[25]

He was with advance elements of the regiment for most of the month of February and was cited for his "faithful services to his men ... fine work and cheerful endurance of hardship."[26] On April 22 he was with the first troops who landed at Tanahmerah Bay which was one of the biggest amphibious operations to date, involving more than 250 boats escorted by battleships and aircraft carriers. Again he made no reference to his participation in the landing in his monthly report, but the adjutant added this comment: "Not apparent in this report is the fact that Chaplain Hallinan landed with assault waves at _____ on D Day. He ministered to all troops on the beach, and his valor and devotion have accounted for high morale of this regiment."[27]

In June he was on the move again, this time to Biak island off the northwestern coast of New Guinea. There he had his closest brush with death. The island was a prime target for the Americans because of its three airfields, the only ones in the area capable of handling heavy bombers. The Japanese garrison consisted of 11,000 men, some of them seasoned combat troops who put up bitter resistance. The climate was better than on New Guinea, but the Biak terrain presented its own special problems. There was very little water on the island, and most of the fighting took place in a heavily forested area with thousands of caves which provided ideal protection for the Japanese defenders.

On Biak he volunteered for temporary service with the 186th Infantry, which had the mission of seizing one of the Biak airstrips. They spent several days marching and climbing across ridges and ravines to reach their objective. On Sunday Hallinan said Mass and held a prayer service for 400 men. Afterward, he asked one of the soliders how close they were to the front lines. He replied: "You were on them." At 9:00 A.M. on the fourth day, they reached the airstrip and were surprised and delighted to find it unoccupied. They began to relax and enjoy their unexpected good fortune when, twenty minutes later, all hell broke loose, as the Japanese opened an artillery and mortar barrage on the Americans from the surrounding hills. The Japanese had allowed the Americans to walk right through their lines and now they had them at their mercy on the airstrip. Hallinan and a medic dove into a large crater where they were pinned down for more than an hour. They quickly turned it into a first-aid station. Some of the shells came so close that he could feel the heat and smell the powder. One shell struck the edge of the crater, wounding seven men, some of them seriously. By chance with the chaplain and medic in the crater were two men from the Graves Registration Service. One wag noted this odd assortment of personnel and said: "Bind 'em, bless 'em, bury 'em—let *us* handle your problem."

Orders came that they were to move the wounded to caves near the beach. They were warned to watch for snipers, but Paul thought that it was rather useless advice: "How do you watch a sniper? He's watching you." With considerable difficulty they managed to get the wounded men to the caves, and they remained there all afternoon and evening under constant artillery and sniper fire. More and more wounded were brought in to them. At one point the beachhead was reduced to a few hundred yards. Four medics were killed instantly when a shell hit them; it reminded Hallinan of a movie which had stopped suddenly, leaving the actors in grotesque poses.

At 3:00 A.M. they were evacuated by sea to the main American positions on Biak, bringing with them almost 100 wounded. Even then they were not out of danger; a lone Japanese plane strafed them, barely missing the boat carrying Hallinan. Although he had been wounded by shrapnel himself, that night he offered a Mass of thanksgiving and spent the next week burying the dead.[28]

He stayed on Biak until the fall of 1944, with one brief excursion to visit elements of the 542nd on Wadke island. The fighting on Biak had been heavy and costly (the Japanese lost 8,000 men) but, once the island was secured, the Americans discovered that it could be a rather agreeable place to rest and recover after the arduous campaigns in New Guinea. The weather was better than anything that they had experienced recently, and the engineers soon built clubs, recreational areas, baseball diamonds and other conveniences. Hallinan repeated his earlier successes and built still another chapel—his third—which was ready for Mass on Thanksgiving Day. Nor did he forget the Jewish soldiers. On Biak as on New Guinea, he arranged for Friday night services for them every week without fail.[29]

On October 20, MacArthur began his recapture of the Philippines—with a surprise landing on Leyte. This was actually a larger operation than the Normandy landing and required a 1,200 mile jump from the nearest American-held island. A few days later the Japanese and American fleets clashed in what Samuel Eliot Morison called "the greatest naval battle in history." Some elements of the Second Brigade took part in the original landings on Leyte; other units, including Hallinan's, remained on Biak until early December, when they were moved to Leyte by sea and air.

The 542nd did not go into combat immediately. Their skills were needed to solve the supply problems of the Sixth Army. The main conduit for these supplies was still the beaches near Tacloban where the landings had occured on October 20, and it was the task of the amphibian engineers to ferry thousands of men and thousands of tons of supplies safely to shore until suitable harbor facilities could be constructed.[30] While these operations went on, Paul was stationed in Tacloban itself, which was enjoying a brief moment of fame because it was there that General MacArthur announced his return and the establishment of the Philippines' civil government. One pleasant new experience was the friendly reception which the American troops received from the Filipino people, and Hallinan made a point of saying Mass each Sunday for the Filipino laborers employed by the army. He spent Christmas 1944 in Tacloban, celebrating four Masses for his men.

By March the supply problems were eased, and the 542nd received a combat assignment: to assist the Eighth Army in the recapture of the central islands of the Philippines—Panay, Negros, and Cebu. The first part of the operation—the landings on Panay and Negros—went smoothly. The Japanese abandoned the city of Iloilo on Panay without a fight and Hallinan spent most of April there, celebrating a memorial Mass for President Franklin D. Roosevelt on April 15 at the request of several Filipino priests from a local parish.[31]

The recapture of the island of Cebu was a different story because the Japanese had mined the beaches. Nevertheless, two days after the landings, on March 25, the American army entered Cebu City, the second largest city in the Philippines. Hallinan was transferred there on April 23, but in May and June he was back at Iloilo. In his efficiency report of Hallinan for that period, his commanding officer, Colonel Fowlkes, wrote: "He possesses a fine understanding of and interest in the problems of the enlisted men, and enjoys their confidence and respect to an outstanding degree."[32]

At this point he finally got an opportunity for a visit home. The boat and shore battalions were taken out of combat once again and given the assignment of training other troops for amphibious landings—part of the preparation for the invasion of Japan. Since the divisional chaplains could cover his duties and he had now spent thirty months in the Pacific, he applied for a leave. He was offered forty-five days in the United States, if he would accept another overseas assignment afterwards. He readily agreed and in July 1945, he and Father Raymond O. Meier, chaplain of the 532nd Boat and Shore Regiment, flew out of Manila together on the long flight home.[33]

He spent most of the time with his parents in Painesville, but Monsignor Daly arranged for him to say the 11:00 o'clock Mass at St. Aloysius on August 5. The church was filled and in the sanctuary were many servicemen from the parish who were also home on leave. In his sermon he spoke with pride of the boys from the parish whom he had met in the army, and he assured their parents that they could be proud of them also. He mentioned that he had met a boy from St. Aloysius only a month earlier in the Philippines. Just a few days before he had met the boy's parents. "Now when I go back and meet Joe," he said, "I'll be able to tell Joe that his mom and dad, his home, his street are unchanged, and that his parish church is still the same St. Al's."[34]

Unlike MacArthur, he did not return to the Philippines. The next day the first atomic bomb was dropped on Hiroshima, and on September 2 Japan surrendered. On October 3 Captain Hallinan was discharged from the army. Apparently he never even considered the possibility of a permanent career in the army as a chaplain. Like millions of other Americans, he served his country in World War II out of a sense of duty, but he had no particular affection for the discipline or bureaucracy of military life. Still less did he have any romantic notions about the glamour of war. Two years later, in an article for the *542nd Alumni News,* he revealed his feelings on this point with unusual bluntness and vehemence. "I hope and pray with you that we never go to war again," he told his former comrades. "War stinks."

> It puts a premium on hypocrisy and hate. There were plenty of casualties besides the dead and wounded; men who came back to busted homes, with busted futures and busted values. Then there were maybe a dozen or two who came back better men than they went over. But the majority, I believe, found that they had to fight to stay on an even moral keel. War stinks.[35]

Despite his loathing for war, Hallinan never thought that pacifism was a realistic alternative. In that same newsletter, he sounded an ominous warning: "The issues over which we go to war again should be crystal-clear," he said. Twenty years later, when the issues surrounding American involvement in Vietnam were far from clear to many Americans, Hallinan became a prominent critic of the war. However, he emphasized that his objections were directed at American conduct of that particular war: he never disputed the right of the United States to defend its vital interests by force. And, no matter how critical he became of United States policy-makers in Vietnam, he never ceased to express his respect and admiration for the ordinary soldiers, who were doing their duty in Vietnam as he had done his in World War II.

4

Newman Hall

After his discharge from the army, ex-Captain Hallinan had the luxury of a two-month vacation while awaiting an assignment from the diocese. He was too young to become a pastor on the basis of the prevailing seniority system, but early in December he got news that would have delighted many young priests—an appointment to the staff of St. John's Cathedral.[1]

By any objective standard it was a reward. If a curate were to be promoted, he could hardly be promoted higher than the cathedral parish, and the pastor, Monsignor Richard P. Walsh, was one of the most affable and best-liked priests in the diocese.[2] However, there was one big disadvantage which someone of Hallinan's temperament would feel acutely. The cathedral was located in a decaying residential neighborhood on the edge of downtown. There were plenty of offices, shops and hotels nearby, but fewer than 100 families lived within the boundaries of the parish, which meant that there was no possibility for Hallinan to engage in the kind of youth work which he had found so satisfying at St. Aloysius before the war.[3]

In any event, he probably would not have had the time for such activities. The cathedral was a very active "business" parish, requiring the services of six priests to care for the workers, shoppers and tourists who came there everyday. One priest who was stationed there with Hallinan, Father Caspar A. Heimann, recalled that it was not uncommon for the priest on duty to be occupied in the office from 9:00 A.M. to 11:00 P.M. Despite the hectic schedule, Hallinan and Heimann started an inquiry class, which offered information about the Catholic

Church to both Catholics and prospective converts. Obviously it met a real need, for, within a short time, they were attracting as many as 140 people to the classes.[4]

Six months after arriving at the cathedral, Hallinan received a second, part-time assignment, as Newman Club chaplain at Cleveland College, which was only a few blocks from the rectory.[5] It was an ideal appointment for someone who liked young people so much and worked with them so well. Moreover, at the same time, his pastor, Monsignor Walsh, was made Diocesan Director of Newman Clubs, making it easier for Hallinan to satisfy the demands of both jobs. From the outset, he liked the new assignment, and during the next dozen years, he helped to make Cleveland one of the most active centers of the Newman movement in the whole country.

In 1946 the Newman movement was just beginning to get the recognition that it deserved from within the Catholic community. Until then, Catholic colleges (and the religious orders who operated most of them) frequently looked upon the Newman chaplain as an unwelcome competitor, likely to lure Catholics away from them and onto secular campuses. Some bishops, like Archbishop Michael J. Curley of Baltimore, were notoriously hostile. One bishop who was more or less neutral quipped that he provided Newman Club chaplains for his diocese on the same basis that he provided prison chaplains— for the benefit of Catholics who should not have been where they were in the first place.[6]

By contrast, in Cleveland, with only three small Catholic colleges for a huge Catholic population, there was a long tradition of episcopal support for the Newman movement. The first club in the city dated from 1922. The chaplain was Monsignor James A. McFadden, later the first Bishop of Youngstown. Another notable pioneer was Monsignor Albert J. Murphy, who made a major contribution to the movement in the late 1920's by organizing all the Newman clubs at local colleges into the Intercollegiate Newman Club of Cleveland. By 1946 this umbrella organization had grown to include local chapters at Adelbert Mather College, Western Reserve University, Case Institute of Technology, Fenn College, Cleveland College and Baldwin Wallace College in Berea.[7]

Hallinan began his career as a Newman chaplain at a time when the need for such an apostolate was more urgent than ever. At the end of World War II, when college enrollments climbed rapidly, there was a sharp increase in the number of Catholics at non-Catholic institutions, many of them veterans taking advantage of the G.I. Bill of Rights. Over five million former servicemen went to college in the late 1940's, and for a brief period, seventy-eight percent of the male students were veterans.

Cleveland College was a good example of the changes that were sweeping through American higher education. A "commuter" college loosely affiliated with both Western Reserve University and Case Institute of Technology, it nearly went bankrupt during the Depression and limped along during World War II with an enrollment of just over 3,000. In 1946-1947, however, the number of students jumped to 12,000, more than 5,000 of whom were veterans. For a time the college had to rent additional space in four nearby buildings, and ambitious plans were made for a fourteen-story tower that was to be a downtown "Cathedral of Learning."[8]

There was little at Cleveland College to remind Hallinan of his own college days at Notre Dame: no tree-lined walks, no lake, no football stadium, no dormitories. The campus consisted of one seven-story building, filled to overflowing with students rushing from one class to another, and then dashing for streetcars to take them home or to part-time jobs. The Newman chaplain's first challenge was to make contact with the Catholic students, few of whom knew him or one another.

He put up posters on bulletin boards and sent personal letters to every Catholic student, but the response was disappointing. He then decided to try another form of communication, which had worked well for him in the past and at which he had considerable experience: he started a newspaper to serve not only Cleveland College but all the Newman Clubs in the city. The first edition appeared in October 1946, a briskly-written tabloid with catchy headlines and numerous photographs and illustrations. He called the paper the *Needle* and he explained the reason for the name on the first page of the first edition:

> A needle may be the cause of many a startled look, sudden movement, sharp embarrassment. A needle can mend something old, create something new. . . . Whether to slow action or to stimulate it, the needle gets under the skin.
>
> These are the reasons why this paper is the "Newman Needle." We want Catholicism felt in our colleges. Therefore as the voice of a

Catholic group, we intend to make like a needle—but you'll never find us hiding in a haystack.[9]

It was hard work attracting students at Cleveland College to the Newman Club when there were so many other competing interests in their lives, much more difficult than filling the ranks of the Alcyon Club at St. Aloysius. For his first membership drive in the fall of 1946, Hallinan set the modest goal of 100 members, less than one percent of the enrollment of the college. One of the obstacles was the perception that the Newman Club was just another social club whose main activity was that of sponsoring dances and parties. That particular allegation made Hallinan furious. "It is exactly one-third of the purpose of the Newman Club," he said, referring to the Newman principle that its threefold purpose was social, educational, and spiritual. All three were very much in evidence at the Cleveland College Newman Club. There were indeed dances and parties, for which Hallinan offered no apology. After all, he said, "it was often natural motives that brought together the crowds that first heard Our Lord." But the Communion breakfasts were just as numerous as the dances, and in the fall of 1946 he began a three-month introductory course on the Catholic faith at St. John's Cathedral.[10]

He put his own special stamp on the *Needle,* always looking for a novel way to present a story. For one issue he invented an imaginary dialogue between Pope Pius XII and an American veteran on the need for religious education in college. He also wrote a series of articles in his best journalistic style chronicling the progress of John Henry Newman's conversion to Catholicism as it might have appeared in the English newspapers a century before. The *Needle* had a lively social conscience too, demanding equal opportunities for white and black students and urging college students to take a sympathetic interest in labor unions. Understandably, the plight of the veterans on campus got special attention, especially that of married veterans with children. "Books or Babies: Must the Married Veteran Make a Choice?" was the melodramatic headline of one article which ended with the rather shrill query, "Does Congress Want to Defy God?"[11]

Cooperation with non-Catholics was another topic frequently aired in the *Needle.* Hallinan persuaded Father John Dearden, then rector of Our Lady of the Lake Seminary, to contribute an article which clearly and logically stated the Catholic position in all its pre-Vatican

II rigor. "We as Catholics know that we have the truth," said the future cardinal, and he discouraged Catholics from participating in any activity which might imply Catholic recognition of another religion. By way of illustration he said that he personally would not speak at a commencement service of a semi-religious nature, if Protestant ministers had done so over a period of years. Otherwise, he said, "the Protestant would be inclined to think that our conception of truth is not as sound and invariable as we claim it to be." The sticking point was any activity of a religious nature. Dearden was quite willing to endorse Catholic cooperation with non-Catholics for other purposes, such as better housing, racial justice and more stringent divorce laws.[12]

Bishop Edward Hoban was generous in providing priest chaplains for Newman work, but a serious handicap in Cleveland was the lack of an adequate Newman center at any of the local colleges. For fifteen years the chaplains had talked and dreamed of establishing a Newman Hall somewhere in the city, but the main obstacle had always been the shortage of money to build and operate such a center. In the fall of 1947, however, Hoban agreed to finance the project. Accordingly the diocese purchased two frame houses on Abingdon Road near University Circle for $38,000. After extensive repairs and renovations, the buildings were opened for business as Newman Hall in February 1948. For the first time the Cleveland Newman Clubs had a permanent home with living accommodations for a chaplain and two dozen students, a chapel, library, offices and meeting rooms. The location was excellent, adjacent to both Western Reserve University and Case Institute of Technology, and close to Severance Hall and the Cleveland Museum of Art. Hoban also agreed that the time had come for a full-time Newman chaplain who would reside at Newman Hall. In November 1947, at the time he bought the property on Abingdon Road, he chose Hallinan for that post.[13]

Hallinan did not lose any time in making good use of the new facility. Rather than wait for the students to come to him, he employed every conceivable device to bring them to Newman Hall. In addition to daily Mass, he offered them a "Novena for Success in Exams" (an old staple of Father John O'Hara at Notre Dame), and days of recollection and retreats. He advertised "Little Pop Concerts," even though the music came from a phonograph, and he started cooking classes and an annual Mothers' Tea and Dads' Night. There were parties, dances and Communion breakfasts, a course in apologetics called

Information Hour, and a weekly discussion series on such topics as racial justice and the role of the Church in politics.[14]

Unfortunately, the statistical results had to be somewhat discouraging for Hallinan and the other chaplains. In 1948 there were about 5,000 Catholics at the various Cleveland secular colleges, but only 480 of them were active members of the Newman Club. Periodically Bishop Hoban issued pastoral letters warning Catholic students that they had an obligation to participate in Newman activities, but the letters obviously did not have much effect. Part of the reason for the poor response was the local situation. The Newman chaplains pointed out to Hoban in their 1948 report that "the soil here is not that of a well-centered state university nor that of a compact private school." In 1955 Hallinan estimated that ninety percent of the Catholics were day students, many of them holding down part-time jobs, and for them, the main contact with the Church, if any, continued to be the local parish.[15]

If Hallinan was discouraged, he showed little sign of it. When some club leaders complained about the poor response from Catholic students, he offered them this encouragement:

> As long as one Catholic engineer is serving Mass, one Catholic nurse studying ethics, one Catholic intellectual turning restlessly from Freud to Aquinas, or any Catholic student loving his neighbor because of God, Christ is not walking the campus alone.

Nevertheless, he was not living in a dream world either and he had to admit: "It's a question of numbers. Not enough Catholics are doing these things; in fact, not enough Catholics are doing anything."[16]

Unlike the man in the Gospel, he could not compel the crowds to come in, but he could and did make sure that few people were unaware of the existence of the Newman Club. Every spring he organized a well-advertised Cardinal Newman Day which began with Mass at the cathedral, followed by a breakfast at a downtown hotel and an address by some prominent local figure. Several hundred students would turn out and each college would usually send a ranking officer, such as the dean or academic vice-president. Another annual event was the Art Show at Newman Hall, which grew out of Hallinan's efforts to foster modern and contemporary religious art. By the late 1950's it was a professional operation, with as many as 300 entries from all over the country and a panel of judges drawn from the faculty of the Cleveland Institute of Art and the Cooper School of Art.[17]

During his second year at Newman Hall, Hallinan suggested staging a musical comedy of the type that had proven so popular a decade earlier at St. Aloysius. He got a favorable response from the club members and they decided to present a musical revue of the 1920's. One of the students, Mary Lou Wurstner, wrote the script and Hallinan composed the music. In October 1949 they rented the auditorium at St. John's College for two performances which turned out to be a huge success and the beginning of still another annual tradition at Newman Hall.

Wurstner and Hallinan collaborated on five other original plays. Hallinan downplayed his own role and gave the credit entirely to the students, but he was the sparkplug here as much as he had been at St. Aloysius. Reflecting on these plays thirty years later, Wurstner marveled at Hallinan's ability to motivate the students. "We were not just satellites basking in his glow," she said, "we all became better and we knew it. He gave us confidence to try." Hallinan's influence on young people, she concluded, was due to something more than intelligence, talent or charm. She attributed it to the same virtue that Hallinan found so attractive in Bishop Romuald Hayes of Rockhampton, an ability to listen and respond to the problems of others. In words that are almost identical with Hallinan's own description of Hayes, she said:

> [Father Hallinan] could listen better than anyone I ever met. He gave his total attention to the person and that person's problems— both the spoken and unspoken ones.... No matter how busy, [he] always had time for us and never made anyone feel guilty about imposing.[18]

The *Needle,* of course, continued to appear every month, and he used its columns and editorial page to comment on almost every topic that was of interest to Catholics in those years. He denounced the show trial of Joseph Cardinal Mindszenty of Hungary in 1949, declared his opposition to the Barden Education Bill of 1950, and warned Catholics that they must be prepared to refute the accusations leveled against the Church by Paul Blanshard. When he thought that moral issues were at stake, he was not afraid to bring politics into the paper. He criticized the naiveté of Henry Wallace in the presidential campaign of 1948, urged support for the United Nations, and deplored the immigration bill sponsored by Senator Patrick McCarran of Nevada. The *Needle* accused McCarran of bigotry against displaced persons, "especially Jewish DP's."[19]

Life was never dull at Newman Hall with so many projects going on at all times, but Hallinan feared that these activities might deflect the Newman Club from its main purpose—that of providing Catholic students with college-level religious education. For him, that was the specific mandate which the bishops had given to the Newman Clubs. "The parish can sanctify," he said, "and the campus can entertain. The Newman Club has the teaching assignment, and clumsily or skillfully, it must do it."[20]

At Newman Hall he tried to fulfill this responsibility through a variety of classes and lectures which evolved into a well-rounded educational program. In the fall of 1951, for example, freshmen or new students could attend a series of Thursday night lectures on apologetics, followed by a question-and-answer period. They also had the opportunity to take a course in basic Catholicism, repeated twice a week, and followed in the spring semester by a similar course in practical moral problems. For those with some Catholic background, he offered an introduction to scholastic philosophy and a companion course in contemporary philosophy. There was also a lecture series on marriage and family life, a seminar on spirituality, and study groups which explored such topics as "The Writings of Cardinal Newman" and "Comparative Religion." Most of these classes and lectures were given by Hallinan himself, but he frequently asked seminary professors or friends like his classmate, Bishop John Krol, to speak at the monthly Communion breakfasts. On special occasions during the year, he invited outside guests, such as Father Philip Hughes of the University of Notre Dame, Monsignor John Tracy Ellis of the Catholic University of America, and Louis Bouyer of the Oratory.[21]

Sooner or later most Newman chaplains found themselves in conflict with some faculty member who used his classroom to make disparaging remarks about religion. One experienced Newman chaplain at the University of New Mexico, Father Richard Butler, O.P., warned that, in such situations, the Newman chaplain needed consummate prudence. Otherwise, his zeal might easily do more harm than good, and he mentioned how often he had written angry letters to offensive professors only to rip them up after a few days' reflection.[22]

Hallinan handled one such situation at Western Reserve University in 1949 with considerable finesse. Dr. Daniel Levinson, professor of psychology, published a six-point manifesto in the university newspaper, asserting that modern science had demonstrated the invalidity of religious belief. He said that modern psychology could not accept any "undiscoverables" such as soul, spirit, free will, which were not susceptible of scientific study. All metaphysical entities, such as God, heaven, the immortal soul, were dismissed as projections of psychological needs. They might be real to those who believed in them, said Professor Levinson, but he denied that they had any objective reality.

Hallinan published Levinson's manifesto in the *Needle* and refuted his contentions point-by-point, not in his own words, but by quoting from the writings of Dr. Vannevar Bush, then at the height of his fame as one of America's leading nuclear scientists. The article contained no abuse and no name-calling, just a well-reasoned argument showing that Levinson's supposedly scientific objections to religion were themselves unscientific. He effectively accused Levinson of reliance on blind faith by citing Bush's remarks about the inherent limitations of science. "Science does not teach a harsh materialism," said Bush. "It does not teach anything at all beyond its own boundaries, and those boundaries are severely limited by science itself."[23]

Years later as Bishop of Charleston, when he was speaking of such controversies before the annual convention of the National Catholic Educational Association, Hallinan gave some excellent advice which he himself followed in this particular case:

> What benefit does either the Church or the world draw from a situation where the Newman chaplain spends his time in controversy and quarrels with the very institution he seeks to penetrate with the word of Christ? Of course there are times when he must oppose a teaching or a trend. This should be done with action that is purposeful, well-considered and decisive. It ought to be done with clarity and it must be done with charity.[24]

Another pitfall which he avoided was that of viewing the Newman center as a beleaguered fortress surrounded by hostile forces on enemy territory. He was well aware that the intellectual climate on campus was often inimical to religion and that, for many professors, as he put it, God was at best an elective. But his solution was not to pull up the drawbridge and offer protection to the Catholic students by creating a

Catholic ghetto for them. Rather he took the position that the best defense was a good offense. In practical terms, that meant providing Catholic students with effective answers to their questions and equipping them to be articulate spokesmen for the Catholic Church on campus.

After a while numbers ceased to mean all that much to Hallinan and he concentrated his efforts on forming young Catholic leaders. Once, when he got a smaller crowd than he expected for a seminar, he said, "It isn't the quantity, it's the quality that counts. I would rather have four interested students than 100 fidgety ones."[25] It was this same concern that led him to organize regular leadership weekends at the CYO camp at North Madison, Ohio, for the student officers of the various Newman Clubs.[26] He told a group of these leaders in January 1949 that "the Newman officer who fails to inform himself on all the basic tenets of the Church is not living up to the trust reposed in him by those who elected him." He compared their situation with that of the Apostles faced with the challenge of converting the pagan Roman Empire and urged them to spread and strengthen the faith among the 5,000 Catholics in the Cleveland secular colleges.[27]

As his experience of Newman work grew, Hallinan became more impatient with those who indiscriminately held secular colleges responsible for the loss of faith of Catholic students. He wondered how many of these had lost their faith before they came to college, and he questioned why the same blame was not leveled at the daily newspapers and television. The answer, as he saw it, was not to lament the presence of Catholics at secular colleges, but to persuade them to join the Newman Club once they were there in order to deepen and develop their faith.[28]

One of Father Hallinan's proudest moments as a Newman chaplain came in 1950, when the National Newman Club Federation held its annual convention in Cleveland and he was invited to celebrate the solemn Mass on the opening day. The convention was one of the largest in the history of the federation, drawing 1,000 delegates from 450 colleges and universities. They listened to a welcoming address from Mayor Thomas A. Burke and speeches by Archbishop Richard Cushing of Boston, Professor Jerome G. Kerwin of the University of Chicago, Clarence Manion, Dean of the University of Notre Dame Law School, and Father John Keogh of Philadelphia, the grand old man of the Newman movement. The highlight of the proceedings was the presentation of the first Cardinal Newman Award to Myron C. Taylor, who had served as special representative to the Holy See under both Presidents Franklin D. Roosevelt and Harry S. Truman.[29] It was a sign of the times that the convention received a gracious tribute from the Jesuits at *America,* who acknowledged the splendid work that the Newman Clubs were doing and referred to the "now abandoned thesis that Newman Clubs somehow make Catholic colleges superfluous."[30]

Hallinan was thirty-six years old when he came to Newman Hall and forty-seven when he left; but, despite some extra pounds and a few more gray hairs, he had all the bounce and energy of a newly-ordained priest. Besides his duties at Newman Hall, he was also responsible for half-a-dozen local Newman Clubs, two of which he served as chaplain: Cleveland College and Western Reserve University. His reputation as a teacher and lecturer brought him many invitations to speak and preach at Catholic functions in Cleveland, and from time to time, he also taught courses at Notre Dame College and St. John's College.

A more mundane but essential job was that of fund-raiser. Newman Hall received a partial subsidy from the diocese but he had to raise $7,000 a year to cover the cost of salaries, utilities and maintenance. Most of the money came from the students who boarded at Newman Hall, but the rest had to be made up through a never-ending round of raffles, rummage sales, theater parties and spaghetti suppers. One sorely-felt need was the lack of an adequate chapel. One sister said that the original chapel was so small that there was no need to bring a missal to Mass; she could read the altar missal over the priest's shoulder. In 1952, however, a building campaign brought in $50,000 and enabled Hallinan to build a new and more spacious chapel (with a large meeting room in the basement) between the two houses on Abingdon Road.[31]

The eleven years at Newman Hall were also a period of personal growth and intellectual development for Paul Hallinan himself. Taking advantage of the G.I. Bill of Rights, he enrolled at John Carroll University and received a master's degree in history in 1953. It was the occasion for his first serious venture in historical writing: a master's thesis on the influence of William James on the political activities of Theodore Roosevelt— a topic in which he never showed the slightest interest thereafter.[32] After John Carroll, his next step was to begin work on a doctorate at Western Reserve University, where his mentor was Professor Carl Wittke, a specialist in nineteenth-century American history. Hallinan charmed him as he charmed everyone else, and (although Wittke was not a Catholic) before long he had signed him up as one of the speakers in his lecture series at Newman Hall.

Another source of intellectual stimulation was his discovery of John Henry Newman. It was certainly helpful for a Newman Club chaplain to be able to quote Newman, but in Hallinan's case, it was to be more than a passing acquaintance. He read widely in Newman's writings and acquired a profound and lasting respect for him. He was very proud of the fact that he had several sets of Newman's collected works and a number of first editions. If the Second Vatican Council really was "Newman's Council," then Hallinan could hardly have prepared himself better for it than by immersing himself in Newman's thought and writings during his years in Cleveland.

One reason why he was able to maintain such a busy schedule was the presence at Newman Hall of Miss Bernadette Williams, whom he hired in 1948 as housemother for the students living in the residence. She agreed to take the job for three months and stayed for twenty years. He came to depend on her heavily for a variety of tasks. She was a combination housekeeper, secretary, accountant and general factotum, miserably underpaid and overworked, but totally devoted to Hallinan and his work at Newman Hall.[33]

Even with the assistance of Bernadette Williams, it is amazing how much work Hallinan could pack into a single day. One of his colleagues, Father Thomas C. Corrigan, Newman chaplain to the graduate students at Western Reserve University, called him the most personable man whom he had ever met. He had a real flair for public relations, Corrigan recalled, which enabled him to become something of a personality on campus, readily identifiable by his trademarks: crew-cut hair, every-ready smile, and ever-present pipe. Equally impressive to Corrigan was the way that Hallinan carefully sidestepped many diversions that would have sapped his time and energy so that he could give his total attention to the work of the Newman Clubs.[34] There were times, to be sure, when Hallinan was pushing himself to the limit of his strength. One former resident at Newman Hall recalled how often he would doze off in a chair at the end of a busy day. On one occasion in Akron, he fell sound asleep at a meeting, woke up to discover that he was being called upon to speak, and did not have the faintest idea where he was or what he was supposed to say.[35]

In 1952, after only five years of full-time Newman work, Hallinan's success in Cleveland brought him national recognition, when his fellow chaplains elected him President of the National Association of Newman Club Chaplains, which in turn led to his appointment as National Chaplain of the National Newman Club Federation. The two posts were as much a burden as an honor, since they involved considerable travel and paperwork, all of which Hallinan did while continuing to live at Newman Hall and look after all his other responsibilities in Cleveland. There were advantages to the new jobs as well, of course; not the least of these was that Hallinan was put in touch thereby with Newman chaplains all across the country and given a national audience and national exposure for the first time in his life.

5

Newman Work in Cleveland and the Nation

The 1950's were the best of times and the worst of times for the Newman movement. Never had there been so many Catholics in secular colleges and universities, nor so many Newman Clubs and chaplains to serve them. Residual opposition from within the Church faded in this decade as it became apparent that there was no way to reverse the flow of Catholic students to non-Catholic institutions. As the apostolate became better appreciated, more priests volunteered for Newman work, and, together with interested students and faculty members, they won acceptance for the Newman Club on many secular campuses.

The dark side of the picture was the rudimentary state of the movement's national organization after fifty years of hand-to-mouth existence. It was totally inadequate to meet the greatly expanded demands of the 1950's, but every effort to strengthen the structure aroused opposition from local clubs jealous of their own autonomy. There was also the perennial problem of how power was to be shared between the students and the chaplains. This issue became especially acute in the 1960's, but Archbishop John J. Mitty of San Francisco, Episcopal Chairman of the Youth Division of the National Catholic Welfare Conference, was already fretting about it in 1952. He warned Hallinan at the time of his appointment as National Chaplain that "because of the immature thinking of youth, much prudent direction is in order."[1]

The Newman movement was anything but monolithic. Many college clubs using the Newman name had no connection at all with the national Newman organization, and many others were affiliated on paper but habitually delinquent in paying dues. On the national level there were two distinct but closely related organizations: the National Newman Club Federation and the National Association of Newman Club Chaplains. The Federation was the older and larger organization, tracing its origins back to 1916 and consisting in 1952 of 30,000 students and chaplains. The Chaplains' Association was much younger and smaller, started at the 1950 Cleveland convention by eight priests who were anxious to emphasize the educational purpose of the Newman movement.[2] Both the Federation and the Chaplains' Association were part of the Youth Division of the NCWC which had its own internal hierarchy, running from the Director of the Youth Division (a monsignor and the real *chef d'affaires*) through the Episcopal Moderator of the Newman Clubs (a bishop) to the Episcopal Chairman of the Youth Division (an archbishop).

The structure looked more coherent than it was. In fact, it was a curious combination of byzantine bureaucracy at the top and near-anarchy at the bottom, leaving many chaplains uncertain of their own authority and of the chains of command within the Federation. Dissatisfaction had been festering for years and reached one of its periodic crises just as Hallinan took office as National Chaplain. Many chaplains wanted to strengthen the authority of the National Chaplain and restrict that of the Director of the Youth Division of the NCWC. In September 1952, shortly after the chaplains elected Hallinan president of their association, they appointed an advisory committee for this very purpose. Their report was ready when the chaplains met again in December 1952 at Boulder, Colorado, and it presented Hallinan with the first test of his leadership.

The chairman of the committee, Monsignor Robert E. Tracy, Newman Club chaplain at Louisiana State University and a close friend of Hallinan, issued a report calling for greater autonomy for the National Chaplain. It was well received by the assembled chaplains and became famous in Newman history as the Boulder Memorandum.[3] The immediate result was still another memorandum, this time from the chaplains at Boulder to the Youth Division of the NCWC, with the request that the day-to-day operation of both the Federation and the Chaplains' Association should be left in the hands of the National Chaplain, who would operate "under a broad policy set by the Youth Division [of the NCWC]."[4]

Hallinan thoroughly agreed with this report, but he showed great tact in presenting it to the man most directly affected by it, Monsignor Joseph E. Schieder, Director of the Youth Division. Far from taking offense at the memorandum, Schieder complimented Hallinan for his objective analysis of the Boulder meeting, thanked him for his handling of the matter, and assured him that he agreed *in toto* with the committee's report. Schieder readily conceded that the old system was not working and hoped that the new arrangement would "forever end the childish superstitions [and] cruel misinterpretations . . . that have held up the Christ-like work of the Newman Federation."[5] In fact, many of the old problems remained and were never completely resolved, but at least, after 1953, the National Chaplain had a much stronger hand in trying to cope with them.

Another difficulty which haunted the Federation to its dying days was lack of money, which severly hampered the operation of the national office in Washington, D.C. Father Thomas A. Carlin, O.S.F.S., the first full-time Executive Secretary of the Federation, wondered how the office had been able to function at all. He discovered, for example, that seventy-five percent of the names on the mailing list were incorrect and he had to write to every chancery office in the United States in order to come up with an accurate list. He also discovered how inflated were the claims sometimes made that the Federation included 300,000 members in 550 clubs; in fact, he said, in 1952 there were 31,705 members in 362 clubs.[6]

The main source of income for the Federation were the dues paid by the individual members, which in 1952 were twenty cents a year, less than the dollar a year paid by the Boy Scouts. The total income for that year was approximately $6,000, roughly the equivalent of the amount that Hallinan raised every year at Newman Hall through rummage sales and spaghetti suppers. There was not even enough money for the executive secretary to visit the local clubs.[7]

At the national convention in September 1953, Hallinan campaigned hard for an increase in dues:

> Financially we get along using sweat and ingenuity instead of cash. But why should our Federation just get along? To maintain a National Office, to promote projects, to enable our leaders to lead— this takes a greater budget. I don't know how student leaders do anything on their Federation allowance. Like all National Chaplains before me, I've spent again as much on my own as the $500 paid me by the Federation.

I think national dues should be raised, but our leaders should match this request with definite purposes: to print a national news organ, program aids, "know how" booklets, to promote such projects as Cardinal Newman Day, to participate usefully in *Pax Romana,* to plan Newman "lecture circuits," etc. I believe that if these projects are properly presented, the delegates to this Convention will increase the budget.

His optimism was misplaced. The best he could get was an increase in dues from twenty cents a year to twenty-five cents a year. It left the Federation, he said, "with probably the lowest member contribution of any national organization in the country."[8]

Some of the resistance came from chaplains who feared that an increase in dues would drive away members and potential members; other chaplains preferred to use the money in their own local clubs rather than send it to Washington. In some other instances genetic stinginess may have been the explanation. In December 1953, the National Executive Committee attempted to cut the National Chaplain's allowance to fifty dollars a year, because someone heard a rumor that Hallinan had considerable money in his own right. The motion was quashed when he threatened to read his income tax returns on coast-to-coast television.[9]

People who quibbled over pennies were not likely to have a broad vision of the Federation's future. Hallinan tried to persuade them, not very successfully, that they had to have "major league financing to get major league results." Without an assured source of income, he knew that the Federation could never realize its full potential:

This is not only a matter of nickels and quarters. It is a matter of providing a national instrument that will *unite* us, that will *serve* us, that will *represent* us. I do not think that it is an exaggeration to say that it is a matter of principle—the principle of the Mystical Body of Christ.[10]

One of the main duties of the National Chaplain was to keep in touch with the troops through personal visits. In his first year in office, Hallinan traveled 15,000 miles, visiting twelve of the sixteen provinces in the Federation and attending most of the provincial conventions. Before his term was over, he had been to thirty-six states, occasionally flying, but traveling mainly by railroad, bus and auto.[11]

A good example of the "Hallinan touch" was his practice after visiting a local club, to write to the bishop, commending the chaplain for his work and asking the bishop for his continued support.[12] Hallinan regretted the many hours on the road and the neglect of his own work in Cleveland, but he enjoyed meeting Newman chaplains all across the country. He pronounced them the most hospitable group of men in the world.

Travel was a chore that went with the job of National Chaplain and came as no surprise to him. What he did not anticipate, however, were the derogatory remarks directed at him and the other national officers by some members of the Federation. "I have been amazed and disgusted with some of the comments," he said after his first three months in office. "Zeal in a Newman Club member is a fine thing, but it is no substitute for justice and charity."[13]

Some of the criticism may have been provoked by his outspoken views about the purpose of the Newman movement. Over the years some clubs had gotten the reputation of being little more than social clubs where Catholics could meet and date other Catholics. Hallinan made no secret of the fact that he regarded this state of affairs as an aberration. As he had done in Cleveland, he pushed hard on the national level to make education the first priority of the Newman movement. "The Newman Club must be concerned about many things," he said in a report in April 1953, "but if the teaching assignment isn't being done, then the other things become rather unimportant." It was a message that he repeated often. "Ours is a three-fold program," he told the national convention in September 1953, "but religious and social activities will help the Catholics we've got and attract the ones we haven't got, only when our intellectural effort is geared to the college level."[14]

He tried to help local clubs meet this responsibility in two very practical ways: by providing them with educational materials, and by sponsoring several specialized summer schools. One of the most basic tools, the Newman *Manual,* had been out of print for years because there was no money to republish it. Hallinan reissued it, together with a thin paperback volume, *The Newman Club on the American Campus,* a collection of essays and addresses on Newman work written in the 1930's and early 1940's by some of the pioneers in the movement. In collaboration with Father Robert J. Welch, Newman Club Chaplain at the University of Iowa, Hallinan himself wrote a small brochure,

The Newman Club in American Education, which listed the religion courses offered by the various Newman Clubs across the country, emphasizing as the ideal the credit courses at several major midwestern state universities.[15] He also sent out to the chaplains a kit with materials for celebrating Cardinal Newman Day. In cooperation with *Extension* magazine, he tried to interest students in a national essay contest on "Religion in American Life."

Summer schools were another educational venture which he supported strongly. For the chaplains, there was an annual two-day Institute preceding the national convention, which gave them the opportunity to hear speakers like Frank Sheed and Vincent Smith of Notre Dame. For priests and lay leaders alike, there was the Newman School of Catholic Thought, which offered two weeks of classes, seminars and workshops in theology, philosophy, Sacred Scripture and church history. Begun in 1952 at Notre Dame, it proved so popular that three other centers were opened in 1957. In 1953 St. Louis University began a National Conference for Newman Club Chaplains, a three-week program designed especially for new chaplains.[16]

The results of these efforts were mixed. The Chaplains' Institute was popular and the Newman School of Catholic Thought prospered and grew. On the other hand, few people bothered to buy *The Newman Club in American Education,* only twenty students entered the nationwide essay contest, and the St. Louis summer school folded after only two years—all of which led Hallinan to warn the National Executive Committee of the Federation that "the intellectual function of the Newman Club will remain an after-thought until we grasp the fact that, without it, we are just another Clam Chowder Society."[17]

Just as Hallinan used his national office to promote the educational work of the Newman movement, he also tried to foster a larger role for student leadership. It was no secret that some chaplains allowed very little student initiative in their local clubs. Hallinan thought that that attitude was a mistake. In Cleveland, where he gave the students ample latitude, he got excellent results, and he encouraged other chaplains to do the same. At the Boulder meeting in December 1952, one chaplain complained about the political horse-trading that went on at national conventions, when the students vied with one another to elect national officers. Hallinan disagreed with the speaker and said, "I happen to think that a live and competitive election is fundamental to a student group."[18]

In Monsignor Robert Tracy he found someone who shared his ideas about the importance of student participation. In one of his tri-monthly reports to the Federation, Hallinan quoted with approval Tracy's description of the proper role of the chaplain:

> The most effective relationship between chaplain and students is not one in which the chaplain issues edicts, solves all problems personally and determines all programs of the club as well as the most minute details of the club's life and activity. It is rather a relationship in which everything is a matter of teamwork in Apostolic adventure between a wise, respected, fatherly moderator and a vigorous group of student leaders. On the basis of such a relationship, ideas for local club action can best come from student thinking, no matter how good the chaplain's ideas may be or seem to him to be.[19]

In his final report as National Chaplain Hallinan minced no words about the unsatisfactory state of the Federation. Only 325 of the 673 Newman clubs in the country were paid-up members of the Federation, and these 325 clubs generated the paltry sum of $7,537 in dues in 1954 for a national organization of 30,148 students. No long-term projects or plans for expansion were possible under such conditions. "It is hardly a moment or a posture for resting" was Hallinan's considerable understatement. Nevertheless, he thought that both the Federation and the Chaplains' Association were working more smoothly than two years before. He professed to see on the horizon signs of a second spring, which, in Newman's words, would bring them "keen blasts and cold showers" but also "bright promise and budding hope."[20]

Hallinan's successor as National Chaplain was Monsignor Robert Tracy and their friendship alone was enough to assure his active participation in Federation affairs. He continued to attend every national convention, as he had done since 1946, but the focus of his attention was once again Cleveland.

Throughout his years at Newman Hall, Hallinan had remained close to his family. Shortly after his parents celebrated their forty-fifth wedding anniversary in September 1952, his mother's health began to fail and he got permission to say Mass for her at home. After her death at the age of seventy-six on December 21, 1952, he brought his father from Painesville to live with him at Newman Hall. The elder Hallinan put his gardening skills to good use, landscaping the grounds and building an outdoor shrine to Our Lady Seat of Wisdom. He continued to live with Paul until his own death at the age of eighty on October 7, 1955.

Hallinan's brother, Arthur, lived nearby with his wife and family, and Paul was a frequent visitor at their home. Father Hallinan also remained especially close to Agnes Lynch and Clare McIvor (and her husband Lawrence McIvor), two first cousins with whom he had grown up in Painesville. Whenever he had the chance, he loved nothing better than to dine out with them or with other relatives and friends and Newman alumni.

He also had a wide circle of priest friends of every age and background, such as the rector of the cathedral, Monsignor Richard Walsh; his seminary classmates, Father Norman Kelley and Bishop John Krol; fellow Newman chaplains Fathers Thomas Corrigan and John Kilcoyne; and younger priests, like Father James Reymann, who had once been a resident at Newman Hall while a student at Case Institute of Technology. Like many of his clerical contemporaries, Hallinan was a faithful devotee of the Forty Hours' Devotion, which not only fostered the Eucharistic piety of Catholics, but—perhaps unknown to many of the devout laity—did at least as much to promote the conviviality of the clergy, and Hallinan's charm and wit were always welcome at such gatherings.

He was always on the lookout for ways to make the Newman movement better known to a wider public. In the fall of 1957, however, the Catholic chaplain at Princeton University received more publicity in the space of a few weeks than most Newman chaplains received in a lifetime, with results that disturbed Hallinan and many of his colleagues on secular campuses. Father Hugh Halton, O.P., Director of the Aquinas Institute at Princeton, had been at loggerheads with the university for some time, criticizing school policies and accusing one professor of "robbing students of their minds and souls." He charged that another professor had been associated with Communist-front organizations and called it Princeton's darkest hour when Alger Hiss gave a speech on the campus at the invitation of a student group. Halton's highly confrontational style provoked criticism from two distinguished Catholics on the Princeton faculty, Jacques Maritain and Dr. Hugh Stott Taylor, Dean of the Graduate School.

In September 1957 Dr. Robert F. Goheen, President of Princeton, withdrew university recognition from Father Halton, accusing him of irresponsible attacks on the intellectual integrity of faculty members.

Halton responded by charging that the pseudo-liberal administration had excommunicated him for daring to criticize them. Bishop George W. Ahr of Trenton refused to remove Halton from his post, saying that the basic issue was the right of a priest to speak in defense of faith and morals.[21]

The newspapers and weekly newsmagazines picked up the story and gave it considerable coverage. The *National Review* and the *Homiletic and Pastoral Review* both came to Halton's defense, while *America* and *Commonweal* were critical of the priest's provocative *modus operandi*.[22] Many Newman chaplains across the country were upset at the repercussions of the controversy, and at their January 1958 meeting, the advisory board of the Chaplains' Association asked Hallinan and Robert Tracy to write an article presenting their view of the matter.[23]

Hallinan was anxious to get the article into print with some sort of approval from the NCWC, because he found himself defending the very existence of Newman Clubs in conversations with priests who sided with Halton on the basis of information that they got from sources such as the *Homiletic and Pastoral Review*. What irked Hallinan particularly was that Halton, who had never been active in either the Newman Federation or the Chaplains' Association, was fast acquiring a reputation as the archetypal Newman Club chaplain. After Halton claimed that many of the Catholic graduates at Princeton had lost their faith, some priests concluded that any secular college must be an occasion of sin for Catholic students. Moreover, William F. Buckley Jr., took up the cudgels for Halton, contrasting his aggessiveness with the intellectual timidity of other chaplains. Many college chaplains, Buckley claimed, were more concerned with justifying themselves than with combating infidelity: he seemed to be completely oblivious of the religion courses sponsored by the Newman Clubs at several hundred secular colleges and universities. Father Aidan Carr, O.F.M. Conv., raised the question whether other chaplains should imitate Halton. If the circumstances were exactly the same as those at Princeton, then said Carr, "we would say 'yes'—the chaplain would *per se* be obliged to take up the gage in defense of his lambs." What Hallinan feared most was the effect of this rhetoric on the bishops:

> We are sure that our bishops would not appoint chaplains to Newman Clubs, if the campus of our colleges and universities were a

universal and proximate occasion of sin. And we are equally sure
that our bishops would replace most of us, if the Father Halton
response were deemed the most appropriate.[24]

Hallinan and Tracy called their joint article "The Chaplain and the
University" and submitted it to their respective bishops for clearance.
Both Archbishop Joseph F. Rummel of New Orleans and Archbishop
Edward F. Hoban of Cleveland approved it warmly and recommended
that it be published in some magazine with a large circulation among
priests. The two authors also got the approval of Bishop Maurice
Schexnayder, Bishop of Lafayette, Louisiana, and Episcopal Moderator of the Newman Clubs.[25] Their one remaining hurdle was to get the
approbation of Archbishop Leo Binz of Dubuque, Episcopal Chairman of the Youth Division of the NCWC.

Binz seemed well disposed, when he was first approached in May
1958 through Bishop Schexnayder. He suggested some minor changes,
such as dropping any explicit references in the article to the Princeton
controversy, which the two authors were quite willing to do. When
Hallinan and Tracy sent the revised article to him in June, however,
they got a flat refusal. Binz now claimed to have discovered that the
article was controversial. As the Archbishop of Dubuque, he said that
he might approve the article, but he could not do so as Episcopal
Chairman of the Youth Division, because he felt compelled not to
sanction any article which "any group of bishops would deem objectionable."

He then admitted to Hallinan and Tracy: "The article may not in
fact be objectionable to any bishop. If that be true, the fault lies in
large measure with yourselves." What he meant was that he was not
about to make inquiries among the interested prelates. Hallinan and
Tracy should have submitted the article to him, not through Bishop
Schexnayder, but through the Youth Office of the NCWC, where
"they employ certain priests at their Washington headquarters for just
such work."

Having resolutely refused to approve the article, Binz then did a
splendid job of buck-passing by suggesting several options to the
authors:

> It is possible that you will wish to appeal to the Administrative
> Board against my judgment as an Episcopal Chairman. It is possible
> that you will wish to reopen the question when there is a new

Episcopal Chairman. It is possible your Ordinaries will offer some other counsel to you.[26]

What was not possible was to get Binz to assume any responsibility. The article finally appeared a year later in *Our Sunday Visitor* under Hallinan's name as Bishop of Charleston without any reference to the NCWC.[27] The only oblique mention of the Princeton controversy was Hallinan's praise of Jacques Maritain as someone who had helped to awaken non-Catholic scholars to the Catholic intellectual tradition.

In the fall of 1956 Hallinan was becoming more and more concerned about completing his own education. By then he had finished his course work at Western Reserve Univesity and was prepared to take oral comprehensive examinations for the doctorate. At least, he thought that he was prepared, but the examiners failed him and told him to come back again in six months. He called the day, November 12, 1956, "Black Monday" and attributed the failure largely to his weakness in English history. He was understandably disappointed and drove around the park that evening before returning home to Newman Hall.[28] The very next day, however, he went to the library and began to prepare a bibliography on English history.

His failure in the comprehensives upset him more than he had at first realized. A few days later he put down on paper his options for the future. He recognized now that it was hardly possible for him to get his Ph.D. by the following June or September as he had originally planned. He toyed with the idea of asking for a year of study at the Catholic University of America, or for a year there and a year in Europe on a Fulbright scholarship, or for a transfer to the faculty of the diocesan seminary. Still another possibility was "to forget about [the] whole thing."[29] He chose none of these options but worked hard at his books in his spare time, even for a good part of Thanksgiving Day, resolved to do better on the second round. When he held a *post-mortem* meeting with the examination board, he found them very encouraging. One professor said that he had seemed exhausted on the day of the examination (Hallinan had spent the two previous days at a Newman convention in Cincinnati.) and assured him that half of the doctoral students in the country failed the comprehensives on their first attempt.[30]

Hallinan quickly regained his confidence. In January he was already doing preliminary work in the Cleveland diocesan archives for his dissertation on Richard Gilmour, the second Bishop of Cleveland.[31] On April 22, 1957, he took his comprehensive examinations for the second time. He walked into the room calm and confident, but he soon realized that he had made what he called certain tactical blunders. This time he was not prepared for the questions on Greek history and American colonial history, and he had to admit that his performance in those two areas was very weak. He waited outside the examination room for almost an hour, saying the rosary and expecting to hear that he had failed for the second time. Then Professor Wittke came out of the room to tell him that he had passed. Publicly Hallinan thanked the professors and privately he thanked the Blessed Mother.[32]

With the comprehensives finally out of the way, he started in earnest on the dissertation, methodically going through Bishop Gilmour's diary in the Cleveland archives. During the summer months when he had more free time, he tried to spend three days a week there, and by October he had almost finished with Gilmour's correspondence. He then continued his researches in the Cleveland newspapers at the Western Reserve Historical Society, and in the summer of 1958 he made a trip to Washington and Baltimore, conferring with Monsignor John Tracy Ellis and tracking down more material in the archives and libraries of those two cities.[33]

He was not pleased with the pace of his progress and was anxious to finish the dissertation, but he did not see how he could do it with all the distractions of Newman work. As far back as November 1956 (shortly after failing his comprehensive examinations), he had mentioned to Bishop Krol the possibility of getting some time off but nothing came of it.[34]

When he was made a papal chamberlain in June 1957, Archbishop Hoban asked Hallinan what he would like to do when his Newman days were over. Hallinan replied that he would prefer to spend a year at the Catholic University of America, taking courses in church history and finishing his dissertation, and then to teach church history at the diocesan seminary. In the spring of 1958, before he left for Washington on his research trip, he raised the issue again with Bishop Krol, this time more aggressively. "If I am to finish the dissertation properly, and do it within the next year," he said, "I can see it now only in terms of a year at Catholic University." He emphasized to Krol that he was not unhappy with Newman work; he was merely taking advantage of the invitation from Hoban and him to speak his mind about possible future assignments.[35] Five months after he sent this letter, he got another assignment, but it was not the one that he had been seeking.

6

Dixie

When the new academic year began in the fall of 1958, Paul Hallinan was still at his old post, resigned to spending at least one more year in Newman work. On his way home from a short vacation in Kentucky, he stopped in Columbus, Ohio, to attend a Newman convention. The next day, September 3, 1958, in the middle of a meeting with other Newman chaplains, he received an urgent telephone call from Bernadette Williams with news that Archbishop Hoban wanted to speak to him.

He called Hoban, and the archbishop told him that the Apostolic Delegate, Archbishop Amleto Cicognani, had been trying to reach him at Newman Hall. Swearing him to secrecy, Hoban then disclosed that Hallinan was about to be appointed a bishop, although Hoban did not know where. Hallinan was to return home at once to await a formal letter from the Apostolic Delegate.

Hallinan was so shaken by the news that he went to a motion picture and sat in the balcony, trying to sort out his thoughts. That evening he gave a talk at the convention as if nothing had happened. The next morning he left for Cleveland with Robert Tracy in a driving rainstorm.

At three o'clock on the following afternoon, the letter came. Hallinan opened it in the chapel at Newman Hall and discovered that he had been appointed Bishop of Charleston, South Carolina. He could not share the news with anyone until the Apostolic Delegate made a public announcement in Washington, but Robert Tracy immediately guessed the contents of the letter, and, as soon as his friend left that evening,

Hallinan went to see Hoban at his Bratenahl residence. The arch-bishop told him that his name had been under consideration for the episcopacy for some years and that the appointment was a tribute to the Newman movement. They discussed possible replacements for Hallinan in Cleveland and the missionary character of the Church in South Carolina. Finally, Hoban told him to relax and not to worry about the details until some future date.[1]

Hallinan could not tell anyone where he was going, although he was free to announce that he was leaving Newman work. For the next two weeks he fended off all questions with smiles and riddles. On the evening of September 16, he had dinner with Clare and Larry McIvor. After dinner he told them that he would like to take a drive and talk. He discussed many topics with them until midnight, and then—ab-solved from his obligation of secrecy—he broke the news to them about his appointment to Charleston. Later that morning Archbishop Cicognani made the formal announcement in Washington.[2]

During the next few days, hundreds of telegrams and letters poured into Newman Hall. Hallinan was gratified that many of them came from the Charleston clergy. He was particularly pleased at the con-gratulations that he received from the two former Bishops of Charles-ton, John J. Russell, his immediate predecessor who had just been transferred to Richmond, Virginia, and Russell's predecessor, Emmet M. Walsh, the Bishop of Youngstown, Ohio.

He used the next few weeks to wind up his affairs at Newman Hall and to attend to a number of practical matters, such as sending out invitations to his consecration. The two Cleveland auxiliary bishops, Floyd Begin and John Krol, were both helpful in initiating him into the *arcana* of the *stylus episcopi,* but one convention which Hallinan found hard to master was the art of wearing a hat. His first attempt in many years ended in ignominy, when a sudden gust of wind lifted a new fedora off his head and sent it sailing down Abingdon Road, to the delight of the students watching the scene from the windows of Newman Hall.[3]

For his episcopal motto, he first considered *Ut Omnes Unum Sint,* but then decided on *Ut Diligatis Invicem.* In selecting his coat-of-arms, he showed a fine eclectic sense of history. He began with the coat-of-arms of Pope Pius VII (who had established the Diocese of Charles-ton), and appended to it a golden "lion of England" (to commemorate both King Charles II and John England, the first bishop of the see); he then added two red roses from the coat of arms of Cardinal Newman and an oak tree in honor of his father and paternal grandfather, both of whom had been nurserymen.[4]

His episcopal consecration took place in St. John's Cathedral on October 28, 1958, with Archbishop Amleto Cicognani as the consecrator, and Archbishop Edward Hoban and Bishop John Krol as co-consecrators. Two dozen other bishops and over 500 priests were present. The preacher was Bishop Floyd Begin, who likened the condition of the Church in South Carolina with that of the whole American Catholic Church at the time of the American Revolution. Before the long ceremony was over, a murmur went through the crowd, as word was passed from person to person that in Rome the cardinals had just elected a new pope—Angelo Roncalli, who had taken the name of John XXIII.

Afterwards, at the dinner in the Hotel Carter, Hallinan described what was going through his own mind during the ceremony. "I listened to the ancient litanies and I knew you were praying for me," he said. "I joined my prayer with you, for myself. I felt unworthy and unable."

> Then I remembered, Paul sinned against the Church. James and John were ambitious, Thomas was doubtful, yet God strengthened them. Then I knew God's work must go on in spite of human frailty. So I took heart.

Several speakers at the dinner alluded to the challenges that faced him in his new diocese. Monsignor William Gallena, his boyhood pastor in Painesville, spoke confidently of his ability "to associate with men and women of every shade and kind of belief." Monsignor Michael J. Murphy, the rector of St. Mary's Seminary in Cleveland, recalled how often the first bishop of Charleston, John England, had traveled to Europe in search of priests and money for his diocese, and he assured Hallinan that he would be equally well received on similar visits to Cleveland.

One of the last speakers was Monsignor John J. McCarthy, the administrator of the vacant see. He revealed that, when Hallinan's appointment became known in Charleston, "we got calls from Protestant boys who knew him in the South Pacific." McCarthy observed provocatively that the Catholics of Charleston had not buried a bishop in thirty-two years. Bishop Walsh had been transferred shortly after moving the site of the chancery office; Bishop Russell had been transferred at the time that he decided to enlarge the chancery office. Consequently, Monsignor McCarthy pleaded with Hallinan: "When you get down to Charleston, don't mess with the Chancery! We'd like to have you for as long as you live, and I promise you we won't bury another bishop for more than thirty-two years."[5]

It was another four weeks before Hallinan left Cleveland for his new home. Much of that time was consumed with Masses and farewell dinners sponsored by various groups in Cleveland and Painesville, but Hallinan was also busy traveling and learning about his diocese. Two days after the public announcement, he had gone to Youngstown and spent several hours with Bishop Walsh. He had attended Bishop Russell's installation in Richmond on September 29, where he had the opportunity to speak with Russell and also with Father Joseph Bernardin, who at the age of thirty had already been chancellor of Charleston for several years.[6]

Bernardin went to Cleveland to brief Hallinan on the state of the diocese, and he came away impressed with the new bishop's inquisitive mind and his desire to learn all that he could about the Church in South Carolina. Bernardin noticed too that Hallinan was surprised that he had been made a bishop, genuinely surprised, unlike some clerics who affect shock and dismay when they receive the mitre that they had confidently expected.[7]

A few days before his consecration Hallinan had visited the NCWC offices in Washington and called on Archbishop Cicognani, receiving from him the formal bull of appointment and the unsolicited advice that he ought to convert the Negroes of his diocese. He was back in Washington again in mid-November, this time to take part in the annual meeting of the bishops of the United States. The sessions were especially relevant for Hallinan, since the prelates spent much of their time discussing the question of race relations and, at their final session, they issued a strong and unequivocal condemnation of segregation, which they criticized as incompatible "with the Christian view of our fellow man."[8]

One week later Hallinan was in Chicago to attend the meeting of the Catholic Church Extension Society; on November 23, he left for Charleston by car with John Krol and Norman Kelley. He got his first glimpse of his diocese next morning, as they rolled down Route 52 in the rain through the thick pine forests around Cheraw. An hour later they reached Florence, then headed south into the heart of Low Country South Carolina across the cotton and tobacco fields of Williamsburg County. They passed Kingstree, once famous as a center of the Ku Klux Klan, and then Moncks Corner, where the Trappists had established a monastery on an estate donated by Clare Boothe Luce. They reached Charleston in the early afternoon, arriving at the cathedral to be greeted by the rector, Father Louis Sterker, and Joseph Bernardin, together with a delegation of school children and several reporters. Later, there were more greetings and introductions and a meeting with the diocesan board of consultors. By the end of the day, Hallinan was so tired that, when he went upstairs to retire for the night, he locked himself out of his room.

Next morning, Tuesday, November 25, 1958, the cathedral was filled with clergy and laity who had come to witness Francis P. Keough, Archbishop of Baltimore and Metropolitan of the province, install Hallinan as the eighth Bishop of Charleston. The students from The Citadel provided a trumpet fanfare. After the Mass, there was a dinner at the Francis Marion Hotel. At a civic reception in the evening, Mayor William Morrison welcomed the new bishop to Charleston. It was another exhausting day, but Hallinan was thrilled and delighted with the beauty of the ceremony and the warmth of his reception.[9]

He was jolted back to reality the next day when he met with a group of volunteers who were trying to raise $300,000 for an addition to Bishop England High School. Tactfully describing himself as a new general taking command in the middle of a campaign, he refrained from interfering with the management of the drive. Within two weeks the fund-raising committee reported that they had easily surpassed their campaign goal.[10]

Not all of his problems could be handled so easily. Charleston was a large diocese in territorial extent, ten times the size of the Diocese of Cleveland but numbering only one-twenty-fifth as many Catholics. It included the whole state of South Carolina, 30,989 square miles, which stretched from Beaufort to Myrtle Beach in the hot, humid Low Country along the Atlantic Coast to the Up Country cities of Greenville and Spartanburg in the foothills of the Blue Ridge mountains 300 miles inland. At that time South Carolina was one of the poorest states in the union, with a per capita income that was only fifty-nine percent of the national average. Local boosters had frequent occasion to say: "Thank God for Mississippi." Agriculture, long the backbone of the economy, was notoriously backward and inefficient. As late as 1954, horses and mules outnumbered tractors on South Carolina farms by a ratio of more than three-to-one. Cotton growers found it increasingly difficult to compete in the national market, and the cotton crop of 1958 was the smallest since Reconstruction days. Almost two million acres of farmland had been taken out of cultivation between 1940 and 1958, and, between 1950 and 1959, the number of farms shrank from 140,000 to 78,000.

The influx of industries from the North more than compensated for the decline in agriculture, but many of the new jobs were in textile mills where wages were low and unions were vigorously discouraged. In 1959 the average weekly factory wage in South Carolina was $62.02, compared with the national average of $90.32, and in 1960 only seven percent of the textile workers had been unionized.[11]

Most alarming of all, perhaps, was the wretched state of the educational system. Less than twenty percent of the adults had completed high school in 1950 (compared with the national average of 34.5%), and the median school year completed for blacks was 5.9—record lows for the South, including Mississippi.[12] The state of higher education was not much better. In 1960 one Southern historian was sharply critical of the academic standards at South Carolina colleges. He wrote off the five black colleges as "notoriously weak" and said that "no South Carolina college has the academic atmosphere or resources to inagurate a first-rate graduate program."[13]

Nevertheless, at the time that Hallinan arrived in Charleston, a major economic and social transformation was taking place in the state and throughout much of the Old South. A common expression at the time was: "Cotton moving west; cattle moving east; Negroes moving north; Yankees moving south." The 1950's were industrial boom years, when South Carolina finally began to emerge from the economic doldrums where it had languished ever since the end of the Civil War. Twenty-five large new factories were opened in the year 1955 alone, a prelude to the massive industrial development of the 1960's. In 1945 there were 1,300 factories in the whole state: in 1968, 2,540 factories, and the new plants were worth more than double the value of all the plants built until then. Along Interstate 85 in the Greenville-Spartanburg corridor a whole new industrial complex took shape, as a half-billion dollars (much of it foreign capital) were invested in plants producing textiles, chemicals, pharmaceuticals and metal products. At the other end of the state, L. Mendel Rivers used his position on the House Armed Services Committee to saturate Charleston with military bases and supply depots to such an extent that the city rivaled Norfolk and San Diego in the number of defense establishments; by 1970, the Department of Defense was spending almost 400 million dollars a year in the Charleston area. Between 1950 and 1970, the urban population of South Carolina grew from 36.7% to 47.6%, and per capita income leaped from $893 to $2,590.[14]

An equally profound social transformation was just beginning to take place in the late 1950's, as South Carolina blacks started to respond—more slowly and cautiously than blacks elsewhere in the Deep South—to the promptings of the Civil Rights Movement. Blacks constituted 38.8% of the population of South Carolina in 1950, a percentage exceeded only by that of Mississippi. In fact, from 1810 to 1930 blacks outnumbered whites in South Carolina, a trend that was only reversed by the massive migration of blacks to the north, beginning after World War I and continuing until the present day. Between 1940 and 1960, for example, the black population of South Carolina increased by only 15,127, while the white population grew by 466,127, and the percentage of blacks in the total population steadily declined from 42.9% in 1940 to 34.9% in 1960 and 30.5% in 1970. Unlike some other Southern states, moreover, blacks were fairly evenly distributed throughout South Carolina: only nine counties had less than a thirty percent black population, and in twenty-two of the state's forty-six counties blacks constituted a majority.[15]

The political scientist, V.O. Key Jr., observed forty years ago that "the degree to which the race issue influences political life varies almost directly with the proportion of Negro population," and with good reason he entitled his chapter on South Carolina "the politics of color."[16] In the early decades of the twentieth century a succession of demagogic politicans repeatedly invoked the racial issue to win election to the governor's mansion and the United States Senate; in the 1950's, Senator Olin Johnston and Governor George Bell Timmerman were still winning elections by using the same old techniques. Despite their numbers (or, perhaps, because of their numbers), blacks in South Carolina had virtually no political power from the end of Reconstruction to the mid-1960's. Before 1948 only whites could vote in the Democratic primary election, and, as late as 1958, only fifteen percent of the adult blacks were registered to vote.[17]

James Francis Byrnes, South Carolina's senior statesman and "the state's most significant political figure in the twentieth century" was determined to preserve this way of life as long as he could. He came out of retirement in 1950 to run for governor in an effort to defend segregation very much as John C. Calhoun had once retired from the national scene to defend the doomed institution of slavery. As governor, Byrnes initiated a three percent sales tax in 1951, hoping to improve black schools with the money and so ward off court challenges to the doctrine of "separate but equal" facilities. "We should do it because it is right," he said, when proposing the new tax. "For me that is a sufficient reason. If any person wants an additional reason, I say it is wise."[18]

Between 1951 and 1954 the state spent $100,000,000 on education (the bulk of it going to improve black schools), but this failed to prevent the United States Supreme Court from outlawing school segregation in the historic *Brown v. Board of Education of Topeka, Kansas,* decision of May 17, 1954. One of the cases involved in that decision had originated in Clarendon County, South Carolina in 1950, when the NAACP, on behalf of forty black parents challenged the legality of school segregation on the grounds that it violated the Fourteenth Amendment.[19] There was no immediate change in South Carolina schools after the Supreme Court decision or even after the implementing decision of the Court on May 31, 1955. At the time of Hallinan's appointment to Charleston, there was not a single integrated public school anywhere in the state. The black parents in Clarendon County simply declined to push the case for fear that, if they did so, the entire public school system in the county would be closed down.

Nevertheless, the handwriting was on the wall for the "Southern way of life" and everyone knew it. One historian at the University of South Carolina thought that the verdict in the Clarendon case "momentarily stunned the white citizenry of South Carolina."[20] Among other results, it led directly to a spate of anti-integration laws by the state legislature.[21]

Elsewhere in the Deep south, the reaction to the Supreme Court decision was equally negative, especially after President Eisenhower sent federal troops to Little Rock, Arkansas, in September 1957 to enforce court-ordered integration of a Little Rock high school. A short while before Hallinan's installation in Charleston, Ernest Vandiver won the Democratic gubernatorial primary election in Georgia with a pledge that "neither my three children nor any children of yours will ever attend a racially mixed school or college in this state."[22] In Alabama that year, a young county judge lost his bid for the governorship partly because he was perceived by many white voters as too luke-warm on racial issues, and, according to his biographer, George Wallace vowed that he would never again be "out-nigguhed" by his political opponents.[23]

The following year Ross Barnett, the hand-picked candidate of the Citizens' Council, was elected Governor of Mississippi with a campaign song that proudly announced: "He's for segregation one hundred percent; he's not mod-rate like some other gent."[24] In the South Carolina Democratic gubernatorial primary in 1958 the two leading candidates vied with each other in professing their commitment to segregation, and the winner, Ernest F. Hollings, took office with a promise to "resist the dictation of a power-happy federal government."[25]

On that November afternoon in 1958 when Hallinan came to Charleston, he found a curious mixture of old and new existing side by side. Outside capital and modern industry were rejuvenating the economy; the interstate highway system was about to revolutionize transportation as thoroughly as had the railroads a century earlier; and the educational system was finally beginning to improve after decades of neglect. But the legacy of the past was very much in evidence also. It was commonplace for newspapers to run want-ads for white-only help and to print headlines such as "Negro Arrested for Hardware Store Robbery." Not a single Republican sat in the state legislature or had sat there since the turn of the century. Political power in Columbia was still heavily weighted in favor of the rural counties,[26] and another endearing example of old-fashioned values came to light in September 1958, when federal agents in Horry County seized a still which contained 40,000 gallons of rye mash whiskey.[27]

The winds of change had hardly touched the elaborate system of segregation, and one historian described how pervasive and insidious the system was:

> Does a Negro go into a Charleston drugstore? He may buy a magazine, but he may not drink a milkshake. Why not? Law? No. Custom. Custom, not law, excludes Negroes from white hotels, restaurants and theatres. The Jim Crow signs are down in the union halls, but in many plants Negroes may hold only menial jobs because their white

brother unionists wish it so. "You can count on the fingers of one hand," says a lawyer at lunch in a fine South Carolina restaurant, "the actual laws prescribing segregation in South Carolina—they cover schools, transportation, restaurants at railroad stations, seating in carnival tent shows, separate entrances at textile mills—but, even though there is no law, Nigras may not patronize white hotels, restaurants or theatres. This restaurant here could legally serve anyone, but he won't serve a Nigra because he doesn't want to run a Nigra restaurant. If he serves a Nigra, he'll never serve another white man, except someone from Kalamazoo that doesn't know any better."[28]

Bishop Hallinan's first real encounter with segregation came in January 1959, when he visited the little city of Aiken and discovered two Catholic churches, two schools, and two halls (one for whites and one for blacks), and he admitted that he found the reality of segregation even more confusing than the theory.[29]

His home in Charleston was the cathedral rectory, a stately red-brick building with twenty-two foot ceilings, built in the 1790's by some wealthy planter seeking relief from the heat and humidity of his Low Country plantation. The rooms were large and comfortable, but simply furnished and far from luxurious. Hallinan used the building exclusively as a residence; his office was across the street in the chancery building, a three-story structure with an unusual marble facade. In typical Charleston fashion, the main entrance led not to the interior of the building, but to an elegant piazza or veranda which ran along the whole southern side of the building, opening on to a tree-shaded garden, which not only was a visual delight, but provided a natural form of air-conditioning during the long steamy summers.

Like the city of Charleston itself, the diocese was rich in history. Founded in 1820, it was the seventh oldest see in the United States, outranked in seniority only by Baltimore, New York, Boston, Philadelphia, Louisville and New Orleans. Its first bishop, John England, was one of the most imaginative and dynamic figures in the history of the American Catholic Church. At the time of the Civil War, Charleston produced another famous bishop, Patrick Neisen Lynch, who rivaled some of the local firebrands in his defense of the Confederacy.

The diocese was large in size, rich in history, full of charming towns and villages, but it was desperately short of Catholic people. The total population was 2,370,000, of whom 30,000, or one-and-one-half percent, were Catholics. Even these statistics were deceptive, for fully half the Catholic population was concentrated in and around three cities, Charleston, Columbia and Greenville. Only in Charleston County did the percentage of Catholics rise above five percent; in seven other counties the Catholic population ranged between one percent and five percent. In the remaining thirty-six counties, the percentage of Catholics was less than one percent; in ten of these counties Catholics constituted 0.1% of the population, and in four others there was not a single resident Catholic.[30]

In sharp contrast to the meager Catholic population was the impressive strength of the Protestant churches. The twenty-nine white Protestant denominations had 3,700 churches and claimed a membership of more than 800,000, or sixty-three percent of the white population. There was no doubt that this was part of the so-called Bible Belt, for Protestant clergymen constituted more than ten percent of all white professionals in the labor force.[31] The largest denomination was the Southern Baptist Convention with more than 430,000 members. The Methodists followed with 206,000 members. Moreover, these figures do not include several hundred thousand black Protestants, who belonged to a wide variety of their own churches, many of which kept no permanent records.

Remarkably, this small diocese of fifty-seven parishes (fourteen of them black parishes) was able to maintain a permanent Catholic presence throughout the state. The bigger cities were relatively well supplied with churches: Charleston alone had ten parishes; Greenville and Columbia, three each; but it was a different story in the rural areas. St. Mary's Church in Edgefield, a beautiful, century-old stone building, had sixty-three parishioners; St. Catherine's Church in Lancaster in the Piedmont had forty-five parishioners; and St. John's Mission at Bishopsville in the north central part of the state had twenty-one active members. Fifty years earlier, Bishop Walsh had said that self-supporting parishes were "very, very scarce in this diocese." In many rural areas, conditions were not much better in 1958.[32]

In fact, there were really two Catholic Churches co-existing within the Diocese of Charleston: large city parishes in a few places which were not very different from their counterparts in many northern cities, and a fragile string of rural parishes with their missions and Mass stations in out-of-the-way places like Walhalla, Moncks Corner, Hardeville, Ware Shoals and Holly Hill.

It annoyed the bishop that Northern tourists saw only the urban part of his diocese. After attending Mass in an air-conditioned modern church in Charleston or Greenville, the typical visitor left for home, wondering if South Carolina really was mission territory. In an article for the Cleveland diocesan newspaper, Hallinan invited them to come back to South Carolina, drive fifty miles in any direction, and discover for themselves the other face of South Carolina Catholicism. He described what any tourist would find:

> He will come to a neat, wooden church, shingled roof, seating about 80 people, built probably in the twenties or thirties. Twenty-three parishioners are present—23. The rest are tourists. The twenty-three have come miles for Mass from homes that are spread over one or two counties.
>
> The tourist keeps driving. Another fifty miles and he sees a small Catholic church, built recently with faith, good taste, imagination and contributions from all over the United States.
>
> In case of a fire, the pastor knows just what he would do. He would carry out the sacred vessels in one arm and his mailing list in the other. If that were lost, his thirty Catholics could never rebuild his beautiful church.
>
> Off the main roads, another kind of mission church appears. Rebuilt and repainted many times, it is a link with the early Catholicity of the Carolinas. It is as poor as its people, but they love it. An elderly farmer proudly announces that his great-grandfather built it.
>
> What the visitor does not see, even as he gets deeper into the story of the Carolina missions, is the "Church Intermittent."
>
> This means the Masses said regularly in private homes, funeral parlors, scout-rooms, theatres, even garages.
>
> For a few minutes each week, Christ becomes present in the most unlikely places. After Mass is over, the building goes back to its everyday use. But another handful of Catholics have taken part in what Cardinal Newman has called "the greatest action of all."[33]

The new bishop had come from a diocese where it was common to have four or five priests assigned to a single parish. That was a luxury which the Diocese of Charleston could not afford anywhere. There were sixty-one diocesan priests and fifty priests from various religious orders available for the needs of the whole diocese. Unlike some other Southern dioceses which relied heavily on Irish-born clergy, many of the diocesan priests were native South Carolinians, reflecting the long history of the Church in the state.[34]

Many priests had more than one assignment: the Superintendent of Schools, the Director of Hospitals, the Vicar for Religious and the editor of the diocesan newspaper all did double duty as pastors. Monsignor John L. Manning, Pastor of Sacred Heart Church in Charleston, also served as Director of Bishop England High School. More than two-thirds of the parishes were one-man assignments, and some covered enormous areas.

Father Nicholas Bayard, Pastor of Our Lady of Lourdes Church in Greenwood, had a parish with fewer than 200 people, which stretched over 1,250 square miles in three counties. Father John Gallagher, C.O., had a parish which was almost as extensive near the North Carolina border: at St. Joseph's Church in Chester he had 177 parishioners, but in neighboring Fairfield County he had only thirty-two parishioners at two Mass stations and one mission. In Orangeburg, the Redemptorists had two parishes (one white and one black) with four priests and 650 people. From there they staffed five missions and one Mass station scattered over 2,100 square miles in four counties. One of the missions was St. Andrew's Church in Barnwell, originally dedicated by Bishop England, repaired and restored many times but never replaced with a newer building.

It would have been impossible for the diocesan clergy alone to meet the needs of the diocese. Twenty-one of the fifty-seven parishes were entrusted to religious from nine different orders and congregations. Proportionately the most generous of all the religious were the Oratorians, who established their first American foundation at Rock Hill in 1934 at the invitation of Bishop Walsh and eventually took over the care of five parishes in the north-central part of the state.

The contribution of the religious orders was especially evident in the black apostolate, which had been a special concern of Bishop Walsh, a native son from Beaufort, South Carolina. As bishop from 1927 to 1949, he did more to promote the evangelization of South Carolina blacks than any other bishop of Charleston, including John England. When he came to Charleston, there was only one black parish in the whole diocese, St. Peter's in Charleston. With only thirty-eight diocesan priests and two religious (both Holy Ghost Fathers at St. Peter's), he simply did not have the resources to establish more black parishes, which—given the circumstances of the time—was the only practical way of expanding the black apostolate. Consequently, he appealed to the religious orders to provide both priests and financial assistance, anticipating by several years a similar plea in 1936 from the Sacred Consistorial Congregation to the bishops of the United States on behalf of American blacks.

Walsh established ten new black parishes, and by 1958, there were approximately 3,000 black Catholics in fourteen black parishes, all staffed by religious orders: Holy Ghost Fathers, Franciscans, Dominicans, Oblates of Mary Immaculate, Oratorians, Redemptorists, the Society of African Missions, and Missionary Servants of the Most Holy Trinity. The religious communities of women were equally generous in responding to Bishop Walsh's pleas, establishing parochial schools in ten of the fourteen black parishes.[35]

The total number of black Catholics was, of course, still pitifully small (approximately .003% of the black population), and a local newspaper reporter could still profess astonishment in 1961 at discovering the existence of a black Catholic parish in the state capital. "The Negro Roman Catholic Church is something of a collector's item anywhere in the United States," he said, "but especially in the midlands of South Carolina."[36] A more perceptive observer, Ralph McGill of the Atlanta *Constitution*, noticing the slow but steady growth of the Catholic Church among Southern blacks, stated: "There was a saying that, if one encountered a Negro in the old cotton states who was not either a Baptist or a Methodist, some white man had tampered with his religion. This comment . . . has ceased to have validity."[37]

One of the most surprising features of South Carolina Catholicism was the extent of Catholic education, at least on the elementary level. Thirty of the fifty-seven parishes maintained parochial schools. They ranged in size from tiny St. Andrew's School in Myrtle Beach with three teachers and fifty-one pupils to Blessed Sacrament School in Charleston with 900 students, fourteen sisters and five lay teachers. All told, there were over 8,000 students in Catholic schools, a higher proportion than in most northern dioceses.[38] Part of the incentive for Catholic education was the heavily Protestant atmosphere in many of the public schools, and also the poor quality of public education in many areas. Such an extensive network of Catholic schools would never have been possible without the services of over 200 teaching sisters, the great majority of them from outside the diocese.

Hallinan himself was amazed at the diocesan school system and remarked admiringly that "it is as though the whole history of Catholic education in the United States were cut open and seen in layers." He explained what he meant in more detail:

> Here is Bishop England High School, a modern 700-pupil institution provided by the generous Catholics of Charleston. But still evolving are dozens of mission schools, in private homes and other makeshift places.
>
> In one place children have their catechism in a former barber shop; in another two army barracks are linked together. And in one town three ramshackle frame houses make up what some of the townspeople admiringly call the "university."[39]

The one missing element was Catholic higher education. There was not a single Catholic college or university in the whole state, but the Newman apostolate was well developed with seven active clubs. Most of the chaplains were diocesan priests who also had other assignments, but the Paulist Fathers staffed the Newman Club at Clemson College, and two Franciscan friars operated the Thomas More Center at the University of South Carolina in Columbia.

Health care was another field where the Catholic Church in South Carolina was surprisingly well represented. In the 1950's the Church operated six general hospitals in the state (in Charleston, Columbia, Greenville, Dillon, Rock Hill and York), another legacy from the days of Bishop Walsh, who had been instrumental in the establishment of five of these institutions, often with the enthusiastic support of local civic leaders who appreciated the work of the nursing sisters in their communities.

Just before Hallinan came to Charleston, the Sisters of the Third Order of St. Francis decided to close their hospital in Rock Hill.[40] Hallinan could do nothing to block the move, but he regretted the sisters' unwillingness to reconsider their decision. Like Bishop Walsh, he recognized the goodwill which these hospitals generated in heavily non-Catholic areas, and he told the sisters:

> From my own personal view, as Bishop of the Diocese, I deeply regret that the hospital is no more. We need every possible Catholic

agency working in our state, both for the apostolic good of the Church and the social and community good of our people.[41]

The longer that Hallinan was in Charleston, the more he appreciated the value of the Catholic hospitals. A few years later he said:

> The wisdom of Bishop Walsh in encouraging our hospitals has borne fruit—more than any other feature of the Church, the hospitals (besides doing their work of mercy) have been an instrument of good will, an apostolate that even the most ignorant and bigoted could appreciate.[42]

Thanks to Joseph Bernardin, Hallinan was well aware of all these statistics before he ever set foot in Charleston on November 25, and for the next few weeks, he did little more than bide his time and absorb them. By the first of the year, he was well acquainted with the needs and resources of his diocese, and he described himself as "satisfied, grateful and ready."[43]

7

A Southern Bishop 1958-1960

During the early days in Charleston, Hallinan trod warily, trying not to offend local sensitivities. For personnel information and financial advice about the diocese, he relied heavily on Bernardin who lived with him in the cathedral rectory. After one long session together, he discovered that the building needs of the diocese came to over a million dollars. Almost invariably Bernardin accompanied him on his Confirmation tours and visits around the diocese, and occasionally they would stop for dinner in Columbia at the home of Bernardin's mother. The young chancellor gave the bishop the local perspective which he so badly needed, and he also doubled as master of ceremonies. "An eyebrow-raising MC," Hallinan said, "not a finger-snapping MC." The professional relationship ripened into a close personal friendship, although Bernardin never ventured to address him by his first name until he himself became a bishop.

Hallinan needed no reminding of the delicacy of his situation as a Northerner in one of the grand old cities of the South during a period of mounting racial tension and increased pressure on the South from the burgeoning civil rights movement. One pastor reported to him the comments that he frequently heard on visits around his parish: "What's the new bishop going to do—mix us up?" When he raised the racial question at the February meeting of the board of diocesan counsultors, three of them asked a few questions; the other three responded with a stony silence.[1]

In October 1958, the Episcopal Bishop of South Carolina, Thomas N. Carruthers, a native Southerner and Chancellor of the University of the South at Sewanee, Tennessee, publicly criticized the endorsement of the Supreme Court decision on school integration by his own church's House of Bishops.[2] And not far from Hallinan's home on Broad Street was the office of the Charleston *News and Courier,* which, under the editorship of Thomas R. Waring, was one of the most articulate and truculent apologists for segregation to be found anywhere in the South. The newspaper blithely maintained that "relations between whites and blacks are more harmonious in the South than in any other place on earth where the proportions are so great. The reason is segregation." Three weeks before Hallinan arrived in Charleston, the *News and Courier* gloated over the attempted assault on Dr. Martin Luther King Jr., by a deranged black women in Harlem and noted with relief that "[if] Dr. King [had] been bodily wounded by white persons in the South, he would have become a martyr in the struggle for racial equality."[3]

Hallinan was intensely conscious of the moral challenge which these attitudes posed for him as a Catholic bishop. At the last Forty Hours celebration which he attended in Cleveland (three days before the public announcement of his elevation to the episcopacy), he went around the room asking his fellow priests: "What would you do to solve these problems? How would you handle the problem of integration, if you were the bishop of a Southern diocese?" Once in Charleston, he concluded that there were no ready-made answers and that he would first have to establish his own credibility before he could attempt to offer effective leadership to his own flock or to society in general.[4]

At the reception following his installation, the spokesman for the clergy, Monsignor Alfred Kamler, a former Marine Corps chaplain, commented that Charleston apparently had become a "boot camp" for the training of American bishops. During the inaugural of Governor Ernest F. Hollings in January 1959, Hallinan met one of the *grandes dames* of Charleston society, who chatted amiably with him for a few minutes, then asked where he was from. When he said, "Cleveland," she replied: "Oh well, I suppose that we are all Americans."[5] Both incidents amused Hallinan, but they were also pointed reminders of how vulnerable he was during his first few months in Charleston.

He frequently discussed the question of integration with his priests, especially with Bernardin, but he was circumspect in his public pronouncements. When he spoke at the prestigious Hibernian Society on

St. Patrick's Day, he criticized segregation without mentioning it by name, and at a day of recollection for the Catholic women of Charleston, his allusions were so indirect that one sister said: "He talked about integration, but they didn't understand it." At a speech in Aiken in April 1959 he referred to the "delicate matter" of racial relations ("The silence," he said, "was deafening."). In June at the graduation of Immaculate Conception (the all-black Catholic high school in Charleston) he mentioned the sin of racial discrimination, but he made no overt criticism of segregation, which still permeated virtually every aspect of life in South Carolina.[6]

Racial discrimination was not the only form of bigotry with which Hallinan had to contend. Anti-Catholic prejudice, though far less virulent than in the past, was still capable of arousing considerable emotion in some quarters. In December 1958, Dr. Stanley Lowell, associate director of Protestants and Other Americans United for Separation of Church and State, made a speaking tour of South Carolina, alerting citizens to the machinations of the Catholic Church and urging them to be on their guard. At a speech at the Citadel Square Baptist Church in Charleston, he was introduced by Dr. John A. Farmer, director of the Baptist Brotherhood of South Carolina, who declared that "Southern Protestants are caught in a squeeze play between the Roman Catholics on the one hand and the Communists on other other," and he allowed that he "didn't know which was worse." Dr. Lowell agreed with him and said that "Roman Catholicism is the strongest center of the Communist conspiracy." For good measure, he denounced President Eisenhower for sending an American representative to the funeral of Pope Pius XII, demanded that American cardinals be deprived of their citizenship for voting in the recent papal election, and predicted that government aid to parochial schools would lead to the curtailment of religious freedom for American Protestants. Only a hundred people attended the talk, but the *News and Courier* sent a reporter to the meeting and gave it extensive coverage in next morning's editions.[7]

Hallinan responded immediately, effectively and adroitly. The issue of the *News and Courier* which carried the report of Lowell's talk also contained a paid advertisement from Hallinan in the form of a personal invitation to "Protestants and Other Americans Fearful of the Catholic Church." He said:

Like most Catholics and Protestants, I grew up with the idea that church was the place where we heard about God, worshipped God, prayed to God. I am always shocked at preachers who attack other churches than their own. Currently such attacks have been made and are being made in South Carolina by a Reverend Mr. Lowell.

Protestants can learn very little truth about the Catholic Church from Mr. Lowell because he keeps busy attacking. But Protestants can learn a great deal about the Church by going to the heart of the matter.

To those who wonder what we preach in church, I invite them to listen to any sermon in any Catholic church any Sunday. To those who wonder what our Sisters teach in school, I invite them to drop in on any school in any place in the state of South Carolina. To those who wonder what our hospitals are like inside, I invite them to visit our hospitals any time anywhere in the diocese.

My motto "That you may love one another" is not a slogan. It is the principle that governs every Catholic in his day-to-day dealings with his Protestant neighbors. We are grieved that an outsider who knows nothing of the mutual charity of Catholics and Protestants in South Carolina presumes to lecture fair-minded people and destroy that mutual charity.[8]

After the first six months Hallinan felt more confident and relaxed. Bernardin told him that he still did not look like a bishop but that he was beginning to act like one. After the first year was over, he felt what he called "a sense of gradual achievement and of acceptance by the people of the diocese." A year after that he said that he would not trade his position for the world.[9]

By that time he had established one new parish, visited most of the others, ordained four priests and acquired a good, first-hand grasp of the state of his diocese. He was now making decisions crisply and efficiently: on a single day he told one pastor to cut back his proposed school addition to two classrooms and prodded another to build three classrooms instead of one. When Monsignor McCarthy of Blessed Sacrament Church in Charleston asked to send a parishioner over for a dispensation, he said no and told him to do the work himself. He admitted to himself that, a year earlier, he would have been worried about McCarthy's reaction.[10]

Without the luxury or burden of a diocesan bureaucracy, he tackled many jobs that would be left to subordinates in a larger diocese, such as processing complicated marriage cases. On a visit to Florence he discovered that the rectory at St. Anthony's Parish was a shambles, and the next day he drove around the city with a realtor and the pastor, looking for better accommodations for him. When two teenagers wanted a dispensation to get married despite their parents' objections, he spent an hour with them, listening to their arguments before turning down their request. On a visit to St. Mary's Parish in Greenville, he went through every classroom in the parochial school, asking the youngsters questions from the catechism. When he asked the children in the third grade, "Who is the head of the whole Church?" they replied: "Monsignor Baum," the pastor.[11]

Father Henry Tevlin, C.O., a transplanted New Yorker, who spent almost forty-five years in South Carolina working in poor black parishes, recalled that Hallinan would send him a check for $100 at Christmas.[12] He showed other sensitive pastoral touches also. The Dominican pastor of St. Martin de Porres Mission in Columbia unintentionally provoked the wrath of some of his black parishioners by careless remarks in an interview with a local newspaper reporter. Hallinan offered his help by volunteering to meet with the parish leaders on his next visit to Columbia and he told the upset priest: "Keep your chin up and be assured that you can count on my support always."[13]

It was fortunate that he liked to travel, for he had plenty of opportunity for it, not only in South Carolina but outside the diocese. One way that "missionary" bishops raised funds for their dioceses was by begging trips to more affluent Catholic areas of the country. Hallinan made a fine art of the practice, usually combining several different objectives into every trip. For example, on Saturday, June 20, 1959, he left Charleston for Baltimore, where he spoke on Sunday at all the Masses at Little Flower Church (netting $2,465 for his diocese). That night he drove to Denville, Pennsylvania, and on Monday persuaded the superior of the Sisters of St. Cyril and St. Methodius to send two more sisters to Charleston. Later that afternoon he went to Pottsville to confer with Father Patrick J. Foley as part of his research on Bishop Gilmour. On Tuesday he said Mass for the novices in Denville, flew out of Scranton, and on Wednesday took care of a full round of appointments in Charleston.[14]

The Catholics of South Carolina were rightly proud of their schools and hospitals, but these institutions were a heavy financial burden and absorbed a good deal of the bishop's time and energy. The Catholic school enrollment had more than doubled in the decade before Hallinan came to Charleston, and the growth continued during his years there. Between 1959 and 1962, three of the four Catholic high schools received major additions; and, for elementary school children, the diocese constructed two new parochial schools, expanded seven other schools, and built three catechetical centers and five convents for teaching sisters.

Hallinan's biggest educational project, however, involved the construction of a new Catholic high school in Columbia to replace an old school condemned by the fire department. At a meeting in that city on June 5, 1959, he won the approval of the local clergy for the project. Inevitably the question of integration came up, especially the effect that any such decision would have on fund-raising. Hallinan sidestepped the issue by saying that no announcement would be made about integrating the new school, but that "when a qualified Catholic Negro asks for admittance, the case will have to be handled on thoroughly Catholic principles."[15] In January 1960 the bishop launched a campaign for $400,000, which enabled him to replace the old structure with the new and much larger Cardinal Newman High School.[16]

For the Catholic hospitals, Hallinan's brief tenure was also a period of extensive growth and development. St. Francis Xavier Hospital in Charleston, Providence Hospital in Columbia, and St. Francis Hospital in Greenville all embarked on major building programs which cost more than three million dollars eventually, half of it raised locally by the hospitals themselves and the other half supplied by the federal government under the Hill-Burton Act. For Hallinan it meant many hours spent at hospital board meetings and many anxious moments worrying about the success of the fund-raising drives.

The most ticklish issue was the admittance policy of the hospitals, only two of which (St. Eugene's in Dillon and Divine Savior in York) accepted black patients. At a meeting with hospital administrators on February 17,1959, the bishop said that "all of us should move toward . . . full acceptance [of black patients] on the same basis as white."[17] He saw an opportunity to make this wish a reality when the three hospitals began to enlarge their facilities. He refused to give permission for the expansion programs unless the hospitals agreed to open their doors to blacks.[18] He had little difficulty in persuading the sisters at the hospitals to accept this change, but he did meet resistance from the lay advisory boards in Charleston and Columbia.

In Charleston, the president of the board at St. Francis Hospital resigned in protest, claiming that "such a program ... was not necessary to serve the colored sick but was a step in the furtherance of integration of the races." Aside from this incident, there was no other opposition and the racial barriers were dropped at St. Francis Hospital without further controversy.

In Columbia Hallinan anticipated greater difficulties with the largely non-Catholic board of advisors, but he was determined to bring Providence Hospital into line with the other Catholic hospitals in the diocese. He told another hospital administrator why:

> The urgency of this was made painfully clear last year when a report was made to me by a woman who was criticized in Confession because she did not have the foetus baptized in a miscarriage, and when asked by the priest why she had not gone to a Catholic hospital, had to reply: "I couldn't—I'm Negro."[19]

The sisters at Providence Hospital left it to Hallinan to win over the advisory board. He attended the board meeting on June 21, 1960, and found them more conciliatory than he had expected. They agreed that blacks would be admitted, not immediately, but at some future date when a second expansion program would enable the hospital to build a separate wing for them. Hallinan reluctantly accepted the compromise because it at least committed the hospital to accepting blacks as a matter of principle.[20]

Five months later, to the surprise of everyone and the chagrin of some, additional government money suddenly became available and Hallinan insisted that Providence Hospital proceed with its pledge to build a wing for blacks. The sister administrator of the hospital was anything but enthusiastic but Hallinan was adamant. He told her: " I do not see how I can stretch the meaning of our diocesan policy to permit the addition of new acute general beds ... and yet continue to exclude Negro patients."[21] A week later he lectured her even more severely:

> The times are changing rapidly—so are customs of long standing. Our people are preparing themselves for changes now that they

would not accept when Providence Hospital was established. If conflict comes—and the newspapers indicate daily that it certainly will—the Diocese of Charleston (with its institutions all over the state) must present an image that everyone will recognize as fully Christian. I do not believe that any thinking person would try to justify a Catholic hospital turning away sick people merely because they have black skin.[22]

Hallinan's toughness paid off. At the December meeting of the advisory board, the bishop's decision was announced and only one member indicated disapproval. By Christmas 1960, all five Catholic hospitals were committed to serving both black and white patients.[23]

In the spring of 1959 Hallinan made an announcement which indicated his interest in a field with which he would become increasingly identified. He revealed that the clergy conference for that spring would be devoted to the liturgy, more specifically to the practical application of the *Instruction on Sacred Music and Sacred Liturgy,* issued by the Holy See on September 3, 1958, which called for the establishment in every diocese of a liturgical commission and greater participation by the laity in the celebration of the liturgy.

Hallinan left nothing to chance. He began planning for the conference in December 1958, asked the diocesan consultors for suggestions, and discussed the agenda over the telephone with Monsignor Martin B. Hellriegel of St. Louis, a nationally known liturgist. There were actually two clergy conferences, one in Charleston on April 28, 1959, and the other in Columbia on April 29. On both days, the principal speaker was Father Frederick McManus, professor of canon law at the Catholic University of America, whose explanation of the new decree in the *Pilot* of Boston had caught Hallinan's attention. McManus spoke for an hour each morning, followed by a question-and-answer period. In the afternoon there were workshops and a Mass at which school children demonstrated the technique of participating in the Latin Mass. It was Hallinan's hope that the clergy would then conduct similar meetings for the people of their parishes, and that the decree would be fully implemented in the diocese by October.[24]

The bishop was delighted with the response of the priests to the clergy conference. He followed it two weeks later with a directive to pastors, urging them to train their people in the use of the simple Latin responses at Mass. He also wanted the gradual introduction of hymns at Mass and a series of sermons to be preached which would explain the reasons for the new emphasis on greater participation in the liturgy. All these efforts were to culminate in a diocesan-wide celebration on the feast of Christ the King at afternoon Masses in each of the four deaneries.[25] Hallinan told the people of the diocese that the purpose of the celebration was

> to worship God in a body, publicly, socially, liturgically. To demonstrate to the good people of our state that the deepest bond of our unity is our bond of loving God together. To encourage all our people in every parish to speak up and become an active part of the Mass.[26]

Over 8,000 people came to the four Masses on October 25, 1959. In Charleston 5,700 people were present at the pontifical low Mass celebrated by Hallinan in Johnson Hagood Stadium. They recited together the *Kyrie, Gloria, Credo, Sanctus, Pater Noster* and *Agnus Dei,* sang appropriate hymns, and watched several of their number bring the bread and wine to the altar in a procession at the offertory. The ceremony was as liturgically correct and progressive as the law allowed, down to the fine detail of two choirs singing the Gelineau psalms antiphonally. Hallinan called the day "a mighty act of adoration and homage ... offered to God by the Catholic people of South Carolina," and reminded the assembled faithful that "our prayers at Mass are never our own pipelines to God. They are part of a mighty chorus, a conversation with God through Christ Our Lord, who is Our Head."[27]

Father Roy Aiken, the first chairman of the diocesan liturgical commission, suggested an even more ambitious project for the following year: a week-long liturgical conference followed by a field Mass for all the people of the diocese. Hallinan liked the idea and began preparations for it a year in advance. He asked Cardinal Richard Cushing of Boston to celebrate the Mass and he invited Bishop Fulton J. Sheen to preach, but both were unable to attend.[28] However, he did secure the services of Father Godfrey Diekmann, O.S.B., of St. John's Abbey, Collegeville, Minnesota, Father Francis X. Weiser, S.J., of Emmanuel College, Boston, and Father Shawn Sheehan of St. John's Seminary, Brighton, Massachusetts. For six days they presented a series of lectures on the liturgy to the priests, sisters and laity, and on May 1, 1960, the conference ended with a pontifical Mass in Johnson

Hagood Stadium celebrated by Archbishop Egidio Vagnozzi, the Apostolic Delegate to the United States. Bishop Hallinan had originally hoped to use the armory on the grounds of The Citadel, but General Mark Clark refused permission for fear that the state legislature would object to the presence of blacks at the Mass at a time when racial tension was running high in the state.[29] Up until the last minutes, the worried bishop had visions of a sudden downpour ruining the day, but the rain held off despite the threatening clouds, and he pulled out all the stops for the occasion. The preacher was Monsignor Martin Hellriegel, and the Diocesan Council of Catholic Men arranged to have the Mass televised over five local stations. More than 8,000 people attended—one quarter of the whole diocese, and the *Catholic Banner* announced that it was the largest gathering of Catholics in the history of the diocese.[30]

Archbishop Vagnozzi also got the red-carpet treatment, including a civic reception attended by the mayor and local military officials (at which the usually unflappable Bernardin introduced him as Archbishop Cicognani). Hallinan observed his distinguished guest closely and admired his ability to get others to do most of the talking. When Vagnozzi asked about the method of processing complicated marriage annulment cases in the diocese, the bishop held his breath until he could change the subject. Overall his impression of the Delegate was that he was "pleasant, casual-appearing, but shrewd, devout and, if necessary, ruthless."[31]

One reason for the success of the liturgical conference was the care with which Hallinan had prepared it. He explained to his priests that it was not "a rally nor pageant nor window-dressing nor something designed to interrupt a busy priest from pastoral care or teaching." Its purpose, he said, "lies deep in the fibre of our priesthood and in the layman's daily life."[32] He showed the same sensitivity in his approach to the laity on liturgical matters, eschewing the fanaticism and intolerance of some liturgists who seemed bent on making Catholics pious in rather the same fashion that Robespierre had once tried to make the French virtuous. At the first meeting of his diocesan liturgical commission in September 1959, he warned the members against changes that would shock or discourage the laity. As a chaplain in the South Pacific, he had seen for himself the value of traditional Catholic devotions and he was not about to jettison them now. While recognizing the paramount importance of the Mass, the sacraments and

Divine Office, he vigorously defended the legitimacy of such devotions as Benediction, Forty Hours, the rosary, the Stations of the Cross, and novenas. "These practices of piety," he said, "are not to be changed or discontinued, but they must be influenced by the spirit and principles of the liturgy." Afterwards he heard rumors that Father Aiken regarded him as an arch-conservative.[33]

In the fall of 1960 he sent a questionnaire to the pastors, asking them for their reaction to the liturgical innovations. One priest complained of "constant changes," and Hallinan replied that none had been made since April 1959. By this time about ten parishes were using lay readers at Mass, and thirty had introduced English hymns. Three-quarters of the pastors said that they welcomed the liturgical changes and expressed a desire for greater use of the vernacular. Two-thirds thought that the changes had already had a favorable impact on the spiritual life of their parishes. The results pleased the bishop, but he also sensed the need for caution, lest he push his clergy too far too fast. "The Holy See has pointed out the way," he told them, but "the pastors (and the assistants) know the parish best and can best direct the details."[34]

During 1960 Hallinan was out of the diocese almost a quarter of the time, mainly on fund-raising trips which took him to six different dioceses. That September, he told a Columbus, Ohio, congregation that he needed to raise $200,000 each year from outside sources in order to keep his diocese solvent.[35] By now he was also receiving invitations from all over the country to speak at Catholic functions. He accepted requests to speak at Greensboro, Columbus, and at Cleveland where he gave the keynote address at the National Newman Club convention in September 1960.

Whenever possible, he would add a few extra days to these trips so that he could visit relatives and friends in Cleveland. In December he paid a call on the ailing George Williams, the father of his former housekeeper at Newman Hall. At Bernadette's request, he gave him a few brief instructions in the Catholic faith, baptized him and confirmed him.[36] Another reason for travel was his desire to finish his doctoral dissertation on Bishop Gilmour. He started work on it again in January 1960 after a lapse of more than a year and hoped to finish it by the end of 1960. At times he wondered if it was worth the effort. "I am dreaming of the degree for September," he wrote, "but what in hell is the point of it? Guess it's partly pride, partly a real interest in Gilmour himself." As time allowed, he conferred with Professor Carl Wittke and Father Nelson Callahan in Cleveland, worked in the archives there and at Notre Dame, checked the holdings of the American Catholic Historical Society at St. Charles Seminary in Philadelphia, and sent inquiries to places as far away as Nova Scotia. In July he had the pleasure of spending a few days retracing Gilmour's footsteps in the Ohio River towns where he had served as a missionary and he found the Presbyterian church in Portsmouth, Ohio, where Gilmour had said Mass in 1852 and 1853.[37]

Early in August he had a bad scare. While on vacation with Clare and Larry McIvor, he suffered several attacks of severe abdominal pains. Doctors at the local hospital could offer no positive diagnosis and he returned home to Charleston, entering St. Francis Hospital for a week of tests. His personal physician told him that he was suffering from kidney stones. Two weeks after leaving the hospital, still in considerable discomfort, he flew off to New Orleans where he had a fund-raising engagement at St. Charles Church. While there he experienced an almost miraculous cure, due, he said, to the strong New Orleans coffee which "dissolved the stones and maybe the kidneys too."[38] He was in and out of the hospital before most people knew that he was ill, but something he had said when he was stricken was quoted all through the diocese. "My first thought," he said, "was to get home." Both clergy and laity were delighted to have a bishop who thought of Charleston as home.[39]

Ecumenism was a word that was rarely used favorably in Catholic circles before the Second Vatican Council, and Hallinan himself had shared the traditional Catholic suspicion that ecumenism invariably led to religious indifferentism. Old habits died hard. When he attended the funeral of Mayor William Morrison in St. Philip's Episcopal Church, he said the rosary during the service; however, his views began to mellow during his years in Charleston. When Archbishop Athenagoras, Greek Orthodox Exarch of Central and Western Europe, paid a visit to Charleston in December 1960, Hallinan invited him to his cathedral where they prayed together. Later they had coffee in the rectory.[40]

He was well aware of the social pressures on his flock in many heavily Protestant areas. When a priest asked advice about allowing Catholic Boy Scouts to attend a Protestant service or permitting Catholic graduates to attend baccalaureate ceremonies in Protestant churches, the bishop said: "Go prudently, but assert our position firmly. A passive attendance might be tolerated, but not if it canonizes an indifference or a 'Protestant-control' mentality among our Catholics."[41] He was more cautious when a Newman Club chaplain inquired about appearing on a panel with a minister and a rabbi to discuss religion at a public forum. Here Hallinan saw a real danger of indifferentism and told the priest to "request separate billing" and "insist courteously on sufficient time and proper setting."[42]

However, a few months in Charleston had been enough to convince him that there was a fund of goodwill toward Catholics in South Carolina, and he wanted to take advantage of it by promoting a clear and positive image of the Church among non-Catholics. Somewhat impractically, he told a local convention of the Diocesan Council of Catholic Men in April 1959 that "we need to keep open every channel of information: newspapers, radio and television. Catholic books and magazines could be placed in the public library of every city and town."[43]

A more effective way of reaching the non-Catholic public was the annual custom of Goodwill Sunday. Once each year, Catholic churches held open house for their non-Catholic neighbors, inviting them to tour the church, hear an explanation of the Mass and sacraments, and stay for a social hour in the church hall. Hallinan did not introduce this practice, but he gave it his complete support, encouraging his priests to advertise the event in local newspapers and to be on hand themselves to meet the visitors. He was perhaps more enthusiastic than some of the pastors, for in 1961 he announced that he wanted a report from each parish on the success of the program.[44]

The last pastoral letter which he issued in Charleston was devoted to the subject of Christian unity and it revealed how far his thinking had evolved on the subject. The letter was a remarkably generous and optimistic document, taking its inspiration from the example and attitude of Pope John XXIII. Describing Christian unity as the duty and responsibility of every Catholic, he said that the day of the Ecumenical Catholic had arrived:

> Certain of his own belief, yet humble lest he betray it by his conduct, he faces the religious challenge of our time not with scorn nor indifference, but with authentic charity. His whole life is dedicated to the absolute integrity of Catholic doctrine. He cuts no corners in his

creed; he brooks no compromise with truth. But the Ecumenical Catholic, like St. Paul, practices the truth in love.[45]

In the summer of 1959, when it became likely that the Democrats would nominate John F. Kennedy for President at their national convention, some Catholics feared a resurgence of anti-Catholic feeling, especially in the South. In June a Methodist newspaper editor warned Governor John Patterson of Alabama (a Kennedy backer) that "the people of Alabama, whose attitudes are basically Protestant, do not intend to jeopardize their democratic liberties by opening the doors of the White House to the political machinations of a determined power-hungry Romanist hierarchy." The following February, Dr. Ramsay Pollard, President of the Southern Baptist Convention, told a Mississippi audience that he would not "stand by and keep my mouth shut when a man under the control of the Roman Catholic Church runs for the Presidency of the United States."[46]

In the more refined world of South Carolina politics there was little of this blatant bigotry, but an editorial in the *News and Courier* provided a fine example of a more subtle and genteel type of prejudice which appealed to the worst fears of many Protestant Americans. In November 1959, when the Pope appointed two new American cardinals, South Carolina's "most outspoken newspaper" noted that some Protestants were alarmed at the rapid growth of the Catholic Church in the United States and said:

> We recognize sound historical grounds upon which fears of Roman Catholic domination rest.... In our opinion it would be disastrous for the nation if any religious group ever grows big enough and strong enough to impose its beliefs—spiritual and otherwise—on the people of the United States.[47]

Hallinan made no comment, but the *Catholic Banner* accused the *News and Courier* of reviving the old canard that an American Catholic could not be a loyal citizen and replied with an eloquent quotation from the first Bishop of Charleston:

> We know of no tribunal in our Church which can interfere with our proceedings as citizens. Our ecclesiastical authority existed before our Constitution and is not affected by it. There is not in the world a Constitution which it does not precede and with which it could not

> coexist. It has seen nations perish, dynasties decay, empires prostrate. It has coexisted with them all and is not dependent on any one of them. They may change and it will still continue.[48]

Shortly after this exchange Hallinan gave an address in Cleveland in which he declared that he did not care whether the next President of the United States was a Catholic or a Protestant. He said, however, that he cared mightily "whether he practices honestly the faith that he professes to be true." He warned Catholics that, in a pluralistic society such as the United States, it was inevitable that conflicts would arise from the interplay of rights and duties, privileges and responsibilities. He urged Catholics to choose their ground wisely and to distinguish between "issues of justice," like aid to parochial schools, and "issues of diplomacy," like an ambassador to the Holy See.[49]

When John Kennedy won the West Virginia primary election in the spring of 1960, beating Hubert Humphrey in an overwhelmingly Protestant state, the religious issue faded and Catholics hoped that it would play no further role in the campaign. Their hopes were dashed, however. On September 7, 1960, Dr. Norman Vincent Peale assembled a group of 150 Protestant ministers and laymen in Washington. They called themselves the National Conference of Citizens for Religious Freedom and issued a statement asserting that the Catholic Church has "repeatedly attempted to break down the wall of separation between Church and State," and that the Church "insists that [Kennedy] is duty bound to admit to its direction." The unresolved conflict, they said, leaves doubt in the minds of millions of our fellow citizens.[50]

This statement immediately revived the religious issue and moved it once again to the center of the campaign. No one recognized this more quickly than Kennedy himself. The next day, he accepted an invitation to speak on the following Monday before a group of Protestant ministers in Houston, Texas—an appearance which may well have been crucial to his victory.

Meanwhile, many religious leaders who were unhappy with the activities of Peale and his friends decided to issue a declaration of their own. It appeared on September 11, signed by 100 prominent Protestant, Catholic, Greek Orthodox and Jewish spokesmen. The Catholic signatories included Cardinal Richard Cushing, Bishop Robert Dwyer of Reno, Father Thurston Davis, S.J., editor of *America,* and Father

Robert Drinan, S.J., Dean of Boston College Law School. They suggested ten principles or guidelines for Americans to follow during the campaign, the first of which was that it was unconstitutional to exclude anyone from public office because of his religion.[51]

Hallinan thoroughly approved of this statement. In a speech before the Diocesan Council of Catholic Men in Greenville on October 16, 1960, he called upon all religious leaders in South Carolina to endorse the ten principles. He got no response from them, but his challenge at least served to put the bigots on the defensive. In the same speech he assured worried Protestants that there was no "Catholic party" or "Catholic line." For Catholics, he had a message too: to ignore aspersions on their loyalty and to follow three simple rules:

> 1. Be calm—leave the anger and hate to others.
> 2. Be accurate—leave the sweeping generalizations and twisted texts to others.
> 3. Be as fully American as you are Catholic. Each of us knows that he needs no split personality to serve his Church and his country.[52]

He repeated the talk a week later before another group of Catholic men in Columbia. This time he amplified his remarks about the incidence of anti-Catholic prejudice in the press and Protestant pulpits. It was the latter source of bigotry which especially disturbed him. "These [clergymen] are doing the real damage," he said:

> These attacks, I believe, will tear down a very precious framework—that of friendship between Catholics, Protestants and Jews.... But we thank God that the vast majority of our Protestant people, together with many of the clergymen, are not following this line. We wish more of them would speak out so that the whole framework of good Catholic-Protestant-Jewish relationships will not be wrecked before November 8.[53]

Other Catholic bishops made similar statements in an attempt to prevent the religious issue from becoming a dominant factor in the 1960 presidential election. Bishop Leo A. Pursley of Fort Wayne-South Bend, for example, warned his priests carefully to avoid any mention of partisan politics in the pulpit, and Archbishop William O. Brady of St. Paul reffirmed American Catholic commitment to the teaching of Pope Leo XIII about the legitimate authority of both the ecclesiastical and civil powers.[54] But at the very time when these prelates were reassuring the public that the hierarchy did not seek to dictate the political choices of the laity, the Catholic bishops of Puerto Rico issued a controversial pastoral letter, warning Catholics on the island not to vote for the Popular Democratic Party of Governor Luis Muñoz Marin.[55] The letter was read at Mass on Sunday, October 23, and caused widespread repercussions both on the island and in the continental United States, where it threatened to become an issue in the presidential election campaign.[56] This was the last thing that the American bishops wanted to happen, and, in a most unusual move, several of them publicly disassociated themselves from the statement of the Puerto Rican bishops. Cardinal Spellman of New York said that Catholic voters would not be sinning and would not be penalized, if they ignored the pastoral letter. Cardinal Cushing stated that it was "totally out of step with the American tradition for ecclesiastical authority here to dictate the political voting of citizens." Even more unusual and more significant was the intervention of the Apostolic Delegate. Speaking in Mobile, Alabama, a few days after Hallinan's talk in Columbia, Archbishop Vagnozzi disclaimed any responsibility for the pastoral letter of the Puerto Rican bishops (Puerto Rico was not part of his jurisdiction.). He noted that the United States bishops had never taken such a position, and added: "I am confident that no such action would ever be taken by the hierarchy in this country." Hallinan did not make any public statement, but he was appalled at the action of the Puerto Rican bishops and told a group of priests: "Apparently [they have] no sense of responsibility."[57]

In his celebrated appearance before a group of Protestant ministers in Houston in September 1960, John Kennedy defended the right of any elected official—Protestant, Catholic or Jew—to follow his conscience in the performance of his duties, yet he stressed his own independence of ecclesiastical authority to such a degree that he seemed to imply that his religion would have little or no influence on his performance in public office. During the summer, Archbishop Karl J. Alter of Cincinnati, in a lengthy magazine interview, had discussed the same question, but he had answered it by showing that the Republic would benefit if Catholic officials carried out their duties conscientiously on the basis of their religious convictions. He said succinctly: "There is no doctrine of the Catholic Church which is in conflict with the Constitution of the United States, and hence there can be no conflict between the obligations imposed by the Church and those imposed by the Constitution."[58]

Hallinan took a similar approach in an article in *Our Sunday Visitor* which received national attention. The Bishop of Charleston observed that nobody's conscience existed in a vacuum and expressed the hope that every religious person, whatever his creed, would apply God's law to everyday problems. He saw nothing objectionable in this, provided that every person

> use[s] his religious principles, not as a substitute for personal conscience, but as a guide for it. Thus the Protestant, the Jew, the Catholic. The important point here is that the American Catholic finds nothing in his religion that conflicts with his duty as an American.... Dozens of Catholic bishops have frankly declared that no such obstacles exist or could exist. No pope has ever contradicted them.

He invited non-Catholics to discover for themselves the real nature of the Catholic Church. He told them to visit a Catholic church or school or hospital, or to read a Catholic newspaper or magazine. Or, "if you wonder what a Catholic bishop is up to," he said, "I invite you to drop in at my office for a visit. Here is the Catholic hierarchy, or at least a small part of it."[59]

Kennedy carried South Carolina in 1960 (by 10,000 votes), and, as Hallinan had predicted, Catholics in South Carolina as elsewhere emerged from the minor crisis more assured and confident of their place in American society than ever before.

8

School Integration 1960-1961

It became evident to Paul Hallinan during 1960 that he would have to take a stronger stand in favor of racial justice. Of course, he was not starting from scratch. Much had been done long before he ever set foot in South Carolina. There had been no Jim Crow laws in any Catholic church in the Diocese of Charleston for many years. In any community where there was only one Catholic church, all Catholics were *bona fide* members; wherever a black parish existed, blacks were free to go there or to any other Catholic church. Ten years earlier Bishop Russell had integrated the Diocesan Council of Catholic Men, the Diocesan Council of Catholic Women and the Confraternity of Christian Doctrine on the diocesan and deanery levels, with the result that any meals served in connection with their meetings and conventions had to take place on church property because no restaurant or hotel would serve them.[1]

The only integrated school in the state was a parochial school—St. Anne's in Rock Hill, actually an old rectory that the Oratorians had converted into a two-room school-house. In September 1954, despite threats of violence, they opened their little school with five black students and twenty-nine whites, and they managed to keep it functioning despite horrendous financial difficulties. Hallinan was very proud of the school and was determined to keep it open at all costs.[2] Hallinan himself had already made a major contribution to racial justice during 1960 by preparing the Catholic hospitals to accept black patients, but he realized that much more still remained to be done. All over the South the flashpoint for both blacks and whites was rapidly becoming the issue of school integration—or "mixing," as critics preferred to call it. It was on this issue especially that Hallinan felt the need for the Church to take a stand and to offer effective moral guidance.

At a New Year's Day gathering at the Hibernian Society in 1960 he was puzzled that everyone was so cordial and so jovial, even though most of the members stood poles apart from him on the racial issue. One elderly gentleman telephoned him afterwards, afraid that he had offended the bishop by saying: "We've lost our freedoms, one by one." Hallinan assured him that he had given no offense and added: "We are all for justice and freedom for all."3

The bishop was more forthright with the governor, Ernest F. Hollings—an episode which provoked him into his first confrontation with the state government. It began when the governor criticized the Civil Rights Advisory Committee for South Carolina. Hollings refused to cooperate with the committee and said: "I don't see how anybody in South Carolina in good conscience can serve on that committee."4 One of the members happened to be Father Allan R. Jeffords, Pastor of Our Lady of Perpetual Help Church in Camden, who had received Bishop Hallinan's hearty approval to serve on the committee. He now came to the priest's defense and (in a confidential letter which he assured the governor he would not release to the press) he asked Hollings if he had been quoted correctly. He then inquired "if one of our most respected priests is to be tagged with the stigma of a false conscience," and he asked if "these attacks on the personal motives of the committee members are to continue?"5

Hallinan got results. The very next day the governor replied in a courteous, four-page letter. Obviously stung by the bishop's criticism, he said that, while his statement had been quoted correctly, "it was quoted in some coverages out of context with the thought in mind." What he meant was that, in his opinion, anyone on the committee claiming to represent the views of South Carolina should be a segregationist, since that was the view of the majority of the citizens of the state. "Perhaps," said Hollings, "I should have stated: I don't see how he can seriously contend that he represents South Carolina."

The governor got in a few barbs of his own. He wondered how Hallinan could claim in "good conscience" that thousands of Catholics in South Carolina were opposed to Hollings' stand on racial matters, when in the city of Charleston the diocese operated a totally segregated school system. "Though the exact wording of [your] statement is correct," he told the bishop, "I can't imagine the 'learning' being far off from the 'teaching.'" Basically, however, Governor Hollings was conciliatory in his answer to Hallinan. He assured him that there would be no personal attacks on members of the committee and suggested that he and Hallinan meet to discuss their differences.[6]

They spent an hour-and-a-half together in the governor's office in Columbia on January 28, 1960. They failed to agree on the purpose of the Civil Rights Committee and Hollings continued to insist that Father Jeffords did not even represent the views of most Catholics in South Carolina on the question of integration. Hallinan replied that most Catholics in the state accepted the Church's teaching intellectually, but they found it hard to accept it emotionally because they had always lived in a segregated society. He pointed out that no Catholic church in the state excluded blacks from Mass or the sacraments or imposed a Jim Crow section on them, and that no Catholic organization excluded them on the deanery or diocesan level. The governor again brought up the existence of a completely segregated Catholic school system in Charleston. To this Hallinan replied that the policy of the diocese was to admit black pupils as soon as it could be done without endangering either the schools or the students. Hollings admitted confidentially that the public schools too would eventually have to admit black pupils, but he could not say this publicly as yet.

The governor was being more candid than the bishop, for the diocesan integration "policy" which he cited was unknown to anyone else in the diocese but himself. He may have been contemplating such a policy for a long time, but apparently the first time that he ever mentioned it to anyone was in this conversation with Hollings.

The governor asked the bishop to understand the difficulty of his position and to recognize the quiet efforts that he was making to improve the condition of blacks in the state. He did not think that Hallinan appreciated the ferocity of white opposition to integration or the limited power of the governor's office in South Carolina politics. Finally he mentioned the Catholic bishops' statement of 1958 with its warning against a "rash impetuosity which would damage the good that had been done." Hallinan (who had signed the statement) reminded him that the bishops had also warned against a "gradualism that is nothing else but a cloak for inaction."

Hallinan came away from the meeting with a greatly enhanced

opinion of Hollings' idealism and courage. "You know now what I am trying to do and I believe that I know what you are trying to do," Hallinan told the governor. "You have my prayers and best wishes." He felt enough confidence in Hollings' friendship to tell him: "Another governor and another bishop will be around at the final solution of this problem, but it is important that you and I take what steps we can to advance towards it."[7]

During the spring of 1960, as sit-in demonstrations and violence became more widespread in South Carolina for the first time since the civil rights movement began, Hallinan became increasingly worried. On March 7, on his way home from Confirmation at the Parris Island Marine Corps base, he told Bernardin what he had already told Hollings, that he intended to open all Catholic schools to qualified blacks as soon as public schools did the same. The ever practical chancellor suggested that he should start to build up an emergency fund to meet any financial crisis that such a decision might precipitate.[8]

As civil disobedience spread throughout the state, leading to the arrest of many young blacks, Hallinan feared that the situation would deteriorate into serious violence. "It appears to me," he wrote, "that we are sitting on a powderkeg while Hollings keeps saying 'No,' [Senator] Olin Johnston says 'Go home quietly now,' and [Thomas] Waring says 'Look at how bad it is up North.'" He decided to draw up a letter to Hollings, outlining his own solution.[9]

He told the governor that the tension and hatred of the previous few weeks would produce scars that would last for generations. The situation was so grave, he said, that it required the civil authorities to do more than merely enforce law and order. While disclaiming any intention of forcing Catholic moral principles on non-Catholics, he explained the reason for his letter:

> My purpose in writing to you is to pledge cooperation to you and other leaders in our state in a program of mutual consultation and prayer, leading to necessary action. Our Catholic people, both white and Negro, are mainly Southerners by birth. They understand the customs and usages of the South.... Can we not, those of us entrusted with positions of responsibility, meet the present tension, and even more the ominous threat of violence, with a program of forward movement rather than just a plea to "calm down and go about your business in an orderly fashion?"

Basing his analysis on a recent book by a veteran South Carolina political journalist, William D. Workman Jr. (who was also an out-spoken segregationist), Hallinan suggested to the governor a three-point program:

> 1. Relax the legal barriers which now obstruct the voluntary association of those whites and Negroes who wish to work together towards solutions through consultation.
>
> 2. Provide for Negro representation in every area of community betterment, especially in the areas where the Negro is affected.
>
> 3. Guarantee to every qualified Negro the right to vote in all elections.

He offered to cooperate in any way that he could and told Hollings: "I believe that the greatest danger to our way of life is not the tension nor the violence, not the unsympathetic Northerner nor the protesting Negro. It is our own fear, our reliance upon repression, our failure to grasp our opportunities."[10]

It was one of the most eloquent letters that Hallinan ever wrote. Unfortunately and inexplicably, he never sent it to Hollings, and the only one who ever saw it was himself. Shortly thereafter, however, he condemned segregation publicly for the first time in a speech in Greenville and he unequivocally refused a request from a white group in Kingstree who wanted separation of whites and blacks at Mass. Not many of his priests echoed his forthright stand, and he told Bernardin in the fall that, unless the clergy started to educate people toward racial justice, he was going to act on the issue alone.[11]

One opportunity for a bolder stand came with the centennial observances of the outbreak of the Civil War. The celebration began (appropriately enough) in Charleston on January 8, 1961. Hallinan wrote a lengthy pastoral letter in which he lashed out at the Citizens' Councils and attributed the disorders at Little Rock, Montgomery and New Orleans to fear and ignorance. The issue, he said, was no longer slavery or white supremacy or even segregation. The most critical issue now, he said, was the unfinished business of a century ago: "How shall white and black live in Christian justice in the nation?"[12] It was stirring rhetoric, but Southerners were used to rhetoric, and he still had to face Hollings' reproach that the Church which officially preached racial equality maintained a segregated school system throughout the state.

He was not the only Catholic bishop faced with this problem. Vincent S. Waters, Bishop of Raleigh, had desegregated Catholic schools in his diocese in 1953, but the climate in North Carolina was considerably more liberal than that in South Carolina. As yet no bishop in the Deep South had dared to desegregate his diocesan school system.[13] Archbishop Joseph F. Rummel of New Orleans, whose archdiocese contained the largest Catholic school system in the South with 75,000 students, had condemned school segregation as "morally wrong and sinful" in a pastoral letter in 1956. But even he, in a heavily Catholic area, hesitated to order desegregation until 1962, two years after the public schools had introduced it.[14]

In fact, all during the summer and fall of 1960, the school situation in New Orleans was the center of attention all over the South, as United States District Judge J. Skelly Wright ordered public school desegregation and Governor Jimmie Davis tried to stop it. Between November 1960 and February 1961, the governor called five special sessions of the state legislature, and Judge Wright, for the first time in American history, placed a restraining order on an entire state legislature. When legal action failed to stop desegregation, white parents resorted to a massive boycott of the public schools, leading to weeks of violence and street clashes between blacks and whites. Leander Perez, the Catholic political boss of Plaquemines Parish (County), became nationally famous as he paraded before television cameras denouncing blacks, Communists, Zionist Jews, Judge Wright, and the "weasel, snake-headed mayor of New Orleans."[15]

Some 300 Klansmen gathered in Montgomery, Alabama, in late November and vowed to prevent school desegregation in that state, by force if necessary.[16] In Charleston itself, black parents appealed to the State Supreme Court in December to prevent the construction of additional classrooms at a black school and to force the transfer of black students to under-utilized white schools.[17]

It was against this background that Hallinan pondered what to do at the beginning of 1961. His fellow bishops across the border in Georgia, Francis E. Hyland of Atlanta and Thomas J. McDonough of Savannah, were in a similar dilemma. Governor Ernest Vandiver had committed the state government to resisting integration at all costs. Serious rioting occurred in Athens, Georgia, on January 11, 1961, two days after a federal judge ordered the University of Georgia to accept two black students.[18]

On January 3, Bishop McDonough had telephoned Hallinan, inviting him to meet with him and Bishop Hyland for a discussion of the racial problem in the hope that it might lead to a joint statement by the three of them. Hallinan agreed to come and started to work on a rough draft of his own statement. Later that day, a package arrived with microfilm copies of documents for his dissertation, and he wished that he could spend some time writing history instead of making it. He admitted, however, that the latter was more satisfying.[19]

His own statement was ready the next day, and at the heart of it was the policy that he had mentioned to Hollings, a commitment to open the Catholic schools to all children as soon as it could be done safely, but certainly no later than the public schools did so.[20] The first hint of trouble appeared when he circulated the statement among the diocesan consultors. Several approved, but Monsignor J. Lawrence McLaughlin, pastor of Stella Maris Parish on Sullivan's Island, advised against publishing it on the grounds that it would crystallize the opposition. Father J. Fleming McManus, Diocesan Superintendent of Schools, was also less than enthusiastic and Hallinan got angry at him for his "weak-kneed and vacillating" stand. The bishop himself began to consider some of the unpleasant consequences that might follow: a financial boycott by the laity, state action against the teachers and the schools, violence in the streets, heckling and bombing. He prayed in his chapel for a while, then decided that he was right and that he had to leave the rest to God.[21]

The three bishops met in Savannah on January 12 and spent three hours discussing their common problems. Hyland frankly admitted that he had no solution and asked the other two for their ideas. McDonough had drafted a tentative public statement similar to Hallinan's, but, after listening to the misgivings of his superintendent of schools, he had decided not to use it for the present. Hallinan agreed that a statement might be unwise, but he suggested that they consider issuing a pastoral letter, combining his own statement with that of McDonough. He recognized that this might crystallize the opposition, but, said Hallinan, it also had the advantage of crystallizing "our side." The three of them then agreed to publish a pastoral letter at the beginning of Lent, each bishop issuing the identical letter in his own diocese under his own name.[22]

Hallinan composed the pastoral letter and sent copies to his two colleagues on January 18. He was having second thoughts about the whole business himself, especially in view of the impending fund-raising drive for St. Francis Hospital in Charleston. A telephone call from McDonough also worried him and left him wondering if Mc-Donough were about to withdraw his support.[23] Then, on January 26, he received a special delivery letter from Hyland, saying that he and McDonough were in substantial agreement on the text of the letter. He suggested a few minor modifications, but he was all in favor of prompt action. Said the usually unassertive Hyland:

> I agree that it is time for us to speak up, and, acting in concert gives us a strength which none of us possesses alone. . . . Personally I do not think the reaction will be an unfavorable one on the part of some as we may fear. I am inclined to think that a substantial number of the people of the South want this issue settled justly as well as peacefully.[24]

Hallinan sent the revised text to Hyland and McDonough on February 7. The two Georgia bishops discussed it over the telephone on February 8 and agreed to accept it without further changes.[25] Hallinan also felt better after a long conversation with Henry Tecklenburg, a prominent Charleston layman and close personal friend, who agreed that the pastoral was needed and promised his support. Hallinan also wrote a catechism-like commentary of fifteen questions and answers to accompany the pastoral. Two weeks before the scheduled publication date, he wrote that he was talking, sleeping, breathing nothing but the pastoral. He prayed, "Dear God, thanks for your steady help. Please keep it up."[26]

Then, on the Monday before the pastoral was due to appear, the Charleston *News and Courier* published a front-page photograph of Father Henry Tevlin, C.O., leading a group of black parents to visit jailed civil rights activists at the York County Prison Farm. The newspaper identified Tevlin, the pastor of St. Mary's (black) parish in Rock Hill, as the only white man to participate in the demonstration. Hallinan telephoned Tevlin and told him not to worry. Two days later he saw the pastor in his office. He listened to Tevlin's explanation of the situation in Rock Hill, cautioned him a little, but endorsed his whole course of action even though the publicity might jeopardize the success of the forthcoming pastoral letter.[27]

The letter became public on Sunday, February 15, 1961. Although liturgists might wince, Hallinan told the priests to read the letter at all the Masses in place of the regular Sunday homily.[28] It followed closely Hallinan's original draft statement, invoking the authority of Sacred Scripture, the Declaration of Independence, and the United States bishops' statement of November 1958 as the basis for its arguments. The letter made no reproaches for the past practice of segregation, admitting that "millions of people have accepted this way of life in good faith." But now, said the bishops, "both whites and Negroes face a tremendous challenge to live in a community with full Christian justice for both."

To demonstrate the commitment of the Catholic Church to full racial equality, each bishop announced the following policies for his diocese:

> 1. Catholic pupils, regardless of color, will be admitted to Catholic schools as soon as this can be done with safety to the children and the school. Certainly this will be done not later than the public schools are opened to all pupils.
>
> 2. The Negro schools will be continued as long as there is need for them. Their purpose is to reach and teach the Negro, not to segregate him.
>
> 3. During 1961, this diocese will undertake a program of preparation for its people. Pastoral letters, sermons, study clubs and school instructions will explain the full Catholic teaching on racial justice.[29]

Hallinan was out of town that Sunday, on a begging trip to Lafayette, Louisiana (where he spoke at all the Masses at Bishop Tracy's parish, starting at 5:45 A.M. and finishing at 6:00 P.M.), but he kept in touch with the local scene through Bernardin. A few people walked out of church, but Hallinan was relieved and pleased with the general reaction. "The priests have rallied," he said, "the die-hards are protesting, the politicians are sore, the Protestants generally agree it was inevitable, and I am confident that Catholics are proud that we acted."[30]

He was back in Charleston on Monday evening and ready to face the storm on Tuesday morning. One elderly gentleman spent an hour in his office, ranting and raving at him. When he accused the bishop of "brain washing" the laity, Hallinan finally lost patience. Bernardin wondered if Hallinan would eventually surrender to public pressure, as others had. He told the chancellor: "I have only started and I never give up." Henry Tecklenburg brought him a letter from the governor, who had read the letter five times and pronounced it brilliant.[31] Hollings told the bishop: "Were I with your responsibility, this inspiring letter would give me satisfaction that I had done the right thing." But then he also reminded Hallinan of the difference in their responsibilities:

> You are the religious guidance and inspiration to two percent. I am the political leader of one hundred percent. In trying to promote progress, in trying to educate, in trying to maintain law and order, I could not in good conscience issue a similar decision or letter as yours. As you, I will have to "prudently judge the appropriate time and conditions" that such a course can be taken.[32]

He got fewer letters of protest than he had expected, but some reeked of venom and fury. One Catholic mother in Aiken told him: "You are a Northern [*sic*] and I am a Southern [*sic*]. Our worlds are far apart.... Will you also integrate the social gatherings, the white children dancing with the Negro children?" An anonymous letter from a self-styled "X Catholic" told him that he should be ashamed for advocating the mingling of the races. "The Pope is trying to undo God's work, wanting to make the Negro white," this person said, "because Earl Warren and Kennedy ... want it." A barely literate letter from the director of the Charleston County Citizens' Council complained that he had shattered the morale of their Catholic members and vowed that they would oppose any government aid to parochial schools.[33]

Not all the mail was negative by any means. A woman from North Charleston wrote: "Good thing you have come along to Charleston. Maybe at long last something will be done which will be wise and right for all of us, both Negro and white." A man who boasted that both grandfathers had fought for the Confederacy congratulated him on the fair and Christian stand that he had taken. And the music director of the Charleston Symphony Orchestra wrote that "many of us are terribly proud of your action in setting forth the Catholic stand on segregation."[34]

In Atlanta, Hyland received similar letters, one from the diocesan attorney who had been born in Georgia in 1886 and had lived through many years of anti-Catholic discrimination. He described himself as a "Cracker born and bred" and complimented the bishop on the pastoral letter. "This does not mean that I welcome it," he explained, "nor does it mean that I will like it; but let's say that it is the proper thing to do and that it is inevitable."[35]

In Savannah the cautious diocesan superintendent of schools seemed less enthusiastic than ever. He explained that the purpose of the pastoral was to announce that the Catholic schools would not be the last bastions of segregation. However, he said, even after the public schools were integrated, some Catholic schools might remain segregated because of the danger of racial strife. Besides, he said, "it is very possible that no Negro will ever apply to enter a white Catholic school here."[36]

Some thought that the bishop had not gone far enough. One man wrote from the safety of Toronto, Canada, urging Hallinan to bolder action.[37] He received a similar letter from another man which could not be dismissed so easily. It came from Mr. James Sulton, a black convert in Orangeburg, who asked:

> Since when does the Church follow? I always thought it led on all moral issues. Some people will never accept anything that is good for the Negro unless it is forced upon them. I can't understand the prejudice that now exists in our Catholic hospitals, when all it would take is an order from the Bishop. It is always the Negro who has to wait until the white man is educated to enjoy a human right. The only way to solve this problem is directly from you. Those people who are real Catholics will obey any order from the Church. Those who do not are not real Catholics to begin with.[38]

This was one letter which Hallinan answered at length. He said that, in delaying integration temporarily, he was not following the public schools, but following God's law, to prevent the kind of violence which had erupted in New Orleans and Georgia. "I will not risk the lives or the dignity of little Negro children (or white children) in this manner," he told Mr. Sulton, and he invited him to come to Charleston to discuss the matter further with him.[39]

Hallinan had arranged with Monsignor Paul Tanner, Executive Secretary of the NCWC, to release copies of the pastoral letter to the newspapers through the press department of the NCWC in Washington.[40] The *New York Times* covered the story the next day (with lengthy excerpts from the text of the letter),[41] and both *Newsweek* and *Time* mentioned it a few weeks later.[42] It was front-page news in many newspapers throughout South Carolina and Georgia.[43] A typical headline was the one in the Columbia *State*: "South Carolina Catholics Set For Mixing."

Few newspapers made any editorial comment, but those that did were surprisingly restrained. The *State* predicted that many Catholics would resist the bishops' decision but seemed relieved that there were no plans for immediate integration. "There is due recognition here," it said, "of the strength and depth of custom and the risks of basic change." The Charleston *Evening Post* merely noted that many people did not think that segregation was a moral issue at all. Even the Charleston *News and Courier* was uncharacteristically irenic (for the moment), paying tribute to the "authoritarian influence" of the Catholic Church and hoping that future generations would not have to regret decisions made by the bishops now with the best of intentions.[44]

The most positive reaction came from Ralph McGill, the widely respected publisher of the Atlanta *Constitution,* who commended the bishops especially for their effort to educate their people in the principles of racial justice. He thought that it would be a wise policy for all churches and all communities to do the same, and he ventured the opinion that "[the Catholic bishops] say what many a silent Protestant minister would like to tell his congregation, if he had apostolic authority behind him."[45]

A week after the pastoral appeared the mail had subsided and Hallinan thought that the worst was over. It was the calm before the storm. At six o'clock on Sunday, March 4, a reporter from the *News and Courier* called the cathedral rectory to ask for a statement about the protest meeting of the Organization of Catholic Parents which was scheduled for Monday evening at Simon Baruch Auditorium. This was the first confirmation of the existence of a group professing to resist integration from within the framework of the Catholic Church. He sent Bernardin down to the office of the *News and Courier* with a strongly-worded statement:

> Catholics who attend meetings called to oppose the teaching of the Church do so in contempt of the Church's authority. . . .
>
> Protest meetings are not the Catholic way of expressing concern

over measures which affect the life of the Church as well as the lives of its members. There is ample time for all loyal Catholics to discuss the matter with their pastors.

Those few Catholics who persist in acting against the Church's teaching cannot expect that their membership in the Church will indefinitely remain unchanged.[46]

The protest meeting never took place. The organizers cancelled it at the last minute, partly in response to Hallinan's strong stand, but partly out of loyalty to the Church. They feared that extremist groups, such as the Citizens' Councils and Save Our Nation, would try to use the meeting for their own purposes.[47] A spokesman for the parents denied that they wished to offend the bishop and said that they would now explore other approaches to preserve segregated Catholic schools in South Carolina. In fact, with the cancellation of the meeting, the opposition crumbled and most of the leaders met with Hallinan individually during the next few days to make their peace with him. He treated them with great forbearance, despite his aversion to one of them who kept muttering about the mongrelization of the race. He reminded Hallinan of Chester, the addlepated deputy marshal in the television Western "Gunsmoke." Actually, said Hallinan, he talked like Chester and argued like Chester's horse.[48]

When the protest movement of the Catholic parents collapsed, the *News and Courier* published a mischievous editorial, commiserating with those who had to choose between long-held personal convictions and "current instructions from church leaders."[49] A few days later, when President Kennedy clashed with Catholic leaders over government aid to parochial schools, the *News and Courier* tried to link the issue with the Church's stand on integration:

Racial integration of schools became a constitutional matter in the judgment of the Supreme Court. The Church now makes it a matter of morals. Will the Church also declare federal aid to parochial schools a matter of morals? If so, will President Kennedy jeopardize his standing in the Church by continuing to oppose it?[50]

Hallinan composed a letter of protest, but he decided not to send it.[51] Perhaps he thought that enough had been said on the subject already, since the correspondence columns of both Charleston dailies had been full of letters commenting on the pastoral. He could not have been displeased with this development, for those who came to his defense easily had the better of the argument. Indeed, they often expressed themselves with touching simplicity. One woman asked: "How can a person love his Church without loving people? We are all part of the Mystical Body of Christ," she said. "If we chop off some of the members, how much Body would be left?" When an irate Catholic complained that the Church had forgotten God's work, he provoked another Catholic into replying: "Is it forgotten? Or does it only seem to be because it requires a difficult application of principle on the part of him who hears it?"[52]

By the middle of March tempers had cooled and Hallinan gave his own assessment of the situation to the priests of the diocese in a circular letter. First of all, he thanked them for their cooperation in explaining the pastoral letter to the people. The overall reaction, he said, was somewhat milder than he had feared, although he correctly predicted that he had not heard the last from the more irresponsible elements among the opposition. He reaffirmed his promise that there would be no immediate integration because of his fears for the safety of both the children and the schools, and he asked the pastors to explain this decision to their people.[53]

An essential part of the pastoral letter of February 1961 was the promise of an educational program in the principles of racial justice. Almost immediately Hallinan appointed a committee to draw up a syllabus on the subject for the Catholic schools. The document was ready in the fall of 1961, a forty-eight page guide to help teachers present Catholic teaching on racial justice in grades seven through twelve.[54]

The presentation was built around three basic Catholic truths: the universality of the Church, the Mystical Body of Christ, and the virtue of justice. The conclusions were stated more bluntly than in the pastoral. Racial segregation was declared unacceptable, not only because the Supreme Court had outlawed it as unconstitutional, but because the United States bishops had condemned it as unjust and therefore immoral. Teachers were urged to counteract stereotypes about blacks and to stress that "there is absolutely no scientific proof to support the contention that the Negro is of an inferior race."

In a state where religion was often invoked to justify racial discrimination, the syllabus flatly declared that "there is no section of the Bible,

Old or New Testament, which can be used to justify racial segregation today." In the hometown of John C. Calhoun, even the touchy question of states rights was met head on: "The issue of states rights cannot be invoked here to defend racial segregation since the state has no power to uphold a law or custom that is unconstitutional and unjust."[55]

The syllabus was the work of Father Leo Croghan, Sister Mary Bernard, O.L.M., and Father J. Fleming McManus, diocesan Superintendent of Schools. Hallinan wrote the introduction and stressed the need for prudence in using the syllabus:

> We must give careful consideration to parental feelings, both of white and Negro parents. The teacher can only build on the child's respect and obedience to the parents.... Where parents disagree with the practical application of a Catholic truth, it will be necessary to use great care not to lessen the child's honor and obedience....
>
> A century ago slavery was defended. Today no American citizen would defend it. A century from now, none will defend the present structure of segregation. The Church, especially when Catholics are in a minority, may have to live with a system at odds with her teaching. But she must protest its inequities and teach her children to move toward their just solution....
>
> What we are doing can help our state move with courage in these changing times. We would be judged lacking in our Christian duty to God, to our fellow men, to our community, if we were to remain silent.[56]

As long as he remained in Charleston, Hallinan took no further steps to integrate the Catholic schools, and St. Anne's School in Rock Hill remained the only integrated school—public or private—in the whole state.[57]

The pastoral letter of February 1961 was probably the most important pronouncement that Hallinan made during his three-and-a-half years in Charleston. It did not please everyone. Die-hard segregationists rejected its arguments and impatient Northern liberals thought that it failed to provide the decisive leadership which the times required. Many blacks must have echoed the words of Mr. James Sulton ("Since when does the Church follow?"), and there was always the nagging example of St. Anne's School, showing what could be done.

Nevertheless, it is hard to blame Hallinan and his fellow bishops for erring on the side of caution. If they had ordered immediate integration of their schools in February 1961, they might have reaped a harvest of favorable headlines in Northern newspapers, but the Catholic people of their diocese—both black and white—might have paid a terrible price for it. The lasting damage from such unilateral action lay not in the threat of violence from a few reckless hotheads, but in the loss of goodwill patiently built up in the community over many years by the small Catholic minority. The fact of the matter is that knowledgeable Southern moderates, such as Ralph McGill and Ernest F. Hollings, thought that the bishops had struck exactly the right note.

Edmund Burke once said that "it is no small part of wisdom to know how much of an evil ought to be tolerated." By that standard, the bishops' decision seemed both wise and eminently practical: by waiting a year or two longer to end a practice which had lasted for many decades, they assured that integration would be a success when at last it came.

9

The Newman Apostolate

On April 18, 1961, Paul Hallinan celebrated his fiftieth birthday. For the first time in his life he admitted that he was beginning to feel his age, but he did not cut down on his schedule in any way. Two weeks later, he noted that he had travelled 10,000 miles so far that year attending meetings, giving speeches and sermons, administering Confirmation, and inspecting sites for future churches and schools.

A typical two-day trip early in 1962 took him from Charleston to St. Anne's in Kingstree for Confirmation, and then on to St. Andrew's in Myrtle Beach for a speech and a chat with a group of priests. The next day he said Mass for the sisters in Myrtle Beach and toured their school, drove to Dillon where he inspected the new equipment in St. Eugene's Hospital, made a flying visit to St. Peter's Parish in Cheraw, hurried on to St. Denis' Mission in Bennettsville for Confirmation, then returned to Charleston that evening—a circuit of at least 350 miles.[1] Traveling conditions had changed a great deal, of course, since the days of John England, but his *modus operandi* would remind anyone of the peregrinations recorded by Charleston's first bishop in his *Diurnal.*

His trips outside the diocese were as frequent as ever. He spent much of November dashing for planes and trains. He flew to New Orleans on November 6 for the installation of John Cody as the Coadjutor Archbishop, went on to Baton Rouge the next day for the installation of Robert Tracy as the first bishop of that see, left immediately for a two-day Newman Club convention in Buffalo, made a brief visit to Cleveland, spent five days at the bishops' meeting in

Washington, gave a speech in Richmond, then attended the meeting of the Catholic Church Extension Society in Chicago where he barely got to the airport in time to catch his flight to Charleston. He admitted that he felt "tired" after he got home on November 20, when he described his odyssey as one long round of "celebration, installation, conflagration, exhilaration, relaxation, concentration, exhaustion, explanation, trepidation, exhortation."[2]

Whenever he could, he made time for his work on Bishop Gilmour. One of his difficulties was that Professor Wittke had originally narrowed the scope of the dissertation to Gilmour's educational work. Hallinan, however, decided to do a full-length biography, necessitating additional research in some of the archives which he had already consulted.[3]

On his way back from a fund-raising trip to Detroit in July 1961, for example, he spent two days in Toledo reading old newspaper files. Wittke told him that summer that he was planning to retire within a year, so Hallinan was more anxious than ever to complete his research. On July 30, 1961, he had done so and wrote the first two pages—at midnight after a full day reading and mulling over the material. By November he had finished the first chapter and sent it off to Monsignor John Tracy Ellis for his evaluation. At the time of the bishops' meeting in November, he spent two hours with Ellis, who recommended major revisions and helped him to write a new outline.[4]

The second version was ready before Christmas, received Ellis' approval, and was in Wittke's hands by the beginning of January. Wittke too was pleased both with the research and the style and he urged Hallinan to finish the dissertation as quickly as he could. Encouraged by Wittke's response, Hallinan hammered away at chapter two for the rest of the month, on one occasion, at least, working until two in the morning.[5]

The subject matter was congenial: Gilmour's labors as a missionary priest in the Ohio River Valley in the 1850's and 1860's. But there were problems too, such as trying to reconstruct Gilmour's twelve years in Cincinnati on the basis of a few letters and newspaper clippings. It was also frustrating that Gilmour, at least in his writings, virtually ignored two of the most contentious issues of his time—nativism and slavery— since Hallinan was making a conscious effort to describe the historical context in which Gilmour lived and worked. Gilmour's reticence made him appreciate more than ever before one of the most unhappy and unhealthy features of the period: "the general Catholic isolation from the mainstream of American political and cultural life."[6]

Like any author, he had his good days and his bad days. After a month of hard work in January 1962, his enthusiasm was running low and he wondered if anyone but Ellis, Wittke, and Robert Tracy would ever read what he was writing. By this time he had two desks: one which he used for ordinary business, and a smaller one which he used exclusively for Bishop Gilmour. No matter how late he arrived back home after a busy day on the road, he tried to spend some time each evening at work on the dissertation. It is an interesting sidelight on his motivation that he would never use the honorary D.D. which the Catholic Church automatically accords to all bishops in recognition of their role in the *ecclesia docens*. He said that either he would have a real doctorate or he would have none at all.[7]

At this point in his life, the last thing that Hallinan wanted was more responsibilities but he could hardly refuse them when they came from his fellow bishops. Archbishop John Dearden called him in November 1960 to tell him that he had been elected Assistant Chairman of the Youth Division of the NCWC (Dearden was the Chairman) and Episcopal Moderator of the Newman Clubs.[8] He readily accepted the appointment. Through Monsignor Alexander Sigur, the National Chaplain, he sent a message to the winter meeting of the National Executive Committee of the National Newman Club Federation, saying: "I will try to do what a Moderator does. He moderates." He told the student leaders that, as Episcopal Moderator, he had a double role: to represent them to the bishops and to represent the bishops to them.

He also tried to communicate to the students something of his own optimism about the future of the movement. He told them:

> We are at the threshold of an era. The first thirty years of the Newman movement were pioneer days, "fighting Indians." The next thirty were the period of maturation, "growing pains," Now we move to consolidation, the most heroic task of all. There are signs all around: more centers, more full-time chaplains, more accredited courses, the newly established Newman Foundation. You are serving the national student apostolate at its most challenging time.[9]

Many of the chaplains were personal friends from the dozen years which he had spent in the movement. He met with them for the first time as Episcopal Moderator in Baton Rouge on January 23, 1961, where he also had a chance to discuss his forthcoming pastoral letter on integration with Bishop Tracy, a native of New Orleans. In his address to the chaplains, he avoided the usual generalities and showed how well informed he was about the issues which were percolating within the movement.

First of all, he reminded the chaplains of the support which they now enjoyed from the hierarchy, symbolized by Cardinal Spellman's tribute to them at the last bishops' meeting and the decision of the bishops to establish a National Newman Foundation to raise money for the movement. "Today there is no question," he said, "that the bishops, singly and collectively, consider the Newman movement as the official instrument of Catholic education on the secular campus."

Secondly he warned the chaplains not to downgrade the importance of the Newman Club in their laudable desire to reach every Catholic student on campus. He predicted that "if we lessen the role and prestige of the Newman Club, it will become either a clique of career yes-men under our direction or else a band of young rebels." Finally, and somewhat surprisingly, he came out strongly against the suggestion that the Newman movement should be transferred from the Youth Division to the Education Department of the NCWC. "Future progress will depend," he said, "not so much upon procedural arrangements as upon the substance of the movement itself."[10]

The creation of the National Newman Foundation in June 1960 promised to solve one of the difficulties which had plagued Hallinan during his tenure as National Chaplain in the early 1950's: the lack of adequate funding. Another problem from those days still remained, however, and was getting worse: the haphazard organizational structure of the whole movement. There were now six separate units in the movement, and no one really knew what the relationship was among these six units, or between each of them and the Youth Division of the NCWC.[11] Throughout his life Hallinan had a penchant for organizational tidiness, and he found this amorphous and overlapping structure a hindrance to the progress of Newman work. So did many other leaders, who had been discussing plans for reorganization for years. Every time that the issue came up, however, it led to a *brouhaha* between those who wanted greater centralization and those who were anxious to preserve local autonomy. Another perennial source of disagreement was the relationship between the students and the chaplains, and how power should be shared between them.

These tensions had been present in the Newman movement from the very beginning and Hallinan had had ample experience of them during his two years as National Chaplain. Eventually they contributed to the breakup and disappearance of the Newman movement in the late 1960's, but no one could have suspected in 1961 that the end was so near. At that date the Newman Federation seemed healthier than ever with 576 Newman Clubs (an increase of fifty-three over the previous year) and episcopal support had never been so strong or so widespread.[12]

It appeared to Hallinan and others, like Monsignor Sigur and Father Charles Albright, C.S.P., Executive Secretary of the Federation, that the time was ripe for a judicious overhaul which would ensure the success of the movement for years to come. Hallinan himself saw reorganization as the most important service that he could render the movement as Episcopal Moderator. He began to fashion a plan early in 1961 with which he approached John Dearden, his old friend, who was now Archbishop of Detroit and his superior as the Chairman of the Youth Division of the NCWC. He spoke to Dearden briefly in June 1961, and then at much greater length in Baltimore in September, when they stayed at the same hotel on the occasion of the installation of Lawrence J. Shehan as Coadjutor Archbishop.[13]

Essentially Hallinan wanted to bring together the six separate Newman organizations as constituent members of a new "Newman Apostolate," which would itself be a branch of the Youth Division of the NCWC and the counterpart of the National Federation of Catholic College Students. Each of the six organizations would have specific objectives, membership requirements and responsibilities. A coordinating secretary would manage the day-to-day operations and would have the right to attend staff meetings of the NCWC. The "Newman Apostolate" would be directly subject to an Episcopal Moderator, who would himself be an assistant to the Episcopal Chairman of the Youth Division. For the first time all aspects of Newman work would be coordinated within the Youth Division of the NCWC, and there would be clearly-defined lines of communication and command throughout the structure.[14]

Hallinan thought that this would be a vast improvement over the previous makeshift arrangement. After getting Dearden's approval on

October 6,1961, he told Sigur:

> For the first time, a new total concept of the Newman movement has been agreed upon: in which all play a well-defined role, all coordinate and communicate, and it has come from the discussions of the chaplains and the agreement of the bishops.[15]

The next step was to test the reaction of Sigur and Albright. Both favored the reorganization, although Sigur wanted to strengthen the role of the National Chaplain, since, as he told Hallinan, "the movement has arrived where it is primarily through the strong collaborative operation of the chaplains." Hallinan accepted Sigur's recommendation and specified that the National Chaplain (in addition to his role in the Student Federation and the Chaplains' Association) should also be the liaison officer between the whole Apostolate and the NCWC on policy matters.[16]

At the bishops' meeting in November 1961, Hallinan made no mention of the projected reorganization but he declared confidently that the Newman movement stood at the beginning of a new era and predicted that there would be a vast expansion of membership and activities during the next forty years. He announced the first results of the National Newman Foundation: the establishment of two training schools for Newman chaplains which would begin operations the next summer at the University of Michigan and Louisiana State University. He also repeated for the bishops' benefit the remarks that he had made at the National Newman Club Convention the previous August about public controversies between Newman chaplains and university authorities. While he mentioned no names, he was obviously thinking of the tempest over Father Hugh Halton, O.P., of Princeton University, which was still fresh in everyone's mind. "When a disagreement in such cases degenerates into a bitter public quarrel," he said, "solutions do not result: only headlines." To prevent a repetition of the Princeton episode, Hallinan a few months earlier had made several recommendations to the Newman chaplains with the full approval of Archbishop Dearden, and he now shared them with the bishops:

> At the beginning of real conflict between our Newman work and any person or department of the college or university, confer with the bishop immediately. In this way the chancery will be kept informed

of developments and not suddenly faced with a *fait accompli.* There are many ways of meeting an adversary—a private conference, a helpful third party, perhaps a clear-cut, well-reasoned presentation of our position. . . .

There are times to speak out and times to be silent. If the Newman chaplain is working closely with the bishop who is responsible for Catholic education, he will be sharing both the prudence and the courage that are urgently needed.[17]

The next pressing item on the Newman agenda was the need to put the National Newman Foundation in working order. After eighteen months the Foundation did not even have a permanent board of directors. On December 6, 1961, the temporary board met for the last time to elect a permanent board which included Hallinan as an *ex-officio* member. Hallinan attended this meeting in Washington and also persuaded General Alfred M. Gruenther, President of the American Red Cross, to serve on the board. Others members included Frank Folsom, Chairman of RCA Corporation, Senator Eugene J. McCarthy of Minnesota, Professor Raymond J. Sontag of the University of California at Berkeley, Professor Helen C.White of the University of Wisconsin, and Professor Carlton J.H. Hayes of Columbia University. Andrew P. Maloney, Vice-President of the Bankers Trust Company of New York was elected President of the Newman Foundation, and the board approved an operating budget of $35,000 for the following year (although there was only $14,625 in the treasury).[18]

Hallinan got the job of raising the rest of the money from the bishops. He had mixed feelings about his role: "[I am] both sorry and exhilarated to be in the Newman movement again," he wrote. "[It] takes time, but it needs now more than ever those who love it." His goal was $50,000, but he told Sigur that he would settle for $35,000, and that was the amount which his letters brought in from the bishops.[19]

In December 1961 he got a new superior at the NCWC, when Dearden left the Youth Division of the NCWC and was replaced by John Krol, the new Archbishop of Philadelphia. Hallinan was, of course, even closer to Krol than to Dearden and they worked together harmoniously on Newman affairs. On April 18, 1962, came the announcement from Krol that the National Newman Apostolate had been established as a new section of the NCWC's Youth Division.

Hallinan greeted the news with the statement that "this new structure for the first time officially and formally recognizes the growth and development of the Newman movement to a vigorous arm of the Church in Catholic higher education. . . ."[20]

Unfortunately, the Newman Apostolate lasted only six years. The 1960's were a difficult decade on American college campuses and the Newman movement was one of many casualties caused by changes in society and the Church. The apostolate of the campus ministry survived and even expanded its efforts, but the idea of a national organization of Catholic student clubs—the dream of Father John Keogh and his successors—hierarchically structured and functioning under the aegis of the NCWC, lost much of its appeal to young Catholics in the 1960's.

There were signs of trouble from the beginning. The new President of the National Newman Club Federation (the largest of the six constituent members of the Apostolate) was a self-confident and assertive young man named Edward Orlett. Even before he took over the reins, he announced that the next president "must be prepared to exercise the fullest power of his office."[21]

He quickly demonstrated that he was prepared to do so. A few days after taking office, he told Monsignor Sigur, the National Chaplain: "The Newman Apostolate needs to involve a great many more lay people. These people must be given the authority and responsibility for helping carry out the Newman Club's goals on the secular campus." One of his first projects was to suggest the convening of a high-level meeting of representatives of the clergy, students, faculty and alumni to coordinate the work of the various elements in the apostolate.[22]

Sigur was impressed and, in an unguarded moment, told Orlett: "Do not worry about tact. Your motives are clear and the rest will follow in time."[23] Father Albright, the Coordinating Secretary of the new Apostolate, was also well disposed to the idea and said:

> I like your plans for a "summit meeting." I personally feel that this can be of the utmost value. By and large the chaplains do not want to lessen student initiative and responsibility; unequivocally, Bishop Hallinan, Monsignor Sigur and I feel very strongly on this. We do feel though that we need to clarify areas of responsibility. . . .[24]

As preparations went forward for the meeting, it became apparent that Orlett had his own ideas on how it should be structured. "Anything that would tend to indicate that the meeting was chaplain-planned or oriented would be detrimental to its success," he told Sigur, and he insisted that, to ensure a successful outcome, "each element—clergy, students, faculty and alumni—must eventually share equally in responsibility and authority."[25] The next day, on his own authority, he sent invitations to thirty-three people to attend a "summit meeting" in June.[26]

Sigur, Albright and Hallinan were all furious—for several reasons. They resented Orlett's presumption in calling the meeting on his own initiative, and they were suspicious of his insistence on the need for an equal voice for all participants. Most of all they were angry because they wanted such a meeting themselves, and Hallinan was actually drawing up the agenda for it, when Orlett's invitation arrived in the mail. Now they were afraid that Orlett's high-handed maneuver might make such a meeting impossible.

Albright told Orlett that he "was nothing short of floored" that he would take it upon himself to summon this gathering, when it seemed so obvious that the invitation should come from all six member organizations, or at least from Sigur and Orlett together. Furthermore, he bristled at the demand that all participants have an equal voice in the proceedings. "Such a statement," he complained, "even meant in a proper Catholic sense, is prejudging one of the primary conclusions that the meeting is being called to decide."[27]

Hallinan was upset too, although not to the same degree as Albright. He told Sigur that "Ed's mimeo circular ... [may have] prejudiced this whole thing. I hope not." He readily admitted that "there is much that is good in his letter," but he was not about to surrender control of the meeting to Orlett. "It is important," he said, "that the meeting be called by the Newman Apostolate ... that the agenda be prepared by you and Ed, and approved by me, then Charlie." He checked first with Albright and Sigur, then sent Orlett a stern rebuke:

> Your single-handed issuance of an invitation to various people to attend a "summit meeting" surprised and disappointed me.... I think that after you sent the ill-timed letter you probably realized the impropriety of having the invitation come from one head of a single organization within the Newman Apostolate, rather than from joint action or from a higher authority.[29]

Despite this *faux pas,* Hallinan was still willing to work with Orlett and sent him a copy of the memorandum that he had been preparing when his invitation arrived. Hallinan proposed a two-day meeting in June of thirty representatives from the six Newman organizations. He said that he would be happy to issue the invitations himself and that he would be present for at least some of the sessions. His main concern, however, was not any of the specific objectives which he listed in the memorandum, but the growing rift between students and chaplains. "The tone of the meeting, that is, the spirit in which it is held," he said, "is more important than the agenda." He had high hopes that this meeting could bring greater unity and harmony to the Newman Apostolate and he held out an olive branch to both students and chaplains:

> If, in the history of the Newman movement, the names of priests are better known, it is only because they have been able to work longer in the movement. Beside them, working closely with them, have been some of the best qualified student leaders in the country. The high points of this history have been those periods when both priests and students cooperated closely; the low points have been when either group tried to go its own way.[30]

Orlett, Sigur and Albright met in mid-April to draw up preliminary agenda,[31] and, shortly after Easter, as promised, Hallinan invited the presidents of the six Newman organizations to send representatives to the summit meeting at Ann Arbor, Michigan, on June 21-23. He gave full credit to Orlett for suggesting the idea in the first place and said that it had the hearty support of Albright, Sigur and himself.[32]

When the three dozen Newman representatives met at the Gabriel Richard Catholic Student Center, the atmosphere was tense. A number of student leaders, following Orlett, feared that the Newman Apostolate would seriously diminish their relative importance within the movement and subject them to greater clerical control. Hallinan and Sigur were both well aware of this feeling, and in their opening remarks they stressed the need for a spirit of cooperation among all the participants. Orlett spoke on Saturday morning, June 23, paid tribute to the contributions of the Newman Foundation and the chaplains, but added: "This detracts from our singular reponsibility and thus our authority. We must decide the Newman Apostolate's role and goals."

That afternoon he asked the delegates to adopt his definition of the Newman movement (one which pointedly ignored the hierarchical structure of the new Newman Apostolate as a component of the Youth Division of the NCWC): "Be it moved that the definition of the Newman Apostolate be ... the association of those who are sent— chaplains, students, faculty and others who are committed to serve— to bring the Church to the total secular campus community." The motion was defeated by a vote of twenty-five to fifteen, and with that the threat of a student challenge to the new structure subsided.[33]

Hallinan was, of course, delighted. Before he left, he congratulated the participants on the high level of the discussions. Sigur was pleased too, and a young priest, arriving for the first Newman Chaplains' Training School and mingling with some of the delegates, noticed "a spirit of optimism and general satisfaction" among those present. The recording secretary observed with youthful astonishment that "there are few places in the world where college students could take on an archbishop in public discussion. .... Archbishop Hallinan respects us genuinely."[34]

The Ann Arbor meeting should have been the end of the beginning, the organizational meeting which eliminated the flaws and rough edges in the new Newman Apostolate. Instead, it was the beginning of the end, and the historian of the Newman movement dates the decline and disappearance of the movement from the period immediately after the Ann Arbor meeting. What happened, he suggests, was this:

> Flushed with the victory of Ann Arbor, the fashioners of the New-man Apostolate could be forgiven for thinking that they had hastened the dawn of a new era and had only to carry out their recently approved plans. They had been so preoccupied with working on the system that they had failed to notice that, although the sky was indeed brightening, its color was red.[35]

There had always been two schools of thought within the Newman movement: those who favored greater centralization and those who wanted more home rule. The Newman Apostolate of 1962, crafted and sponsored by Hallinan as much as by anyone in the opinion of Father Albright, represented the last and apparently the definitive victory of the centralizers after fifty years of struggle. It was indeed their last victory, but it was hardly definitive. Almost at once, sentiment within the movement started to run strongly in the opposite direction, away from a highly-structured national organization and toward more local leadership and local control. The Second Vatican Council also had its effect, producing a desire for a stronger emphasis on pastoral care and liturgical activities, and by the end of the decade, the traditional Newman "club" and the national Newman organizations were moribund.[36]

The establishment of the Newman Apostolate was the last great service which Hallinan rendered to the movement, and neither he nor anyone else suspected that its success would be so ephemeral. He continued to take a close interest in the movement, frequently speaking at meetings and conventions;[37] but, a few weeks after the Ann Arbor summit meeting, he told Archbishop Krol that he wanted to be released from his position as Episcopal Moderator. It had involved more work than he had anticipated, and by the summer of 1962, other and more urgent matters were demanding his full attention.[38]

Back in February he had observed the silver jubilee of his ordination with the kind of lavish celebration which he loved. Governor Hollings paid a courtesy call at the rectory, and in the afternoon the cathedral was filled for a Mass of Thanksgiving during which he expressed the hope that he would be able to celebrate his fiftieth anniversary in the same church. Afterwards there was a reception at Bishop England High School, attended by over 700 guests, including the Mayor of Charleston and the Episcopal Bishop of South Carolina. The day ended with a dinner for the clergy at the Francis Marion Hotel at which the vicar general presented him with a check for $3,000. It was, he said, "a wonderful day," and he gave the credit to Bernardin, who had managed all the arrangements.[39]

At noon the next day he flew to Cleveland to address a Newman convention. Before the day was over, Bernardin called him at the cathedral rectory in Cleveland to say that the Apostolic Delegate wanted to speak to him. When he telephoned Archbishop Egidio Vagnozzi, he was told that Pope John XXIII had selected him to be the first Archbishop of Atlanta. He was as stunned as he had been when he first heard of his appointment to Charleston. He knew, of course, that Bishop Hyland had resigned the see of Atlanta the previous October but he never expected to replace him. The transfer of an ordinary from one small Southern diocese to another would be highly unusual. The situation was changed dramatically, however, when the

Pope raised Atlanta to the rank of an archdiocese, making it the metropolitan see for the southeastern United States. Apparently, Bishop Hallinan had no advance notice that this change was under consideration in Rome, and hence his surprise, when the new post was offered to him. At first, he hesitated to accept it, and Vagnozzi asked if he were going to refuse the wish of the Holy Father. Hallinan then asked if he could wait until the next morning to give his answer, but Vagnozzi replied that the Holy See wanted the appointment made immediately and that he had to send a cable to Rome that evening.

Hallinan wondered what people would think. Only twenty-four hours earlier he had waxed eloquent about his desire to end his days in Charleston! He mentioned his limited abilities, but Vagnozzi told him to trust in God. At no point in the conversation did Hallinan actually say "no," and Vagnozzi evidently was not prepared to accept any answer but a "yes." By the time he put down the telephone, Hallinan was the Archbishop-elect of Atlanta.[40]

The public announcement came six days later. In his statement to the press, he softened the blow as much as he could by protesting that "part of my heart will always remain in the Diocese of Charleston." He said that the Holy See had raised Atlanta to the status of a metropolitan see (only five years after becoming a diocese) in recognition of the new vitality of the Catholic Church in the Carolinas, Georgia and Florida, where the Catholic population had increased from 200,000 to 638,000 in the past ten years. (He did not add that most of this growth had taken place in Florida.) He also reached back to biblical precedents to justify his transfer and compared it to St. Paul sorrowfully taking leave of the Christians in Caesarea.[41]

The reaction in Charleston was not as critical of him as he had feared. His genuine popularity meant that many would be pleased with his promotion for his sake, even as they complained about the frequent changes of leadership in their diocese—three times now in thirteen years. Even his old nemesis, Thomas Waring, wished him well and observed that he had made many friends and admirers—including the *News and Courier*—during his years in Charleston.[42]

He spent the last five weeks there fulfilling his usual rounds of parish visitations and Confirmations, and tying up loose ends in the chancery office with Bernardin. On March 8, he visited Bishop Hyland in Philadelphia and came away with a good deal of useful information about his new see. The next day he saw the Apostolic Delegate in

Washington and emphasized the need for a strong person as bishop in Charleston. He recommended Bernardin as his successor, but Vagnozzi thought that he was too young and feared that, if he were turned down now, it might hurt his chances at a later date.[43]

Paul Hallinan spent a total of only forty-one months in Charleston, too short a time to put his own stamp on the diocese. Nonetheless, in an age when bishops were often measured by their accomplishments with brick and mortar, he did surprisingly well with the limited resources of his small diocese. He left nine new churches and chapels, either built or planned, and completed four new schools, including Cardinal Newman High School in Columbia. He also enlarged ten other schools, built four convents, and encouraged three of the Catholic hospitals to undertake major expansion programs. In an area where few bishops felt comfortable—liturgical reform—he showed imagination and a high degree of common sense in the way he introduced the liturgical movement to the clergy and laity of his diocese.

Despite his Northern background, he had quickly adapted to his role as the religious leader of a tiny minority. Avoiding both truculence and timidity during such sensitive periods as the 1960 presidential campaign, he became a respected community leader. His outstanding contribution was the prudent manner in which he brought the Catholics of his diocese to face the issue of racial justice, especially in their schools and hospitals. While showing due regard for local customs, he taught clearly that segregation was a moral issue that the Church could not ignore or condone indefinitely; and, when he left Charleston on March 28, 1962, all the Catholic schools and hospitals were committed to opening their doors to blacks.

Integration was still a highly volatile issue all across the South in the spring of 1962, and it was one of the first challenges that he had to face in Atlanta. If Hallinan needed any reminder, he had only to look at the front page of the newspaper which showed him boarding the plane in Charleston for his new see. Its headline broke the news that Archbishop Joseph Rummel had announced that very morning that he would desegregate the parochial schools of the Archdiocese of New Orleans in September.[44]

10

Atlanta

When Hallinan got off the plane in Atlanta, the reporters were waiting to pepper him with leading questions. He had no intention of using the airport tarmac for making major policy statements and he handled them like a seasoned politician. He said that it would be "highly improper" to comment on Archbishop Rummel's decision to integrate the parochial schools in New Orleans, and "highly improper" for him to comment on his own plans for the Atlanta Catholic schools until he had been formally installed as archbishop.

It was a virtuoso performance. He never lost his temper, kept smiling, announced his desire to walk arm in arm with those of other religions, and professed an aversion to the terms "left wing" and "right wing." "I believe in the vital Christian center," he explained. His smile turned to a frown briefly, when a reporter asked about the problems facing the Church. He parried the question by smiling again and saying that he preferred to talk about opportunities.

The more he talked, the more adeptly he smothered the reporters' questions with vapid banalities, which was what he intended to do. He told them that he liked to talk in terms of facts, "always with the idea of moving forward," and he offered them this comforting advice: "We must be optimistic, confident, and trust in God, our country, our civil officials, the Supreme Court, and state officials.... Hope is a Christian virtue, which ranks with faith and charity."[1]

After his escape from the press, he rode to the Cathedral of Christ the King to meet a delegation of school children and the diocesan consultors. The next day he was installed as the first Archbishop of Atlanta by Archbishop Vagnozzi in the presence of thirty-two archbishops and bishops. In his sermon, the new archbishop addressed many of the questions put to him on the previous day, but on his own ground and in his own terms. First, he traced the history of the Catholic Church in Georgia, describing it as a "heroic account of staunch faith and daily struggle." He looked forward now, he said, to the springtime of Catholicism in America's Southland, and, borrowing from Newman, he exclaimed: "It was a long winter, and the world grows old, but the Church is ever young."

Facing squarely the question of racial justice, he said that the Church must put into practice its own clear teaching, and he called upon the people of his archdiocese to implement that teaching "with prudence, with courage, with determination." He made it clear too in his sermon that he took a wide view of his responsibilities and hoped to offer his services to the whole community as well as to his own Church. Perhaps his research on Bishop Gilmour had prompted the remark, for he privately lamented the isolation of the nineteenth-century American Church from the mainstream of political and cultural life. On his second day in Atlanta, he announced what his own attitude would be:

> Our Catholic people, speaking their deepest Catholic convictions, will work side by side with citizens of other faiths toward a community approved by God. Our first task is to save our souls, but we cannot save them in heaven, nor in the sanctuary. We can save them only in Atlanta, in Georgia, in America, in the world in which we live.[2]

Later that day, at the dinner held in the Dinkler Plaza Hotel, Archbishop Vagnozzi called Hallinan a "great optimist" and likened him to another ecclesiastical optimist, Pope John XXIII.[3]

A week later Archbishop Hallinan gave an interview to Sally Sanford, the religious news editor of the Atlanta *Constitution*. She described him as a short, stocky man with greying crew-cut hair, a ready smile and a firm handshake. He repeated his pledge to work with other religious leaders and civil officials for the good of the city. Then he said to her: "Does that make sense? I have the habit of asking that whenever I say something pompous."

He still refused to comment on the situation in New Orleans, and he declined to give a date when the parochial schools in Atlanta would be integrated. "We must move prudently," he said, "but we must move. I mean it." He also pointed out to her that integration was not and could not be his first priority: "The first thing is the good of the Church and this [racial problem] has to be worked out in that context."

Once again he staked out his own position as representing the vital Christian center and criticized both "professional liberals who blur the difference between right and wrong" and "professional reactionaries who would have us move only backward." He was particularly scathing in his comments on the proponents of unilateral disarmament. "I'm against war. I'm for peace," he protested, but he warned that the United States Government should never "expose our own position by fuzzy dreams. That's carrying naiveté to an extreme."

On spiritual matters, he expressed concern at those who were offering the public a painless popular Christianity. "My notion of the spiritual life," he explained, "is one of struggle—for the individual and the community. It's not an easy thing. Christ didn't say: 'Take up your pillow.' He said: 'Take up your cross and follow me.' "[4]

When he saw an advance copy of the printed interview, he was pleased but fearful that the readers might think that he was too flippant and too cocky. Much to his surprise, it caused very little comment and it made him appreciate one pleasant change from Charleston: the difference between the *News and Courier* and the Atlanta *Constitution*. From now on, instead of having to spar with Thomas Waring, he found himself usually in agreement with the editorial views of Ralph McGill. Before long they became good friends.

There were other differences which were not so pleasant. Bishop Hyland had never established an adequate chancery office and Hallinan had to work out of cramped quarters in the basement of the cathedral. Another problem was the finances. Charleston was a poor diocese, but at least the finances had been well managed; and in Bernardin, Hallinan had someone who was thoroughly familiar with the whole financial picture. After spending a day with his chancellor in Atlanta, Harold J. Rainey, Hallinan was in despair at the lack of a financial system. He did not blame Rainey; rather he concluded that Hyland had tried to do too much too soon and had allowed financial control to slip into too many hands. Two days later he brought in accountants to conduct an audit and set up a coherent financial system for the archdiocese.[5]

As his interview with Sally Sanford indicated, he was far more confident and self-assured now than he had been in November 1958 when he arrived in Charleston. After three and a half years he thought that he knew the mind and the temper of the South fairly well. "Most Southerners love the Bible," he said, "they identify religion with life, they reverence their churches." In Charleston he had waited two years to issue a pastoral letter, promising school integration at some unspecified future date; in Atlanta, after only two weeks, he had just about made up his mind to order the integration of the parochial schools in September.[6]

It must have been immediately obvious to him how similar Georgia was to South Carolina. Both states had been desperately poor until World War II: in 1940 per capita income in Georgia was only 57% of the national average; in South Carolina, it was 52%. Both states had large black populations, although in Georgia they were concentrated in a black belt which ran through the center of the state. Four northern counties did not contain a single black person. As in South Carolina, and for the same reasons, large numbers of blacks had been migrating to the North, and the percentage of blacks in the total population fell steadily from 33% in 1940 to 25% in 1970.

Other parallels were equally striking. Agriculture declined as rapidly in Georgia as it did in South Carolina after World War II, and the number of farm families decreased from 220,000 in 1949 to 47,000 in 1979. In both states public education had long been a scandal: as late as 1950 one-third of all public schools in Georgia were one-teacher institutions, and two-thirds of the schools had fewer than five teachers. The following year both state legislatures imposed a three-percent state sales tax to raise funds for much needed educational improvements (and also to try to preserve a system of "separate but equal" schools for blacks).[7]

Georgia was as firmly rooted in the Bible Belt as its next door neighbor. Only 0.9% of the total population was Catholic in the late 1950's. There were forty Catholic parishes in the whole state—compared to 5,614 Protestant churches. As usual in the South, the two largest denominations were the Southern Baptists (with almost one million members by 1968) and the Methodists (with 392,000 members). Surprisingly, the Catholic Church became the third largest denomination in Georgia during the 1960's, surpassing the Southern

Presbyterians; but it was a poor third indeed with 84,000 members.[8]

Georgia also had its counterparts to L. Mendel Rivers in two veteran politicians, Senator Richard B. Russell and Congressman Carl Vinson, both of whom used their influence on the armed services committees of their respective Houses to benefit the state handsomely. By the 1970's there were fifteen military installations in Georgia, employing over 40,000 people. Together with defense contracts, military spending amounted to over two billion dollars a year and generated about 10% of the state's total personal income.[9]

Racism had long been a staple of political life in both states, exploited with equal cleverness and equal viciousness in the early decades of the twentieth century by "Pitchfork Ben" Tillman in South Carolina and Tom Watson in Georgia. Eugene Talmadge carried on the same tradition from the 1920's to the 1940's, saying on one occasion: "I like the nigger, but I like him in his place, and his place is at the back door with his hat in his hand." In 1946, at a Ku Klux Klan dinner, he asked: "Why should Nigras butt in and tell white people who should be elected in a white primary?" Not only demagogues like Talmadge defended the racial status quo. Even the relatively liberal and tolerant businessman Ivan Allen Jr. said in 1953: "Negroes have got to learn to respect the traditional rights of segregation."[10]

One historian at the University of Georgia explained why it was so difficult to induce white Georgians to change their racial attitudes:

> By the World War II years, Georgia's segregated social system had hardened into a rigid caste structure accepted by virtually all whites and substantial numbers of blacks as the ordained and proper way of doing things. The ubiquitous words "white" and "colored" that adorned virtually every public facility from drinking fountains and rest rooms to the Bibles used in Georgia courtrooms for administering oaths were an accepted part of the Georgia scene like red clay and kudzu. To many whites, segregation was an element of social stability in a rapidly changing world; it was both an identification with the past and an opportunistic method to limit economic and social opportunities to themselves and their children.[11]

The first serious blow to this system was the Supreme Court decision of 1954, mandating the end of segregation in public schools.

The reaction in Georgia was stronger than in South Carolina; the state legislature promptly passed a resolution declaring the court decision "null, void, and of no force or effect." It also made it a felony offense for any school official to allow the operation of an integrated school. The State Board of Education went even further and threatened to revoke "forever" the license of any teacher who "supports, encourages, condones, offers to teach or teaches" integrated classes. However, it backed down and revoked the policy in the face of widespread criticism from teachers.[12]

Despite these and other similarities, however, by 1962 the differences between Georgia and South Carolina were becoming more pronounced every year, and most of them could be summed up in one word—Atlanta. The city acted as a magnet to pull the rest of the state forward economically and culturally if not politically. There was simply no city in South Carolina, or anywhere else in the South, which could rival Atlanta as a regional capital, and the growing wealth of the metropolis had repercussions throughtout the state.

Between 1959 and 1970 the economy of Georgia entered what one economist identified as a "take-off growth status." Per capita income in Georgia grew more rapidly than in the United States as a whole, and population growth exceeded the national average for the first time since the 1840's.[13] Most of this progress was directly traceable to the economy of metropolitan Atlanta, which was far more developed than that of the rest of the state.

Atlanta had long been famous as a railroad hub, but now it was becoming the center of high-wage manufacturing industries, transportation, finance, insurance, real estate, and government administration for the whole South. Even in 1959, at the very beginning of the boom years, per capita personal income in the Atlanta metropolitan area exceeded the national average and was twice that of some other regions of Georgia.[14] Between 1950 and 1970, the population of metropolitan Atlanta doubled from 750,000 to 1,440,000 and by the latter year, the metropolitan Atlanta area contained 33% of Georgia's population, 38% of its jobs, and accounted for 42% of its personal income. Thanks largely to Atlanta, per capita income for the state as a whole reached 84% of the national average by 1970, and, according to one estimate, the income of the typical Georgian doubled between 1950 and 1970.[15]

Atlanta had a special significance for black Americans. If Hallinan found the blacks of Atlanta more confident and self-reliant than those of Charleston, it was understandable. Nowhere else in the South, or in the whole country, was there such a concentration of black business and black capital. Auburn Avenue had long been called "the richest Negro street in the world" because of its numerous black banks, insurance companies and stores. Atlanta also boasted the largest cluster of black educational institutions in the country: four undergraduate colleges (Clark, Morehouse, Morris Brown, Spelman), the Interdenominational Theological Seminary, and Atlanta University. By the late 1940's, blacks had begun to make a dent in Atlanta politics, and the first black was elected to the state senate the year that Hallinan came to Atlanta. In 1960 Martin Luther King Jr. returned home to Atlanta from Birmingham, Alabama, and for the rest of the decade, Atlanta was the headquarters of the civil rights movement throughout the South.[16]

Economically Atlanta was pulling the rest of the state to new levels of wealth and prosperity, but political power remained firmly in the hands of the rural counties, where the "wool hats" often looked with suspicion on the progressive proclivities of the big city. Even more than in South Carolina, the old order and the new stood uneasily side by side, much of the tension arising from the clash between the capital and the provinces.

The year 1962, however, was a turning point in the political history of modern Georgia. Not only was the first black elected to the state legislature since Reconstruction, but two crucial court decisions delivered a fatal blow to the archaic system which had given disproportionate power to the rural areas. A few weeks before Hallinan's arrival in Atlanta, a federal district court declared unconstitutional the county-unit system. The immediate result was that, for the first time in fifty years, the voters, not the politicans, decided the outcome of the Democratic gubernatorial primary election (the only election which mattered). They selected a moderate, Carl E. Sanders. A second court decision in May had even more serious consequences, for it ordered the reapportionment of the state legislature on the basis of population.[17]

Six months earlier, in the Atlanta mayoralty election, Ivan Allen Jr. had given a demonstration of the politics of the future when he formed a coalition of blacks and white moderates to defeat the rabid segregationist Lester Maddox. Allen's predecessor as mayor, William

Hartsfield, had coined the phrase that Atlanta was a city that was "too busy to hate," but the 1960's were a difficult period in Atlanta, as they were in most large cities. During the decade, 60,000 whites moved out of Atlanta and 70,000 blacks moved in, many of them settling in delapidated slums like Vine City and Buttermilk Bottom which provided a stark contrast to the gleaming glass and steel office buildings and hotels that were transforming the face of downtown Atlanta. Black prosperity did not keep pace with that of the whites, and by 1970 the black family income in Georgia was $4,743, while white family income was $9,179.[18]

Allen described the situation that he found when he took office in 1962:

> Atlanta in the early sixties possessed all of the elements that could lead to full-scale racial bloodshed and turmoil: headquarters for the civil rights organizations and white-racist groups alike ... an abundance of old-school segregationist politicians like Lester Maddox, a growing school of impatient young Blacks such as Stokely Carmichael. Consequently I was never far away from my next race issue. There would be what I call "indignation meetings" of white neighborhood associations, demanding a hearing and telling me Negroes had moved into their block and asking what the city was going to do about it. ...
>
> There would be picketing from Black students, demanding to be allowed to eat in certain restaurants, and outraged cries from the restauranteurs themselves. There would be visits from out-of-town Blacks who had been denied access to a hotel, followed by outright threats from the hotel owner, if my reaction was not to his liking.[19]

Some desegregation had taken place in Atlanta by 1962: the color bar had been dropped on buses and golf courses, at downtown hotels, restaurants and department stores; and token integration had been introduced at four public high schools the previous September. But Allen described the city as "still almost totally segregated" and nowhere more so than at City Hall, where there were still separate rest rooms and drinking fountains for blacks and whites. Most significant of all perhaps was the fact that there were forty-eight black policemen, but they did not have the authority to arrest whites.

Allen gave Hallinan a cordial welcome on his arrival in the city. Like many Atlantans, the new mayor had never met an archbishop and was not sure how to address him, but he shared the general feeling that the Catholic Church was honoring his city and enhancing its status by making it the seat of an archdiocese. Later Allen said that he had known few men in his lifetime "who fitted into the pattern of a community better than the new archbishop."[20]

Archbishop or not, Paul Hallinan found many of the same ecclesiastical problems in Atlanta that he had left behind in Charleston. In some respects, the situation was even more difficult. For one thing, his see was only six years old. Until 1956 the Diocese of Savannah-Atlanta had included the whole State of Georgia, but the growth of metropolitan Atlanta led the Holy See to establish a separate diocese for northern Georgia in that year and to raise it to the status of an archdiocese six years later. Both decisions were based on the expectation of a large increase in the Catholic population, which never really materialized.[21] The Archdiocese of Atlanta even today has barely 135,000 Catholics, and has lagged far behind Florida and, to a lesser extent, Virginia, in the size of its Catholic population.

The first ordinary of Atlanta, Bishop Francis E. Hyland, could be pardoned if he looked upon his diocese as something of a statistical nightmare, for it contained a Catholic population of 23,000 people in twenty-two parishes spread over seventy-one counties. To care for this widely scattered flock, he had only twenty-five diocesan priests. Fortunately, there were also seventy-two religious order priests resident in the diocese, but many of them were engaged in teaching and other activities.

Six years later in 1962, conditions were not appreciably better. Hallinan inherited an archdiocese of 33,000 Catholics, who were all but submerged in a general population of 2,150,000. Even more than in the diocese of Charleston, the Catholic population here was concentrated in one place (Atlanta and suburban Fulton and DeKalb counties), which contained fifteen parishes, while the other sixty-nine counties had only fourteen parishes.

Hallinan commissioned a census for the whole archdiocese early in his administration, and the results disclosed that, in 1963, there were 43,243 Catholics in the archdiocese, an increase of 85% over 1956. Of this number, 36,168 (or 83.4%) lived in metropolitan

Atlanta, and fully one-quarter of those counted in the census had lived in the archdiocese for less than one year.[22]

Even in 1971, when the Catholic population had climbed to 56,000, there was not a single resident Catholic in one-third of the counties of the archdiocese, and in another third of the counties, the Catholic population was less than one percent. To be sure, there were several thousand Catholics in and around the cities of Dalton, Rome, Gainesville, Athens, Milledgeville, Washington, Griffin and LaGrange, but the vast majority of Catholics still lived in metropolitan Atlanta.

Diocesan priests contined to be scarce. In 1962 religious order priests outnumbered them by a margin of almost three to one, and they staffed ten of the twenty-nine parishes. The Marists were especially prominent, administering two parishes and Marist College, a high-school military academy. The Franciscans operated Immaculate Conception Church, a downtown "business" parish, and the two black parishes were also in the hands of religious, the Society of African Missions at Our Lady of Lourdes and the Passionists at St. Paul of the Cross. In the eastern reaches of the archdiocese, the Sons of the Sacred Heart of Jesus ministered to a widely dispersed Catholic population from two parishes at Toccoa and Washington.

Hallinan was especially grateful to the Redemptorists, who cared for parishes at Dalton and Fort Oglethorpe along the Tennessee border, and for a third parish near the southern boundary of the archdiocese, Sacred Heart in Griffin, which had four missions and extended over nine counties. At one of these missions (McDonough in Henry County), the "chapel" was a small rented room up a flight of stairs in the local Masonic Hall. On a visit there early in 1963, Hallinan took an instant dislike to the place, but he enjoyed the tactics used by the pastor and parishioners, who wanted to build a proper church. As Hallinan explained afterwards:

> The best way to convince a bishop that a new church is needed is to put him with a congregation of about 100 in a room built for 50—cold and forty steps up from the sidewalk. From this point I was whisked to see an attractive piece of land where they hope to build. Then a fine fish dinner, lots of good coffee, and a chance to read a newspaper account of my weekend visit. This was especially interesting because I learned that we were planning not only a new

church, but a new school! This is like asking the boss to treble your salary when you really only want to double it.[23]

At Cleveland, in the scenic Georgia mountains in the northeastern corner of the state, one Glenmary missionary, Father Francis Ruff, began a mission parish in 1964. There were no known Catholics in three counties for which he was responsible. Three years later, he counted twenty-eight parishioners in White County, two parishioners and twelve college students in Towns County, and, in Union County, eight Catholics in the winter and twenty in the summer. The Sunday collection gradually rose from three dollars to thirty dollars, but his main problem was the attitude of non-Catholics. "Some of them look upon Catholics not as a different Christian Church," he explained, "but as a different religion like the Moslems." "But, thank God for Pope John," the priest added, "he had a special grace and it got through up here."[24]

In the city of Atlanta, as in Charleston, several of the larger parishes could rival their counterparts in any northern diocese, both in numbers of parishioners and the size of their facilities. The Cathedral of Christ the King was a handsome stone building, erected by Bishop Gerald P. O'Hara as the co-cathedral in 1939 (after the Diocese of Savannah had become the Diocese of Savannah-Atlanta in 1937). The site was the former headquarters of the Ku Klux Klan, and, in a famous gesture, O'Hara invited the Imperial Wizard, Hiram Wesley Evans, to attend the dedication. He sat there, Ralph McGill reported, "his face beaming like a Halloween pumpkin as High Mass was said before him."[25] In addition to the two black parishes in Atlanta, there were also two Eastern Rite parishes, one Maronite and the other Melkite. The archbishop's first interview with the Maronite pastor did not go well. When he began to moan and groan about the plight of his poverty-stricken people, Hallinan reminded him that the blacks were worse off economically and did a better job of supporting their parishes.[26]

Two-thirds of the parishes maintained parochial schools with a total enrollment of more than 6,000 students. All but five of the schools were in metropolitan Atlanta where an astonishingly high percentage of Catholic children—76.2%—attended parochial schools. Some of them were quite large, such as Our Lady of the Assumption with 900 pupils and St. Thomas More in Decatur with more than 700 students.

Atlanta was also well supplied with Catholic high schools, too well supplied, as it turned out, for Hallinan had to close several of them before his death. In addition to Marist College (really a military academy opened in 1901), the Grey Nuns had recently opened D'Youville Academy for Girls, and Bishop Hyland had built three diocesan high schools (two white and one black) at a cost of $1,750,000. Annual operating expenses for the three schools came to $750,000, one-third of which came from the parishes of Greater Atlanta as a direct subsidy. There was also an active Confraternity of Christian Doctrine in the archdiocese, and, as one would expect, the archbishop took good care of the Newman movement, assigning four full-time chaplains and eight part-time chaplains to the work.[27]

In Charleston, Hallinan had seen the contribution made by Catholic hospitals in the South and he was quick to appreciate and praise the work of the nursing sisters at St. Joseph's Infirmary in Atlanta and St. Mary's Hospital in Athens. He had the pleasure of blessing a third Catholic hospital in 1964, when the Medical Mission Sisters converted their Catholic Clinic (originally the Catholic Colored Clinic) into Holy Family Hospital in the southwestern part of the city. In addition to these three general hospitals, the Dominican Sisters operated a unique institution, Our Lady of Perpetual Help Free Cancer Home.[28]

By the 1960's, therefore, Catholics were no longer an exotic species, at least in Atlanta, and they were making a real, if modest, contribution to the city with their educational and charitable institutions. In his installation sermon, Hallinan mentioned the long history of Catholics in Georgia and emphasized the good relations which had generally existed between Catholics and Protestants since the beginning of the nineteenth century when the first Catholic communities appeared in Augusta and Savannah. In Atlanta itself, there had been a Catholic presence from the very beginning of the city. Atlanta was a quintessential railroad town, and with the railroad had come the Irish Catholics who built it. They erected Immaculate Conception Church at the same time that the Baptists and Methodists were building their first churches—and only months after the Town of Atlanta had become the City of Atlanta.[29]

In November 1864, when General William T. Sherman burned much of Atlanta, the pastor of Immaculate Conception Church, Father Thomas O'Reilly, became a popular hero because of his successful intervention with the Union army to prevent the destruction of his own church, four Protestant churches, the City Hall and a number of private residences. Relations between Catholics and Protestants in Savannah were so good that for forty-six years the Board of Education directly subsidized the Catholic schools of the city.[30]

This era of good feeling came to an abrupt end in 1916, when a wave of anti-Catholic feeling swept across the state, much of it orchestrated by Tom Watson, an embittered populist demagogue, and the revived Ku Klux Klan (founded in Atlanta on October 16, 1915). In Savannah the Board of Education promptly terminated the subsidy for Catholic schools; in Atlanta the Klan tried to fire Catholic teachers and ban "pro-Catholic" textbooks from the public schools. Watson, running for the United States Senate, made the preposterous claim that President Woodrow Wilson had become the catspaw of the American Catholic hierarchy; the Georgia Legislature passed a "convent inspection" bill; and hate literature was spread throughout the state.[31]

At his installation ceremony, Hallinan made no mention of this sad chapter in Georgia history, preferring to regard it as an aberration. He was not interested in fighting old battles in the spring of 1962 but in preparing for a new battle which he knew was inevitable. The most sensitive racial issue at that moment in Georgia was the segregation of public accommodations and segregated classrooms. Young black activists had already begun to stage sit-in demonstrations and had gone to jail in an effort to end the system. The system was indeed beginning to crack and crumble, but too slowly for many blacks and too quickly for many whites.[32]

By that time it was almost four years since the United States bishops had condemned segregation as incompatible with human dignity; it was almost two years since Hallinan himself had promised to end segregation in the Catholic schools no later than the public schools did so. In Atlanta, the time for decision had now arrived, since nine black students had been admitted to all-white public high schools the previous September.

The archbishop made his move on June 10, only ten weeks after his arrival in Atlanta, when he announced the desegregation of all Catholic schools in the archdiocese. It was far from a snap decision. He had spent those ten weeks carefully taking readings and preparing the ground before he acted. There were 6,900 whites and 735 blacks in the Catholic schools. Hallinan wanted to know how many black students would choose to transfer to white schools. At registration time for the Catholic high schools in the spring of 1962, six black eighth-graders applied for admission to white Catholic high schools which indicated that there would be no massive influx of black students into the white schools. As a result Hallinan decided to act. On the next day he drew up a draft statement announcing the opening of all Catholic schools to students of both races.

Before he published it, however, he went through a lengthy series of consultations with several prominent Catholic laymen, including Judge Sam P. McKenzie of the Fulton County Superior Court, and the two archdiocesan attorneys, Hughes Spalding Sr., and Robert Troutman, both members of the leading Atlanta law firm of King and Spalding. In his conversations with them, he hammered away at the theme that this was the "optimum moment" for change and he won the backing of all three of them. He also had a conference with former mayor William Hartsfield and showed him the text of his proposed announcement. Hartsfield liked the statement and assured him that both the police and the newspapers would support him fully. The former mayor also made several practical suggestions: to read the statement first in church; to limit integration initially to a small number of students; and to involve more lay people in the decision. It was advice that the archbishop appreciated. That evening at St. Joseph's Church in Hapeville, he told the parishioners of his plan, although he did not mention any specific date.

There were also the priests and religious to consider. Father Michael McKeever, S.M.A., the pastor of the largest black parish school in Atlanta, was in complete agreement with the archbishop's plans, and, after a three-hour discussion, so was Father Vincent P. Brennan, S.M., the principal of Marist College. Another three-hour meeting was held on May 21 with the nineteen members of the Archdiocesan School Board. It ended with their endorsement of the archbishop's plans.[33]

A few days later Hallinan raised the issue with the diocesan consultors. He did not precisely consult them: he announced that he had decided to integrate the schools in September and asked them for their reaction. One priest warned that caution would be necessary in areas outside of Atlanta; another asked the archbishop to add a sentence to his statement "easing the conscience of segregationists." Hallinan objected to the latter suggestion on the grounds that it would weaken the force of the announcement and contradict the stand already taken by the United States bishops. The senior consultors, Monsignors Joseph E. Moylan, Joseph G. Cassidy and Patrick J. O'Connor, gave him strong support and the board voted to back his stand.[34]

At the beginning of June the archbishop was back again at Marist College, this time to meet with the parents and advisors. Since Marist was the most prestigious Catholic high school in Atlanta, it was crucial that integration work smoothly here. Hallinan mentioned his plans (again without specifying a date) and he was pleased with the reaction. One enthusiastic priest who was present exclaimed: "Damn the torpedoes!" It was the wrong thing to say and Hughes Spalding replied: "Yeah, but he was a Yankee."[35]

Sunday, June 10, was the date set for the announcement. Judging from his diary, Hallinan seemed less concerned about this statement than he had been about the pastoral letter of February 17, 1961. Yet this was really a much bigger step. In 1961 he was merely declaring that segregation would end in the Catholic schools of Charleston at some future date. It was difficult to whip up opposition to a statement of that nature. Now, however, he was about to take the plunge and open the Catholic schools of Atlanta to blacks in the next three months. Only one other bishop in the Deep South had dared to do the same—Archbishop Joseph Rummel of New Orleans, and he had provoked widespread and bitter opposition.

At 8:30 A.M. on June 10 the archbishop held a press conference at the cathedral rectory and read a brief statement. Among those present was Charlayne Hunter, the young black woman who had helped to integrate the University of Georgia in January 1961. The *New York Times,* the wire services, *Newsweek,* and the local radio stations and television channels all sent reporters. Someone asked the archbishop how the civil authorities would react to his decision. Hallinan knew that he had nothing to fear from the city officials. They would welcome his move, since they themselves were about to announce a further step in the integration of Atlanta's public schools.[36] It was another matter with the state government, however, which was still officially committed to preserving racial segregation in education. In answer to a reporter's question, Hallinan conceded that he had some apprehension that the state officials might attempt to end the tax-exempt status of Catholic schools and to deprive teachers of their licenses. However, he said, "I believe that it is less likely now than it would have been a year ago." If the state did try to impose sanctions on the Catholic schools, he admitted that "it would be a major struggle for us."[37]

At all the Masses that day in the archdiocese the congregation heard the archbishop's letter. It happened to be Pentecost Sunday and Hallinan used the occasion to stress the universality of the Church. He mentioned the pastoral letter of February 1961 and said that it was time to act on the principles contained in it. Consequently he announced that, as of September 1, 1962, "Catholic children, regardless of race or color, will be admitted to the Catholic schools of the Archdiocese.... The same norms of admission, registration, transfer, residence, tuition and academic qualifications [will] apply to everyone."

The letter was short and its message unequivocal, but it also included an eloquent appeal to the best traditions of Georgia's Catholics. "Our churches have always been open to everyone regardless of race or color. White and Negro Catholics have attended Mass and received the sacraments side by side for generations." Therefore, said the archbishop, "the logical step in 1962 is a school admission policy without regard to color."

There was also a pointed reminder that Atlanta was not Mississippi. Hallinan expressed his gratitude for "the climate of law, order and justice in which we live" and he declared that "Catholics are part of that community, proud of its tradition, faithful to its highest law." Finally he hoped that "every Catholic in the Archdiocese will stand loyal and firm with his Church as we move toward the full measure of justice, with faith, with prudence, and with courage."[38]

The next day the letter was a major news item all over the state, even in south Georgia where it had no direct application.[39] Even those newspapers which had ignored the pastoral letter of February 1961 gave it extensive coverage. The only editorial comment came from the Atlanta *Constitution*, which greeted it in a tepid sort of way, and the Atlanta *World*, a black daily, which welcomed it with considerably more enthusiasm: "At last a move on the part of at least one church to stand up and set a worthy example for the state."[40]

Ralph McGill adopted the same tack in a long column two days after the letter appeared. A Presbyterian himself, McGill lamented the lack of Christian leadership in the area of racial justice. But, he said:

> The Roman Catholic Church is the one most strongly and most intelligently on the move in the sociological jungle of racist prejudices where the agents of the White Citizens' Councils roam with poison darts of slander and abuse.

He noted that the pastoral letter appeared on Pentecost, the day when the Holy Spirit helped the first disciples to overcome their fears and prejudices to make Christianity a world religion. "The Archbishop was saying to his flock," McGill explained, "that they must put aside prejudices and stand for Christian morality. Protestant churches and schools can hardly avoid some move. They must either affirm or deny the immorality of segregated religion and citizenship."[41]

If Hallinan feared the same reactions which the pastoral letter of February 1961 had provoked in Charleston, he must have been pleasantly surprised. There were a few angry telephone calls and a few nasty letters, but no real opposition and certainly no threats to establish a segregated "Marian Academy." The following day, at lunch in a restaurant, an elderly lady approached Hallinan with a scowl on her face. He thought that now at last he would get a barrage of criticism, but she only wanted to complain about recent changes in the liturgy.[42]

The archbishop was beginning to like Atlanta. A recent Confirmation tour had given him the opportunity to see much of the archdiocese and to meet many of his priests. The renovations at the rectory were proceeding on schedule; his office was ready and the book shelves in his room were filling up. "It's mighty nice around here these days," he admitted. School integration had been his first big challenge; once that had been successfully met, he said that he felt ten feet tall. If he needed any further persuasion that Atlanta now was home, it came when he returned to Charleston for the installation of his successor, Bishop Francis F. Reh. Much as he enjoyed the occasion, he said that it was "like visiting an old flame and finding her married to a successful businessman who has charmed everyone."[43]

11

The Second Vatican Council

Except for the integration of the parochial schools, Hallinan's first six months in Atlanta were uneventful but not without worries. The deeper he delved into the finances of the archdiocese, the more concerned he became. Bishop Hyland's fund-raising campaign of 1960 had fallen far short of its goal and he had dipped into the Diocesan Development Fund to meet ordinary operating expenses. Parishes had been slow to pay their debts and assessments. Some pastors owed the diocese a great deal of money.

Hallinan took several immediate steps to bring the situation under control. He ordered an audit of all diocesan expenses since 1956, terminated the languishing fund-raising campaign, told pastors to send their assessments and collections to the chancery office within ten days, mandated a uniform system of bookkeeping for all parishes, and instituted monthly financial reports for the pastors. He spent several days reviewing the diocesan high school budgets himself, "slashing and patching," as he said, to pare expenses wherever he could.[1]

There were two other problems which he began to tackle: the lack of a proper chancery office and the lack of a diocesan newspaper. In both cases the main difficulty was money, yet in September he bought property from the Marists on which he hoped to build a Catholic Center in the not too distant future. As he dreamed about it, his plans became more and more elaborate. Finally, he had in mind a structure which would not only house the diocesan offices but provide meeting rooms, a library, a chapel and an auditorium for all the people of the archdiocese. He even thought of building a new cathedral alongside it. All that he could do in 1962, though, was to dream about such things, for both he and the diocesan consultors agreed that it would not be wise to undertake another fund-raising drive until 1964 at least.[2]

The establishment of a diocesan paper was an easier matter to handle. He estimated that it would cost $60,000 a year and that he could raise $31,000 through subscriptions and $24,000 through advertising revenue. This would leave the archdiocese with a deficit of only $4,000 a year. A bigger problem was finding the right editor. Father Donald Kiernan recommended an Australian-born journalist named Gerard Sherry. Before the end of the summer, Sherry met with the archbishop, accepted his proposal, and agreed to start a diocesan newspaper for the new year.[3]

Hallinan did less traveling now than he had done in Charleston. Six months went by without a single begging-trip. He accepted only one engagement outside the diocese—the Ann Arbor Newman Club "summit meeting." But early in October he packed his bags, flew to New York City for a few days of vacation, and then left for Rome.

He arrived there on October 9, for the opening of the Second Vatican Council. Next day, he attended a meeting of the United States archbishops at the North American College to select a list of American candidates for the various conciliar commissions. Along with Archbishop Krol and Coadjutor Archbishop John Cody of New Orleans, he suggested that the archbishops draw up an international list of names. The suggestion was turned down. Nonetheless, Hallinan was pleased with the list that the archbishops agreed upon, and, if he had any doubts, they were erased when he saw and heard Cardinal James Francis McIntyre of Los Angeles bellowing fruitlessly about the results of the meeting.[4]

The Council opened at eight in the morning of October 11 with the procession of 2,300 cardinals, patriarchs, archbishops, bishops, abbots and major religious superiors from the Vatican Palace to St. Peter's Basilica. The Archbishop of Atlanta was one of the last prelates to get on line, but even then he had to wait an hour before he began to move forward. Once inside St. Peter's, he sat with Krol and Bishop John Mark Gannon of Erie. He was overwhelmed by the magnificence of the occasion—"grand, simply grand," he wrote in his diary—but his mood changed that evening when he had dinner with Martin H. Work, Executive Director of the National Council of Catholic Men. The conversation turned to the press coverage of the council, and Hallinan became quite angry when he discovered how inadequate were the press facilities.[5]

Other American bishops were angry too. The subject came up the next day at the meeting of the Administrative Board of the NCWC at the North American College and Archbishop Patrick A. O'Boyle of Washington, on behalf of the NCWC, agreed to spend $10,000 for a press office. But, according to Hallinan, Monsignor Paul Tanner, General Secretary of the NCWC, did not show the slightest interest in the proposal.[6]

On Saturday, October 13, Hallinan donned his choir robes for the first working meeting of the council, the general congregation (i.e. plenary session) which was to select the members of the ten conciliar commissions. He compared it irreverently to the Sonny Liston fight, which had ended a few seconds into the first round with a knockout. On this occasion, immediately after the opening Mass, Cardinal Achille Liénart of Lille asked for a postponement of the voting so that the various episcopal conferences could caucus and discuss the selection of candidates. Cardinal Joseph Frings of Cologne seconded the motion at once. The applause was so overwhelming that no vote was taken, and Cardinal Eugene Tisserant adjourned the meeting after only fifteen minutes.[7]

For the next three days, Hallinan, like the other Council Fathers, was busy with the mundane business of politics. On October 14, he met with Bishop Tracy, Bishop Leo Dworschak of Fargo and Father Frederick McManus, and together they drew up their own international list of names for the conciliar commissions. When they brought the list to the next meeting of the United States bishops, however, they discovered that they were too late. Three other bishops—Archbishop Cody, Archbishop Lawrence Shehan and Auxiliary Bishop James Griffiths of New York—had already produced a complete international list for all ten commissions, and Hallinan and his friends dropped their list in favor of this one.

Both Hallinan and Dworchak were on the accepted list, and they were the two prelates finally selected by the American bishops as their candidates for the Liturgical Commission.[8] On October 15, Frederick McManus relayed another bit of news to Hallinan; he was also likely to be the North American candidate of the French, Dutch (and possibly) the German bishops for the Liturgical Commission.[9] The balloting took place on October 16. Next day, Krol (one of the undersecretaries of the Council) tipped him off that he had been elected to the Commission by a large majority.[10] He noted in his diary that he was "surprised, delighted and scared."

The elections results were announced on October 20 (Hallinan received over 1,400 votes), and on the following day he attended the first meeting of the Commission. It was a difficult hour-and-a-half. He sat there listening to the others speaking fluently in Latin, while he grasped at nouns and verbs, getting only the general drift of the discussion and hoping that his command of Latin would improve.[11]

Not only was his Latin rusty, but, at this stage of his life, he had no extensive expertise in liturgy either, as two of his closest friends, Bishop Tracy and Father McManus, both recognized.[12] He had shown an interest in the liturgical apostolate both as a Newman Club chaplain and as a bishop, but only now did he begin to read and study the liturgy in depth, relying heavily for advice upon Frederick McManus whom he saw almost every day.

On October 22, at the fourth general congregation, the debate began on the *schema* on the liturgy—that is, the preliminary draft for the Constitution on the Sacred Liturgy. Hallinan was impressed with the speeches of Cardinal Montini of Milan, Cardinal Giacomo Lercaro of Bologna and Cardinal Laurena Rugambwa of Tanganyika, all of whom spoke in favor of the *schema*. On the other hand, he thought that Cardinal Spellman, who wanted to retain the Latin Mass intact, was "incredibly out of step," and that Archbishop Vagnozzi was "using a smokescreen of inexact and verbose theology" when he criticized the draft of the *schema*. The next day, Cardinal McIntyre made an impassioned defense of Latin, and Hallinan heard comments that the speech had advanced the cause of the vernacular in the liturgy by twenty years. On October 25, he decided to speak himself in favor of the *schema*. He wrote out a speech in longhand, showed it to McManus, and then asked Father William Leahy of the North American College to translate it into Latin for him.[13]

Meanwhile, he enjoyed himself at the news conference for the American correspondents on October 26. He answered most of the questions himself and told the reporters that in the debates in the general congregations "there have been very few extremists. . . .

Everyone of the speakers has conceded the merits of the other side." He said that he had been amused to hear bishops using Ciceronian Latin to defend the use of the vernacular in the liturgy.

Someone asked about the time limit of ten minutes imposed on speakers in the general congregations. The archbishop admitted that it had been largely ignored, but "a certain restraint is imposed on speakers by the expressions on everyone else's face." On the other hand, he said, occasionally a prelate will simply say *iam dicta sunt,* meaning that someone else has already said what he was going to say. Then, said Hallinan, "there is a feeling of applause in the Council even if nobody actually applauds."

As to the American bishops, he denied reports that they were not interested in the liturgy and emphasized that they had not taken a unified position on the subject. He mentioned that they were holding informal study sessions on the liturgy and would probably do the same for other topics as they came before the Council.[14]

After waiting all Tuesday morning for an opportunity which never came, he addressed the Council on Wednesday, October 31. He was not nervous but fearful that Cardinal Tisserant might cut him off, as he had done to two other speakers before him, when they had exceeded the ten-minute time limit. He was the first American bishop to preface his remarks by saying that he spoke for "many bishops (although not for all) of the United States of America." The words were interpreted by some as a declaration that Cardinal Spellman and Cardinal McIntyre did not speak for the whole American hierarchy.[15]

The Archbishop of Atlanta strongly advocated a simplified, vernacular liturgy:

> The liturgy of the Church must be public, but this can have real meaning for our people only if they understand enough of it to be part of it. They must be united to God not alone as in private prayer, but together with the whole Church in our Head who is Christ. . . .

He mentioned another reason why numerous American bishops favored the proposed *schema,* a reason which startled some of the Council Fathers:

In a particular manner this is desired by the bishops of those regions in which there are few Catholics. For example, in my own Archdiocese of Atlanta, scarcely two percent of the population is Catholic. The more we can do to render the Mass understandable to all, not just to those equipped by learning or formed by habit, the more we open new avenues to the minds and hearts of Christians who are not Catholic.[16]

Hallinan was pleased with the way he delivered the talk and with its reception afterwards. Krol told him that it was excellent, as did Cardinal Ritter and Bishops Griffiths, Reed and McDevitt, Father McManus, and a number of the Australian bishops. A week later he was still getting congratulations and concluded that he had not misjudged the degree of support that he enjoyed among the American bishops.[17]

Matters were not proceeding so smoothly in the Liturgical Commission, however. Hallinan was becoming increasingly frustrated with the dilatory tactics of its president, Cardinal Arcadio Larraona, C.M.E., a Spanish-born Claretian who had become Prefect of the Congregation of Rites only in February 1962 after spending most of his life teaching canon law and serving as Undersecretary and Secretary of the Congregation of Religious.

Hallinan hoped that the Fathers would be able to vote on the revised *schema* before they went home, but the reactionaries on the Liturgical Commission were deliberately stalling for time in the hope of limiting the scope of liturgical reform. They were especially anxious to prevent a vote in the general congregations, where the supporters of the *schema* were likely to score an impressive psychological victory. Cardinal Larraona unquestionably favored the reactionary faction, and their ranks were considerably strengthened at the end of October when the pope appointed Archbishop Enrico Dante to the commission as an additional member.[18]

The unofficial leader of the progressive bloc in the Liturgical Commission was not any of the episcopal members, but one of the *periti* (expert advisors), Father Annibale Bugnini, C.M. He had served as the Secretary of the Preparatory Liturgical Commission under the chairmanship of Cardinal Gaetano Cicognani from November 1960 to January 1962, and he was the man mainly responsible for the *schema* on the liturgy. Alone of all the secretaries of the preparatory commissions, he was not appointed secretary of the corresponding conciliar commission. When Larraona succeeded Cicognani as president of the commission upon the latter's death, he deliberately passed over Bugnini and appointed as secretary Father Ferdinando Antonelli, O.F.M. Bugnini used what leverage he had left, however, to keep careful watch over his *schema* and to prevent Larraona and his friends from eviscerating it.[19]

Through Frederick McManus, Hallinan came to know and to appreciate the role of Bugnini in the preparatory commission. Like Bugnini, he realized that the work of the conciliar commission was being delayed intentionally and he became more and more anxious to move the emendations through the commission more promptly. He decided on a twofold plan of action. First he drew up a proposal that the commission should change its procedure so that the members could vote immediately on each proposed revision and then send it on to the General Secretary of the Council at once, rather than wait for each chapter of the *schema* to be completed. He drafted a proposal outlining the procedural changes in detail, showed it to Tracy and McManus, and asked Father Leahy to translate it into Latin.[20]

The second part of Hallinan's plan was to take his case to a higher level than Larraona. He asked for an appointment to see Cardinal Amleto Cicognani, the Papal Secretary of State and former Apostolic Delegate in the United States. On the afternoon of November 7, as they walked in the Vatican Gardens, Hallinan explained to him the situation on the Liturgical Commission and gave him a copy of his proposal. He told Cicognani: "We need something specific approved by the Council before we go home."

Cicognani was receptive and candid in his replies. He told Hallinan: "You are right in pushing for a vote on the liturgy. I try to push but I can only do so much. The curia is not all bad—only out of touch. We need bishops here." He was aware of the problems with Larraona. He asked Hallinan: "Can you understand him? I can't." He also criticized the secretary, Father Antonelli, as too conservative, but praised Bugnini as an "excellent man" who had done "good work" for his brother Gaetano.[21]

While Hallinan was conferring with the Secretary of State, Archbishop Francis Grimshaw of Birmingham was presenting the proposal to Larraona; but, as Hallinan said afterwards, he "flubbed it." Instead of reading the proposal at the meeting, he showed it to the cardinal beforehand and the result was total confusion.[22]

On the following day Hallinan tried to salvage the situation. During the general congregation in the morning, he persuaded thirteen members of the Liturgical Commission to sign a petition endorsing his recommendation that they should vote on each proposed revision of the liturgical *schema* as soon as possible. He produced it at the afternoon meeting of the Commission. The members voted unanimously to accept it and then proceeded to follow the new procedure by taking three votes on a report from Lercaro's subcommission. But just when Hallinan thought that he had won, Larraona showed that he too was a resourceful politician. There was no urgency in sending the results to the General Secretary, he said, because the Council Fathers would not vote on the various emendations until the whole *schema* had been completely revised by the commission. As if to emphasize his point, he then cancelled the meeting scheduled for the next day.[23]

Only three weeks were left now before the end of the first session. Time was working in favor of those who wanted to sabotage the *schema* and Hallinan was more frustrated and angry than ever. He sent off a bluntly-worded letter to Cicognani, contesting Larraona's interpretation of the Council's rules and telling the Secretary of State:

> The bishops want to vote as well as to listen; they prefer the voting closely connected with the pertinent discussion. . . .
>
> The Holy Father has made possible this *aggiornamento* by convoking the Council. We are all sensitive to his appeal to us to work with him that our beloved Church may meet the crisis of our times. . . . We will continue doing what we can to carry out this responsible role, but I do not feel that the efforts in our commission over the past three weeks have matched the spirit of profound concern and the yearning for this renewal that are so evident in the words expressed daily in the Council by the Fathers.[24]

Over the weekend Hallinan's spirits improved as he heard rumors that Cardinal Montini was about to intervene, that the French and German bishops were angry, and that Cardinal Cicognani had been to see the pope over the lack of progress in the Liturgical Commission. Krol telephoned with a report that Archbishop Pericle Felici, the Secretary General of the Council, had told Larraona to speed up the pace of the proceedings in his Commission. Supposedly, Larraona's reply was: "*Nulla difficultas.*" At the meeting of the American bishops on Monday, Hallinan gave them a frank account of the situation but said that the revised text of the Introduction to the *schema* could reach the Council floor by the end of the week—if Larraona would move it through the Commission.[25]

During the next few days, developments in the general congregations increased Hallinan's optimism. First was the test vote on November 13, when Cardinal Bernard Alfrink of Utrecht called for a standing vote on whether to conclude the discussion of the final chapters of the liturgical *schema* and the Fathers overwhelming approved the clôture motion.[26] The next day, at the suggestion of Cardinal Tisserant, they voted to send the whole *schema* to the Liturgical Commision by a majority of 2,162 to 46. Referring to the minority, Hallinan said: "I didn't know that Dante and Vagnozzi had that many friends."[27] On November 16 the four paragraphs of the amended Introduction reached the Council floor, and the next day, the Fathers approved them by lopsided margins. Larraona crowed about "*magna nostra victoria.*"[28]

The Liturgical Commission did not entirely absorb Hallinan's attention. He also watched closely as the Council took up the controversial *schema* entitled *De Revelatione,* prepared under the direction of Cardinal Alfredo Ottaviani of the Holy Office. The ensuing debate produced a clear division among the Council Fathers between those who were willing to accept Ottaviani's theology and those who were not. Among the latter were Cardinals Liénart, Frings, Koenig, Alfrink and Ritter, the last of whom said of the *schema*: "What a tedious and unrealistic attitude it betrays toward the Word of God which we call the Scriptures." Hallinan thought that their interventions were magnificent.[29]

There was so much dissatisfaction with this *schema* that, on November 22, Archbishop Felici suddenly announced a snap vote to decide whether to continue with the discussion. Many of the Fathers were confused about what they were voting for, but those who wished to drop the *schema* came within a hundred votes of the two-thirds majority needed to do so. The fact that over 1,300 Fathers voted for the resolution was proof of the lack of confidence in the *schema*. The next day, in a surprise announcement, the pope ordered the *schema* withdrawn and the appointment of a new mixed commission to revise it. Hallinan was pleased to see the original *schema* scrapped and happy that Cardinal Bea would be part of the new commission. But his reaction also indicated the degree to which he had become conscious of the doctrine of collegiality, for he said: "I don't like the abdication of conciliar authority. Why can't we do sensible things like the Holy Father?"[30]

Meanwhile only two weeks remained of the first session of the Council and the log-jam in the Liturgical Commission seemed as bad as ever. Hallinan decided on another two-pronged attack. With Krol's help, he composed a new order of procedure for the commission and drew up a petition to the Presidency of the Council which he hoped the American bishops would sign.[31]

Essentially Paul Hallinan was in the position of a congressman who wants to get a bill out of a committee where its prospects are dim and onto the floor of the House where he knows that he has the necessary votes for passage. After listening to the speeches in the general congregations and watching the voting there, he was certain that there was a majority in the Council in favor of the *schema* on the liturgy. The crucial thing was to give the Fathers an opportunity to vote on it. There was no chance of having the whole revised *schema* ready by the end of the first session, since there had been 625 oral and written interventions, each one of which the Liturgical Commission would have to consider. But there was a strong possibility of having the first chapter (with its endorsement of some vernacular in the liturgy) ready by the end of the session, and many bishops wanted to return home with at least this much accomplished.

Hallinan's new proposal was more radical than the one he had suggested on November 7. This time he wanted a major change in procedure both in the Liturgical Commission and in the general congregations. First of all, he thought that it would save time in the commission if the theological, juridical and Latin subcommissions reviewed the emendations before they came before the full commission (the procedure that had been adopted at his suggestion in processing the Introduction). The members of the commission would then be required to vote *placet* or *non placet* as soon as a subcommission submitted its emendations to them. There would be no discussion unless a proposed revision failed to gain a majority of votes.

Next, the secretary of the commission would send the emendations to the Council Fathers with specially prepared ballots. Each ballot would have three columns, listing (a) the original text of the *schema,* (b) all the revisions which the subcommissions had recommended to the commission, whether accepted or not, (c) the new text of the *schema* approved by the commission. Obviously this was designed to expedite the process of revising the *schema* by putting more power into the hands of the Council Fathers and lessening the power of the commission.[32]

The same day that he drafted this proposal he had his petition mimeographed at the NCWC office in Rome. It was a simple, courteous plea to the Presidents of the Council for action:

> We the undersigned Bishops of the United States of America request that Chapter One of the *Schema de Sacra Liturgia* be brought to the General Congregation for the necessary vote, so that (if approved) the final text can be submitted to His Holiness, Pope John XXIII, before this session closes.
>
> Chapter One contains most of the principles on the renewal of the Sacred Liturgy; subsequent chapters can be deferred to subsequent sessions. The almost unanimous approval of the *Schema in genere* and the *Proemium* leads us to believe that the Fathers of the Council desire to vote on this fundamental chapter.[33]

Neither Felici nor Vagnozzi liked what Hallinan was doing. Felici told Antonelli that Hallinan's procedural changes just would not work. Vagnozzi met Hallinan at one of the coffee bars at St. Peter's and said: "You are a politician," to which he responded: "It takes one to know one." In the Liturgical Commission other members were beginning to speak up. The Yugoslav Bishop Alfred Pichler of Banjaluka berated Larraona for failure to do his duty. The shocked cardinal replied: "I go to confession. I don't confess that."[34]

At the meeting of the United States bishops on November 26, Bishop Tracy and Bishop William Connare of Greensburg took charge of collecting signatures for Hallinan's petition. Cardinal McIntyre and Archbishop Joseph P. Hurley of St. Augustine refused, but 132 bishops signed the petition. The next day, Archbishop Shehan and Hallinan gave it to Cardinal Spellman for presentation to the Presidency of the Council.[35]

The pace of work in the Liturgical Commission suddenly picked up at this time and Hallinan wondered if the Presidency had put pressure on Larraona. In any event, Antonelli unexpectedly produced the texts for the first nine articles of Chapter One. The effect, said Hallinan, was electric, and the members of the commission promptly approved them. When they got along to article 24 and a discussion of the vernacular, Archbishop Dante began to scream, but Larraona reminded him that an Ecumenical Council was superior to the Sacred Congregation of Rites.[36] Even more reassuring was the fact that the revised *schema* was making its way piece by piece to the floor of the Council. On November 28, the Fathers received the printed copies of the nine articles approved by the Liturgical Commission two days before. They voted in favor of all nine of them by wide margins on November 30. On the same day, the Liturgical Commission wound up its task of revising Chapter One. "We have done our work," said a satisfied Paul Hallinan.[37]

This was the first weekend in a month that he did not spend worrying about the fate of the *schema*. He used the opportunity to catch up on his correspondence with Harold Rainey in Atlanta and with Charles Albright of the Newman Apostolate. He also did some shopping, went to confession at Santa Susanna, and on Sunday—a fair, cool day—went to St. Peter's to hear Pope John recite the noonday *Angelus* and bless the crowd in the square.[38]

On Monday, as usual, he went to St. Peter's for the general congregation, prepared to savor the fruits of Friday's victory in the Liturgical Commission. He expected that the Fathers would receive the printed texts of articles 16-31 at any moment, but as the speeches continued on the floor and the minutes ticked away, there was no sign of the missing texts. He became uneasy, then apprehensive, then furious. He seems to have jumped to the conclusion that this was a deliberate ploy by the obstructionists on the Liturgical Commission to prevent key sections of Chapter One from coming to a vote at this session of the Council.

By noon, Hallinan was boiling. "What in hell has gone wrong?," he wrote in his diary. He saw McManus, Krol and Felici, and tried to get in touch with Cicognani. Blaming Antonelli for the delay, he confronted him directly at the afternoon meeting of the Liturgical Commission, but got no satisfaction. He also saw Spellman and asked him what good it had done to present his petition to the

Council Presidency. When he came away, he was convinced that Spellman had never formally presented the petition at all.[39]

He poured out his frustrations and his suspicions to the American bishops, when he addressed them that evening at the North American College. He called the missing articles "the heart" of Chapter One, since they sanctioned the use of the vernacular in the liturgy and gave considerable power in liturgical matters to episcopal conferences. The work on the articles had been completed the previous Friday at 7:30 P.M., he reported, and "every bishop on the committee fully expected [that they would] reach the floor today for a vote on Tuesday or Wednesday." But now, he continued, it is apparent "that nothing at all was done on making a few simple corrections."

There were only four days left in the first session, and Hallinan warned his fellow bishops that, unless the missing articles were brought to the floor in the next two days, there was no hope of completing Chapter One before its close. He asked his confrères to consider two reasons why it was important to finish this particular chapter at the present session of the Council.

First, he reminded them that they had worked all through October and November and had produced almost nothing. Three other *schemata* had been rejected for extensive revisions, and only the *schema* on the liturgy seemed to command the respect of the Council Fathers. If they were going to accomplish anything at this session, it would have to be in this field. Secondly, he brought up a very practical matter: "If we leave here on December 8 with Chapter One approved ... we will be free to speak about it in the United States— to continue and to intensify the educational preparation of priests and people." But, if Chapter One did not receive the approval of the Council Fathers, Hallinan pointed out that "we will be in no position even to discuss it. It will remain *sub secreto*. We can't even print the Introduction on a holy card and pass it out."

In closing he asked the bishops to pray for the help of the Holy Spirit. He said that the situation reminded him of his days at Notre Dame, when the football team was trailing by three touchdowns with three minutes left to play. "It is still humanly possible to win," he said, "but a miracle of grace would be awfully helpful."[40]

The next morning the missing articles finally appeared and the Council Fathers gave them a round of applause as they were distributed at the general congregation. The *relatio* (the formal presentation of the material) was scheduled for the next day and Bishop Karel Calewaert of Ghent said that it would be long and intricate. When Hallinan asked him to summarize it, he said that he could not; it had to be read in its entirety. Hallinan now began to wonder if he had acted unfairly on the previous day. Once he saw the *relatio,* he admitted to Krol that it could not have been completed on the previous Saturday as he had supposed. Perhaps, it had been rash of him to attribute the delay to the reactionaries on the Liturgical Commission.[41]

On December 5 and 6 Calewaert explained the revisions, and the Fathers approved thirteen amendments to Chapter One. (Hallinan wondered what had happened to the Italian bloc.) Then, on December 7, came the definitive victory. The Fathers gave their approval to the whole revised introduction and Chapter One of the *schema* on the liturgy by a vote of 1,922 to 11, with 180 Fathers voting *placet juxta modum.*[42]. Hallinan hoped that the pope might promulgate the two sections next day, when he brought the first session of the Council to a close. He did not do so. Hallinan was a bit disappointed, but he enjoyed repeating the story that was making the rounds in Rome: Pope John had intended to promulgate both sections but was unable to do so because Archbishop Dante (his master of ceremonies) had hidden the book.

As the first session of Vatican II was drawing to a close, Hallinan conceded that he felt nostalgic about the past two months. The Council had been a remarkable educational experience for him, as it had been for many bishops. For one thing, he had come to know his fellow American bishops better through their frequent meetings at the North American College, and also his service on the Liturgical Commission had introduced him to Catholic prelates and scholars from all over the world. One handicap which he bitterly regretted was his ignorance of other modern languages, and he "cussed out" the educational system which had left him so poorly equipped in this respect. Of necessity, his contacts had been limited mainly to English-speaking bishops; Archbishop Grimshaw of Birmingham became a friend, as did Archbishop Guilford Young of Hobart, Tasmania. There were others whom he met only once, such as Cardinal Bea, but who had left an indelible impression. He was deeply moved at the papal audience which Pope John gave to the American bishops on November 17, when the pope praised the American Church for the solidarity of its priests and people, bishops and priests.

Frederick McManus was a person whom Hallinan had known for many years, and he had invited him to speak on the liturgy to his priests in Charleston, but at the Council they became close friends. It was the beginning of a collaboration which lasted until Hallinan's death and paid handsome dividends to the American Church as it coped with the implementation of the liturgical reforms in the United States over the next several years. Two other liturgical scholars for whom Hallinan developed great admiration were Bugnini and Dom Cipriano Vagaggini, O.S.B., whom he described as a genius.[43]

His own election to the Liturgical Commission seems to have been largely accidental, but, once elected, he took his responsibilities seriously, educating himself in the liturgy, and nudging the Commission in a forward direction. Sometimes more than a nudge was required. On those occasions, he showed intelligence, courage and good American horsesense in combating the maneuvers of the reactionaries on the Commission. If he overreacted at the final delay in moving Chapter One of the liturgical *schema* through the commission, his suspicions were understandable and plausible, if not altogether justified.

Bishop Tracy explained another way in which he and Hallinan made the most of their two months in Rome:

> While Archbishop Hallinan was busy at Liturgical Commission hearings, I agreed to take care of certain business that we had in common. One of the items of this business was the arranging of evening meals with various groups we wanted to become acquainted with. And so from time to time I set up a dinner with the Observers, then I would set up a "French" dinner, an "Irish" dinner, a dinner with the young newspaper correspondents and journalists, a dinner with Council experts and the like.[44]

On his way back from Rome, Hallinan stopped for a few days in New York City, attended a meeting of the Newman Apostolate in Washington, and arrived home in Atlanta by train on December 14, where about forty priests welcomed him at the railroad station. Like the other bishops returning from a two months' absence, he found a pile of mail awaiting his attention and began to tackle it the next day. Unlike the other returning bishops, he also found on his desk his unfinished dissertation on Bishop Gilmour. The very next day he picked it up again and put the finishing touches on chapter three.[45]

12

Hopes and Plans

When Paul Hallinan returned from the Council in December 1962, he had every reason to feel confident and optimistic. He was the youngest archbishop in the country, in vigorously good health, with a wide circle of friends, an excellent writer and speaker, well known in the South as an advocate of racial justice and increasingly prominent as a spokesman for the progressive wing of the American Catholic hierarchy. He wrote in his diary on New Years's Day: "Another year begins, as always, quietly, warmly, confidently, but full of wonder." In fact, he had exactly twelve months left before the first attack of the disease which eventually killed him, and never again did he enjoy the strength which enabled him to put in sixteen-hour days and to hopscotch around the country from one meeting to the next.

In 1963, however, he was still running at full throttle, bubbling with plans and projects for his archdiocese and for the renewal of the Church in this country. His role on the Conciliar Liturgical Commission gave him a wider perspective than ever before and the opportunity not only to influence his fellow bishops but to affect the religious life of every Catholic at its deepest level. At home he was anxious to tackle the problems which his absence in Rome had forced him to neglect, such as launching a diocesan newspaper, building a Catholic Center in downtown Atlanta, overhauling the parochial school system, desegregating the Catholic hospitals, and involving the Catholic Church more actively in the life of the community. Among all these hopes and plans there was one very personal one which he was determined to realize in 1963, if he possibly could. That was to finish the doctorate which he had started ten years before.

He had never had the opportunity for full-time study and there had been several lengthy interruptions in research and writing. After going to Charleston in November 1958, he dropped work on the dissertation for a whole year, and his transfer to Atlanta in March 1962 again forced him to give up work on it temporarily. At times he wondered why he bothered to pursue the degree. Part of the incentive was an interest in Gilmour himself; part of it a natural desire to finish something that he had started. But Father Charles Albright, C.S.P., a close friend and colleague in the Newman Movement for many years, thought that he detected another reason why Paul Hallinan was anxious to earn a Ph.D. degree. According to him, Hallinan thought of Newman work in the broadest possible terms— as an apostolate to the university as well as to the Catholic students on campus. Thus he saw his own pursuit of a doctorate at a secular university as a way of showing the academic world the Church's recognition of the value of learning and scholarship.[1]

Not until the end of July 1962—almost four months after his arrival in Atlanta—had he been able to give any attention to his dissertation. Between then and the beginning of October, when he left for the first session of the Council, he worked hard revising the first chapter and writing part of two additional chapters. After five years, he had now barely written 100 pages, and he had come back from Rome with the additional responsibility of his membership on the Liturgical Commission. From his return to Atlanta in December 1962 until the following spring, he made an all-out effort to complete the rest of the dissertation and to have it ready for the defense in May 1963.[2]

The problem was not any lack of material; in fact, he said, there was "just too darn much material" for some topics. The real difficulty was finding blocs of time when he could concentrate and organize his thoughts. Often the only time available was in the evenings. On some occasions, he stayed up working on Gilmour until two or three o'clock. In the two months after his return from Rome he wrote more than in the previous five years. When he went to Chicago for a Newman Apostolate convention in the middle of January, he brought a sheaf of papers with him and spent the better part of two days at work on Gilmour in his hotel room. "It is going well," he wrote in February, "and I am really encouraged." He was on familiar ground now, chronicling the growth of the Diocese of Cleveland in the 1870's and 1880's. The work was proceeding so well that Rainey had to find a second typist for him, and Ellis had to remind him that he was writing the biography of a bishop and not the history of the diocese of Cleveland.[3]

Gilmour was beginning to grow on him. He told Ellis:

> The hours I've been able to get in on the work have been the most peaceful and satisfying of the recent months. Gilmour has been a teacher to me in more ways than one. Rough and tumble, which I am not, but humble and patient, which I need to be. It is remark-able, given a century time-differential, how much a close study of a man's episcopate can teach another.[4]

Some of Hallinan's own preoccupations are evident in his growing admiration for the dour Scot. In Charleston, Hallinan had com-plained once that it was impossible to do anything with a rude, crude pastor of fifty who was set in his ways. When Gilmour met a similar clerical type in his diocese, he had known what to do: he sent the man a curt note, saying: "Your own character is a little too angular, and with the best of intentions it brings you into trouble. Round the corners a little."

Cleveland in the 1880's had three times as many diocesan priests as Atlanta in the 1960's. Churches, schools, hospitals and charitable institutions were springing up then at a rate which the latter see could never match. For Hallinan, about to embark himself on a major building campaign, Gilmour had some sobering advice. "We think we are strong because we are laying up brick and stone," he had said, "but the mortar—virtue—is weak, and our buildings, I fear, rickety."

Hallinan paid considerable attention to a running battle between Gilmour and Manly Tello, the mercurial lay editor of the diocesan newspaper, the *Catholic Universe.* Although intensely conservative in many matters, Gilmour had given Tello a surprising amount of independence. Hallinan's interest in this was more than academic. At the time that he was describing the early days of the *Catholic Universe,* he was launching his own diocesan newspaper, the *Georgia*

Bulletin. The editor was also a layman, Gerard Sherry, whose outspoken views on many subjects forced Hallinan to confront the same issue that Gilmour had to face: to what extent is the bishop responsible for whatever appears in the diocesan newspaper.

Hallinan set a record for productivity early in March, when he completed a long chapter of ninety pages in two weeks. The topic was one of deep interest to him personally—Catholic education—and the more he learned about Gilmour's views on the subject, the more respect he had for him. "Gilmour was as strong a champion of the parochial school as any Catholic bishop in the United States," Hallinan claimed, but:

> he was not a promoter of what has been called the "Catholic roof" theory of education, the assumption that all pupils were receiving a proper Catholic education as long as they were in Catholic schools. To child and teacher, pastor and seminarian he urged excellence— not for the prestige of the Church, but for the advancement of the child.[5]

The words were the words of Gilmour, but the sentiments were those of Hallinan as well. He proved it, a month after he wrote those lines, when he said the same thing himself at the convention of the National Catholic Educational Association in St. Louis. In his address he was as blunt as Gilmour himself and pleaded with Catholic educators not to continue multiplying the number of Catholic colleges when they did not have the resources to make them first-rate institutions. He said:

> There is a real danger in the "Catholic roof" theory of education— that everyone is better off under a Catholic roof no matter how many leaks are in it. Unless we are ready to subscribe to that theory, we might well practice a neglected Christian virtue which is sometimes as meritorious as zeal—the virtue of forbearance.[6]

There was another, little-known facet of Gilmour—a concern for the Blacks and Indians—which Hallinan discovered and which further increased his admiration for him. He quoted with delight a comment which Gilmour had made in a pastoral letter of 1883:

> We owe to the Negroes of the South more than so far the Catholics of the North seem to have recognized. We pre-eminently owe to

the ill-treated Indians a united effort to save them from destruction of body and soul.... In the hurry and press of caring for the immigrants as they have arrived on our shores, the Indians and Negroes have mostly been lost sight of.[7]

During the spring of 1963 he was keeping the Post Office busy, sending rough drafts to Ellis for comment and then dispatching the final copy to Wittke as soon as he had made the last revisions. In mid-March he noted that he had four weeks left and two-and-a-half chapters still to finish. Unfortunately, during those four weeks, he also had to send a report to Cardinal Larraona on the draft of the Constitution on the Liturgy, prepare a St. Patrick's Day address for the Hibernian Society in Savannah, compose a speech for the convention of the N.C.E.A., write an introduction to Ellis' *Perspectives in American Catholicism,* figure out his income tax, negotiate the refinancing of several diocesan loans and do a "few hundred other odd things."[8]

He was reasonably confident that he could finish the dissertation on time but he was concerned about the final examination: whether it would be limited to the dissertation or include the entire period of American history since the Civil War. He told Wittke: "Much as it would hurt me to give up now, I could not in conscience take the time from my duties here to prepare for it." Then he added:

> I have considered the possibility of not pushing for this June, but frankly I cannot continue it into the years ahead.... I've been pushing these three months and can continue under the circumstances noted above. But if it is not practically possible, except by doing a rush job in quality as well as in timing, and by sacrificing either my duties or my health here, the sensible thing (it seems to me) is to complete it for my own satisfaction ... forget about the degree and be grateful for all I've received from WRU and especially you.

> I started on the Ph.D. in the fall of 1953 and had the privilege of sitting in classes with some of the best minds in history now alive. I've read and studied far more than I ever would have done without the stimulation of the academic prod. I've attended seminars and history conventions, read the journals, used the libraries and archives of a score of institutions, and enjoyed every bit of it. So that, if the decision must be to forget it, and get on with the job of being a proper Archbishop, I will have no regrets.[9]

He told Ellis at the same time that "he had to come to some sort of showdown with myself on this." If Wittke advised him that there was not time to do it properly, he was prepared to forget about the degree, finish the work on Gilmour, and look for someone to publish it, content, as he said, to have the "substance without the symbol." When Wittke assured him that the examination would be limited to a defense of the dissertation, he was immensely relieved and more determined than ever to meet the deadline. Despite his other distractions and a stormy meeting with his high school principals over budget cuts, he wrote three chapters in four weeks. On April 8, his fifty-second birthday, he completed Chapter Ten and finished his dissertation at 2 A.M.

There were still numerous loose ends to wrap up between then and May 20, the date of the final examination, and he accomplished this with his usual flair but with barely minutes to spare. John Tracy Ellis came to spend Easter with him in Atlanta and read the final chapters. On the following Tuesday Hallinan flew to Cleveland to see Wittke, making the last revisions of the work in the airport lounge. Wednesday he spent with his typist, Miss Frances Goff of Western Reserve University, proofreading the final pages as she typed them. On Thursday he went to St. Louis for a Newman Apostolate dinner. He addressed the convention of the N.C.E.A. on Friday, and left for New York on Saturday, where he took a flight to Rome for the spring meeting of the Conciliar Liturgical Commission. He still had not finished the bibliography, but he did so the next day in Rome and had it typed by Jerry Hardy, an Atlanta seminarian who was a student there.[10]

Two weeks later he flew back from Rome to Cleveland, deposited his bibliography at Western Reserve University, and returned home to Atlanta. He was back in Cleveland the following weekend and spent Monday morning in the library making last-minute preparations for the defense of his dissertation. Then he went to Wittke's office to meet him and the three other professors on the examination board. It was the same room where he had taken his comprehensive examinations six years before. This time, however, the examination lasted only a few minutes. After some perfunctory questions, the professors started to ask him about the progress of integration in Atlanta. It was obvious they liked the dissertation and that all was well. He then filled out a few questionnaires (including one about what he planned to do in his "post-doctoral career") and that night was back in Atlanta, ready to welcome his suffragan bishops to a meeting at his residence the following day.[11]

The actual conferral of the degree took place on June 12—a blustery, overcast day, more like November than June—but the weather did not dampen Hallinan's spirits. Dressed in academic robes, he marched in procession to Severance Hall for the convocation. At the end of the ceremony, Dr. John S. Mills, the President of Western Reserve University, took note of Hallinan's presence and said that, to his knowledge, this was the first time that an archbishop had earned a doctoral degree at any American university. Then he called Hallinan to the stage and asked him to give the benediction.[12]

He proceeded next to Epworth Methodist Church for the diploma ceremony. Wittke, the retiring Dean of the Graduate School, spoke briefly (the same speech as fifteen years before, Hallinan noted) and then awarded the doctoral degrees. There was a dinner afterwards for family and friends at Newman Hall, and a reception later, when hundreds more turned out to congratulate him. Many of them were former Newmanites, who knew better than most how much the degree meant to him.[13]

The people of his archdiocese could hardly complain that their shepherd was neglecting them while he finished his dissertation. With the new year the first issue of the diocesan newspaper, the *Georgia Bulletin,* had appeared. He contributed a thoughtful essay to it, outlining his own hopes for the paper and disclaiming any intention of competing with the Atlanta dailies or the local newspapers. "We are in competition," he said, "with only two things: religious ignorance and religious prejudice." He assured the readers that the *Georgia Bulletin* would not be a "house organ" or a "trade sheet"; nevertheless, he made it plain that "there is a sense in which the *Georgia Bulletin* is an official newspaper of the archdiocese."

> It will carry all official announcements. And when it is engaged in the task of teaching religion, it will teach as the Church teaches. In its larger framework of reporting, its spirit and mood will be in keeping with the large pattern of Catholic ideas and Catholic culture.

Beyond these stipulations, he said, there was a vast area of freedom open to the editor and to every Catholic, as the proceedings of the

Vatican Council had recently demonstrated. He promised that the news-reporting would be honest and fair, and that the paper would be catholic in the fullest sense of the term. "The religious journal which is excessively narrow, unfairly slanted, unduly cautious, or indifferent to the human society around it," he said, "is badly out of step with both good journalism and the cause of religion."[14]

Gerard Sherry made the *Georgia Bulletin* a lively newspaper and he did not shy away from controversy. Indeed, he seemed to thrive on it and even to provoke it with his editorials. When the rector of the Catholic University of America barred four prominent Catholic theologians from speaking at the university, Sherry lamented that "there were still some men in the Church who are fascinated with the past because they are scared to death of the present and dare not think of the future." He was equally outspoken on civil rights, saying that "the Christian conscience cries out for justice for the Negro, not only in Birmingham, Alabama, but anywhere he is denied recognition of his divine dignity."[15]

It was not long before there were angry responses from some readers. A businessman from Marietta canceled his subscription "for the protection of my children" and told Sherry that "your editorial policy continues to slur and slander our state and our region, its people and its past." One irate woman wrote from Brooklyn, New York, complaining that Sherry had voted to give the annual award of the Catholic Press Association to Xavier Rynne. Harold Rainey, the chancellor of the Archdiocese, blandly assured her that Hallinan would appreciate hearing her views on the matter. In fact the archbishop made no effort to gag Sherry. His only complaint was that he wanted more extensive coverage of local news.[16]

Not everyone was critical of the archbishop's style. Few people were more respected in the Atlanta Catholic community than Hughes Spalding, Sr., and, just as the diocesan newspaper was beginning to arouse controversy, he gave Hallinan a strong vote of confidence:

I devoutly hope that you will be a permanent fixture here. I am afraid that, if you display too much talent and ability, you may be transferred to what may be considered a more important location. However, with the potential advantages of the Southland, I personally consider Atlanta one of the most important posts in this country.

Our section of the country has been classified for many years as one of intolerance and bigotry. In a sense this is true, but nothing like it was formerly. We are making a breakthrough here; and you seem to be the unanimous choice to perform this function.[17]

The integration of public facilities was still a highly charged issue in 1963 as barrier after barrier continued to fall. The Catholic schools had been integrated in September 1962, but there was still one area where the Church had not brought its policies into line with its teaching—the Catholic hospitals, both of which were still segregated. In February, the archbishop spoke to the administrators at both St. Joseph's Infirmary in Atlanta and St. Mary's Hospital in Athens, and both of them agreed to integrate their facilities by May 1.

At St. Joseph's Infirmary the doctors were willing to accept the change but they asked that it be done quietly. Hallinan agreed, but in reply to black press criticisms of the Catholic Church for operating segregated hospitals, he decided that a public statement was necessary.[18] He issued it at the end of March, mandating the full integration of the hospitals and explaining why this had not been done when the Catholic schools were integrated. "The Catholic hospitals, as distinct from our schools, are dependent upon the support of the entire community," he explained, and "they must make changes carefully to insure their continued effective service." He made it clear, however, that a Catholic institution could not continue indefinitely to practice segregation:

> Because it is Catholic, it reflects the full teaching of the Church, not only in works of mercy and charity, but in the demonstration of social justice. Whatever concessions are made to local custom, no Catholic hospital in our archdiocese could be permanently bound to segregation as a matter of fixed policy.

His ruling went well beyond the decision that he had taken in Charleston. There he had let Catholic hospitals temporarily maintain separate wings for black patients. Here he announced: "Assignment of hospital space to patients will be made on the basis of medical and surgical need, not on the basis of race or color. There will be no separated section for any racial group."[19]

It was relatively easy to integrate the Catholic hospitals: a much more difficult problem was finding the money to keep the diocesan high schools financially afloat. The biggest of the three was St. Pius X with 650 students, whose priest-principal proved to be a difficult person to deal with over financial matters. When he resisted Hallinan's efforts to cut operational expenses in the spring of 1963 in order to raise teachers' salaries, the archbishop called a special meeting of the administrative council of the school. He found them equally unreceptive to his arguments and came away disgusted at their inability to grasp the overall financial picture of the archdiocese.

He had several other meetings with all three priest-principals that spring and worked out an agreement with them that called for both an increase in tuition and larger diocesan assessments. These were only temporary expedients and did not solve the long-term financial problems inherent in running the schools. Nor was money the only problem. Hallinan had serious reservations about the suitability of the three principals. "We will need God's grace in abundance," he said, "to get a first-rate educational team out of the three."

By the end of the year he thought that he had a solution: to persuade Monsignor Patrick J. O'Connor to take over the post of Superintendent of Schools. O'Connor was not only one of the senior pastors and a man with considerable administrative experience; he had the reputation also of working well with young people from his years in vocation work. The decision was a "bombshell," to use Hallinan's word. However, it appeared, for a while at least, as if one more problem were on the way to a solution.

The pleasantest chore that Hallinan had all year was mapping plans for the Catholic Center which he was anxious to build in downtown Atlanta. When he brought the matter up at the consultors' meeting in June, he was agreeably surprised by their favorable reaction. Even Moylan and O'Connor, from whom he had expected opposition, voted for the project and agreed to a two-million-dollar fund-raising campaign in 1964. Hallinan had already purchased the property that he wanted from the Marists and now he invited architects to bid on the project. Over the next few weeks, six of them submitted designs, one of them proposing a sixteen-story tower, which was not at all to Hallinan's liking. Impressed with the plans of a local architect named Richard Aeck, he reached a preliminary understanding with him early in September before he left for the second session of the Vatican Council.

When he returned to Atlanta briefly in November, Aeck had a

mock-up model ready for his inspection. At that time he also bought additional real estate to round off the property on Ivy Street, and during a meeting of the consultors, Moylan exploded a bombshell of his own. Since the Center was to be located next to Sacred Heart Church, he suggested that the archdiocese take over that parish from the Marists. To facilitate the transfer, he offered to give them his own parish of Our Lady of the Assumption in an affluent suburb of Atlanta.[20] It was as bold a move as making Patrick O'Connor the Superintendent of Schools. Hallinan eventually followed Moylan's advice (and made him pastor of Sacred Heart), but not just yet. His main concern at year's end was to launch a successful fund-raising campaign without which there would be no Center at all.

His duties as a member of the Conciliar Liturgical Commission had kept him busy throughout the spring and summer even though the Vatican Council was not to reconvene until the fall. He made three trips to Rome in 1963, the first in late April for a two-week meeting of the Liturgical Commission. Before he left, McManus warned him of reports that Cardinal Larraona was determined to derail the *schema* on the liturgy and even to undo Chapter One, which had already received the approval of the Council Fathers.[21]

Even earlier Hallinan himself had seen a story in the *Saturday Evening Post* that Bishop van Bekkum would not be in Rome for the meeting because he had been told that his presence would not be required. Since the bishop was a member of Hallinan's Subcommission on Sacraments and generally voted with the progressives, he suspected skulduggery and sent an anxious letter to Larraona, praising van Bekkum's work on the subcommission and saying: "I hope that you can assure me that the report was wrong."[22]

When he saw Larraona on the day after he arrived in Rome, all was sweetness and light. They had tea together and exchanged small talk, although Hallinan admitted later that some of it was double talk. The two weeks that he spent in Rome this time were quite a contrast to the two months in the fall. Gone was the excitement which had marked the first session of the Council, as he was reminded every morning when he and McManus celebrated Mass in St. Peter's Basilica. In fact, he said, "the *aula* looks haunted." But it was also a relief not to be forever shuttling between the general congregations, the meetings of the Liturgical Commission and the gatherings of the United States bishops. The Liturgical Commission usually met now for about three hours in the morning and made such rapid progress that Hallinan quickly concluded that "the die-hard opposition's back is broken," an observation which proved to be premature.[23]

His afternoons and evenings were usually free, allowing ample time to do some sightseeing and sample the Roman restaurants while he put the finishing touches on his dissertation. He had dinner with Archbishop Grimshaw at the English College. Together with McManus he paid a call on Cardinal Bea and Monsignor Jan Willebrands at the Secretariat for Promoting Christian Unity to inquire about the Council's projected statement on religious liberty. A visit to the Archives of the Congregation for the Propagation of the Faith was fruitless but hilarious. A clerk told Hallinan that Cardinal Agagianian, the perfect of the congregation, would prob-ably waive the "hundred-year rule" so that he could consult the dossier on Bishop Rappe. However, he advised him that no one, not even Cardinal Agagianian, could change the rule that students could work there only in the mornings. Hallinan was more amused than angered and said that the incident was "worthy of a *New Yorker* article."[24]

His most memorable moment came on May 1, when, on the spur of the moment, he decided to attend the general audience that day at the Vatican. Much to his surprise, he was whisked up to the chairs reserved for the archbishops. The pope entered the hall on the *sedia gestatoria,* said a few words about Our Lady, St. Joseph and the Church, and then spoke individually to the archbishops and bishops. He had a limited command of English but enough to say "Atlanta" and "Georgia," and he paused for a photograph with Hallinan. One month later he was dead.[25]

Hallinan's work on the Liturgical Commission went smoothly, largely because he and McManus had done their homework. The Subcommission on the Sacraments had worked hard all during the first session of the Council, keeping abreast of the oral and written interventions of the Council Fathers and making almost daily revi-sions in the part of the *schema* for which they were responsible, so that, by the time that they went home for Christmas, they had completed most of what they had to do.[26] Frederick McManus became Secretary of the Subcommission on the Sacraments in December. During the next four months he had borne the brunt of the work, corresponding with Hallinan, the other three bishops on the subcommission (van Bekkum, Jop and Spülbeck), and the *periti* in Rome. After gathering their comments, he put together a revised draft of Chapter Three and sent copies to the bishops and *periti*. Accordingly, when they met in Rome in April, they had only to iron out some minor details. It took Hallinan himself the better part of four mornings to present his *relatio* to the full commission, but it went reasonably well and he received many compliments about the style of the material.[27]

On May 7 he held a press conference at the Columbus Hotel which was not his finest hour, for he complimented Larraona for conducting the meetings of the Liturgical Commission in a democratic manner and giving everyone an opportunity to express his opinions, as was duly noted in *Osservatore Romano* two days later. He must have gulped hard when he said: "We had at all times full opportunity to speak freely and to develop our own thinking," a claim which can hardly be squared with his own activities the previous fall, when he twice felt it necessary to challenge Larraona's tactics as chairman.[28]

If Hallinan thought that the cardinal had mellowed or changed his stripes, he got a rude awakening during the last three or four days of the spring meeting. First, Larraona appointed a new *Subcommissio Praesidum* (composed of the chairmen of the other thirteen subcommissions), which served no purpose, said Hallinan, except "to foul things up." Then Larraona decided that the commission would vote by secret ballot, and, most importantly, he changed the voting procedures. Instead of giving the commission members the opportunity to vote on each revision in every article of the *schema* (as they had done in the fall), they were now restricted to voting on the completed version of each article, rejecting it or accepting it *in toto*.[29]

Another disappointment was the lack of support for a vernacular breviary, not only from the reactionaries, but even from European bishops who generally favored the other liturgical changes. Hallinan returned home from Rome at the beginning of May apprehensive about this issue and angry at what he and McManus regarded as last-minute tricks on the part of Larraona and his cronies.

At the meeting of the American bishops in Chicago in August, Hallinan gave a lengthy report on the status of the liturgy *schema*. The bishops were understandably curious to hear what amendments they would be voting on in the fall. Hallinan had to admit that he could not tell them, because the commission had not decided which changes were important enough to submit to the Fathers for a vote. However, he revealed that the commission was prepared to recommend the use of the vernacular for large portions of the Mass as well as for the administration of the sacraments and sacramentals, although the form of the sacraments would remain in Latin (except for matrimony).[30]

A topic of great interest to the bishops was the practical question of the use of the vernacular languages in the breviary. The original draft of the *schema* had made no provision at all for this, and the Liturgical Commission now proposed to make a grudging concession that the local bishop could allow its use "in individual cases to those clerics for whom the use of the Latin language is a grave impediment to their due celebration of the office." Hallinan did not like the supercilious way that this amendment was worded, and he knew that the American bishops would not like it either. Several of them had spoken in favor of the vernacular breviary at the first session, and they had offered positive reasons for it, namely, the spiritual advantages for the clergy, and the pastoral and ecumenical benefits. Hallinan anticipated their objections by saying that it was the best that they could hope for under the circumstances. There was so much sentiment in favor of retaining the Latin breviary, he explained, that only a limited concession such as this could muster the necessary two-thirds majority on the floor of the Council. And he reminded the bishops that, if this amendment failed, then the original text of the *schema* would prevail—with no provision at all for a vernacular breviary.[31]

Some bishops wrote to him immediately after the meeting, expressing their desire for more vigorous action on behalf of a vernacular breviary. Bishop Clarence Issenmann of Columbus said that, if the Council rejected a motion to this effect, then the bishops of the United States would present a petition in favor of it. Bishop John Carberry of Lafayette, Indiana, made the same point, remarking that the proposal of the Liturgical Commission "is so worded that it casts a certain amount of reflection on the individual priest who would wish to have this privilege." Bishop William Connare of Greensburg objected to the whole notion of granting dispensations for the use of the vernacular. "Why not, then, be more positive from the very beginning," he asked, "allowing a choice either of the Latin or of the vernacular in its fulfillment?"[32]

Before Hallinan left for Rome in September, he wrote to Larraona concerning the bishops' meeting in Chicago. About 140 bishops had been present, he told the cardinal, and he stressed how unhappy they were with the Liturgical Commission's draft *schema* on the breviary:

> The text is completely unsatisfactory to the majority of the bishops of the United States because it in no way corresponds to the problem described by the Fathers of the Council in the debate on the subject. The concession was sought for the clergy of large areas, not for individual cases, and for spiritual and pastoral reasons, not for the reasons of ignorance. Furthermore, the negative and condescending tone of the article is offensive to many bishops and out of touch with the whole stress of the liturgical schema on the value of the Church's public prayer and not the value of a particular language.
>
> I urgently request, on behalf of the bishops of the United States, and I am certain, of many bishops of other lands, that this matter be re-examined at the preliminary meeting of the Commission on the Sacred Liturgy to be held September 27-28 1963. I further propose that ... the emendation made in the aula on November 9, 1963 by His Eminence Albert Cardinal Meyer be submitted to the members of the commission for discussion and vote.[33]

Meyer had proposed that clerics be allowed to recite the breviary in the vernacular "for the sake of greater piety," not because of a "defective knowledge of Latin," adding that many who had an excellent command of Latin would be delighted to receive such permission. An unlikely but powerful ally was Cardinal Spellman, who was as anxious to permit the vernacular in the breviary as he was to retain Latin in the Mass. He told Hallinan: "I intend to make every endeavor possible so that both religious and diocesan priests may have the opportunity of saying the breviary either in Latin or in the vernacular as they choose."[34]

At the beginning of the Council the American bishops had been criticized for their apathy about the liturgy. Whatever the truth of that observation in 1962, it was not true a year later. They went back to Rome in the fall of 1963 deeply interested in the *schema* on the liturgy and anxious to see how it would emerge from the Liturgical

Commission. As the only American prelate on the commission, Hallinan had a key role to play at the second session in representing their hopes and fears on this issue to the rest of the Council Fathers.

13

The Constitution on the Sacred Liturgy

Tracy and Hallinan traveled to the second session of the Council in style—on the last of the great American ocean liners, the *United States*. It was a voyage to which both of them had long looked forward but their disappointment began as soon as they boarded the ship in New York. "[It] looks sea-worthy," said Hallinan, "but singularly dull." So it turned out were the other passengers, except for Paul Tillich and his wife who happened to be aboard *en route* to Europe. Hallinan had several conversations with them, read Hans Küng's latest book (*The Council and Reunion*), watched a few motion-pictures, and, for the first time in years, sat down at the piano for a pleasant workout. "How long it's been," he wrote, "and how tired I get now." The last day out, the two bishops tried sitting on deck but the North Atlantic in mid-September was hardly the place to get a sun tan. They sat there shivering and thinking how they had expected so much of the ocean trip and what a letdown had been. When the ship docked at Le Havre, they could not wait to get off and take the boat train to Paris.[1]

In Paris, they rented a car, made a one-day excursion to Chartres, and then drove east to Meaux, Verdun and Trier. In Trier they visited Monsignor Johannes Wagner at the Liturgical Institute. They also paid a call at the monastery of Maria Laach, where they discussed the liturgy with the abbot, an affable man with a disconcerting habit of winking or blinking "like a Buick getting ready to turn left."

They traveled by steamer up the Rhine from Coblenz to Mainz, enjoying the trip far more than their trans-Atlantic voyage. There they took the Rheingold Express to Lucerne, where they stopped for a few days and met several Canadian bishops, one of whom said to Hallinan: "You're the one who spoke up at the Council when all the other Americans were silent." They lingered longer than they should have in Switzerland, and on reaching Milan on September 26, they abandoned the train, rushed to the airport, and took a flight to Rome where the Liturgical Commission was scheduled to meet the following day.[2]

Both Hallinan and McManus were apprehensive as the commission resumed its work on the rest of the *schema*. In a position paper that Hallinan prepared for the meeting on September 30, he criticized the changes in procedure that Larraona had pushed through during the last week of the spring meeting, pointing out that they prevented members from voting on individual amendments and left further revisions to the *Subcommissio Praesidum* rather than to the proper subcommissions. "The members of the commission did not have a true choice among the amendments," he claimed, "and it is impossible to know their mind with regard to individual amendments."

There were five specific changes that he asked for at this meeting and he got the commission to accept four-and-a-half of them. First, they agreed to restore the *declarationes* (the explanations of the Preparatory Liturgical Commission) which the reactionaries on the commission had succeeded in eliminating from the *schema*. Secondly, they did a turnabout on Roman approval of liturgical changes by local episcopal conferences, suppressing the "*actis ab Apostolica Sede confirmatis vel probatis*" in favor of the original "*actis ab Apostolica Sede recognitis.*" Thirdly, for the Sacrament of the Sick, they restored the name "Anointing of the Sick," specifically saying that it was preferable to the term "Extreme Unction." Fourthly, they left open several questions about the manner and conditions of administering this sacrament in order not to preclude further theological speculation about the sacrament.

Only on the fifth point, regarding the rite of religious profession, did he meet with a partial rebuff. The commission restored the recommendation of the original *schema* that religious profession take place during Mass, but only in some instances. It failed to make this the norm for all rites of religious clothing and profession with the result, Hallinan predicted, that "the change will not meet the needs and desires of large numbers of religious, especially women religious, who want a more truly liturgical context for their important acts."[3]

Despite his dissatisfaction with this last point, he was pleased with his overall success, and Larraona asked him: "*Contento?, contento?*"[4] He also had the satisfaction at this time of having Father Godfrey Diekmann, O.S.B., appointed as a *peritus* to the Liturgical Commission; when he approached Larraona about it, the cardinal replied, true to form: "*Nulla difficultas.*"[5]

The question of the vernacular breviary was still unresolved. Support of it in the Liturgical Commission was so soft that he did not bring it up with the other items on September 30. Instead, after speaking privately with Bishop Albert Martin, the Chairman of the Subcommission on the Divine Office, he concluded that the only hope was still Amendment Twelve, authorizing bishops to give such permission to their priests in individual cases.

Knowing how dissatisfied the American bishops were with this amendment, he urged them to accept it nevertheless as "the best and widest concession possible because of the great strength of the pro-Latin breviary sentiment." He also told them that, if they read the whole *relatio,* they would see that "Ordinaries may employ the faculty ... liberally as to its contents and generously as to its application." As a practical matter he pointed out to the bishops that the issue of the vernacular breviary would come before the Council twice: first in the form of the twelfth amendment to Chapter Four, and then as part of the whole chapter. He urged them to vote *placet* the first time (assuring at least some minimal concessions) and then to vote *placet juxta modum* on the whole chapter, indicating their desire to send it back to the Liturgical Commission for more liberal revisions.[6]

In the second week of October, the Fathers interrupted their discussion of the *schema De Ecclesia* to vote on Chapter Two of the liturgical *schema.* On October 8, 9, and 10, as expected, they overwhelmingly approved nineteen amendments[7] and then confounded everyone on October 14 by failing to give the chapter as a whole the needed two-thirds majority. While 1,147 bishops voted for it, 36 voted against it and 781 voted *placet juxta modum* (for it, but with reservations) which meant that the chapter would be returned to the

Liturgical Commission for further work.[8]

At the United States bishops' press conference the next day, Hallinan explained this vote by claiming that there actually were 2,198 *placet* votes, since those who voted *placet juxta modum* really were voting for the *schema*. Minimizing the concern expressed by others, he said that the Liturgical Commission would examine the qualifications (*modi*), combine them and send them back to the floor of the Council as amendments. "If they are approved," he explained, "they will be simply inserted in the text of Chapter Two, which has now been approved."[9]

What Hallinan did not mention was his role in forcing Chapter Two back to the Liturgical Commission for further revisions. Three days before the vote, he distributed a mimeographed circular to the American bishops, urging them to vote *placet juxta modum* in the hope that, if Chapter Two were sent back to the Liturgical Commission, the use of the vernacular would then be extended by the Commission to the Collect, Secret, *Libera* and Postcommunion Prayers and the reception of Holy Communion under both species would be allowed for the spouses at a nuptial Mass. Since Chapter Two fell short of the two-thirds majority by only seventy-nine votes on October 14, it seems likely that the American bishops played a major role in returning it to the Liturgical Commission for revision.[10]

Hallinan got an opportunity to address the Council on October 15, when he presented the *relatio* on Chapter Three.[11] The Fathers approved ten amendments that day and on the two following days, but then, on October 18, they repeated what they had done with Chapter Two and refused to give Chapter Three the necessary two-thirds vote of approval. Over 1,000 bishops voted *placet juxta modum* that day. Hallinan, as already noted, had recommended this strategy to the American bishops in his circular as a way of pressuring the Liturgical Commission to extend the use of the vernacular to the form of the sacraments. McManus conjectured that many of the bishops who voted *placet juxta modum* did so for precisely that reason.[12]

Twice in one week now the Fathers had failed to approve successive chapters of the liturgical *schema*. The next item to be considered was Chapter Four (the Divine Office), and Bishop Martin, president of the subcommission and *relator* of the chapter, was fearful that it would suffer the same fate. The American bishops were known to be dissatisfied with the limited concessions made for the use of the vernacular, and Hallinan had twice recommended to them (on October 4 and October 11) that they vote *placet juxta modum,* when the crucial vote came up on October 24.

The day before this vote Martin distributed an open letter to the Council, pleading with the Fathers not to add any *modi* to their vote on Chapter Four. He argued that the Liturgical Commission was already overwhelmed with work and claimed that the breviary was such a delicate topic that any tampering with the text would lead to the unraveling of Chapter Four and jeopardize the whole *schema.* The signatories of the letter included twelve members of the Liturgical Commission, among them Bishops Spülbeck and van Bekkum, and eminent scholars such as Monsignor Johannes Wagner, Father Aimé-Georges Martimort and Dom Cipriano Vagaggini, O.S.B.[13]

Hallinan's initial reaction was to draw up a sharp protest to the Liturgical Commission, accusing Martin of using scare tactics and misrepresenting the work load of the Liturgical Commission. On second thought, he did not present the protest to the commission. Instead, he had a long, unsatisfactory talk with Martin during which he told him that the American bishops resented his "quasi-official" effort to influence the voting.[14]

Martin received powerful support from Archbishop Felici, who also asked the Fathers not to cast *juxta modum* votes, saying that such votes "are a real cross for the members of the commission." The pressure had its effect. When the votes were tallied on October 24, Chapter Four was approved by a majority of 150 votes.[15]

The remaining four chapters of the *schema* were less controversial and received the approval of the Council Fathers during the last few days of October. On November 21, a few final amendments were disposed of and on November 22 the Council gave its approval to the entire *schema*—2,158 voting for it, 19 against, and one null vote.[16] That evening there was a party in the dining room of the Cavelieri Hilton, at which Godfrey Diekmann, Vincent Yzermans and others were celebrating the victory of the *schema* after so many obstacles and delays. The laughter stopped suddenly when Archbishop John Cody walked into the room and announced that President John F. Kennedy had been assassinated in Dallas.[17]

Hallinan had only one confrontation with Archbishop Vagnozzi at this session of the Council but it was an embarrassing one. The

Georgia Bulletin carried a cartoon of a cardinal with a strong resemblance to Ottaviani trying to isolate the Council from the rest of the world by means of a "Spaghetti Curtain." Vagnozzi complained to Hallinan about it and a week later he got a call from Cardinal Cicognani. When he saw the Secretary of State the next day, Cicognani told him that both he and the Pope found the cartoon offensive.

By this time Hallinan had been briefed by Sherry and he explained that the cartoon did not originate with the *Georgia Bulletin*. It had been offered to many diocesan newspapers by a syndication service and an assistant editor had inserted it in the *Georgia Bulletin* during Sherry's absence. Sherry had since written an editorial apologizing for the incident. When Cicognani heard this explanation, Hallinan said that he was kind and understanding. "Such things can happen," he commented, and asked to see a copy of the editorial. A few days later he stopped Hallinan in the *aula* to tell him that the pope was pleased with the editorial and with his own explanation.[18]

When Sherry came to Rome in mid-November, he had difficulty obtaining approval for his press credentials and Archbishop Martin J. O'Connor, President of the Pontifical Commission for Motion Pictures, Radio and Television, said that it was due to the furor over the "Spaghetti Curtain" cartoon. Hallinan had to intervene directly with O'Connor, who straightened out the situation and sent Sherry his credentials the next day. When Hallinan wrote to thank O'Connor, he told him:

> Gerard Sherry is an excellent Catholic, and an outstanding editor and journalist. When he speaks up or enters controversy, he has only one objective—the good of the Church. In his stand on integration, social justice and the principles of the papal encyclicals, he is certain to have enemies, the same enemies the Church has. What is disheartening is that one or two of them fire off bitter letters to high-ranking prelates (not excluding those in the Curia) on the slightest provocation. This is a most vicious form of slander. I have already had occasion to defend his loyalty to the Church in a letter to the Apostolic Delegate who was also the target of anti-Sherry harangues from the same source.
>
> The Church needs more and more Gerard Sherrys, and Catholic journalism will be the poorer if men of his quality can be slandered and eventually brought to silence.[19]

The second session of the Council disappointed many who had been thrilled by the first session. The debate on the *De Ecclesia schema* dragged on and on in the general congregations with no end in sight, and Cardinal Ottaviani's Doctrinal Commission (which was responsible for the *schema*) showed little evidence of expediting matters. One bishop said: "If things continue to go on like this, we might as well all pack up and go home." Cardinal Cushing did just that and did not come back.[20]

Hallinan himself decided to return home after receiving word from Harold Rainey about the opportunity to buy additional property for the Catholic Center. He was present in the *aula* on October 29, when the Fathers voted by the thinnest of margins (1,114 to 1,074) to include the doctrine on the Blessed Virgin Mary in *De Ecclesia* and not to make it the subject of a separate *schema*. He was present again the next day—which Bishop John J. Wright of Pittsburgh called a turning-point in the Council—when the Fathers overwhelmingly approved the concept of episcopal collegiality and the restoration of the permanent diaconate. The following day, however, he left for Atlanta and did not return until November 10.

The situation had not improved in his absence. Ten days after his return, the Fathers were still bogged down in a repetitious discussion of the principles of ecumenism. "The Council drones on," said Hallinan, "all of us are impatient. What about chapter four [of the *schema* on Ecumenism] (the Jews)? What about chapter five (religious liberty)?"[21]

The Fathers never got a chance to vote on either topic at the second session. They spent the whole ten weeks debating three *schemata* (*De Ecclesia,* Bishops and the Government of Dioceses, and Ecumenism) and voting on two others (Liturgy and Communications). Many of the bishops regarded the Communications Decree as inadequate and three American newsmen publicly castigated it as "a classic example of how the Second Vatican Council failed to come to grips with the world around it." At the final vote on December 4, Hallinan was one of 164 Fathers who persisted in voting against it to the bitter end. When Pope Paul VI promulgated it the same day, he referred to it cryptically as "not of small value."[22]

By contrast, the promulgation of the Constitution on the Sacred Liturgy that day received a warm welcome both inside and outside the Council. Back in October, when it appeared likely that the

Fathers would approve the Constitution at this session, Hallinan and McManus turned their attention to the next step: the implementation of the new laws after the end of the Council. Other English-speaking bishops were grappling with the same problem, and on October 2, during a lull in the morning's general congregation, Archbishop Denis Hurley, O.M.I., of Durban, South Africa, held what he called a "liturgical caucus" just outside the *aula* with Hallinan, Grimshaw and Archbishop Guilford Young of Hobart, Tasmania. They made Grimshaw the chairman of their little group and asked him to get in touch with bishops from other English-speaking countries.[23]

The result was a meeting at the English College on October 17 attended by representatives of the bishops of the United States, England and Wales, Scotland, Ireland, Canada, Australia, New Zealand, South Africa and India. Grimshaw explained that the purpose of the meeting was to "explore the idea of a uniform vernacular text acceptable in all English-speaking countries." He said that an official of the Congregation of Rites had told him that it would take ten years to prepare the new Latin texts for the Mass. Rather than wait so long, he suggested that they think in terms of material that was already available.

Archbishop Gordon Gray of St. Andrews and Edinburgh wondered if there was a need for a new English translation of the Missal. Archbishop Young mentioned four translations of the Bible which they might consider using: the Confraternity of Christian Doctrine Version in the United States, the Knox Bible, the Jerusalem Bible and the Revised Standard Version. Archbishop Hurley suggested that they aim at establishing an international body to provide the translation of the liturgical texts. The question of "Americanisms" came up, and some wondered if it were possible to have a single translation for all English-speaking countries. Archbishop Hallinan offered his opinion that a common text was possible, citing the example of Abraham Lincoln and Winston Churchill as authors who transcended national boundaries. He then proposed that (1) they should implement the Constitution in their own countries as soon as possible on the basis of whatever texts were available; and (2) they should support the formation of an international body to prepare a common acceptable English text. The bishops accepted Hallinan's proposals and decided to set up a governing body consisting of Grimshaw as chairman and Hallinan and Young as vice chairmen. It was an historic occasion, the formal beginning of what would later become I.C.E.L.—the International Commission on English in the Liturgy.[24]

This international episcopal committee (or the "Common Market," as Hallinan liked to call it) met three more times during the second session of the Council. Their discussions centered on the suitability of the various English versions of the Bible, with most favoring a Catholic edition of the Revised Standard Version, for which Archbishop Gray offered to give an *imprimatur.* Hallinan was away in Atlanta for two of the three meetings; nonetheless, he was elected secretary and asked to set up a permanent coordinating secretariat.[25]

During the last few weeks of the Council, he himself practiced the good advice which he had given the other bishops at the October 17 meeting. While supporting long-term efforts at international cooperation, he urged the American bishops to get started immediately with the process of liturgical reform. In a memorandum of November 10, he called to their attention the extensive power over liturgical matters now given to the national conferences of bishops and he asked them to use this power at once in the United States.[26]

The American bishops were scheduled to hold their annual meeting in Rome in mid-November and Hallinan wanted them to face this issue before they went home. McManus urged him to make a strong case with the bishops for immediate action. He calculated that fewer than half of the 130 articles in the liturgical Constitution had to await the approval of the Holy See. The rest of it (including the articles on the vernacular in the Mass) was effective upon promulgation—leaving implementation squarely in the hands of the local episcopal conferences. He told Hallinan:

> If in all that wealth of conciliar legislation—the first pastoral and documentary constitution of a Council in four centuries—the bishops can only find one article to emphasize (art. 22, n. 3 [forbidding unauthorized changes in the liturgy]), then their influence will be minimal.[27]

Hallinan agreed and decided to use the bishops' meeting for a dramatic presentation of his case. First, his hand was strengthened when Bishop Griffiths proposed that he be appointed to the Bishops' Commission on the Liturgical Apostolate and the motion was accepted by acclamation. Then Archbishop Krol assured them that the

Constitution on the Sacred Liturgy would be promulgated before the end of the second session. Hallinan now had his opening. He took Krol's announcement as his starting point to warn the bishops that, once this happened, they would have to take the lead in implementing the Constitution or others would take matters into their own hands. He told them frankly:

> Let us be, above everything else, honest with ourselves. Some bishops do not want any vernacular in the Mass, sacraments or Divine Office. Others want it in the breviary, but not in the Mass or sacraments. Others hesitate because, although they want the vernacular, they question whether we have the authority to implement the decrees.
>
> But many of the American bishops (a majority in my opinion) want to move with the Church; they want to use the entire concession granted in the Constitution, a concession voted by the overwhelming majority and soon to be promulgated by the Holy Father in a solemn session.

He pointed out that the American public knew what had happened at the Council, and that the bishops could not conceal the liturgical reforms from them:

> In the United States many priests and laymen are fully aware that the adoption of the vernacular is within our immediate authority. Perhaps some of these priests and laymen are extremists; that is not the point. The majority of them are good, intelligent Catholic priests and laymen. They are following the Council carefully, *and they know we have the power....*
>
> If we only warn them to be patient, if we only tell them what cannot be done, then our influence will be minimal because it will be entirely negative. If we assure them that we are the source of teaching, government and sanctification, that we will lead the way to the renewal so dear to the heart of Popes John and Paul, and the whole Church, if we lead and not merely follow, then we will have their confidence, their loyalty and their full cooperation.

Anticipating objections from those who feared a breakdown of law and order in the Church if the changes were made too rapidly, he said:

> I agree fully with those bishops who want to prevent the clergy from taking undue initiative into their own hands, but only on condition that we take the initiative into ours. . . . I believe strongly (and many other American bishops believe the same thing) that we the Bishops must lead the way. We do not lead by simply issuing negative prohibitions. We lead by demonstrating clearly to our American priests and laymen that we are one with the Church universal. We must *legislate,* we must *direct,* we must *lead.*[28]

He got a respectful hearing from the bishops, and then the cardinals present asked him several questions. Spellman wanted to know how much English would be used in the liturgy; McIntyre protested that he had *not* voted for the changes in the liturgy; Meyer thought that the only alternative to Hallinan's proposal was chaos; and Ritter said: "Let's vote."[29]

The bishops then approved four resolutions on a motion by Dearden and seconded by Krol: (1) to make full use in the United States of the vernacular concessions in the liturgy; (2) to authorize the Bishops' Commission on the Liturgical Apostolate to prepare translations for interim use; (3) to hold a special meeting of the bishops in the spring of 1964 to discuss the liturgy; (4) to authorize cooperation with other episcopal conferences for the preparation of a common liturgical text for all English-speaking countries.[30]

Before the Council adjourned, Hallinan attended a meeting of the Bishops' Commission on the Liturgical Apostolate in Dearden's room at the Hilton Hotel, where they discussed such topics as the preparation of a new Missal, Ritual and Breviary, the use of the vernacular in sung Masses, and the need to emphasize to the other bishops the importance of diocesan liturgical commissions, not only to implement the Constitution, but to prevent abuses on the parochial level. Someone raised the question of the use of the vernacular in national parishes. It was reluctantly agreed that some provision would have to be made for languages other than English, but they hoped that the use of an English liturgy would hasten the end of national parishes in the United States.[31]

On December 4, at the close of the second session of the Council, when Pope Paul VI promulgated the Constitution on the Sacred Liturgy, Hallinan had more than a spectator's interest. He found it, he said, "an historic moment and a thrilling experience" to share the event with the Holy Father and 2,200 other bishops. He could take pride that some of his recommendations had been incorporated into the document. Even on those points where he had suffered defeat, such as a more extensive use of the vernacular at Mass or the option for clerics to recite the breviary in their own language, he would be vindicated within a few years when the Holy See granted all that he had asked and more. Another source of satisfaction for him was the knowledge that, in his battles on the Liturgical Commission and his efforts to organize I.C.E.L., he had not been playing the role of a maverick but acting with the authorization and approval of the majority of the American bishops. At the bishops' meeting they demonstrated their confidence by electing him to the Bishops' Commission on the Liturgical Apostolate and endorsing his proposals for immediate implementation of the Constitution on the Sacred Liturgy in the United States.

The second period of the Vatican Council may have been a disappointment to many of the Council Fathers after the heady days of the first, but Hallinan had more reason than most to feel that his two months in Rome had been well spent. Pope Paul closed the session with a carefully nuanced address that Hallinan found disturbing because it was so ambivalent and elusive on crucial issues such as collegiality. The next day, December 5, he was off to the United States on a special, non-stop flight which even had a segregated section for the archbishops.[32]

Press coverage of the Council had been considerably more critical during the second period. *Time* called it "a parliament of stalemate, compromise and delay." But Hallinan was quick to defend the Council as soon as he got home. At a reception for him at the cathedral on Sunday, December 15, he gave a lengthy address, admitting the dissatisfaction that many of the Fathers felt over procedural matters but denying that the pessimism of the journalists was justified.

He pointed to the Constitution on the Liturgy, the acceptance of the doctrine of collegiality, and the lively debate on religious liberty as examples of the progress that was being made. Those who wanted the Council to move faster reminded him of William George Ward, the ultramontane lay theologian in Victorian England who wanted an infallible encyclical at the breakfast table each day with his copy of the *Times*. "Today," said Hallinan, "we have those who apparently would like a brand new conciliar pronouncement each morning with their morning newspaper."

He said nothing about his own role in the Council, but he mentioned that the liturgical changes would soon begin to affect every Catholic in the archdiocese and he appealed for charity and forbearance during this period of transition. Whether people liked the changes or not, he pointed out that only four bishops had voted against them on the final tally and he predicted that "gradually we will all come to wonder how we really worshipped God in any other way."[33]

14

A Horizontal Archbishop

The archbishop spent the rest of December catching up on diocesan business. Over the next few weeks he complained several times of fatigue and exhaustion, but he still managed to maintain a normal schedule of visits and appointments. A major preoccupation was the fund-raising campaign which was scheduled to begin in January. He stayed up until eleven o'clock one night discussing details with Frank Clines whose firm was to direct the drive. Christmas Day was especially taxing for him: he celebrated the Midnight Mass in the cathedral and said two additional Masses later that morning in two other Atlanta parish churches. By the time he returned home in the early afternoon he was so exhausted that he slept until seven o'clock.

He flew to Cleveland next day for a brief vacation with his family, but his condition did not improve. That night at the McIvors' home he was sick three times, and the next day at his brother's house he became ill again. All that he could eat for dinner was a bowl of cream-of-wheat cereal, and he slept from nine o'clock until two o'clock the next afternoon. At that point he decided to return to Atlanta at once. Harold Rainey met him at the airport and drove him to the office of his personal physician, Dr. Joseph Wilber. As soon as Wilber saw Hallinan's yellow complexion, he ordered him to St. Joseph's Infirmary where he spent 270 days over the next twelve months.[1]

He described the first three weeks in the hospital as a nightmare; he was often confused and could neither sleep nor eat. The jaundice grew worse. He became badly bloated as he began to fill up with fluids. Dr. Wilber brought in two specialists and their working hypothesis was "subacute hepatic necrosis." They could not rule out the possibility of cirrhosis or liver tumors, however, and they dared not risk a biopsy in his weakened condition. Both depression and anorexia also became serious problems. The doctors resorted to feeding him intravenously, but he kept dislodging the tube in the middle of the night, and he slept poorly even after receiving fifty milligrams of a sedative each evening.

Harold Rainey came faithfully every day. Sometimes he found the archbishop alert and capable of discussing diocesan business; on other days he was hopelessly confused. There were other visitors too: Bishop McDonough and Bishop Hyland came and John Krol stopped in to see him on his way home from Florida. His brother Art spent a long weekend with him in mid-January, followed by Larry and Clare McIvor, Agnes Lynch, Robert Tracy and Norm Kelley, and their visits sent his spirits soaring. For the next month he seemed to be improving. His abdomen and ankles were still swollen, but he had no pain and he was able to sit in the solarium for long periods, reading newspapers and watching television.

His doctors were not as optimistic as he was about his condition. Dr. Wilber thought that he looked bad on February 21 and noted his weak voice, slurred speech and poor memory. "No improvement," Wilber wrote on the hospital chart two days later, "he is euphoric and doesn't realize how sick he is."

The next day Hallinan suffered a severe relapse, which left him in great pain and more confused than ever. The doctors observed a marked deterioration in his mental condition and, fearful that he would slip into a coma, they ordered special nurses around the clock. For several weeks his situation was critical and the doctors made repeated blood tests and fed him a diet of forty pills a day. By the second week in March the worst was over and the real recovery began, but it was agonizingly slow. A liver scan on March 19 ruled out cancer, but he still faced many more weeks of rest to recover from the hepatitis. Dr. Wilber would only allow him out of bed for four hours a day. On March 29, he observed the second anniversary of his installation with a sad little ceremony sitting in a wheelchair in the hospital chapel while Harold Rainey said Mass.

On April 18, for the first time in almost four months, he felt like his old self. Two weeks later, his doctors allowed him to move from his room to the hospital guest suite. He was still restricted to twenty hours of bed rest every day, but he was pleased with the change of scenery and he now had the luxury of saying Mass twice a week.

During the next three months he resumed more and more of his duties, turning the hospital room into his office, holding a meeting of the diocesan consultors in his bedroom, and having the School Board hold its spring meeting at the hospital so that he could attend it.[2] At the end of May he told Frederick McManus:

> I feel fine and am chafing at the bit to get back to a full schedule, but the doctors say I can't until the liver has reached a near-as-perfect functioning. That makes sense, so I'm trying to turn impatience into the holy virtue of obedience, and here I am without even a vow to that effect.[3]

With his doctors' permission he was now venturing out of the hospital for brief trips. Early in June he drove to the Trappist monastery in Conyers and spoke for forty-five minutes to the diocesan priests on retreat there. When he tried to repeat the performance the following week at St. Ignatius House, however, he felt dizzy and spoke only briefly. He later regretted going at all—when he heard how shocked the priests were at his appearance. At long last, he was discharged from the hospital on July 15 after a stay of six-and-a-half months.[4]

It was no wonder that he shocked many of the priests who saw him at the retreat house in June. He was only fifty-three years old, but he looked twenty years older when he emerged from the hospital. He had lost forty pounds and the change was especially noticeable in his face; once so chubby and cherubic, it was drawn and gaunt now. Gone too was the crewcut which had been a Hallinan trademark since Newman Club days. He let his hair grow longer and combed it straight back in a way which revealed how grey he had become. In some respects he looked more episcopal than ever before, but he was obviously no longer the exuberant young archbishop whose physical endurance had seemed limitless.

One of his great regrets was that his illness occurred at a time when crucial decisions were being made in implementing the changes in the liturgy. The United States bishops discussed these changes on four different occasions in 1964, but Hallinan was unable to attend any of the meetings and he apologized to Dearden for letting him down at this critical time.

The Bishops' Commission on the Liturgical Apostolate was scheduled to meet in Philadelphia in the second week of January to make preparations for the special meeting of the bishops in April—one which was to be devoted exclusively to liturgical matters. Although he could not attend this preliminary meeting either, he sent Dearden a detailed list of recommendations about English translations of the Missal, Breviary and Ritual. He was particularly anxious that the Bishops' Commission should set up a working committee of *periti* under the direction of McManus and Diekmann to analyze and compare the proposed vernacular texts. He warned Dearden that some bishops would undoubtedly prefer to drag their heels on the grounds of caution and prudence. Such stalling tactics, he said,

> would not only be fatal to the liturgical renewal in the United States: it would be a grave failure on the part of the United States Episcopal Commission on the Liturgical Apostolate. We are charged with having all things in readiness for the spring meeting of the American bishops.[5]

In the meantime, Hallinan received word that he had been appointed to the *Consilium ad Exsequendam Constitutionem de Sacra Liturgia,* the new commission created by Pope Paul VI in February 1964. The appointment came at a moment when he needed something to lift his spirits and he recognized it for what it was: a tribute to his growing reputation in the field of liturgy. (The ony other American appointed to the Consilium was Cardinal Ritter.) Although he could not attend the first meeting in Rome in March, he thanked Cardinal Cicognani for selecting him as a member.[6] Still another honor and burden came his way in June, when Dearden asked him to take over the post of Secretary of the Bishops' Commission on the Liturgical Apostolate, left vacant by the recent death of Bishop James Griffiths. Although he was still in the hospital, he agreed to accept the post as of August 1.[7]

On April 2, 1964, 189 American bishops met at Caldwell Hall on the campus of the Catholic University of America for their special session on the liturgy. Hallinan told Dearden: "If there is any place in the world I want to be this week, it's Washington ... [but] hepatitis is cured apparently by rest, rest and more rest." His note to

Dearden was cautious and cordial, and he did not raise a question which was bothering McManus and many other American liturgists at the time: whether to petition Rome for more extensive use of English in the Mass, particularly in the Collects and Postcommunion prayers. Most English-speaking hierarchies had already submitted requests for such concessions, and there was mounting pressure on the United States bishops to do the same. But Hallinan said nothing to Dearden about it despite a broad hint from McManus that he should do so.[8]

As McManus feared, the topic of further vernacular concessions did not come up at the meeting, but the bishops passed several decrees authorizing the use of English in the Mass, sacraments and Divine Office within the limits allowed by the Constitution on the Sacred Liturgy. They also tackled a number of practical problems peculiar to the United States, such as norms for the use of vernacular languages other than English.[9] They approved a single text for the altar Missal, restricted the use of Scriptural texts at Mass to the Confraternity of Christian Doctrine version (on a temporary basis), authorized the use of two English translations of the Breviary (those published by Benziger Brothers and the Liturgical Press), and gave approval to two Rituals (the bilingual *Collectio Rituum* and the *Roman Ritual* published by the Bruce Publishing Company).[10]

The decrees were sent to Rome immediately and received the approval of the Consilium on May 1.[11] The only question still to be settled was when the changes would take effect in the United States, and the bishops decided to set that date at their next meeting in the fall. Before the April meeting ended, however, two of Hallinan's friends proposed a project that he had been anxious to promote for some time: the establishment of an Institute of Liturgical Studies which would emphasize the teaching of pastoral liturgy. Auxiliary Bishop Joseph B. Brunini of Natchez made the proposal and Bishop Tracy seconded it. The bishops passed it by a voice vote, but no practical steps were taken to implement it.[12]

One of the inherent problems in liturgical renewal was the piecemeal manner in which changes were authorized by Rome. It was a particularly risky business for liturgical publishers, who faced the possibility that their books might be obsolete almost as soon as they were printed. In the spring of 1964, Dearden told the publishers that the life expectancy of the new Missal and Ritual would be about five years.[13] His estimate was overly generous. During the summer Hallinan heard that the Consilium was about to issue a new Instruction with a list of further changes. "If we get word of Phase II changes this fall (or before)," he warned Dearden, "it is going to look odd if we go ahead on Phase I for the First Sunday of Advent." He promised to make inquiries about the date of the new changes. "If it is to be soon," he told the Archbishop of Detroit, "I would favor a mail ballot to the United States bishops asking approval to include these new changes, even though it may mean delaying the new edition for a few months."[14]

Another concern of Hallinan's was the need for a "vast educational program" in the United States on the liturgical changes. A number of bishops had asked him if the Bishops' Commission on the Liturgical Apostolate would sponsor such a program. He was heartily in favor of it and told Dearden: "It seems to me that we might well use the remaining six months of 1964 to make available, under the sponsorship of the Bishops' Committee, as much material, etc., as possible." He also recommended closer cooperation with the Liturgical Conference, a private organization which some of the bishops regarded with deep suspicion as a hotbed of radical agitators. Hallinan, on the contrary, liked much of the material that they were producing and wanted the Bishops' Commission to make use of it as part of the proposed educational program.[15]

While he was unburdening himself privately to Dearden, he had several opportunities for public comment. His Lenten Pastoral for 1964 (written in St. Joseph's Infirmary) was a clear and simple explanation of the new meaning of liturgy. It appeared on the front page of the *Georgia Bulletin,* looking for all the world like the manuscript of one of his talks, with the key words and phrases underlined. "You are asked to come out from behind the pillar and put away your rosary," he told the laity, "*you are asked to join with the priest in a community prayer and action,* first drawing in the riches of the Bible, then participating in the Eucharist, participating by receiving Christ's Body and Blood."

He deplored the artificial distinction between spirituality and liturgy. Liturgy used to be considered a set of rules, he explained, while spirituality was regarded as a strictly private affair, summed up in the phrase: "I have a soul to save—by myself." Now, he said, the Church called for a new understanding of liturgy: "a full and active participation by all the people is the aim to be considered before all else."[16]

In August he was invited to speak at the National Liturgical Week of the Liturgical Conference in St. Louis. It was his first public appearance outside the archdiocese since his illness. He was still weak and easily fatigued, so much so that he considered omitting a whole section of his talk, and, when he referred to the two American prelates on the Consilium, he identified Cardinal Ritter as the vertical or working member and himself as the horizontal or consultative member.

He called his talk "The Church's Liturgy: Growth and Development," and he traced the modern liturgical movement back through Pius XII, Dom Virgil Michel, O.S.B., Dom Lambert Beauduin, O.S.B., to the reforms of Pope Pius X, and he included a gracious tribute to Monsignor Martin Hellriegel, the St. Louis pastor and liturgical pioneer, who was celebrating his golden jubilee that year. As he well knew, Hallinan was speaking to an audience that was impatient with the pace of change and his historical excursus was meant to deliver a message to them. "The landmarks show," he said, "that the Church has labored a long time for this harvest. And the renewal now in progress will not be just a matter of months."

He thanked the members of the Liturgical Conference for the contributions which they had made to the progress of the liturgy. "This long thin line of heroes," he said, "has occupied the real frontier of the liturgical movement in the United States," but he also urged them to be magnanimous in the hour of victory and to show tolerance for those who did not quite share their enthusiasm for liturgical reform:

> The resistance is not made up of elderly ladies in devotional tennis shoes nor of ecclesiastical generals and admirals retired from clerical reality. Many of those who are holding back are devout and dedicated Catholics who love God and serve their fellow men. Your role among them calls for special tact, a sub-virtue under the gift of charity. Zeal we need: indeed zeal for the liturgy is a sign of the providential disposition of God in our time. But we also need tact and courtesy, and kindness and persuasion, and all these are the ways of charity. The law of love has not been repealed by the new Constitution, but it would be blasphemy to act as if it had.[17]

On more than one occasion over the next few months Hallinan found it necessary to practice this good advice himself. By now he had given up hope of attending the third period of the Council because he still required twelve hours rest each day, a sodium-free diet, and bi-weekly medical checks and tests. He noted ruefully that he would probably be the only American bishop under the age of eighty who would not be in Rome that fall.[18] McManus kept him well informed about the course of events there, but Hallinan did not always like what he heard and he grew more and more impatient with his inability to influence events from this side of the Atlantic.

Other friends wrote to him from the Council also. John Krol described the progress of the Council's work on collegiality, including a surprisingly positive contribution made by Archbishop Pietro Parente, the Assessor of the Holy Office. He also regaled him with the story of Cardinal Cushing's presence at the silver jubilee of a Maryknoll bishop. There were to be no speeches, but Cushing made "a few remarks"—which ran to fifty-two minutes.[19] Bishop Tracy reported how Cardinal McIntyre had collapsed at the opening Mass, overcome (he quoted some wags as saying) at the sight of concelebration. According to him, many of the American bishops were annoyed at the condescending way that Archbishop Felici treated them during the general congregations, and he said that Archbishop O'Boyle "would like to send some shoe leather in the right direction."[20]

Tracy was more revealing in a letter to Gerard Sherry, saying:

> The Archbishop is greatly missed in Rome, as you may surmise. Not only Americans, but bishops from many parts of the world have expressed the sentiment that his absence is a distinct and serious loss to this session. This is one of the compensations of getting laid up: you would never know otherwise how much you are missed. And yet for some people here I would imagine the Archbishop's absence is met with feelings such as attend the engagement of an efficient baby-sitter for an especially active child. The tempo of life around here will be distinctly reduced this go-around.[21]

The nicest message that Hallinan got from the Council was a hand-written letter from Cardinal Cushing. "You are certainly missed at the Third Session," he told Hallinan, adding, "this is not my opinion, for that would not mean much, for I have spent few days at formal sessions. It is the opinion of the members of the hierarchy of the United States whom I have met." The Cardinal described himself as "representing the Church in Silence at this Council," but he told Hallinan that he definitely intended to speak on the subject of the Jews and religious liberty. "Say a prayer that I don't make a fool of myself," he asked.[22]

During the third session, the United States bishops met three times in Rome to discuss the forthcoming changes in the liturgy. The long-awaited Instruction from the Consilium (dated September 26, 1964) appeared during the second week of October, listing a number of structural changes in the Mass (none of which *per se* required further use of the vernacular) which were to take effect on March 7, 1965.[23] The bishops held the first of their three meetings immediately after this Instruction became public. Dearden assured them that both Benziger Brothers and the Catholic Book Publishing Company would have new altar Missals available by the end of November, and he proposed that they set November 29, the First Sunday of Advent, as the date for the introduction of the changes which they had approved at their last meeting in April. They voted overwhelmingly to accept this date, and two days later Dearden submitted their formal petition to Cardinal Lercaro, the President of the Consilium.

The bishops also discussed the new Instruction from the Consilium and agreed that it would be a mistake to wait until March 7 to implement it. Thereupon, they passed a second resolution asking the Consilium to make this Instruction effective also as of November 29 on the reasonable grounds that, if these changes were introduced into the United States at the same time as the use of the vernacular, the total transition would be easier. The Consilium readily granted the first request but turned down the second.[24]

Bishop Charles Buswell of Pueblo raised the question of greater use of English in the Mass. At this point Rome had already granted permission for the use of English in the Collects and Postcommunion prayers to the hierarchies of Australia, Canada, England and Wales, Scotland, New Zealand and South Africa. Among English-speaking countries, only Ireland, India, Pakistan and the United States still retained Latin for those parts of the Mass. Diekmann and McManus had been trying to get Dearden to reverse himself and come out in favor of the vernacular, but he consistently refused to do so on the grounds that it would be unfair to the publishers who had their Missals almost ready for distribution. "We are bound to keep good faith with the publishers," he told the bishops at the October meeting, "who have ventured to invest several million dollars in this project."[25]

McManus thought that the problem could be solved by printing supplementary inserts or booklets for the new Missals. Initially, Hallinan had the same misgivings as Dearden about possible financial damage to the publishers. After listening to McManus' arguments, however, Hallinan came over to his position and agreed that the bishops should ask for this concession at their November meeting but keep it quiet until after November 29 lest they jeopardize the sale of the new Missals.[26] By that date, he reasoned, everyone who was going to buy a new Missal would have done so.

A second meeting of the bishops on October 26 was devoted largely to an explanation of the new rites for the sacraments. Then, at the final meeting of the bishops on November 12, the question of more English in the Mass came up again, with Cardinal Ritter, Archbishop Shehan and Bishop Floyd Begin of Oakland joining Bishop Buswell in speaking for it. However, on a motion of Bishop Connare, seconded by Auxiliary Bishop Francis J. Furey of Philadelphia, they voted not to ask for further use of English in the Mass *at that time*.[27]

Hallinan regretted their decision, especially after the First Sunday of Advent when he saw how smoothly the initial changes had been introduced into the liturgy. In January 1965 he asked Dearden to seek an indult for the use of English in the Collect, Secret and Postcommunion prayers, and to do so immediately, so that it could take effect on March 7 along with Phase II of the liturgical changes. "It seems to me," he said, "that now is the time."

> The Italian and Mexican hierarchies—notably not as progressive as our own—have received the permission.... The latest is now Portugal.... We are fast becoming the only hierarchy in the world without it, and if we ever begin the March 7 period with this sore thumb in our text, I think it will be judged inexcusable by everyone.
>
> While we are at it, we might try to seek permission for some other parts: the *Orate Fratres,* the Preface and the *Libera Nos.* They are all surely about to come in the course of the next few years, and I think it would be wise to take the lead again.

> I am certain that the inserts could do the job as far as the Altar Missals are concerned; but in any case, we should not tie ourselves to the publishers, cooperative as they have been. The issue is the integrity of the whole liturgical renewal and the pastoral formation of it for our priests, religious and laity.[28]

Dearden, however, replied that it was impossible to meet the March 7 deadline because the Bishops' Commission on the Liturgical Apostolate did not have authorization from the hierarchy to ask for more English. Moreover, he complained to Hallinan of his own frustrations in dealing with the Consilium. Rather than request minor concessions every few months, he preferred to find out how much of the vernacular the Consilium was ultimately disposed to allow and then to ask for that at one time.[29]

Another source of concern for Hallinan was the running battle between the Consilium and the Congregation of Rites for control of liturgical reform. It was an open secret that the original *Motu Proprio* of January 25, implementing the Constitution on the Liturgy, had been doctored by the Congregation of Rites. Protests from the French, German and Belgian bishops had led the pope to revise it before it was printed in the *Acta Apostolicae Sedis* of February 15.[30] Now, in the spring and summer of 1964, however, there were indications that the Congregation was again gaining the upper hand and replacing the Consilium as the dominant liturgical authority in Rome.

In May rumors were circulating that henceforth the Consilium's role would be limited to that of preparing decrees: the promulgation and execution would be the exclusive prerogative of the Congregation of Rites. The French liturgist, Abbé Aimé-Georges Martimort, had no doubt about the effect of such a change. In a confidential memorandum to Hallinan and other episcopal members of the Consilium, he warned that:

> The decisions of the Consilium could be altered by the people in [the Congregation of] Rites. A few of these functionaries in the curia would be able to stymie the unanimous wishes of the Bishops on the Consilium .... The indults issued could wreck the reforming work undertaken by the Council.[31]

From England, Clifford Howell, S.J., complained about the need for the national conferences of bishops to send vernacular texts to Rome for approval. It was reasonable enough, Howell said, that the *acta* of the bishops' meetings should be sent to Rome for confirmation. What he objected to was "the implication that some curial official is better qualified than the local bishops to judge whether a given translation is accurate and suitable for local use—which is nonsense. It puts the bishops back in the position of office boys handing out orders from the Curia."[32]

Early in October, Hallinan wrote to Cardinal Lercaro about the rumors that the actions of the Consilium were to be subject to the approval of the Congregation of Rites. "I am convinced," he told the Cardinal, "that such a step would be disastrous to liturgical development and would be totally opposed to the spirit of the Council Fathers." Therefore, he continued,

> as a member of the Conciliar Commission on the Sacred Liturgy and the Consilium for its implementation, I am strongly in favor of retaining the present juridical competence of the Consilium. Acting with the Holy Father's approval and with the support of the majority of the Fathers of the Council, the Consilium is fully capable of guiding the development of the Sacred Liturgy. With the exception of the unfortunate incident of the translation of the *Motu Proprio* in January, this procedure has been eminently successful in guiding the development of the renewal, and in giving hope to bishops, priests and laity all over the world.[33]

His American colleague on the Consilium, Cardinal Ritter, was delighted with Hallinan's intervention. "It is becoming more and more like Congress," he wrote from the Council, with the "give and take." He was confident, however, that the Holy Father favored the progress of reform and he assured Hallinan that his letter would be a great encouragement to Cardinal Lercaro, "who seems to be the right man for the job."[34]

One of the problems which Hallinan had agreed to handle while the other bishops were in Rome was the establishment of a Music Advisory Board for the Bishops' Commission on the Liturgical Apostolate. The idea originated at a meeting of church musicians in Pittsburgh in December 1963, when several of the participants, including Archabbot Rembert Weakland, O.S.B., of St. Vincent's Archabbey in Latrobe, Pennsylvania, Father C.J. McNaspy, S.J., and Professor Robert Snow of the University of Pittsburgh, volunteered their services to the bishops.[35] At the time, it appeared that such an advisory body would be absolutely necessary, for it was thought that all the new melodies for the vernacular parts of the Mass would require approval by the bishops at the national level. Hallinan was bracing himself for a deluge of manuscripts and wondering how to process them, when word came from Rome which caused an abrupt change of plans. The Consilium informed the United States bishops in the fall of 1964 that any ordinary could give authorization for most of the new melodies: only the chants sung by the priest required the approval of the national conference of bishops.

Dearden seemed relieved to be rid of the responsibility, but for Hallinan, it meant that he had wasted much time devising plans for a situation which would never eventuate, since any problems could be handled at the local level. Both he and Dearden were anxious, however, to continue the advisory board. Dearden suggested that the members should now concentrate their attention on producing original compositions for the parts of the Mass sung by the priest.[36]

For a brief moment in October Hallinan thought that he might be able to go to Rome for the final weeks of the third session, but a severe blood infection forced him back into the hospital.

McManus told him that it was just as well that he stayed at home rather than involve himself in the squabbles over the liturgy which continued throughout October and November.[37] Some American bishops persisted in fighting a rearguard action against further use of the vernacular, and Connare and Furey (who had proposed and seconded a motion to this effect at the November meeting) were both elected to the Bishops' Commission on the Liturgical Apostolate.[38] On the other hand, when Dearden suggested the establishment of a secretariat in Washington for the Bishops' Commission—a move which Hallinan strongly favored, especially when it became evident that McManus was Dearden's first choice for the post—Bishop Reed objected that it was a slap at the Liturgical Conference. Many of its members, he predicted, "will be antagonized and determined to continue the Conference as a rival organization."[39]

The state of the "Common Market" (I.C.E.L.) was also far from satisfactory. Bishop Connare filled in for Hallinan at the meetings in Rome. The I.C.E.L. representatives agreed to the plan which Hallinan had proposed the previous year and voted to establish a secretariat of their own in Washington headed by an English priest. It was estimated that the cost of this operation for the first year would not exceed $28,000, two-thirds of which would come from the United States. Difficulties began when Connare (who had initially opposed the secretariat) made his report to the American bishops and they failed to approve it.[40]

Without American participation the plan was unworkable, although all the other English-speaking hierarchies had approved it with the exception of Ireland. The bishops on the International Committee then suggested an alternative plan which involved a meeting of the members of the International Advisory Committee in London in January. McManus was disgusted with the meager results of so much hard work and told Hallinan: "It seems very wasteful for us to start in a preliminary and imperfect way what should really be done by a secretary concentrating on the whole task. In a sense, the London meeting is just marking time, but we will do our best with it." He reported to Hallinan the disappointment of Archbishop Young and Archbishop Hurley at the decision of the American bishops and said dejectedly: "If the United States is not going to take any leadership, we should get out of it entirely so as not to hinder the rather good plans which the other bishops have worked out."[41]

Even before he received this last report, Hallinan was becoming increasingly upset at the news that was filtering back from Rome. He told McManus in an unusually frank letter:

> There is so much confusion at this point I really don't know what to think about it all. I wanted to get to Rome desperately and to try to help weld some unity into the liturgical picture (United States), to assure the Common Market of our whole-hearted interest and support, and to help fight the tortuous path of the Consilium. But God kept me at home and among the fringe benefits is that I was spared the ignominy of blowing my top which I know I would have done.[42]

The same day he wrote to Dearden, expressing alarm that the American bishops were losing their taste for liturgical reform and retreating from positions that they had previously taken:

> I am convinced that the bishops will either lead the United States liturgical renewal or it will end in a checker board of diocesan

drifting with frustrated priests and laymen. What I hope for fervently is that the Liturgical Committee uses every good means right now to take the lead. There are certain bishops, we all know, who are fighting the spirit of the constitution, limiting the use of the new Missal, delaying the new Ritual, making the vernacular option so opprobrious that it totally evades the mind of the legislator. . . . It is up to you and me and others entrusted with the liturgy to change it. We can't do it by mandate, but we can do it by leadership as was evident in the November 1963 meeting in Rome.[43]

The year 1964 had been a rough one, and Hallinan was back in the hospital again at this time when he was pouring out his fears and frustrations to Dearden and McManus. The situation was not quite as bad as he depicted it; at least Dearden did not think so, and he had been present at most of the important meetings in Rome when Hallinan had been 3,000 miles away in Atlanta. While admitting that some of the bishops were giving only a grudging and marginal acceptance to the liturgical changes, Dearden pointed out that no bishop could block the use of the vernacular in his diocese and he predicted that the spirit of the times would compel even the most reactionary bishops to move faster than they wished. He also gently reminded his friend in Atlanta of the limited power of the Bishops' Commission, which could prod and encourage the bishops but could not order any of them to do anything.[44]

On several matters Hallinan failed to show that sharp grasp of the situation which had made him such an efficient politician at the first two sessions of the council. Initially, at least, he seems to have overlooked the enormous potential of the secretariat in Washington, which in subsequent years fulfilled many of his aspirations by bringing a high degree of professionalism and unity to the liturgical renewal in the United States. And he showed a curious blind spot in underestimating the extent of the opposition in the hierarchy to the Liturgical Conference. Dearden, who was in daily contact with the bishops at the Council, knew better. He realized that many of them disliked the influence of the Liturgical Conference on their clergy and even feared that it might become a rival authority to the bishops' own Liturgical Commission. When McManus became secretary of the Bishops' Commission, for example, it was Dearden, not Hallinan, who suggested that he resign as the President of the Liturgical Conference lest there by any ambiguity about the relationship between the two bodies.

Hallinan's concern about the fate of the Consilium and the International Commission on English in the Liturgy was also exaggerated. Both proved to be more resilient than he had feared. With regard to American participation in the latter, Dearden quietly secured from the American bishops the financial backing that Connare had failed to get in November. Hallinan's bad health and absence from the scene of action may account in large measure for his unusually gloomy mood in the fall of 1964 and his failure to judge the situation as shrewdly as he had done at the first two sessions of the Council.

15

On the Home Front

While Archbishop Hallinan was battling *a longe* with ecclesiastical generals and admirals in 1964, he found an outlet for some of his frustrations close at home—preparing the priests and laity of his archdiocese for the first round of changes in the Mass. At a clergy conference for over one hundred priests on September 15, 1964, he stressed the need to involve the laity in active participation in the liturgy. He quoted for them a remark of Cardinal Ritter which was fast becoming a favorite of his: "No priest can ignore the Constitution [on the Liturgy]. If he did so, it would be to his own peril—not the peril of the Church, but the peril of his own soul."[1]

A short time later, he told Frederick McManus:

> Things [are] going on well here.... Father [Lawrence F.X.] Mayhew is Chairman of our newly constituted [Liturgical] Commission with five excellent laymen and three sisters. We published a Priest's Guide and made it the official law of the archdiocese. Charleston and Savannah went in on it with us. Now [we are] working on sermon outlines, school preparation and parish organization programs. Our choir leaders are meeting regularly and a number of parishioners are working with the Course for Commentators and Lectors. Next is the Conference on Worship ... at which we will have ... five Masses in English-Latin and plenty of opportunity for discussion.[2]

Over the next few months he provided his clergy with detailed directions on the implementation of the changes. As of the First

Sunday of Advent all low Masses were to be "dialogue Masses" with the congregation reciting most of the Ordinary, and he strongly encouraged the use of hymns, offertory processions and weekday homilies in addition to the mandatory Sunday homilies. All Sunday Masses were to be celebrated *coram populo* and, whenever possible, with lectors and commentators.[3]

Similar directives followed for the new rites for administration of the sacraments. He recommended that Confirmation be celebrated during Mass but recognized that practical difficulties might often make this impossible. With regard to the Sacrament of Penance he forbade even the use of the term "communal celebration" lest anyone conclude that the individual confession of sins was no longer necessary. On the other hand, he advocated "a more flexible relationship between First Confession and First Communion so that each sacrament may be received with the greatest possible benefit to the child," even if this meant separating First Communion from First Confession. At wake services in funeral homes, he suggested that a Bible service might sometimes be more appropriate than the recitation of the rosary, especially when large numbers of non-Catholics were present, but he left the ultimate decision to the wishes of the family.[4]

His own enthusiasm for the liturgical changes did not blind him to the value of traditional Catholic devotions. During Lent in 1965, for example, he asked every parish to schedule the Way of the Cross services using one of the Scripturally-oriented formats. He saw no contradiction between this request and his own promotion of the new liturgical rites. After all, he said, we are only "following the Gospel maxim to bring out of our treasure 'new things and old.'"[5]

Two young priests in Charleston wrote to him expressing their disappointment that there was still so much Latin in the Mass. "It simply inhibits the reception of the benefits of the Mass," they contended. Hallinan sent them a friendly reply, conceding that a vernacular Mass would probably be of great benefit to both priests and people, but he asked them to remember that

> the vast majority of our people all over the world have not been sufficiently prepared by *Mediator Dei* and the studies of liturgical scholars over the past two decades. The vernacular is a relatively minor point to be fitted into the greater context of true liturgical understanding and participation. It is probably better that the

vernacular proceed slowly in order that our people do not get the impression that it is simply a gimmick. It is rather an important instrument when seen in the light of the full liturgical renewal. In view of that, a gradual process of both education and motivation must accompany dramatic changes such as we will probably have this year.[6]

Whenever he could, he welcomed the opportunity to experience for himself the changes that he was promoting for others. While in the hospital he took to reading the breviary in English and told McManus how much he enjoyed it. On the Feast of the Epiphany in 1965, he concelebrated Mass for the first time with the Trappists at their monastery in Conyers, Georgia. He was so pleased that he wanted to obtain an indult from Rome for a concelebrated Mass at the diocesan ordinations in May. "I can't think of any more appropriate time," he said, "for the expression of the unity of the priesthood."[7]

During the summer his friend Godfrey Diekmann, O.S.B., asked him for a favor to remedy what he called "an almost desperate monastic concern." No provision at all had been made in the Constitution on the Liturgy to allow monks to use the vernacular in the celebration of the Divine Office. Many American monks strongly desired this and Diekmann feared a severe vocation crisis if such permission were not forthcoming. He quoted one abbot who spoke of the likelihood of "corporate suicide" if they were forced to continue with the use of Latin. Most American abbots favored the vernacular, but many of their European counterparts did not—including the Abbot Primate, who was a member of the Consilium.[8]

At Diekmann's request, Hallinan wrote to Bugnini, the Chairman of the Consilium, relaying the complaint and asking that each monastery be allowed to vote on the use of the vernacular. Hallinan considered the request reasonable and thought that it would meet opposition only from those who thought that the preservation of Latin was as important as liturgical understanding. Bugnini, however, politely brushed aside his request on the grounds that the matter was not yet ripe for a decision and would require more detailed study.[9]

The liturgy was not the only subject which preoccupied him during his long stay in the hospital. A couple whom he had known years before in Newman work wrote to him (after reading an article by Rosemary Ruether in *Look* magazine) to ask his advice about the morality of the newly introduced birth-control pill. Basically, Hallinan told them, contraception was wrong because it was against nature—"and to understand this fully, and faithfully," he added, we need "to understand it in the sense in which the Church, aided by the Holy Spirit of God, teaches it." He also offered the couple this personal pastoral advice:

> You both bring to this problem tremendous assets—you love God, your Church; you love each other, your children. Yours is not the cold-blooded approach of a Mrs. Ruether, who simply wants her own definition of right and wrong, uncolored by Christ or the Church. On these assets you can build, as thousands of other couples facing the same problem are building, a Catholic married life. It is not the simple solution of a pill, grabbed at by desperate people, even while a large part of the medical profession still warns of our ignorance of its effects. Yours is the solution of struggle and sacrifice—but with a meaning.[10]

One casualty of the archbishop's prolonged hospitalization was the archdiocesan fund-raising compaign scheduled for that year. He asked the diocesan consultors whether it would be possible to conduct the campaign without him, but they unanimously agreed that he should be the center of the drive. He admitted that they were right and reluctantly decided to postpone the campaign until 1965.[11]

Even in the hospital, however, he tried to keep in contact with his flock through his regular column in the archdiocesan newspaper.[12] Through the newspaper he thanked them for their prayers and good wishes, told them what he was reading, and joked about the note which he had received from an old friend which said: "I wasn't surprised to hear that you were in bed, but I was surprised to hear that you were sick." On one occasion he described for them how he had asked the hospital chaplain to anoint him and how different it was to be the recipient of a sacrament which he had administered hundreds of times himself. Another new role for him was participating in a medical conference in the hospital on the subject of hepatitis. Over one hundred doctors were present and asked him questions from the floor. Far from resenting it, he used the experience to write a column about modern medicine.

He found material for another column in the comment of a young hospital orderly who was studying to become a Protestant minister.

He came to the archbishop's room every morning at 6:30 to tidy up. When Hallinan asked why, he said that he was there to prepare him for the Eucharist. What he meant was that he wanted everything to be in order before the Catholic chaplain came later in the day to bring him Holy Communion. It did not take much effort for an old journalist to turn the incident into a *ferverino* on the need for every Christian to prepare himself for the Eucharist.[13]

When the third period of the Council opened in the fall of 1964, he made no secret in his column of his desire to be there. While discussing the prospects for the third and fourth sessions, he reverted to another old habit from college days and composed a few limericks to depict the lighter side of the Council's proceedings:

> There are Rahner, Ratzinger and Küng
> Whom a few would like decently hung
> Among the *periti*
> Of various *riti*
> But by many their praises are sung.[14]

As his health gradually improved, he started to map out an ambitious writing program for himself since that was the one form of activity that his doctors approved—as long as he stayed in bed. He began work on a book for Random House to be called *The Council in Mid-Passage* and planned a second book for the Helicon Press with the tentative title of *The Parish and the Council*. He hoped to find a publisher for his dissertation on Gilmour and actually completed several articles for *Continuum* and *Ave Maria*. By June he was working until midnight trying to meet deadlines. "It was just like 1962," he told John Tracy Ellis—the time when he was struggling to finish his dissertation. The strain was too much and he had to abandon the projects, although he still hoped to finish the book for Random House at a later date. "I don't want to do just another book on the Council, nor a defense of both sides, nor of neither," he told Ellis, "I would like to use some personal knowledge of events and figures . . . and I would like to bring into the treatment of the liturgy some first-hand knowledge."[15]

For much of 1964, while Hallinan was battling hepatitis inside St. Joseph's Infirmary, civil rights workers outside were often battling police dogs and angry white crowds. During that summer many volunteers from the North came South to assist local civil rights workers in conducting voter registration drives for blacks. The reaction of white Southerners was often violent and bloody, especially in Mississippi where black homes and churches were burned and three Northern civil rights workers were murdered. In Atlanta on July 4 at a patriotic rally, a mob of whites savagely beat several blacks with axe handles. Hallinan immediately condemned the culprits and wondered aloud in his newspaper column about the mentality of such people. "How in God's name," he asked, "do you reach them?"[16]

As the nation watched this drama unfold each evening on television, there were more and more demands for federal intervention to end the violence. In July, Congress passed the Civil Rights Act of 1964 giving the federal government more power than ever before to eliminate discrimination in schools, employment and public accommodations. Despite this law, however, and despite the ratification of the Twenty-Fourth Amendment in January (abolishing the poll tax in federal elections), very few blacks dared to vote in Southern elections and political power remained firmly in white hands. Consequently, the civil rights movement now focused its attention on this grievance, which, in turn, triggered further violence from outraged whites.

Both black and white clergymen were now playing prominent roles in the civil rights movement. One exasperated white citizen wrote to an Atlanta newspaper praising Cardinal McIntyre for supposedly saying that the racial issue was a purely political one in which the Church should not interfere. Hallinan defended the cardinal (in a way that he might not have appreciated) by pointing out that McIntyre had signed the 1958 statement of the American bishops which had emphatically condemned segregation and had declared that "the heart of the race question is moral and religious." What we need, said Hallinan, is more and not less speaking out by the clergy about the evils of our society.[17]

He did precisely that a few months later when he gave the keynote address at the annual convention of the Steelworkers of America in Atlantic City. Some union members were still smarting from the Civil Rights Act of that year, forbidding discrimination in employment, but Hallinan faced the issue squarely. He called upon the labor unions to interest themselves in the plight of three groups: unorganized workers, the blacks, and the destitute. In a remarkably perceptive passage he described the unhealthy economic and social trends which he saw developing around him:

We are permitting a jobless class, impoverished and permanent, to coexist with abundance, more jobs, more wages, more profits, more wealth. The first two questions feed the third—the concern of the Negro and the unorganized simply aggravate the problem of our jobless class.

While praising the contribution of the labor unions to the nation, he called their attention to a flaw which he had noticed in the American labor movement from the beginning: "the fear of competition with minority workers." He cited the opposition of the Knights of Labor in 1882 to Chinese immigration and the support given by organized labor to the restrictive immigration laws of the 1920's, and he pleaded with the steel workers not to repeat the error:

This prejudice against the immigrant, the Puerto Rican, the Cuban and especially the American Negro is unworthy of men of labor. Your long tradition of fighting for what is right cannot afford the luxury of loopholes. For twenty-five years you have struggled to establish the right of all workers to form a union of their own choosing. In the words of Monsignor Edward Head of New York: "The objective must now be the right of all working men to join these unions so formed—all men, regardless of race or color."[18]

In 1964, when Martin Luther King Jr. won the Nobel Peace Prize, Atlanta was presented with an embarrassing dilemma. If the city failed to honor its native son, it would tarnish the carefully cultivated image of Atlanta as an enlightened and progressive oasis in the Deep South. On the other hand, few prominent citizens were willing to take the lead in organizing a public tribute to King when racial tension was running high throughout the South. As Mayor Allen said later: "We had made great strides in civil rights in recent years, but we hadn't come *that far.*"[19] There was deep resentment of King not only among the blue-collar supporters of Governor George A. Wallace of Alabama but also among many people in the Atlanta business community. Nevertheless, Allen and Paul Austin, the President of the Coca Cola Company, met with two dozen leading businessmen and persuaded them to support a bi-racial dinner in honor of King. It was the first such event in the city's history, attended by 1,500 people at the old Dinkler Hotel in downtown Atlanta. There were a number of bomb threats and the

State of Georgia showed its displeasure by failing to send a representative to the affair. Outside on the sidewalk, members of the Ku Klux Klan picketed the hotel; inside, Mayor Allen planted 200 plainclothes policemen in the audience.

Years later, Allen expressed gratitude for the help which Hallinan gave in organizing the event. "I think that history will show," said the former mayor, "that Archbishop Hallinan was a prime mover in seeing that the business community supported that dinner."[20] It came off without incident and King made a stirring address. The leaders of the white Protestant churches in the city did not attend the dinner but Hallinan insisted on leaving the hospital for a few hours so that he could make an appearance. He was still quite weak and spoke only briefly, comparing King to Mahatma Gandhi and praising him for his commitment to love and peace. "Out of this vibrant Biblical truth," he said, "you have helped to fashion an American instrument of nonviolence. You have made it a creative force in the long bitter struggle for racial equality."[21]

Within weeks of this dinner King was back at work again in Alabama, inaugurating a campaign to register three million black voters across the country. He began in the little city of Selma, which soon became the center of national attention (as he knew it would) when the police began to club and arrest blacks who tried to register to vote. Thereupon King decided on a new tactic: a march from Selma to the state capital at Montgomery fifty miles away. Twice he and his followers started from Selma and twice they were forcibly turned back by the police. Television recorded every move and countermove. When King announced a third march, Governor Wallace declared that he could not protect the marchers. At that point, on March 15, 1965, President Lyndon B. Johnson nationalized elements of the Alabama National Guard and ordered federal marshals and agents of the F.B.I. to protect the marchers. On March 21 the marchers finally left Selma, their numbers swollen by many ministers, priests, rabbis and sisters from all over the country. Four days later they peacefully entered Montgomery. On the day that the marchers left Selma, President Johnson appeared before Congress to plead for the passage of new civil rights legislation which would guarantee federal protection for black voters in the South.

The leading Catholic prelate in Alabama, Archbishop Thomas J. Toolen, Bishop of Mobile-Birmingham, disapproved of the march and criticized the clergy and religious who participated in it. At a St. Patrick's Day dinner in Mobile, he complained that the priests and sisters had not asked permission to come into his diocese. "What do they know about conditions in the South?," he asked. "I am afraid that they are only eager-beavers who feel that this is a holy cause." He had forbidden the clergy and religious of his own diocese to take part in the march. As for the "outside Crusaders" who had descended on Alabama, he said: "Certainly the sisters are out of place in these demonstrations. Their place is at home doing God's work. I would say that the same is true of priests." Toolen admitted that the blacks had justifiable complaints and even conceded that he himself could probably not pass the voter registration tests that were administered to them. However, the only advice that he had for blacks was to be patient and law-abiding, because the "things that need correcting ... will be corrected in time."[22]

Approximately two hundred priests and fifty sisters came to Selma in March 1965. A half-dozen Atlanta priests asked Hallinan for permission to go also, but he refused point-blank to let them go—not out of deference to Toolen or concern for public opinion in Atlanta, but because of fear for their safety in Selma. He explained in his newspaper column what he had done and added: "I acted as I honestly judged best. I hope it was the right decision."[23] Twenty-four hours later he reversed himself and allowed the six priests to leave for Selma. Again he shared with his readers the motives for his decision. "There are times," he said,

> when we must risk safety and convenience and protocol—and even lives. This was one of those times—and six priests from our archdiocese took part in the protest. We thank God that they are home safe, and we thank Him too that they took part.
>
> Someone recently called me "that Nigger-loving Archbishop." If I were not, I would be untrue to the motto "That you may love one another." When we all follow this command of Christ, there will be no further need for demonstrations.[24]

His decision to let the six priests go to Selma produced what he called the "usual rash of crazy letters," but there were many other letters endorsing his decision and praising him for taking such a forthright stand.[25] One local Catholic layman said that he had shuddered and almost despaired after reading Toolen's statement. "I do not want to hear sermons about charity, brotherly love and humility," he explained. "I want the leadership of the Church to relate these concepts to our daily lives."[26]

Not everyone was so complimentary. An admirer of the Klan told him: "You are so right: the whole world is watching Catholicism, especially four million members of the Masonic Fraternity. This is a white man's country and no niggers are going to take it away from us."[27] A Catholic said that he was ashamed to see his Church involved in "cheap nigger politics" and announced that henceforth he would send his church contributions to the white police fund in Selma. A Protestant warned him not to be duped by the Communists. "I do not know just how far you have gone down the road to Communism," he said, "but it must be pretty far, for integration ... has been a top objective of the Reds for over fifty years."[28] An angry Catholic told Gerard Sherry that he would not contribute a cent to the archdiocesan fund-raising campaign. "I am disgusted with Hallinan," he said. "I was sickened when he led those ill-advised people who honored this pushing, climbing, arrogant Negro. I would say to him: 'Yankee, go home.'"[29]

Many of the critics wrote more in sorrow than in anger. Some feared the reaction of their neighbors, like the man who said: "It is all very well for priests like Father [Noel] Burtenshaw [the vice-chancellor] to be such heroes; he can retreat to the protective seclusion of your rectory and doesn't have to face life among non-Catholic Southerners every day like [*sic*] we do."[30] Many Catholics were shocked because they thought that Hallinan had ordered priests and sisters to go to Selma, while others sincerely believed that the events in Selma were entirely political in nature and saw no justification for the Church's participation in them, especially when Martin Luther King's tactics involved the deliberate violation of state and local laws. One man was so upset that, for the first time in fifty years, he stayed home from Sunday Mass in protest.[31]

Hallinan printed a fair sampling of these letters (both favorable and unfavorable—with the names omitted) in the *Georgia Bulletin*. To set the record straight he emphasized that no one had been *sent* to Selma. In fact no sisters from Atlanta were present in Selma at all; six priests had asked and received his permission to go there. To squelch another rumor he said that each of the six had paid his own way; not one cent of diocesan money had been used. On the main point at issue—the legitimacy of Catholic participation at Selma—he was adamant. "A demonstration for racial justice is a moral issue," he insisted. Far from apologizing for what he had done, he defended his decision vigorously. "It is because non-violent demonstrations can be acts of virtue," he said,

> that this Archdiocese of Atlanta has approved our people taking part in them.... This is consistent with our standing practice of total integration in our schools, hospitals and institutions.... The Church will probably take part in demonstrations again, if the cause is right and the necessity is urgent, and if they are non-violent.[32]

On Pentecost Sunday the bishops of the Province of Atlanta issued a joint statement much of which was devoted to ecumenism and race relations in the South. On the latter topic, they deplored the discrimination suffered by blacks in housing, education, employment and even the right to vote. They did not go as far as Hallinan in endorsing demonstrations like those in Selma, but, on the subject of the recent civil rights laws, they declared: "Justice has been slow in coming. Now it is written in the law and surely it must be preached in our pulpits and practiced in our lives."[33]

Later that summer Hallinan sponsored a Conference on Social Change and Christian Response which brought together five bishops and several hundred priests, sisters and lay people for three days of speeches and workshops on the significance of the recent civil rights legislation. He delivered the keynote address at the conference, and, with the memory of the Selma events still fresh in everyone's mind, he tried to define the proper role of the Church in the civil rights movement. A week earlier a local black leader had boasted that he could turn out priests and sisters for a demonstration whenever he wished. Hallinan heatedly rejected the notion of clergy and religious as "protective coloration or as an irritant to town and community." The role that he envisioned for them was that of a catalyst, offering moral direction to Catholics and non-Catholics alike. And he reminded the lay delegates at the conference that often they could be more influential than the clergy by bringing the Church's teaching on racial justice into their homes, neighborhoods, offices and factories.[34]

In a pastoral letter issued to publicize the conference he returned to a theme that he had mentioned in his talk to the steel workers: that economic improvement must accompany the political gains being made by American blacks. He claimed that the first phase of the civil rights movement—the Era of the Frontier—was almost over. "Now we enter the Era of the Market Place," he said, and he warned that "unless knowledge grows, many Negroes will find themselves untrained and unprepared for the changing methods of the American economy."[35]

During the summer of 1965 racial disturbances erupted in many cities, providing abundant ammunition for both black and white demagogues. Some of the worst rioting occurred in the Watts area of Los Angeles and received national attention. Hallinan was quick to condemn both the rioters and those black leaders who tried to justify the disturbances as a legitimate form of protest. "They are besmirching a noble and fruitful method," he said and called upon every black leader to condemn the rioters as unequivocally as Martin Luther King Jr. had done. At the same time, he reminded whites that Watts was a symbol of long-standing black grievances which they could no longer afford to ignore.[36]

The controversy over the Selma demonstration came at a bad time because it coincided with the archdiocesan fund-raising drive, which finally began (a year late) in January 1965 with a goal of two million dollars. A few people refused to contribute in protest over the archbishop's stand on civil rights, but they were a small minority, and by the end of April the drive had raised $2,100,000 in pledges. Hallinan was jubilant, especially since his own health was now steadily improving, and on Holy Thursday he was able to concelebrate the Mass of the Chrism with sixteen other priests in the cathedral. The sisters at St. Joseph's Infirmary scolded him for overexerting himself, but he assured them that the Mass had taken only an hour and a half. "I guess it is that word 'pontificating' that looks so impressive," one of them said. That spring he often reflected on the contrast with the year before, when he had been confined to the hospital. Even the sights and smells of spring now seemed more attractive and he frequently remarked how lovely the dogwood and fresh-cut lawns were at that time of year.[37]

He had other reasons for feeling better too. The work of liturgical reform was proceeding smoothly on both the national and international levels. The secretariat for the Bishops' Commission had gotten off to a good start with McManus at the helm; the May meeting of the bishops on the Commission was cordial and constructive, and Hallinan was happy with the way in which Dearden persuaded Connare and

Furey to follow his lead. The meeting of the Music Advisory Board next day was equally pleasant and successful.[38] One of the items discussed at the meeting of the Bishops' Commission had been the now perennial problem of the relationship between the Commission itself and the Liturgical Conference. The establishment of the secretariat seemed the ideal occasion to delineate the role of each and it fell to Hallinan as secretary to break the news to the officials of the Liturgical Conference. He did so as gently as possible, thanking them for their contributions but leaving no doubt that the Bishops' Commission would be the authoritative voice of the hierarchy in liturgical matters.[39] Another proposal approved by the Commission at the same time was an idea long advocated by Hallinan: the creation of an institute of higher liturgical studies comparable to those which already existed in Rome and Paris offering doctoral programs in liturgy. He hoped that the Catholic University of America would provide a home for such an institute and wrote to Cardinal Spellman, the Chairman of the University's Board of Trustees, trying to interest him in the plan.[40]

The fortunes of the International Committee on English in the Liturgy also took a decided turn for the better. The American bishops had left this Committee in limbo in the fall of 1964 when they failed to approve the $22,000 which was the American share of the budget. However, in May 1965, Dearden got the Administrative Board of the National Catholic Welfare Conference to agree to this expenditure, thus saving the International Committee from oblivion. Once the funding was assured, Hallinan set to work establishing a secretariat for them also in Washington, and for the post he secured the services of Father Gerald Sigler, Secretary of the Erie Diocesan Liturgical Commission and a friend of Frederick McManus.[41]

When the fourth and final period of the Second Vatican Council opened on September 14, 1965, Hallinan was present in St. Peter's Basilica. After the usual formalities the Council Fathers proceeded at once to the first item on the agenda: the proposed Declaration on Religious Liberty. Many of the American bishops were still angry that the Declaration had not been brought to a vote at the end of the third session because of last-minute maneuvers by diehard opponents. Now they spoke up forcefully in its favor, led by Cardinals Spellman, Cushing and Ritter.[42] Hallinan spoke on September 17, adding his strong endorsement to the Declaration and offering a clarification about the relationship of the civil government and religion in a constitutional state. Some of the opponents of the Declaration had contended that it necessarily committed the government to a position of religious indifferentism. Hallinan disagreed. "Rather," he said, "where religious liberty is secured, the state simply acknowledges its own limitations over human rights which cannot be relinquished ('inalienable'). In other words the state recognizes that it has no right to constrain the exercise of religious liberty except in the case of civil crimes." As far as he was concerned, "the state best fosters religion when it fosters the free exercise of it."[43]

This was the only occasion on which Hallinan addressed the Council at the final session, but he offered two written interventions during the debate over the *schema* on The Church in the Modern World. The first was on October 4, when he asked for a more explicit condemnation of racial discrimination by the Council as a way of strengthening the position of those Christians who were already working to "remove this moral offense from mankind's catalogue of sins."[44]

Four days later he submitted to the Council Secretariat a similar written proposal about the status of women in the Church and in society in general. He questioned whether the Church in the past could not have done more to promote the political and economic equality of women. "In our society," he said,

> women in many places and in many respects still bear the marks of inequality. This is evident in working conditions, wages and hours of work, and in marriage and property laws. Above all it is present in that gradualism, bordering on inaction, which limits their presence in the tremendous forces now working for universal education, for peace, for the rehabilitation of the deprived, the just and compassionate care of the young, the aged and the needy, the dispossessed and the victims of human injustice and weakness.

Hallinan asked for five specific additions to the *schema:* (1) permission for women to act as lectors and acolytes at liturgical functions; (2) restoration of deaconesses with the power to preach and discharge the other functions of deacons; (3) encouragement for women to become teachers and consultors in theology; (4) provision for women religious to be represented and consulted in all matters concerning their interests in the Congregation for Religious and the Commission for the Revision of Canon Law; (5) recognition that women who are neither wives nor religious may witness in their own way to the universal call to holiness.[45]

Hallinan's third and final written intervention developed out of a meeting that he attended on October 12 with two dozen American bishops to discuss the Decree on the Ministry and Life of Priests. Three American *periti,* Father Frank Norris, S.S., Father Francis X. Murphy, C.Ss.R., and Father Barnabas Ahern, C.P., expressed misgivings about certain aspects of the draft *schema,* notably the failure to define more closely the relationship between the episcopate and the priesthood and the inadequate directives about priestly spirituality. Immediately after the meeting Hallinan suggested to the bishops that they compose a written intervention embodying the criticisms of the three *periti.* Twelve of the bishops signed the document and he submitted it in his name.[46]

During his stay in Rome he also took part in the deliberations of the International Committee on English in the Liturgy, briefly serving as chairman in succession to Archbishop Grimshaw who had died the previous March. By his own admission, the liturgy meetings were heavy going (much of the discussion centered on whether to use "thou" or "you" in the vernacular texts) and he did not stay in Rome until the final close of the Council. Instead he left for home on November 3 and immediately entered St. Joseph's Infirmary for two weeks of rest.[47]

While still in the hospital he wrote a candid assessment of the Council for the *Georgia Bulletin.* He was, of course, pleased with the documents on the liturgy, and with many others too, particularly those on the Church, Divine Revelation and Ecumenism. The Declaration on Religious Liberty was another source of satisfaction. He had recently been reading James Hennesey's book on the American bishops at the First Vatican Council, and he told his readers how Archbishop John B. Purcell of Cincinnati had fought for a similar declaration in 1870. "A magnificent step into the present century," he called it and said: "If Alfred Smith and John F. Kennedy had run for President today, they would have a lot less explaining to do."

On the other hand, he found the Decree on the Oriental Catholic Churches disappointing and singled out the Decree on Communications and the Declaration on Christian Education as the two weakest documents produced by the Council. "There is no fire in them," he complained, "and little relevance to two of the most dynamic areas in today's world—education and public communications." The Council was still in session as he was writing, and he reserved judgment on the final draft of the *schema* on the Church in the Modern World. "It is hard to see how it will turn out," he admitted. "It may be powerful; it may be a gesture. We must wait."

With the Council about to finish its work, Hallinan gave a glowing estimate of the impact that he expected it to have on the Church and on the world at large:

> Our homes and neighborhoods will find a new vitality. In increasing circles the city and state will be invigorated. Deep too will be the profound probing into our parish and the Archdiocese. The Church is changing, and with it, the world.

Like many of those inspired by the Council, he tended to minimize the difficulty of translating the conciliar documents into reality. The world at large proved to be considerably less receptive to the Church's overtures than he and many others had hoped. At the same time the ferment within the Church produced by the Council grew more serious and it became evident that the Council had been an unsettling experience for many Catholics who found themselves with old loyalties shaken and new expectations unfulfilled. Disillusioned progressives like Jacques Maritain would be complaining before long that the world seemed to be influencing the Church to a much greater extent than the Church was influencing the world. At the end of the Council, such a possibility was far from Hallinan's mind. He did seem to sense, however, that there would be many pitfalls on the road ahead, for he tempered his sunny forecast with the warning that: "We are living in rare times. They put upon us not just the joy and the excitement. They increase our responsibilities. Being a Catholic will no longer be easy."[48]

16

Odium Liturgicum

The liturgy of the Roman Rite changed more between 1963 and 1966 than during the previous 400 years. As late as 1959, Gerald Ellard, S.J., noticing the proliferation of missals at Mass, lamented that "we are in this country a Church of Silence during Sunday Mass." Before the Second Vatican Council, only the most sanguine liturgists hoped to see a vernacular liturgy in their lifetime. At the annual Liturgical Weeks, it was customary for them to discuss at length the mechanics of the "dialogue" Latin Mass, the highest form of participation that many of them ever expected to see. On the other hand, few people found the use of Latin oppressive. Even Godfrey Diekmann, O.S.B., one of the more vocal proponents of the vernacular liturgy, made it plain that he did not want to see Latin and Greek disappear entirely from the Mass. Almost all American Catholics agreed with him. Indeed, lay intellectuals often took a snobbish pride in acquiring enough knowledge of ecclesiastical Latin to appreciate the fine points of Gregorian Chant or to quote the Scriptures from the Vulgate or even to read the breviary in the same language as the clergy.[1]

In the mid-sixties such attitudes quickly became outdated. Between 1963 and 1965, the American bishops faithfully executed the Constitution on the Sacred Liturgy, thoroughly changing the shape of Catholic worship. The results were strangely mixed. Public opinion polls reported that most American Catholics welcomed the introduction of the vernacular, but, oddly enough, many of the liturgists were profoundly unhappy—more unhappy than they had been in 1963, despite the fact that many of their fondest dreams had become reality much more quickly than they could ever have anticipated.

John B. Mannion, the Executive Secretary of the Liturgical Conference, complained that Sunday Mass in most parishes was still as dull as ever. "What happened?" he asked. "Where is the bright new day? It has been dawn for several years and the dim glimmer in the East isn't getting any brighter."[2] Some focused their complaints on the fact that the Canon of the Mass was still in Latin. "In the liturgy, as it now stands," said one critic, "we have at the very center a massive hole, a very unfortunate period of silence."[3] The veteran liturgical promoter, Father Hans A. Reinhold, warned that further changes were imperative. "Unless the Mass is made more relevant," he predicted, "it will be passed by as antiquarian."[4] The editor of *Worship*, Father Aelred Tegels, O.S.B., expressed the sentiments of many when he admitted that the use of the vernacular had brought with it a disconcerting revelation: the change of language alone had not been enough to make the Mass accessible to many contemporary Christians. It was also necessary, Tegels said, to make far-reaching changes in the structure and content of the Mass. He thought that it was premature to attempt such changes at that time, however, since the requisite historical and sociological data were simply not available.[5]

Few American liturgists were as patient as Tegels. To many of them the deficiencies of the new Latin-English format seemed more glaring than those in the old Tridentine Rite. Liturgists compared the process of reform to turning on the lights in a neglected part of the house and suddenly discovering that the furnishings were more dingy and threadbare than they had suspected. Just as rank-and-file Catholics were absorbing the first round of liturgical changes in 1965, liturgists began to agitate for three additional innovations: (1) the use of modern music, (2) the use of the vernacular for the entire Canon of the Mass, (3) the freedom to experiment with the basic structure of the Mass in order to devise more appropriate forms of celebration. It was this last demand for "experimentation" that became a particularly sensitive issue, a battlecry for those dissatisfied with the new liturgy and a panacea for those anxious to make the Mass more "relevant" and "meaningful"—two frequently-invoked adjectives in the 1960's.

"The liturgy or liturgies of the future cannot be composed in advance or imposed from on high," said one speaker at the North American Liturgical Week of 1967. "They must emerge out of an authentic development from below." Such language was bound to disturb many bishops trained in a tradition of rubrical precision which specified uniform rules for the most minute details of liturgical celebration. The bishops were not likely to be reassured when the same speaker commented: "We are gradually becoming aware that a single perfectly chiseled and juridically prescribed liturgy may not be quite the thing for all seasons and all types of congregations."[6] Experimentation was a broad and nebulous term. Some scholars welcomed it as a necessary and useful way to identify and eliminate distortions which had crept into the liturgy over the centuries. Others, however, used the term to justify the most bizarre aberrations. This led some ecclesiastical authorities to dig in their heels at the very mention of the word, fearful that it would inevitably lead to anarchy and irreverence.

In the United States, at least, a definite polarization took place over the liturgy in the late 1960's. Observers noted the irony that the Eucharist—the source and symbol of Christian unity—had become one of the most divisive issues in the Church. Archbishop Hallinan was extremely proud of the work accomplished thus far by the American bishops and he was determined not to see it jeopardized by extremists on either the left or the right. As usual he tried to stake out a position somewhere in the middle—what he liked to call "the vital Christian center"—and he attempted to steer the Bishops' Commission on the Liturgical Apostolate in this moderate direction despite opposition from both radicals and reactionaries.

Church music was an area where resistance to change was especially strong and Hallinan found a valuable ally in Archabbot Rembert Weakland, O.S.B., the Chairman of the Music Advisory Board. The members of the board were deeply divided over the question of appropriate church music. Weakland complained that some of the laymen were more "monastic" than he was in their approach to Church music; others were accustomed to working with highly trained professional choirs and showed little interest in promoting congregational singing at Mass.[7] The use of folk music was especially controversial. When the board voted by a narrow margin in February 1966 to recommend the use of folk songs at Masses for high school and college students, one member of the board, Father Richard J. Schuler of the College of St. Thomas in St. Paul, Minnesota, wrote an impassioned protest to Hallinan. He predicted that "if we admit the folksong-guitar-hootennany, we are opening the door to further aberrations from the canons of good taste. . . . " Hallinan supported the decision of Weakland and the majority and explained to Schuler that "the whole spirit of the Constitution permits and even encourages such adaptation."[8]

Weakland and McManus were both concerned about the influence of the *Consociatio Internationalis Musicae Sacrae,* a semi-official organization with headquarters in Rome that was strongly opposed to the modernization of Church music. When the *Consociatio* asked the American bishops to designate a representative to serve on their board, Hallinan submitted the name of Weakland, much to the consternation of the officials of the organization. They pointed out that he was not even a private member and suggested that Hallinan designate someone else. Instead, Hallinan sent a stiff reply and threatened to take the case to the president of the National Conference of Catholic Bishops in the United States, if the *Consociatio* refused to accept Weakland as the American delegate. The acting president of that organization, Father José Lopez-Calvo, S.J., backed down and meekly suggested that "we could leave all this question for the time being."[9]

Since Weakland's own philosophy was so similar to his own, Hallinan gave him a free hand in running the Music Advisory Board and apologized for the fact that his health prevented him from offering more assistance. "I am unable to take on large-scale talks because of doctors' orders," he explained, "especially where some rough infighting would be involved."[10] Nevertheless, Hallinan was able to attend the Church Music Forum in Kansas City in November 1966, a meeting sponsored by both the Liturgical Conference and the Church Music Association of America. It proved to be something of a watershed in the history of Church music in this country. The highlight was an erudite address by Weakland in which he effectively demolished the theory that there was something especially supernatural about Gregorian Chant or Renaissance polyphony. "There is no music of a liturgical golden age to which we can turn," Weakland claimed, "because the treasures we have are the product of ages that do not represent an ideal of theological thinking in relationship to liturgy." He pleaded with church musicians not to seek "the holy in music by archaicism" and not to regard everything new and contemporary "as being somehow secular and profane." Hallinan thoroughly agreed with this approach and thanked the abbot for clarifying his own thoughts on the subject.[11]

Two months later came the long-awaited official Instruction on Church Music, a compromise document which showed clear traces of revisions by opposing factions in Rome. However, the very fact that it did not canonize Gregorian Chant or insist on the exclusive use of the organ at Mass represented a considerable victory for those who favored a more flexible approach to Church music. Hallinan hailed it, with a good deal of hyperbole, as "our last great hope for peace in the liturgical cold war now being waged." He urged all concerned to imitate the tolerant tone of the Instruction. "There is room in God's liturgical celebration for many mansions," he said. "There may be rooms for pipe organs; others for guitars. None of them will have piped-in Muzak."[12]

The archbishop was less pleased when Archbishop Dearden called his attention to another Roman document—an Instruction about the teaching of liturgy in seminaries. After reading it and noticing the heavy emphasis on Latin and Gregorian Chant, he told Dearden that he deplored the general spirit of the document which seemed to have little in common with the Constitution on the Liturgy. He felt so strongly about the shortcomings of the Instruction that he advised Dearden to poll the American bishops for their reaction. He also used the opportunity to outline his own thoughts about the place of Latin in the Church. "In my opinion," he told his friend in Detroit,

> Latin should be the normative language of the Latin Church for doctrinal matters and necessary documentation. As such, all seminarians should be able to read and write capably in Latin. But the basic flaw in priestly formation has been that Latin absorbed their public prayer and worship, as well as their textbooks and even classroom lectures, to the detriment of a sound grasp of the principles involved. Normally priests do not pray nor think nor speak in Latin. Neither do bishops.[13]

When Dearden was elected President of the National Conference of Catholic Bishops in 1966, Hallinan succeeded him as Chairman of the Bishops' Commission on the Liturgical Apostolate and gave the liturgical report at the bishops' meeting that year. It had become an annual ritual at these meetings for the bishops to vote on a shopping list of suggested liturgical changes. On this occasion Hallinan presented them with a list of thirteen changes, all of which they approved. Two were of major significance: a request for the use of English in the Canon, and a request for authorization to experiment with the structure of the Mass (subject in each instance to prior approval by the local ordinary) in "specific and controlled communities."[14]

The request for even this limited degree of experimentation was a bold move on the part of the American hierarchy. Less than a month before, Pope Paul VI had complained to a group of liturgists about unauthorized and arbitrary innovations in the liturgy, and he had called upon the Consilium to exercise vigilance over liturgical experimentation.[15] One of those in the audience was Cardinal Ritter, and on his return home to St. Louis he ordered a halt in experimental liturgies in his archdiocese. "It is obvious," he said, "that no priest or group of priests should presume to experiment with the liturgy."[16] It was precisely to prevent such abuses by individuals acting on their own authority that the bishops now voted for authorized experimentation. "Obviously," Hallinan explained in a statement at the end of the meeting, "the Constitution intends experimentation in order to achieve the most suitable form of liturgy in the light of liturgical research and the contemporary needs of the people."[17] He himself had consistently argued that the best way to counteract the proliferation of underground liturgies was for the bishops themselves to sponsor legitimate experimentation, and their vote on November 17, 1966, gave a qualified endorsement to this position.

He was under no illusions that it would be easy to obtain the permission from Rome. A few weeks later he told a reporter: "If we don't get it this time, I think we should ask again and we should keep asking." He compared himself to the beggar in the Gospel who kept pounding on the judge's door at night. The beggar was ultimately successful in getting a hearing because the judge was annoyed and wanted to get back to sleep. "I think there is no harm in putting ourselves in exactly that position," he explained. After all, he said:

> Ours is a very representative part of the Church universal. It is one of the largest hierarchies, one of the largest groups of Catholic people. And I think that our wishes, our own frame of mind should be given voice. And we should be able to ask questions and get an answer.[18]

While the American bishops were waiting for an answer, he told Dearden: "I suppose those of us who see them [the requests] as essential to American renewal should hold our arms extended in prayer while the battle rages in Rome, we in the role of Moses, the forces for reform in the role of Josue."[19] The Roman authorities were themselves disturbed by reports reaching them about the state of the liturgy in the United States. At the Liturgical Week in Houston in 1966, the secular press had given inordinate publicity to experimental Masses celebrated in hotel rooms by a few priests. The Liturgical Conference was blamed for these and other abuses, although it had not approved them and could hardly have prevented them, as Aelred Tegels noted, "without the active collaboration of the Houston police." Nevertheless, the Consilium, through its official organ, *Notitiae,* deplored the press accounts of the Houston meeting and observed that it was not the first time that such events had happened in conjunction with the Liturgical Weeks.[20]

The editor of *Worship* touched a raw nerve when he attributed the rash of unauthorized experiments partly to the dilatory procedures of the Consilium, which had yet to allow authorized experimentation under the direction of the bishops. A petulant notice in *Notitiae* reminded him that liturgical renewal was "not the work of one day nor a game for children."[21] The President of the Consilium, Cardinal Lercaro, himself entered the lists and urged Hallinan to use his new position as Chairman of the Bishops' Commission on the Liturgical Apostolate to bring the Liturgical Conference under the control of the hierarchy. Lercaro's message came through Archbishop Vagnozzi, who should have realized, even if Cardinal Lercaro did not, that this was really an impossible assignment.[22] The Liturgical Conference was a private lay organization and its leaders were in no mood meekly to surrender their autonomy to the Bishops' Commission.

Hard on the heels of Lercaro's letter came a Declaration from the Sacred Congregation of Rites and the Consilium calling attention to a wide variety of abuses in the liturgy, such as Masses in private houses and Masses "using strange and arbitrary rites, vestments and formulas, and sometimes accompanied by music of a totally profane and worldly character, not worthy of a sacred action."[23] The document got considerable attention in the secular press, which commonly reduced the two-page Declaration to the wildly inaccurate headline: "Pope Forbids Jazz Masses." John Mannion wrote a whimsical reply in the form of a dialogue between Finley Peter Dunne's famous bar-room characters, Martin Dooley and his friend Hennessey. "While I'm on the subject," Mr. Dooley said,

> and while you finish that beer, Hennessey, let me enlighten you a whit on that musical uproar. The only types that can rail against

guitars and folk music are types highly educated to believe that some sounds are holy, Hennessey, and some sounds are not. If they're right, then God have mercy on them orientals with their weird strings and gongs, and on them African drummers and gourd-shakers and on all the music makers outside of Eurpope. Ye'd think God took a music appreciation course at the Sistine Chapel and signed a pledge not to listen to anything His teachers didn't like....

In exasperation poor Hennessey cried: "But the Pope, Dooley, it was the Pope who was behind this!" "Oh," said Mr. Dooley, "someday we'll talk about who speaks for the Pope, Hennessey, and maybe someday we'll even hear from himself on that fascinatin' subject."[24]

Archbishop Vagnozzi was not amused. He sent an angry letter to Hallinan, denouncing the Mannion article as "simply unbelievable" and asserting that it only proved once again the urgent need for the bishops to gain control of the Liturgical Conference.[25] Any such capitulation was far from the mind of John Mannion. At that moment, he was offering, on behalf of the Conference, to launch a major educational effort in 1,000 carefully selected parishes across the country in order to rescue the parishioners from the liturgical obscurantism of their clergy.[26]

When the Bishops' Commission (now renamed the Bishops' Committee on the Liturgy) held their next meeting in February 1967, they had a full agenda and the almost impossible task of satisfying the Roman authorities (who were becoming more vociferous about the supposedly radical drift of the liturgical movement in this country) and disenchanted American liturgists like the editor of *Worship* (who were bemoaning the fact that the liturgical renewal had run out of steam).[27] Since the Roman Declaration of December 29th had caused such a furor, the Bishops' Committee explained that it was aimed at abuses and not at Masses in homes and neighborhood centers which had been authorized by the local bishop. The Committee put the best possible interpretation on the document by saying that "the condemnation of abuses must never obstruct desirable and necessary programs of liturgical renewal."[28]

An even more delicate question was the relationship between the Liturgical Conference and the Bishops' Committee. Lercaro had asked Hallinan to clarify this relationship, but the latter was too realistic to think that he could reduce the Liturgical Conference to an adjunct of the Committee (as Rome wished), nor did he want to do so. At the Committee meeting, Hallinan stressed the contributions of the Liturgical Conference to liturgical renewal in the United States and argued that the existing relationship between the Conference and the bishops was in harmony with the Constitution on the Liturgy and with subsequent Roman documents, including the guidelines issued by Lercaro himself in January 1965. All ten bishops on the Committee agreed with him and he was able to send Lercaro a strongly-worded defense of the Conference's activities. On the crucial question of more episcopal control, he told Lercaro:

> In the light of this splendid record of pioneering and servicing the liturgical renewal in the United States, it is our decision that no changes are needed in our relationship. Indeed it is my opinion, and one shared by many bishops, that the Church could not have introduced or carried out so effectively the spirit of the Liturgical Constitution had it not been for the generous work of the National Liturgical Conference....
>
> We are satisfied that the present situation is best for the Church. It follows the American pattern, so evident among our bishops at the Council, of all necessary consistent freedom. It avoids the precensorship of the activities of such groups. It has set a healthy, thoroughly Catholic precedent for other groups, such as the Canon Law Society and the Catholic Theological Society, which had not had the same experience before the Council.[29]

The question of liturgical experimentation also came up at the February meeting. Bishop Connare thought that every bishop should be authorized to designate some parishes as experimental liturgical centers, but Hallinan urged a more cautious approach. He indicated that experimentation was a more difficult process than many people realized and cited the experience of his own archdiocese and that of the Archdiocese of St. Louis with the experimental funeral rite recently authorized by Rome. The committee also discussed a request from the Passionist Fathers for experimental Masses in connection with their new parish mission program. Dearden told them that the question of liturgical experimentation might be discussed at the forthcoming Synod of Bishops and relayed the news that Bugnini was mildly optimistic about a favorable response to the other requests from the American bishops.[30]

Meanwhile unauthorized experimental Masses continued to make news and bishops continued to fret and fume over the breakdown of episcopal authority. At the suggestion of Archbishop Dearden, the Bishops' Committee decided to send every priest in the United States a letter of explanation. The first draft was composed by McManus: it was then shortened and refined by the bishops on the Committee. Hallinan sent a copy to every bishop and, at the April meeting of the hierarchy, he asked them to approve it. Despite objections from Krol who thought that it was weighted in favor of the innovators, it won overwhelming approval from the bishops and went out to every priest in the middle of May.[31]

The letter unequivocally condemned bizarre aberrations in the liturgy and declared that "unauthorized liturgical innovations are not genuine innovations at all. They are diversionary." However, the overall tone of the letter was constructive and fair; it also condemned the resistance of die-hard reactionaries. "There are still parishes which have almost totally neglected liturgical renewal.... No one should criticize the errors of the liturgical innovators without also criticizing the extreme apathy of the others."[32]

One of the more surprising reactions came from the *National Catholic Reporter:* it praised the bishops for their candor in admitting that further changes were needed and that the pace of change had been unnecessarily slow. Showing unwonted sympathy for the hierarchy, the editors pointed out that, in liturgical matters, the bishops of the country were facing a revolution of rising expectations and compared them to the leaders of many developing countries.[33]

The National Liturgical Weeks reached the height of their popularity in the late 1960's, drawing thousands of participants from all over the United States and Canada. They were a bellwether for the whole liturgical movement, closely watched by friend and foe alike. The 1967 Liturgical Week, scheduled for Kansas City, promised to be even more controversial than the Houston meeting of 1966, since the theme for the Week was "Experiments and Community." In fact the talks and workshops were relatively tame, except perhaps for Father Thomas Ambrogi's presentation of "A Mass of the Future." One of its leaders announced that the Liturgical Conference must be the bishops' loyal opposition (which was hardly the role envisioned for it by Vagnozzi), and at the closing Mass, there was loud applause for the homilist, Father John Corrigan of Washington, D.C., who called upon the bishops to lead the revolution already under way.[34] The very theme of the Week touched off a flurry of articles and editorials in the Catholic press calling for official approval of liturgical experimentation. An editorial in *America* succinctly stated: "The danger is that, if greater latitude is not granted officially ... eccentric or bizarre ceremonies will proliferate underground. Flexible, enlightened guidance, rather than tight regulations or crackdowns, would seem the truly pastoral need at this time."[35]

Unfortunately, neither Hallinan nor the Bishops' Committee could provide this kind of guidance until the Consilium approved their requests for controlled liturgical experimentation. Meantime, Hallinan hoped that he could at least obtain permission for the English Canon, but even here he was not immediately successful. By the summer of 1967, the situation was particularly awkward. Rome had granted permission in principle for the use of an English Canon but had not yet approved any specific version. As a result, many priests were taking matters into their own hands and using one of the many private translations that were available. When bishops and priests wrote to him for permission, Hallinan had to explain that he had no authority to give such permission until Rome designated an approved vernacular text.[36]

One of the bishops making this request was Charles Helmsing of Kansas City-St. Joseph, whose diocese was to be the host for the forthcoming Liturgical Week. As the date for that meeting drew closer, Hallinan became more and more impatient with the lack of a response from Rome. Finally, a week before the beginning of the Liturgical Week, he asked Dearden to intervene in Rome. He told him:

> We have worked hard, you and I and the other bishops to close the credibility gap between the bishops and both priests and laity deeply concerned with liturgical renewal. (I am not speaking of the lunatic fringe. I am speaking of the thousands who are studying, working, speaking and praying that the Church in America will not miss the boat.)
>
> I think that we are closing that gap. They know we are working on a dozen fronts; that we were the first to implement, extend, prepare and vote favorably on the vernacular; that we have kept up with the difficult job of implementation; and have staffed our dioceses with liturgical priests. Your leadership, and our Committee, and many

other United States bishops are getting through.

> Next week ... at the National Liturgical Conference thousands of these priests and laity will come together. They know about the steps we have taken ... and they will be praying and waiting for the first English Mass. Can we provide it both as a tribute to their own fidelity and as a rebuke to those who have jumped the gun, made up their own rules and offered our people a souped-up version of their own, not of the Church....

> As you know, John, I am intensely concerned about this development, and I think we should get loose of the bind in which we are being squeezed—the die-hards in Rome acting way beyond their competence and the irresponsibles at home who are way beyond theirs.[37]

The next day, after a telephone conversation with Dearden, Hallinan himself wrote to Lercaro. It took another month, though,—and a very strong letter from the Episcopal Chairman of I.C.E.L., Archbishop Gordon Gray, to the Pope—before the Consilium replied that it would permit the interim use of a single vernacular text of the Canon, provided that it was approved by the local ecclesiastical authorities.[38] At the next meeting of the Administrative Board of the National Conference of Catholic Bishops, Hallinan proposed that they adopt the I.C.E.L. text of the Canon (which had already been approved by ninety-five percent of the bishops).

He expected a perfunctory vote of approval, but, without warning, Cardinal O'Boyle insisted on reopening the whole question by proposing that the words of consecration be kept in Latin. Dearden repeatedly told him that he was out of order, which only made him more argumentative. Then Cardinal McIntyre came to O'Boyle's defense and both of them turned their guns on Hallinan. As he told his friend Bishop Connare, "There was very little support that an archbishop could call upon in the face of two cardinals, one of whom had simply repealed in his mind the documents of Vatican II, especially the Constitution *De Sacra Liturgia*." Connare and Dearden, together with Krol, threw their support to Hallinan, and the result was a compromise: a decision to poll the entire hierarchy once again—the second time in four months.[39] The ballots went out on September 13. On the following Monday, September 18, Dearden announced that the bishops had given their almost unanimous approval to the I.C.E.L.

text and that the use of the English Canon in the United States would begin on Sunday, October 15 (later changed to October 22).[40]

Hallinan turned next to the more difficult problem of experimentation. By this time Rome had rejected the American request of November 1966 to experiment with the structure of the Mass. Despite this refusal, he now formulated a twofold plan which called for (1) the establishment of experimental liturgical centers at several Catholic universities; and (2) authorization for every ordinary to set up an experimental center in his diocese.[41] In a letter to the other bishops on the Liturgical Committee, he insisted that such experimentation was urgently needed:

> We all know that an undergrowth of unauthorized experiments has spread across the country. Some is caused by willfulness, desire for novelty, impatience with delays and the cumbersome process now used. Many, however, in my opinion, of the most skilled have mistakenly gone underground because the present process is so slow. They love the Church.[42]

Only one member of the Committee, Bishop Leo Byrne of Wichita, voiced opposition to both proposals. There was general agreement on the Committee that the existing procedures for experimentation were inadequate. Most of the bishops gave guarded approval to Hallinan's first proposal about university liturgical centers, but they were considerably more skeptical about his second proposal giving every bishop a free hand to experiment in his own diocese in designated centers.[43] Nevertheless, Hallinan felt that he had enough support on the Committee to sound out the rest of the bishops on the subject.

Meantime, Cardinal O'Boyle was busy too, eclipsing McIntyre as the most visible opponent of liturgical changes when he issued a lengthy pastoral letter denouncing experimental liturgies in his archdiocese. "No one is to proceed faster than the Church authorizes," he warned. He outlawed the use at Mass of "electronically amplified string instruments" without explicit prior approval and announced that any priest who violated the liturgical regulations would *ipso facto* lose the faculty to celebrate Mass in the Archdiocese of Washington. For good measure he sent a copy of the pastoral to every bishop in the country.[44]

The cardinal also found himself on a collision course with Father Joseph Connolly, the newly-elected President of the Liturgical Conference. On September 19, 1967, the Board of Directors of the Liturgical Conference decided to hold the next Liturgical Week in Washington, D.C. When Connolly called upon O'Boyle to tell him the news, the cardinal informed him that the Liturgical Conference was a suspect organization and he forbade them to hold their convention in his archdiocese. Connolly told him that he had not come to ask for his permission, since none was required. None of this got into the newspapers, but Connolly was prepared to hold the 1968 Liturgical Week in Washington even if they would not be able to have Mass in conjunction with the proceedings.

Hallinan tried to play the role of mediator. He told O'Boyle politely but firmly:

> I am writing you, as I am sure you understand, not in any criticism of what you judge best in your archdiocese. I would have no right to meddle in this way. But your pastoral letter was sent to all the bishops and publicized widely. I regret that, due to your prominent position, it has introduced a negative note of disagreement on liturgical progress. Since an overwhelming majority of American bishops have endorsed this progress, many of your priests and people have been shocked and disappointed.

Hallinan asked O'Boyle to "excuse the impertinence of this letter, if it should strike you as such." He explained how much he had admired the cardinal's work for the social apostolate and for racial justice, and he mentioned that he had not forgotten his personal generosity to him in 1964 when he had been gravely ill. "These are the reasons why I am writing you this personal private letter," he said. "In the area which Vatican II called the source and summit of Christian life, I do not want to see you being typed as a bishop opposed to the development of the liturgy."[45]

Neither this letter nor a request to speak with him privately had any effect on O'Boyle. During the next meeting of the Administrative Board of the National Conference of Catholic Bishops, he rebuffed Hallinan's overtures to settle their differences quietly and remained one of the most vociferous critics of the proposals for liturgical experimentation.[46] Anxious to avoid a confrontation between the cardinal and the Liturgical Conference, Hallinan pleaded with Connolly to change the site of the 1968 Liturgical Week from Washington to some other city on the grounds that it would place the Conference, which has done so much good, in the position of a free-wheeling group, ready to disobey the local ordinary. This would be welcome chaff for the extremists on both sides. The irresponsible would cheer and applaud, not your rights but your boldness, and the recalcitrants would have more material for their dislike of liturgists in general.

He told Connolly that several bishops—longtime friends of the Liturgical Conference—had asked him to intervene with the Conference officials and urge them to change their plans. If the Board persisted in its decision to hold the next Liturgical Week in Washington, then, said Hallinan, he would withdraw his membership from the Conference. "I regret putting this so bluntly," he said, "but just as the members of the Board have their conscience, so have I."[47] He sent a copy of this letter to O'Boyle, but it did nothing to soften his intransigence. He remained as frosty as before.

Hallinan got word of another critic in the hierarchy, Archbishop Thomas Connolly of Seattle, who had been grumbling about the "continued machinations" of the Bishops' Committee on the Liturgy and had criticized Hallinan personally for going "too far . . . too fast." Hallinan held out an olive branch to him as he had done with O'Boyle. Expressing dismay and discouragement at Connolly's remarks, he offered to meet with him privately to iron out their differences and asked Connolly to separate the issue of liturgical renewal from his personal feelings toward him:

> I have written you, Archbishop, not to complain about unfair words like "machinations" nor to justify the careful work of the other members of the Bishops' Committee on the Liturgy. I write in the hope that I might induce you to work closely with us, giving of your own liturgical skills for the good of all. Our unity as the American hierarchy should not be something imposed from above. It should be an open and healthy coordination. It should be big enough to receive criticism and resolute enough to answer it.[48]

A full month before the annual meeting of the American hierarchy in November 1967, all the bishops received a brochure from Hallinan detailing liturgical changes that the Bishops' Committee was proposing for their consideration. When the bishops got around to discussing the sixteen proposed changes on the afternoon of November 13, there was anything but agreement. Hallinan's proposals for liturgical experimentation drew the most fire. He spent two-and-a-half hours defending them. He was prepared for opposition from O'Boyle and Connolly, but he was surprised to see Krol lined up against him also. Few of the progressives dared say a word, he complained, leaving him to carry the ball alone. Pickets from Father Gommar de Pauw's Catholic Traditionalist Society were marching up and down outside the building, carrying signs that said "With Shepherds Like These Who Needs Wolves?"

The following morning there was another two-and-a-half hour session on the liturgy during which Hallinan warned his colleagues that a vote to reject liturgical experimentation was really a vote to break off dialogue with the priests most interested in liturgical renewal. His eloquence paid off. The bishops approved both proposals by handsome margins, but he paid a heavy price for his victory. By lunch time he was physically and emotionally exhausted and asked Dearden to appoint an *ad hoc* committee to define the purpose of the Bishops' Committee on the Liturgy. "Was it supposed to furnish leadership, initiative, and experimentation," he asked, "or to ride herd on undisciplined litniks?" Somehow he managed to keep his sense of humor and he told the readers of the *Georgia Bulletin* of an amusing incident in a Washington hotel. One bishop on his way to say Mass saw another in his pajamas at the door of his hotel room. "Listen, Frank," he said, "I'm all for these experimental Masses, but this is ridiculous."[49]

At the end of the month Hallinan flew to Rome for a meeting of I.C.E.L. and he had an opportunity to talk to Cardinal Cicognani. He found the papal Secretary of State as friendly as ever but extremely cautious. Hallinan tried to tell him the facts about the state of the liturgy in the United States as he saw them, but he came away convinced that he had made little or no impression. A few days later, however, he and Archbishop Denis Hurley, O.M.I., of Durban, South Africa, had an interview with Cicognani's chief aide, Archbishop Giovanni Benelli, which went much better, and Hallinan left for home feeling more optimistic about the prospects for liturgical experimentation in the United States.[50]

He set to work at once at the job of selecting three or four universities for the experimental centers. Almost a hundred institutions had expressed interest in the project. The University of Notre Dame was at the top of his list of the most suitable candidates, but he also gave strong consideration to Fordham University, Boston College, the College of the Holy Cross and St. John's College, Collegeville, Minnesota.

When the acting Rector of the Catholic University of America, Father John P. Whalen, said that he hoped to form a liturgical center there, he was delighted. He told Whalen that he had been trying for three years to get the university to sponsor an Institute of Liturgical Studies.[51]

As he carefully explained to the university presidents, all his plans were dependent on receiving approval from Rome. He got some indication of what to expect when the Consilium turned down a similar request from the Canadian bishops at the end of December.[52] Then, while he still awaited an answer, the Liturgical Conference leveled a blow at the American bishops, blaming them in an open letter for the "continuing absence of significantly open, creative, vigorous leadership." At a press conference Father Connolly was especially critical of the hierarchy's unwillingness to permit experimentation. He refused to accept the explanation that Rome had tied their hands. "If the bishops say that Rome won't let us," he commented, "then I would say to the bishops: 'Change Rome!'" Although Connolly specifically exempted Hallinan and the Bishops' Committee on the Liturgy from his criticism, Hallinan was furious at his remarks. "Joe Connolly's latest tantrum," he called it.[53] Publicly, however, he avoided polemics. Admitting that the Liturgical Conference had put its finger on a real problem, he asserted that everyone—not only the bishops—could do more to advance the cause of liturgical renewal. In a conciliatory gesture he invited the Liturgical Conference to submit concrete proposals to the Bishops' Committee.[54]

Hallinan sent urgent follow-up letters to both Bugnini and Benelli early in January, emphasizing that seventy-five percent of the United States bishops had approved the two proposals for experimentation.[55] Two weeks later Bugnini informed him regretfully that the Consilium had turned down both proposals. He was almost apologetic about conveying the bad news. "I am in complete sympathy with the liturgical state of affairs in the United States," he said, "and want to do whatever I possibly can to cooperate with your admirable endeavors." He promised that every individual request for experimentation would receive a response as "quickly as our postal service makes possible."[56] Despite Bugnini's efforts to soften the blow, the refusal was a bitter disappointment to Hallinan. He told Bishop Dougherty that he would take Bugnini up on his offer of prompt service. "The reply will probably be 'No,'" he predicted, "but it would be reassuring not to wait a year to get it."[57] With Dearden he was even more candid and complained that

"Rome's failure to grasp the seriousness of our problem is incredible despite Father Bugnini's soothing words." He feared too that the Consilium would only become more timid and more rigid under the leadership of its newly appointed President, Cardinal Benno Gut, O.S.B. "From my recollection," said Hallinan, "he will be no bargain. As one American bishop characterized it, 'The liturgy has been gutted.'"[58]

By this time Hallinan was back in the hospital again—for the sixth time in four years. He found the strength nevertheless to send Bugnini a long letter, asking him to reopen the whole question with Cardinal Gut and with the Pope. He also called Bugnini's attention to the damaging effect that the decision had had on the whole concept of collegiality, so recently endorsed at the Council. He told Bugnini that many bishops, priests and lay people in the United States were asking: "Of what significance is the collegiality of an episcopal conference, if our reasonable requests, sought by so many, are bluntly refused?" Then he tried to describe the demoralizing effect of the Consilium's decision on liturgical renewal in this country:

> The future of young priests and seminarians, already critical here as it is elsewhere, simply cannot be visualized by someone not in the United States. Our priests are loyal, eager for the renewal, and ready to work hard and faithfully. They have taken seriously the spirit of the Constitution. Now, in their opinion, it is becoming meaningless. Excessive caution, they feel, has been substituted for loyal and orderly, but creative, action.
>
> Many will go underground. Hopeless, unstructured, irresponsible liturgy will thrive. Secret Masses of no sound liturgical tradition will multiply. Some will likely write and speak openly and derisively of the needless dilemma. Others will bury their frustrations in bitterness. A few of the best priests will do as they are told, but with dullness, not joy. I do not exaggerate....[59]

In a newspaper interview at the same time, Hallinan spoke candidly of his difficulties. He still bristled at Joseph Connolly's charge that the bishops were not doing enough for liturgical renewal. "Every bishop in the country is furious at that statement," he said, "because they know what we are doing." While admitting that many bishops could do more (He rated only thirty or forty of them as "top-rate modern renewal men."), he pointed to his own performance at the last bishops' meeting. "I am pretty sure that I am here today [in St. Joseph's Infirmary]," he said, "because of that November meeting of the bishops. That was a real rugged business. I was up there for six hours on the podium fighting for these experimentations." He also revealed how Vagnozzi had pressured him to muzzle the Liturgical Conference. "I was ordered practically to tell them to cease," he said, "but I wouldn't do it. I fought back." Turning to the question of experimentation, he repeated his criticism of those who violated liturgical rules and regulations. That is disobedience, said Hallinan, "and disobedience means that I, John Doe, place myself above the living Church. It can't be anything else." He mentioned how he had alerted Rome to the gravity of the situation in the United States and repeated his fear that "we are creating a generation of disobedient priests."[60] Nevertheless, there was no reprieve, and Hallinan's failure to sway Rome became public early in March.[61]

Despite his deep personal disappointment over the rejection of his proposals, Hallinan had no intention of taking the law into his own hands or encouraging others to do so. He was too honest to pretend that he agreed with the decision of the Consilium but too loyal to countenance defiance of legitimate ecclesiastical authority. In breaking the news of the Consilium's answer to the priests of his own archdiocese, he said: "I realize that it is painful to wait while our liturgy develops and grows; but we must be true sons of the Church, perhaps showing discontent if necessary, but not disobedience."[62] Three weeks later he was dead.

There was near unanimity among the American bishops in the late 1960's that they had a crisis on their hands because priests throughout the country were conducting unauthorized experiments with the liturgy. It came as a terrible shock to them because such behavior would have been unthinkable in the years before the Second Vatican Council when the clergy had observed the liturgical regulations with scrupulous fidelity. The bishops were upset not only at the challenge to their own authority but at the scandal caused by irreverent and even sacrilegious distortions of the public worship of the Church.

While there was near unanimity that they were facing a crisis, there was uncertainty on how to handle it. Some old-fashioned prelates like McIntyre and O'Boyle favored a heavy-handed assertion of episcopal authority and rejected the very idea of experimentation with the liturgy. Others, perhaps a majority of the bishops and certainly a majority of those on the Bishops' Committee on the Liturgy, recognized the inadequacies of the *Ordo Missae* and wanted modifications in it, but they feared that any experimentation might play into the hands of the extremists. Hallinan belonged to neither camp. On the one hand, he saw no merit at all in the authoritarian approach of O'Boyle and McIntyre; indeed, he was convinced that it would only aggravate the situation by swelling the ranks of the dissidents. On the other hand, he did not share the apprehensions of many other bishops that any concessions would be interpreted as a sign of weakness; hence his openness to new styles of music in the liturgy, and his efforts to obtain permission for the Canon in English and for officially approved experimentation. He was convinced that by such measures the bishops could steal the thunder from the radicals and satisfy the legitimate demands of those interested in the liturgy. He hoped that once American Catholics saw the bishops responding to their needs in this way, they would cease to look elsewhere for direction. That was his notion of positive episcopal leadership.

He told a friend in the summer of 1967: "We have built a good rapport now between the liturgists and the bishops. I see my job as one of pushing, and yet holding the confidence of the majority for the tremendous work ahead."[63] His last great service to the liturgical movement in this country was the proposals made at the bishops' meeting in 1967, especially his plans for liturgical experimentation. He convinced the majority of his colleagues (and probably Bugnini as well) that he was right. That he was unable to convince the other authorities in Rome hardly detracts from the wisdom of what he was advocating.[64]

17

Church and Community

During these last two hectic years of his life, while Archbishop Hallinan was struggling with the problems of liturgical renewal on the national level, he was never in good health. He was suffering now from diabetes as well as hepatitis. On New Year's day of 1966, he wrote in his diary: "[I] really don't ask for much except more tolerance of spiritual pain, not physical—to practice serenity no matter what." Dr. Wilber gradually allowed him to assume more and more duties but he never returned to a full schedule. In the spring of 1966, he was still permitted to spend only four hours a day at the office (and ten hours a day out of bed).[1]

He had already asked the Holy See for an auxiliary bishop and Archbishop Vagnozzi had told him in January that he would almost certainly get the man of his choice: Joseph Bernardin, his former chancellor in Charleston. The two of them spent several days together in Atlanta in early March, and formal announcement was made of Bernardin's appointment as auxiliary Bishop of Atlanta on March 9. It was highly unusual for a see as small as Atlanta to have an auxiliary bishop and even more unusual for the ordinary to select one from outside the diocese, but Vagnozzi realized that Hallinan needed help. He told Hallinan that the only opposition had come from one un-named official in Rome who feared that Bernardin would be too much like his new ordinary.[2] Bernardin at once took over many of the routine episcopal chores in Atlanta, which allowed Hallinan more time for a project that he had been considering even before the close of the Second Vatican Council—the calling of a diocesan synod. He had hesitated to pursue the project then because canon law restricted membership in the synod to the clergy, and he wanted to give the laity some voice in the proceedings. The idea occurred to him that nothing prevented the calling of a Laymen's Congress first, at which representatives of the laity would have the opportunity to make recommendations for the synod, and in the summer of 1965 he had chosen thirty laymen to begin the process. He left them pretty much on their own and as free as possible from clerical interference. Each of the four *ad hoc* committees into which they had formed themselves drew up a long list of recommendations. In January 1966, after elections held in every parish, the appointed members on the four committees were replaced by elected members. At open parish meetings, the committeemen explained their work and sampled reactions on the local level. They then rewrote their committee reports on the basis of what they had heard in the parishes, and the whole process was repeated to permit a second round of suggestions from the parishes before the Lay Congress opened in the old Biltmore Hotel on May 20.

Enthusiasm among the lay representatives ran high when they realized that the proceedings were not to be a charade but a genuine attempt to sound out the views and opinions of the laity. Before the opening, they had an opportunity to deepen their own understanding of the issues by attending a series of workshops to which Hallinan invited such specialists as his friend Archbishop Guilford Young, Father Barnabas Ahearn, C.P., Father Joseph Connolly of the Liturgical Conference, and Martin Work of the National Council of Catholic Men.[3]

Hallinan gave the Lay Congress an ecumenical flavor by inviting Dr. William Cannon, Dean of the Candler School of Theology at Emory University, to give the keynote address. He also invited fifty Protestant, Orthodox and Jewish observers to the plenary sessions as well as all the priests of the archdiocese and a large representation of sisters. At the opening session the archbishop welcomed the delegates and assured them that the clergy was present, not to dominate the discussions, but to listen and to learn. He had arranged it this way, he said, because:

> Vatican II calls for it and the tradition of the laity in North Georgia more than justifies it.... Over a century ago this region felt the strong, optimistic force of one of our greatest American bishops,

John England of Charleston. From 1822 to 1842 the diocese was administered by bishop, priests and laymen. Like our own Lay Congress, England's annual conventions brought together elected delegates under the presidency of the bishop. Like our own, each parish had its own board of elected laymen.[4]

Over the next three days the seventy-two representatives discussed the committee reports section by section. The debates were often lively and resulted in extensive revisions of the reports before they were adopted. The final statement of the Lay Congress consisted of forty-four single-spaced pages of detailed recommendations which included such matters as more efficient organization of the central offices of the archdiocese and the establishment of elected councils in every parish. The Lay Congress also requested the appointment of lay auditors who would attend the sessions of the synod and then form an Appraisal Committee to decide (with the archbishop's approval) whether a second Lay Congress should be convened.[5]

The preparation for this Lay Congress stimulated so much interest that Hallinan decided to hold a similar gathering for the sisters. At the beginning of May, over 200 sisters from fourteen different communities took part in a two-day Sisters' Congress, which produced another lengthy report, including a request for an Archdiocesan Sisters' Council. Still a third meeting took place in late September, the Young Adults' Congress, which attracted only a few dozen participants and produced the only radical recommendations—requests for optional clerical celibacy and general absolution in the sacrament of penance.[6]

After these elaborate preparations, Hallinan finally opened the synod with a Mass in the cathedral on Sunday, November 20, 1966. Auditors from the three congresses attended all the sessions as did Protestant, Orthodox and Jewish observers as well as guests from other dioceses. In fact, every Catholic in the archdiocese was invited to be present at the synod so that, in Hallinan's fulsome phrase: "the decree that it will produce will be *of* God's people, *by* God's people and *for* God's people."[7] For three days the 100 priests present voted on a wide variety of proposals, grouped into six chapters: the People of God, the Archdiocese of Atlanta, Parishes, Clerical Life, Christian Formation, and the Church in the Community.

A tense moment occurred early in the procedings when Father Dale Freeman asked the synod to take up the question of clerical celibacy. This was carrying democracy too far for Hallinan. He refused to allow any "casual polling" of the priests on the issue, but he agreed to have the Priests' Senate make a detailed study of it and promised to send the results to Rome.[8] Hallinan attended all the sessions, staying up each day until three o-clock in the morning working with the Steering Committee as it revised and rewrote the draft resolutions.

Perhaps the most impressive work of the synod was the recommendation for "a shared exercise of authority" through elected boards and councils. The creation of a Priests' Senate, Sisters' Council, and elected parish councils was the direct result of this initiative as was the establishment on the diocesan level of a Pastoral Council, Administrative Council, and five boards (responsible for education, social services, development, communications and lay organization). Hallinan lost no time in establishing these consultative bodies. Here he had an opportunity to emulate John England's policy of involving the laity in the administration of the diocese: of the seventy-three members of the archdiocesan councils and boards fifty-nine were laymen (elected to their posts in parish elections on January 29, 1967), and the chairmen of all seven bodies were laymen.[9]

The presence of a dozen Protestant, Orthodox and Jewish observers at the synod—including Randolph G. Claiborne, Jr., the Episcopal Bishop of Georgia—was the result of Hallinan's own involvement in ecumenical activities. By this time he had established friendly relations with many of Atlanta's religious leaders, and he had accepted invitations to speak at several Protestant churches and at the Temple, the city's biggest synagogue. Indeed, within a few months of his arrival in Atlanta, he had set up a Commission on Christian Unity which included both clergy and prominent laymen such as Robert Troutman Sr. and Judge Sam McKenzie. Like most Catholics of his generation, the archbishop was groping for the right approach to ecumenical activities and he told Father Vincent Brennan, S.M., the first Chairman of the Commission on Christian Unity, that the members "must be by temperament courteous and friendly to others, yet absolutely loyal to the magisterium of the Church."[10] A year later, when Hallinan issued ecumenical guidelines to the priests of the archdiocese, he reminded them that the canon law on *communicatio in sacris* remained in force and he ruled out any active participation in non-Catholic worship. Nevertheless, he encouraged his clergy to take part in discussions with non-Catholics (provided that they had the opportunity to present the full Catholic position) and he gave his special blessing to Catholic participation in interdenominational efforts to promote racial and social justice.[11]

During the course of the Second Vatican Council, Catholic relations with Protestant and Orthodox Christians had improved to such a degree that Hallinan felt free to join them in a series of services for the Week of Prayer for Christian Unity of 1966. Six Protestant churches, one Orthodox church, and the Cathedral of Christ the King all scheduled services at eight o'clock each evening and invited the members of all eight congregations to attend them. Hallinan had no qualms about Catholic participation. He himself went to a service at the Covenant Presbyterian Church one evening and he told his priests:

> Our people are urged to attend them all, not just the Catholic service. We go, not out of curiosity or even fellowship—we go to pray that, in God's good time, "all may be one." We go as Catholics, in no way diminishing the certitude of our faith, but we pray as brothers.[12]

The synod had a relatively easy task in defining the Catholic position on ecumenism. It had at its disposal the conciliar Decree on Ecumenism and the guidelines of the United States Bishops' Commission for Ecumenical Affairs as well as Hallinan's own Archdiocesan Directory on Ecumenism, a twenty-one page directive which had appeared earlier that year. As a practical matter, the synod distinguished three areas of contact with non-Catholics and laid down specific rules for each: common prayer and cooperation in civic activities were encouraged; intercommunion was strictly forbidden; and common worship was permitted under certain circumstances.[13] One such occasion, Hallinan thought, was the 450th anniversary of the Reformation. On October 31, 1967, when the Lutherans in Atlanta were preparing to celebrate the anniversary of the posting of the Ninety-Five Theses in Wittenberg, he invited them to hold a joint service with the Catholics at the Cathedral of Christ the King. Over 800 people attended the service conducted jointly by several Lutheran ministers together with Hallinan and Bernardin. As he reflected on the event afterward, the archbishop said: "We have prayed and sung together. Isn't it time we studied and talked and dialogued together?"[14]

The good will engendered by such a gathering was likely to make someone of Hallinan's temperament overly optimistic, tempting him to underestimate the obstacles to Christian unity. But it did not take much to jolt him back to reality. A year earlier, after speaking to a

Greek Orthodox clergyman who was decidedly cool to any attempts at Catholic-Orthodox rapprochement, Hallinan sadly concluded: "A few dialogues here and there, a few theological discussions in the future will not bring us together."[15] The greatest asset that the archbishop brought to ecumenism was his own engaging personality, which won him the respect and friendship of some of Atlanta's leading clergymen. One of them was Rabbi Jacob Rothschild of the Atlanta Temple with whom he worked on many community projects. At Rothschild's request, he gave a talk at the Temple on "The Vatican Council and the Jews." After explaining the background and content of the Council's statement on the Jews, Hallinan candidly expressed his own disappointment at the negative reaction of some Jewish leaders. Then, turning to the local scene in order to end on a positive note, he suggested to the congregation that Jews and Catholics could make a distinctive contribution to Atlanta:

> We happen to be among the smallest of the religious congregations. But we also happen to be sensitive to injustice, both bodies conscious (because of our past) of [the] present sufferings of the Negro, the poor, the foreigners, the oppressed—keen to explore new paths of equality, freedom, justice and love.[16]

The speech was vintage Hallinan and a model for any Catholic prelate addressing a non-Catholic audience: first a clearcut exposition of the Catholic position, then an honest admission of what he found disappointing on the other side, and finally an appeal for joint action in areas where they could find agreement. Unfortunately, he was not always that crisp or that clear on the subject of ecumenism, especially when his own ebullient nature led him to overlook some of the thorny issues which stood in the way of Christian unity. His optimism on the subject was certainly not due to ignorance or superficiality, for he was well aware of the theological obstacles in the path of ecumenism. After a long conversation with Paul Tillich aboard the liner *United States* on his way to Rome in 1963, Hallinan had identified the question of authority as the central issue dividing Protestants from Catholics, and he saw no easy solution to the problem. On another occasion, he warned Catholics that:

> Ecumenism is not a knocking off of rough edges, a watering down of belief. Love of God and fellow man—the heart of the Christian

life—becomes nothing more than sentimentality, unless it is seeking for truth.[17]

Hallinan never repudiated these cautionary warnings, but he sometimes spoke as if he believed that dialogue and good will alone were sufficient to surmount most of the problems associated with ecumenism. "All over the Christian world there are stirrings toward the unity of Christ," he said with satisfaction in 1965. "To a Catholic or Protestant long concerned with the four-century frustration of Our Lord's will, this seems incredible." A year later, he had high hopes for the discussions initiated by the American Catholic bishops with the Lutherans, Presbyterians, Methodists and Episcopalians. At about the same time, he spoke of his own plans for an Ecumenical Center in downtown Atlanta. "It is our task," he said, "to open up new approaches to Protestant and Orthodox churches, and especially to the Jews, and to other non-Christians." Progress proved to be more difficult than he had anticipated; some of his optimism now seems fatuous; yet Hallinan made a genuine contribution to religious tolerance and mutual understanding on the local level simply by his warm and open approach to the problem.[18]

The Ecumenical Center (and the rest of the downtown Catholic Center), which had figured so prominently in Hallinan's plans during his first few years in Atlanta, was never built, partly because of the need to divert funds to the financially strapped parochial school system, and partly because of his failure to come up with a satisfactory development plan. Fortunately, he did live to see two other projects successfully completed: a new Catholic Center at the University of Georgia and new facilities for the Village of St. Joseph, an archdiocesan institution for retarded children.

During Hallinan's years in Atlanta, the Catholic school system in the United States began to show signs of serious trouble. The rapid expansion of the 1950's had come to an end; enrollment reached its peak in the mid-1960's and then began to decline from 5,600,000 students in 1965 to 3,200,000 in 1980. At the same time Catholics were more inclined to take a critical view of their schools and to complain of large classes, outmoded curricula and—a new phenomenon in the 1960's—large numbers of poorly paid lay teachers who were replacing the dwindling numbers of religious. The bishops were as much concerned as any parent. In Cincinnati, Archbishop Karl Alter eliminated the lower grades in some schools in order to provide better education in the upper grades; and in St. Louis, Cardinal Ritter declared a three-year moratorium on the construction of new parochial schools. The situation became so serious that in 1967 the bishops felt the need to issue a statement reaffirming their commitment to the continuation of the parochial school system in this country.[19]

The Archdiocese of Atlanta had to face the same educational problems as the other dioceses across the country but with far fewer resources than most of them. Hallinan did what he could to improve existing conditions: he raised teachers' salaries, instituted new financial and budgetary procedures, limited class size to forty pupils and urged pastors to establish parish school boards. Even after making these housekeeping reforms, however, he had grave doubts about the future of the Catholic school system in Atlanta and he expressed them publicly in a position paper which appeared in the *Georgia Bulletin* in the spring of 1966. He quoted with approval a recent remark of Father Theodore Hesburgh, the President of the University of Notre Dame, that "we Catholics should not take on any education that we can't do well." "You can't serve God with mediocrity," he added. Hallinan's old hero, Bishop Gilmour had made the same point a century earlier, when he had criticized the "Catholic Roof Theory of Education"—the attempt to place every Catholic child in a Catholic school, no matter how poor the quality of the education.

It was a practical matter which led the archbishop to clarify his own thoughts on the subject. He had recently established the new parish of the Holy Cross in the Atlanta suburb of Chamblee and some parishioners had raised the question of building a parochial school. The pastor, Father Leonard Mayhew, was skeptical about the wisdom of the proposal and so was the archbishop. After consulting with the parishioners, Hallinan decided instead to build a School of Religion, a permanent facility to provide religious instruction for the Catholic children in the public schools. The building was to be designed in such a way that it could be converted into a parochial school in the future, if that ever seemed advisable. For Hallinan the experiment had many advantages, and if it was successful, he hoped to repeat it in other new parishes. As he explained to the people of the archdiocese: "We cannot continue to build and operate Catholic schools by an across-the-board assessment on all Catholics only to close our doors to many because of increased tuition and a single academic standard that works against the average student."

When the archbishop inaugurated the experimental School of Religion in Chamblee, he announced that there would be no elimination or "phasing out" of existing Catholic schools, but he promised that the archdiocese would try to make every Catholic school as good as it possibly could be. Even in new parishes, he declared that he would consult the people "by the American process of deliberation" before deciding whether to build a parochial school or a School of Religion. It was obvious, however, that he had high hopes for the Chamblee experiment and thought that it offered a solution to the dilemma faced by more and more bishops throughout the country: how to provide children with Catholic education without depriving them of a good secular education or imposing a crushing financial burden on their parents.[20]

While Hallinan was pondering the fate of his school system, the civil rights movement in the United States was entering a new and more disturbing phase. In 1966 young black radicals like Stokely Carmichael began to promote Black Power in opposition to Martin Luther King's call for interracial brotherhood; white extremists shot and wounded James Meredith, the first black student at the University of Mississippi; during the summer racial riots erupted in many Northern cities. Black violence and threats of black violence spawned a white backlash, which led Congress to refuse President Johnson's request for further civil rights legislation. In Georgia old-fashioned politics enjoyed one last success with the election as governor of Lester Maddox, a die-hard segregationist who had closed his Atlanta restaurant rather than serve blacks. His triumph in November 1966 came, said Mayor Allen, "just when we needed him the least."

A Bible-quoting fundamentalist and high school dropout, Maddox had been a slightly risible figure in Georgia politics for years, twice defeated in attempts to become mayor of Atlanta. His election as governor was an acute embarrassment to the city of Atlanta, where many people regarded his election as the revenge of the "wool hats" in the conservative rural areas. Nobody was more shocked than Allen, who epitomized the new image that Atlanta had created for itself. "I was interested in seeing Atlanta grow," said the mayor, "but he was primarily interested in seeing Atlanta segregated."[21] During the gubernatorial election campaign of 1966, Hallinan never mentioned Maddox by name but nobody who read his column in the *Georgia Bulletin* could have had any doubts about his views. The archbishop pointedly reminded Catholics that they could not ignore moral issues in politics. In the aftermath of racial riots in Cleveland in the spring of 1966, he warned them that the same disturbances could occur in Atlanta unless they improved economic and social conditions in the black communities.[22]

A month before the election, Hallinan issued a statement, declaring that "the honest Catholic cannot support segregation in any way." Still avoiding any mention of Maddox by name, he added: "This is not politics; it is morality." He also pointed out that the Church had not raised the issue of segregation: it had become "the official stand, name and policy of a political candidate and the movement that has suddenly espoused him." When asked by reporters if the statement applied to Maddox, he replied: "It applies to any political candidate with that stand."[23]

Maddox tried to brush off the statement with the claim that he enjoyed widespread Catholic support. "I have Catholics supporting me all over the state," he said. "I don't call them dishonest. I call them good Georgians." Affecting to be more hurt than angry at the archbishop's remarks, he said: "It sounds like maybe he's been getting instructions from Mayor Allen and Martin Luther King."[24] Hallinan received considerable backing for his stand from both Catholics and non-Catholics in Atlanta; but, he commented, "twenty feet outside the Atlanta city limits it's Maddox country and I have had my share of abuse." He got even more abuse when the Los Angeles *Times* carried the story on the front page together with a picture of Hallinan. The story provoked some fifty people in Southern California to write hate-filled letters to Hallinan, including one with a Hitler mustache and haircut painted on his photograph and a note that a copy had been sent to Rome.[25]

Neither Maddox nor his Republican opponent, Howard H. Callaway, won a majority of the popular vote, forcing the election into the state legislature where the huge Democratic majority gave the victory to Maddox. Inauguration Day was a sad occasion for many Georgians, but the *Georgia Bulletin* reminded its readers that every Catholic owed proper respect and obedience to legitimate civil officials. "No citizen has a right to disobey civil law unless the law is clearly unjust," said the newspaper, but "no official may rule on the basis of unjust law."[26]

Lester Maddox surprised his critics by giving Georgia a better administration than they had expected. Some said that he proved that Georgia did not need a governor, since he left administration largely in the hands of the bureaucrats and legislators while he toured the state whipping up publicity for himself. Despite Maddox, Atlanta escaped the worst ravages of the "long hot summers" of 1966 and 1967 which brought havoc to many Northern cities. In the latter year alone racial riots left forty-three dead in Detroit and twenty-five dead in Newark. Atlanta remained relatively quiet throughout this period thanks to an enlightened city government and effective action on the part of both white and black civic leaders. Mayor Allen also attributed the city's good fortune to a generous measure of luck, because Atlanta possessed all the ingredients for a serious racial conflagration. As in the ghettos of the North, the city was full of poor blacks who had migrated there from the rural areas of Alabama and Georgia looking for a better life and often finding only frustration and poverty. In the emotionally charged atmosphere of the late 1960's almost any incident could trigger a serious racial disturbance in a city which never had more than 300 policemen on duty at one time. Twice, on one June evening in 1967, Hallinan nearly found himself in the center of a riot. As he described it later for John Tracy Ellis:

> [I] had just returned from an exciting evening [on] the Mayor's Human Relations Commission at the Tabernacle Baptist Church, crossed swords with an angry Negro preacher-cum-politician and caused a slight riot when a number of the community still wanted to speak. So when I was asked to close with a prayer, I made a motion to continue the meeting instead. A little while after that a rumble started outside. (This is Boulevard Avenue where the riots were last summer.) A six year old Negro boy had been hit by a truck driver (white) and knocked to the street. About seventy had gathered in a foul mood. We got an ambulance, and I drove the mother and grandmother and three other little kids to the hospital. It looked bad when I left after an hour: [I] hope he makes it. Of such stuff are riots made.[27]

Mayor Allen had formed a Community Relations Commission in November 1966, and Hallinan agreed to serve on it. He took his duties seriously and soon became embroiled in a bitter dispute between the Atlanta School Board and local black leaders who were protesting the overcrowding in predominantly black schools. At one meeting the blacks took offense and marched out of the room after a remark by the attorney for the School Board. Hallinan followed them and asked them to return. State Senator Leroy Johnson said the remark had been "an insult to us all." Hallinan replied: "He insulted me too, but if we can't sit down and talk, I don't know in God's heaven who can." At Hallinan's insistence, the blacks changed their minds and told Hallinan: "In deference to you, we will come back, if the school attorney is asked to leave." The attorney left, the meeting resumed and Atlanta moved a little bit closer to the peaceful resolution of a highly volatile problem.[28]

A year after its creation the Community Relations Commission nearly foundered when the members failed to reappoint the Executive Director, Mrs. Eliza K. Paschall, to another one-year term. The black members protested the decision and forced the resignation of the Chairman, Irving K. Kaler, leaving the Commission leaderless and dispirited. Hallinan was very upset and said in his newspaper column:

> As a citizen I deeply regret that the roof fell in. But as a member of one year, I have a more profound sorrow. I knew the zeal of both the Negroes and whites who were associated with us.
>
> Together we visited deprived neighborhoods and tried to ease grievances. We worked with our executive committee during the Dixie Hills trouble. We fought for an end to half terms [in public schools] and other discrimination against Negroes.[29]

He urged Mayor Allen to rebuild the Commission as quickly as possible, pledging his own full support. He told the mayor: "I have never been associated with a program which I felt was more keenly needed." One of the black members of the Commission was the Reverend Samuel Williams, Pastor of the Friendship Baptist Church, who continued to support the Commission despite opposition from more radical black leaders. Hallinan told him how much he admired his courage and said:

> God knows the endless record of injustice to the Negro people and the agonizing slowness of progress even now. But we had begun; we worked together; we even had in a short year, on a limited budget and with little authority, some limited victories.[30]

By the end of 1966 many Americans were turning their attention from the civil rights movement to another and more pressing problem:

American involvement in the war in Vietnam. As the number of American troops there increased, so did domestic opposition to the war. At the beginning of 1965 there were 27,000 American troops in Vietnam; by the end of the year, 185,000; and by the end of 1966, 400,000. The casualty figures also rose dramatically from 2,500 in 1965 to a total of 33,000 in 1966. During 1965 the first serious signs of trouble had appeared across the country: Senator J. William Fulbright, Chairman of the Senate Foreign Relations Committee, publicly urged President Johnson to withdraw American troops; professors and students at the University of Michigan staged the first of many antiwar "teach-ins"; in October a few men ostentatiously burned their draft cards; in November, 30,000 people held an antiwar rally in Washington. In that same' month public opinion polls showed that sixty-six percent of the American people supported President Johnson's policies; by October 1967, only forty-four percent still supported them; and the President himself found it increasingly difficult to appear in public without provoking large-scale demonstrations against him.[31]

The most vocal opposition to the war came from the "New Left" radicals who openly sympathized with the Vietnamese Communists and looked forward to a Communist victory. Other Americans wondered if intervention in Vietnam was doing more harm than good to the people whom we were trying to help. Still others—probably a majority of Americans—hesitated to oppose the war actively because they had no illusions about the nature of the regime in North Vietnam and they knew that the Communists were counting on American disillusionment to bring them victory. Yet even these people increasingly lost patience as the war dragged on and American casualties mounted with no prospect of victory despite reassuring predictions from politicians and generals.

Individual Catholics played a surprisingly prominent part in the opposition to American policy in Vietnam. The activities of the Berrigan brothers, Daniel (a Jesuit priest) and Philip (a Josephite priest), made them familiar names and upset many Catholics unaccustomed to seeing priests in such roles. Then, in September 1966, David J. Miller, a member of the Catholic Worker community in New York, burned his draft card in front of the induction center in New York City—the first person to do so in violation of the new federal law making such acts a felony. Six other members of the Catholic Worker Movement repeated the performance in Union Square three weeks later. On November 9, a twenty-one year old former seminarian doused himself with gasoline and burned himself to death in front of the United Nations. Father Daniel Berrigan, S.J., eulogized the young man as a martyr and was himself reassigned by his superiors to Latin America. A full-page advertisement on his behalf in the *New York Times* drew a thousand signatures (including those of seventy-five priests), and, within three months, Berrigan was back in New York organizing opposition to the war. Later that year his brother Philip, in the first of several raids on local draft boards, gained entrance to the draft board in Baltimore and poured blood over files and records to dramatize the loss of life in Vietnam.[32]

Catholic radicals like these were a tiny minority, but they attracted inordinate attention, earning either the admiration or, more likely, the detestation of their fellow religionists.[33] Until the end of 1965 Paul Hallinan said nothing about the Vietnam war, but he was deeply disturbed by the suicide of the young pacifist in New York. He was outraged when Senator Barry Goldwater said of the victim (and a-nother young man who had imitated him): "They were nuts to begin with." While condemning suicide as a legitimate form of protest, Hallinan also castigated the senator for his lack of compassion. At the same time he made it clear that he was no pacifist himself and defended the right of the United States to curb aggression and injustice in Vietnam. While regretting the self-immolation of the two young paci-fists, he noted that dozens of other young Americans were dying every week in Vietnam. "Most of them are well aware," said Hallinan, "that, if they were not there, the Communists would be there instead." Like most Americans, including the President, he had no solution for the war, and he admitted that it is "a lonely, dirty, savage job," but he was not ready in 1965 to say that American involvement in Vietnam was either immoral or unwise.[34]

As disenchantment with the war increased, so did the pressure on the American bishops to take a stand on the war, which meant, in fact, pressure to take a stand against the war. Early in 1966 the *New York Times* observed that, unlike most American religious leaders, the Ca-tholic bishops had been largely silent on the question of Vietnam.[35] Thereupon the *National Catholic Reporter* sent a questionnaire about the war to 225 bishops but received replies from only three, all of whom supported the war in varying degrees.[36] *Commonweal* expressed dismay at the failure of the bishops to address what it called "the number one moral problem confronting the American people," calling their silence a scandal.[37] During the summer of 1966, Chardinal Shehan issued a carefully balanced pastoral letter in which he warned that American involvement in Vietnam could be justified only as long as the means used to win the war were moral.[38]

A few months later Hallinan and Bernardin jointly issued a similar pastoral letter, which attempted to relate the teaching of the Second Vatican Council to the situation in Vietnam. Unlike some opponents of the war, the two bishops did not question the motives which had led the United States to intervene in Vietnam. Indeed, they said: "American Catholics can put faith in the integrity of our government's aim in Vietnam." They also cited the teaching of the Council that "government cannot be denied the right to legitimate defense," and they went so far as to say that "it can be argued that to the present course of action in Vietnam there may be no visible alternative." Nevertheless, the two bishops did not give the United States Government *carte blanche*, for they quickly added:

> But we cannot stop here. It is the Christian duty to keep looking for other alternatives. We must know as much about the factual situation as possible in order that these alternatives be realistic. To a limited extent, our national security requires secrecy. Except for that, however, we must keep insisting that our leaders fully inform us of the facts and issues involved in the Vietnam War.

It was advice that the Johnson Administration might well have heeded, for the President's failure to explain the situation honestly to the American people was one of the principal reasons for the erosion of support for the war. In their pastoral letter, Hallinan and Bernardin also asserted that the government must recognize and respect the rights of conscientious objectors. They made it clear too that their continued support for the war depended on the kind of war that the United States waged in Vietnam. They quoted Cardinal Shehan's warning: "If our means become immoral, our cause will have been betrayed," and then added their own statement:

> We must protest, therefore, whenever there is danger that our conduct of the war will exceed moral limits. A Christian simply cannot approve indiscriminate bombing, methodical extermination of peo-

ple, nuclear arms designed for "overkill" or disregard for non-combatants.[39]

The Atlanta pastoral was so carefully nuanced that it pleased neither the militant supporters nor the militant opponents of the war, both of whom wanted agreement with their views rather than a careful analysis of the situation from the point of view of Catholic morality, which was what the pastoral letter provided. For example, John Leo, associate editor of *Commweal* and outspoken Catholic critic of the war, praised both Shehan and the Atlanta bishops for holding up "strong moral yardsticks," but he complained that they failed to provide "any specific attempts to measure the war."[40] A month later the American bishops, convening in Washington for their annual meeting, for the first time issued a statement on the morality of American involvement in the Vietnam war. In tone and content their statement was practically a summary of the Atlanta bishops' pastoral letter, offering the same kind of carefully qualified support for the war and receiving the same tepid reaction from both left and right.[41]

As domestic opposition to the war grew ever stronger and louder in 1967, Hallinan tried to maintain a reasoned and objective position. Neither he nor any other Catholic bishop attended the two-day "mobilization" that attracted over 2,500 Christian and Jewish clergy to Washington in January to discuss "Vietnam: the Clergyman's Dilemma." He also refrained from endorsing a public statement against the war signed by 800 Catholic priests and laymen and auxiliary Bishop James Shannon of St. Paul-Minneapolis.[42] In February, however, he travelled to New York to share a platform with a rabbi and a minister at a symposium in a Protestant church sponsored by Clergy and Laymen Concerned About Vietnam. He could hardly have expected Cardinal Spellman's blessing for this enterprise, since the cardinal had recently reiterated his belief that anything less than total victory in Vietnam was unacceptable. Hallinan did not even seek Spellman's permission. He merely informed him what he intended to do.[43]

At this symposium Hallinan sided more strongly than ever before with the opponents of American policy in Vietnam. Quoting the Atlanta pastoral, he declared it a moral evil "to destroy indiscriminately whole cities ... [or to] plan for the methodical extermination of an entire people." He never accused the Johnson Administration directly of pursuing such policies in Vietnam, but he could hardly escape blame if his receptive audience drew that conclusion. In their peace pastoral, Hallinan and Bernardin had mentioned the need to seek alternatives to American military action in Vietnam. The alternatives that Hallinan suggested in this talk, however, seem woefully inadequate, for he urged an end to the stockpiling of weapons and support for the peace-keeping efforts of the United Nations.[44]

Even more questionable was the analogy which he drew between the civil rights movement in the United States and the war in Vietnam. He rightfully identified Selma as a turning point in the history of the civil rights movement because it "challenged Americans to stop talking about the civil rights movement and to do something about it." He then called for a "Selma for Peace," a comparable event that would lead to the end of the Vietnam war. His rhetoric seems here to have gotten the better of his judgment. Selma succeeded because it appealed to the consciences of the American people to correct past injustices. Unless Hallinan's "Selma for Peace" meant unilateral American withdrawal from Vietnam, however, it is hard to see how he could have expected such a moral appeal to have a similar effect on the Communist leaders of Vietnam.[45]

Hallinan's speech in New York was the closest that he had yet come to an outright condemnation of the war; but, in the months following the talk, he drew back from this position when antiwar activists tried to associate him with a project called Vietnam Summer. Its purpose was to elect antiwar politicans and to organize opposition to the war among young blacks of draft age. State Representative Julian Bond of Georgia claimed Hallinan's endorsement for the organization and an advertisement appeared in the *New York Times* on May 5, 1967, listing Hallinan as a sponsor together with such figures as Martin Luther King Jr. and Dr. Benjamin Spock. Hallinan repudiated the use of his name by the organization and denied that he had any connection with Vietnam Summer. He repeated his declaration of support for conscientious objectors but strongly opposed any campaign of massive resistance to the draft. He told a reporter:

> I would hold to the right of the conscientious objector, just as our Church does. But a campaign of mass refusal, which is what King is pushing now—I see a great distinction: I would endorse one and not the other.

Then, in words that won him few friends among the radical left, he added:

> I have heard some strange sentiments put forth lately in the name of peace. The craven fear of death and apathy to moral evil . . . are unworthy credentials for those who sign up or speak up. We have had enough of that.[46]

During 1967 the number of American troops in Vietnam rose to 475,000, and the casualty figures reached a total of 80,000. Antiwar demonstrations became larger also; one in New York City drew 300,000 protesters. Continued American bombing of North Vietnam (on a scale which exceeded the bombing of Nazi Germany during World War II) did nothing to hasten military victory in South Vietnam or to end the frustrations of many Americans with the seemingly endless conflict. Numerous *ad hoc* committees filled the newspapers with advertisements offering their own special solutions to the Vietnam dilemma. One such group was Negotiation Now, whose leaders rejected both escalation of the war and unilateral American withdrawal in favor of a negotiated peace settlement. Since the Communists refused to negotiate as long as the United States continued its bombing of North Vietnam, Negotiation Now advocated an immediate end of the bombing and American efforts to arrange a ceasefire. Twice before, early in 1966 and 1967, President Johnson had temporarily halted the bombing without luring the Communists to the bargaining table. The organizers of Negotiation Now, however, claimed that the results would be different if the United States dropped all preconditions for the peace talks, and they hoped to collect a million signatures for a petition to this effect. Unlike some antiwar activists who favored a Communist victory in Vietnam, the supporters of Negotiation Now wanted free and democratic elections in South Vietnam. Why the Communists should agree to such elections once American military pressure was relaxed was a question they had not asked themselves.

Among the sponsors of Negotiation Now were Norman Cousins, John Kenneth Galbraith, Martin Luther King Jr., Reinhold Niebuhr, Norman Podhoretz and Victor Reuther. Four Catholic bishops added their endorsement: Victor Reed, John Dougherty, James Shannon and Hallinan.[47] In a joint statement, the four bishops said that, in conformity with the plea for peace made by Pope Paul VI at the

United Nations, they called upon the United States Government to set a time and place for negotiations. They also called upon the Communists to respond affirmatively to this offer. They had been led to make this statement, they explained, because:

> With growing dismay we have viewed a public climate increasingly characterized by troubled acceptance of military escalation or by intemperate dissent, which, in condemning the policies of our own country, has too often ignored the obstacles to peace posed by North Vietnam and the National Liberation Front.[48]

Local reaction to Hallinan's stand was very critical. Most of the unfavorable letters, he said, "were savage in their attack, lacking in logic and coarse in language." One exception was the statement of the parish council in St. Luke's Parish in Dahlonega, which vigorously but courteously took issue with their archbishop's position. Hallinan called it "a real contribution to dialogue" and published the full text in the *Georgia Bulletin*.[49] A week later he responded with a lengthy explanation of the reasons which had led him to support Negotiation Now. Beginning with a description of his own experience of war, he said:

> I signed it because, as an Army chaplain in the Southwest Pacific in 1943-1945, I lived with war. Even though our nation had been attacked in 1941, and our cause was clear, I found that war is the total of men who die ugly deaths. And the duty of fighting, being wounded and dying carries no glory. It is a terrible waste of young human lives.
>
> As an American citizen, I hope that my desire for peace with justice is just as consistent with patriotism as that of the leaders of the administration and the armed forces, of all those who conscientiously believe that we should go on fighting a war in which the United States may be winners, in name but hardly in fact.
>
> I honestly believe that our nation is being hourly weakened by the terrible cost of American lives, the loss of American stature in this troubled world, the honest but hurtful division within American opinion, the wasteful diversion of American money and the frightening intensity of accelerated bombing, especially in August and September.[50]

On a related point, Hallinan rejected the complaint of the Dahlonega parish council that he had failed to distinguish adequately between his own opinion and Church teaching. He admitted that what he had said about the war was not official Church teaching, but he insisted that it was more than his own private opinion since it was based on the careful consideration of the statements of two popes, the Second Vatican Council, and the American hierarchy. "My signature," he said, "was offered not simply as a citizen but as a bishop of the Catholic Church obligated to give voice to moral imperatives."[51]

Like many Americans, Hallinan felt the full impact of the war when it finally touched a member of his own family. Early in 1968 one of his relatives applied for a deferment from the draft as a conscientious objector. Although Hallinan had consistently defended the rights of conscientious objectors, it came as a shock to him to find one of his relatives in that category. He tried unsuccessfully to persuade the young man to accept non-combatant medical service and then sent him an anguished letter in which he poured out his own distress and disgust at the effects of the war on American society:

> You don't think I understand. Perhaps not ... but I know this— that human nature does not change between generations; only our vision gets clearer. Maybe I [was] wrong in 1942-1943, and you're right in 1968. Maybe. But your generation, I find, has dangerous blinders like a horse. You are always right—what went before is wrong, pig-headed, bombastic or empty theatrics.
>
> This war, as I have said so often, is a mistake, and the senseless killing of Vietnamese (North and South) and Americans and Koreans has stained our national character indelibly. I think Westmoreland is stodgy and Johnson is all worn out, incapable of fresh insights, convinced that he is like Lincoln. It just ain't true. We are being beaten shamefully and the recovery of our national sanity will take decades.

He wrote these words in the aftermath of the notorious "Tet" offensive of January 1968, when the Communists launched the most brutal attacks of the war against the major cities of South Vietnam. It took a full month to repulse the Communists, whereupon General Westmoreland, the American Commander, hailed it as an American victory. He then promptly asked for 200,000 more American troops and additional planes. A few weeks later—on March 31 (four days after Archbishop Hallinan's death)—President Johnson announced that he would not seek a second term. On April 3 the Vietnamese Communists agreed to peace talks, but the next day Martin Luther King Jr. was murdered in Memphis and American blacks responded with a rampage of rioting all across the country. A confused and angry America now faced the daunting challenge of making peace on two fronts: in the jungles of Southeast Asia and in the ghettos of almost every major American city.

As 1968 began its course, not only was American society in turmoil; the Catholic Church in the United States was experiencing a period of unprecedented restlessness and uncertainty. For the first time in the history of American Catholicism, large numbers of priests and religious were leaving the active ministry; young Catholics manifested the same rebelliousness to authority as their non-Catholic counterparts; and the Catholic laity in general assumed a more critical and assertive attitude toward the clergy and the hierarchy. Symbolic of the new atmosphere was the popularity of the *National Catholic Reporter,* a provocative and sometimes flippant tabloid, which subjected the Church to the same irreverent scrutiny that the secular press displayed toward political leaders.

Hallinan disliked much of what he saw happening around him—the denigration of clerical celibacy and the defiance of ecclesiastical authority, the incivility of antiwar protesters, the dishonesty of politicians and generals who lied about the situation in Vietnam, the antics of white demagogues like Lester Maddox, and the threats of black demagogues like Stokely Carmichael. At no point, however, did Hallinan succumb to nostalgia for a simpler, quieter past, nor did he ever suggest that brute force could solve the problems of the day by crushing those who caused them. Instead, in both Church and society, he looked and worked for positive and constructive solutions, such as calling a diocesan synod (the first American bishop to do so after the Second Vatican Council), inviting the laity to share in the administration of the archdiocese, promoting better relations with non-Catholics and exploring alternatives to parochial schools. His interest in racial justice never flagged, and only weeks before his death he was advocating open housing in Atlanta.[52] The one issue on which he found it most difficult to articulate a clear and consistent position was the Vietnam war, but he had plenty of company, beginning with the President of the United States. Despite poor health and the heavy demands upon his time because of his role on the Bishops' Committee on the Liturgy,

Archbishop Hallinan gave a convincing demonstration of how a diocesan bishop in the troubled 1960's could use his office to offer guidance and direction to both Church and society.

18

The Measure of the Man

When Paul Hallinan was hospitalized for the first time in 1963, his doctors told him that he could expect to live for about five years.[1] He did not reveal this to anyone until the onset of his final illness, and, as late as 1967, it appeared that he might still prove his doctors wrong. For the first time in four years, he managed to stay out of the hospital for a full twelve months in 1967, and by husbanding his strength and relying heavily on Bernardin's help, he was able to remain remarkably active. Both *America* and *Commonweal* published articles by him that year;[2] and he was in greater demand than ever as a guest speaker on special occasions.

One such occasion was the installation in the summer of 1967 of the new Bishop of Savannah, Gerard Frey. Hallinan was the homilist and took as his theme the new image of the Church which had emerged from the Second Vatican Council. For centuries, he recalled, the traditional picture of the Church had been that of a pyramid—with the Pope at the top, the laity on the bottom, and everyone else somewhere in between. Hallinan found that picture far from satisfactory. "It was symmetrical, pleasing to look at, easy to understand," he said.

> But it was closed and tight, a little too smug, a little too secure. It failed to catch the high spirits and daring of fire cast upon the earth, a light burning on a mountain, a fishing boat setting out from shore, a net cast into the sea.

Unfortunately, he said, "in a world grown used to self-reliance, dialogue, involvement and the democratic way of life, the pyramid just will not do."

He suggested instead the image of the Church as the "Open Circle" with the bishop, not at the top, but in the midst of the people whom he serves, guides, teaches, and gathers together for worship. The view is better from the center than at the top, said Hallinan. "Bishops do not take, as the military do, the high ground. They walk and live among the people." Critics might find fault with the boldness of his imagery, but he was not questioning the hierarchical nature of the Church. Rather he was urging his fellow churchmen to avoid the kind of clericalism that would leave them isolated and alienated from the very people whom they were supposed to serve. In case that anyone doubted his orthodoxy, he suggested that they consider the *Last Supper* of DaVinci, where

> the open circle is indicated by the central figure, the High Priest, Christ, turning on either side to His Apostles, speaking with them in everyday dialogue, feeding them with the sacrament of His Body and Blood, climaxing the Eucharistic sacrifice. There is nothing closed or tight or pyramidical in this scene. In fact it has been observed that, for centuries, priests turned their backs on their people at Mass in sharp and ironic contrast to our High Priest, Christ, who stood in their midst, sharing His presence, words and even Himself with them. I recall no artist who ever painted a Last Supper that had Our Lord facing the wall.[3]

Although Hallinan now had little direct contact with the movement, he gave an address to the Newman chaplains at the National Newman Congress that same summer. Well aware of the rebellious mood on campuses across the country and of the uncertain future of the whole Newman movement, he commiserated with the chaplains, contrasting their difficulties with his own halcyon days in the 1950's. "So here it is 1967," he said, "with a new kind of Church, of world, of university, and a new Pandora's box of tensions and concerns in every student's I.D. kit." He recounted for them his own experience at the University of Georgia, where students had recently protested the building of a new Catholic Center as a waste of money. His initial reaction had been one of anger, but, the more he thought about the students' disenchantment with the materialism of American life, the more sympathy he felt for them. "We may avoid the young radicals' weird shapes," observed Hallinan, "but we can hardly shut out of our consciousness their disgust, their frustration, their revolt."

His advice to the Newman chaplains was to admit what was legitimate in the students' protest and to direct their energies into more constructive channels. "Reach them by every new and honest approach," he pleaded. "Share with them, not their hatred, but their agony." Nor did Hallinan think that all the problems on campus were confined to the radicals. He was equally concerned about what he called "the safe Catholic, organized to the hilt, but committed only to the superficial." In order to transform such students into effective Christian leaders, he warned the chaplains, they would need more than a "manual of Thomistic hand-me-downs."

Hallinan also tackled the prickly issue of academic freedom. Far from expressing any fear that it would be inimical to religion on campus, he recalled the vigorous controversies in the medieval universities and Newman's defense of intellectual freedom. He told the chaplains: "True academic freedom could be your most-needed contribution. Urge the freedom to teach, to hold, to dissent, in season and out."[4]

He had had occasion to practice what he was preaching a few months earlier, when the trustees of the Catholic University of America had voted not to renew the contract of Father Charles Curran as an assistant professor of moral theology. (As an archbishop, Hallinan was an *ex-officio* member of the Board of Trustees.) At the April meeting in Chicago, he cast the solitary vote in Curran's favor, when twenty-eight other trustees voted against him.[5] Once the trustees' action became public, students and professors at the university went on strike, shutting down the institution. The Chancellor, Cardinal O'Boyle, had to send urgent telegrams to the trustees, asking them to reverse their decision so that he could negotiate an end to the strike. The rector, Bishop William J. McDonald, was not reappointed when his second five-year term came to an end in the summer of 1967. Hallinan told O'Boyle that, if the next rector were a priest, he should be told at the beginning of his term that he would not be made a bishop. "The hope of such a promotion is dangerous," said Hallinan, "because it easily inhibits the necessary academic freedom of the rector."[6]

The fracas over Curran was not the only controversial issue which kept Hallinan's name in the news that year. In February he gave permission to one of his priests, Father Conald Foust, to start an experimental parish, the Community of Christ Our Brother, similar to one which Bishop Victor Reed had established in Tulsa, Oklahoma. The parish had no territorial boundaries, included Protestants as well as Catholics among its members, and met for Sunday Mass at a local Methodist center. (Needless to say, the Protestants were not permitted to receive Holy Communion.) The parish consisted of no more than fifty people, lasted only a few years, and was one of Hallinan's less happy experiments.[7]

Quite different was the fate of another Hallinan proposal: the establishment of the permanent diaconate in the United States. Within weeks of Pope Paul's restoration of the permanent diaconate on a world-wide basis, Hallinan called upon his fellow bishops to petition for it in the United States. He was anxious to have permanent deacons in his own archdiocese, and after taking a poll through the pages of the *Georgia Bulletin,* he discovered that seventy percent of those who replied were in favor of it also. He realized that his involvement in matters such as these brought him a certain notoriety, but he seemed to enjoy the role of "maverick bishop," as he styled himself, and he noted impishly in the middle of the summer: "I keep things stirred up."[8]

At the very beginning of 1968, however, Hallinan's health suddenly deteriorated. He complained of drowsiness and exhaustion and canceled two talks that he was scheduled to give. On January 9, Dr. Wilber told him that he had to go to the hospital. "[I] dread it," he said, "but [I] know that I have to." He still put it off for another week, but, on January 17, he entered St. Joseph's Infirmary and five days later Bernardin anointed him. On February 1 he underwent emergency hernia surgery but he came through it amazingly well in view of his condition. That afternoon, when Bernardin and Burtenshaw came to see him, they found him reading the latest issue of the *Georgia Bulletin.*[9]

Hallinan recovered successfully from the surgery, but he lost ground over the next few weeks in his fight against a combination of hepatitis, cirrhosis and diabetes. On February 4, he heard of the death in Philadelphia of his predecessor, Bishop Hyland. "A fine guy," he said, "just too scrupulous."[10] Sometime during this period he sent a note to Bernardin in which he told him:

> Our last two conversations have brought me a serenity that I have lacked. Since you know me so well, this does not require another

statement ... I am as determined and probably as stubborn as ever, with the same lack of fear of consequences ... the same will to live coupled (I hope) with a Christian acceptance of death.[11]

He left the hospital on February 19 but he was going home to die and he knew it. He held a meeting with Bernardin and others to discuss how he could best use the time that he had left. After the meeting was over, he pointed to a faded picture that hung on the bedroom wall. It was a picture of the Sacred Heart that had once belonged to his mother. He said: "I have no fear because He is with me."

One concern that he did have was the loss of Bernardin, who was scheduled to go to Washington to replace Bishop Paul Tanner as the General Secretary of the United States Catholic Conference. Archbishop Dearden, the President of the U.S.C.C., was anxious to have Bernardin in Washington. In November, Hallinan had agreed to the change. However, the day after he came home from the hospital, he wrote to Dearden, explaining that the situation had changed drastically since then. "What it adds up to, John," he said, "is that I must withdraw my earlier promise given you then in good faith.... To lose Bishop Bernardin would be the next step to the end for me. I do not intend to be dramatic or self-pitying, only honest."[12]

During the next month he grew progressively weaker but he kept his sense of humor and tried to remain active to the end. He even gave a farewell party for his staff and friends, and he made a series of telephone calls to those who could not attend. He told John Tracy Ellis about the Roman rejection of his proposals for liturgical experimentation, and he assured him: "We will go back again; we will go back again." To another friend in Cleveland, Father Eugene Best, he said: "I'm only being kept alive now by prayer and cortisone, and I don't know how much longer the cortisone will work." On the feast of St. Thomas Aquinas (celebrated on March 7 in those days), three seminarians came to see him. He decided to confer tonsure on one and minor orders on the other two. He used a very ornate mitre for the ceremony and then said to them: "Shades of triumphalism, I guess, but it is the only one that fits." On March 18, he learned of the death of Bishop Emmet Walsh of Youngstown and sent a telegram to Bishop James Malone, expressing his condolences. "He was my predecessor, my inspiration, my friend," he told Malone.[13]

One day Bernardin celebrated Mass in the archbishop's bedroom. Hallinan was too weak to leave his bed but he concelebrated the Mass with Bernardin and preached a homily on the Eucharist. "That one demonstration of faith," Bernardin has said, "did more for me and my appreciation of the Eucharist than all the articles he had written and all the talks he had given."

A few days before his death, Hallinan tried to dictate a talk that he was scheduled to give later that month at the convention of the National Catholic Educational Association. He knew what he wanted to say but he did not have the strength to express his thoughts.

Late on Tuesday, March 26, he slipped into a coma. Bernardin in his funeral homily described the end:

> During the twelve hours preceding his death, even though he was in a coma, he kept calling the name of Jesus, and this was the last word on his lips, when the final breath of life slipped from him just before dawn on last Wednesday.[14]

The following Friday, many of the ministers and rabbis with whom Hallinan had worked held an ecumenical service for him in the Cathedral of Christ the King. The preacher was Dr. William Cannon, the Methodist Dean of the Candler School of Theology at Emory University, one of Hallinan's closest friends among the Protestant clergy. He praised the late archbishop as one "whose personal devotion to God and genuine goodness blessed us and made us all better Christians." Cannon described for the congregation how he had taken leave of Hallinan for the last time only a few weeks earlier:

> The last time I visited him, he asked me for my blessing. To give a blessing is a beautiful and wonderful act. It is a Roman Catholic custom, however. It is not a Protestant custom. So I did not know how to do it.
>
> I asked him, therefore, to give me his blessing first. He knew what I was about but smiled warmly and did so from his sick bed. Then I put my hands on his head and said a prayer for him. Tears streamed down my cheeks, and if unity could be built on what we felt, we would have it.[15]

The funeral Mass took place in the cathedral on the following Monday, celebrated, as Hallinan directed in his will, according to the new experimental rite with white vestments and the paschal candle next to the coffin.[16] *America* recalled that Hallinan had said a few months earlier that there were "about thirty to forty" bishops who were genuine reformers and noted that "about thirty to forty" bishops attended his funeral.[17] Archbishop Luigi Raimondi, the Apostolic Delegate to the United States, was the principal celebrant; Cardinal Krol gave the absolution; and the homilist was Bishop Bernardin, who eulogized his friend as a prophetic figure for his leadership in the liturgy, civil rights, ecumenism, the Vietnam war and the general renewal of the Church. There were two qualities, Bernardin said, which were the key to understanding Hallinan's character and greatness: his "humanness" and his courage. "It was his 'humanness,'" he said, "that made it possible for him to relate to people; it was his courage always to do or say what he thought was right that made him a prophetic figure." Bernardin described Hallinan's sufferings over the previous four years and the heroic way that he had accepted that cross, especially during the last three months. Aware that not everyone shared his admiration for the archbishop, he defended his depiction of him as a prophetic figure by saying:

> There may be some who say that he was ahead of his time. Perhaps he was. But I think his genius was that he saw that time was running out. He had the courage to take a bold step—that necessary, decisive step needed to bring the Church into the mainstream of contemporary life. It was for this reason that he was a prophetic figure. It was for this reason that his influence will long be felt.[18]

Others felt the same way, although they had only met him briefly or knew him mainly through his talks and writings. Father Timothy S. Healy, S.J., Executive Vice-President of Fordham University, recalled several conversations with him and revealed how impressed he had been with Hallinan's grasp of the problems of young people and of the need for the Church to respond to them in an effective way. Hallinan's death, said Healy, "leaves me with the sick and low feeling that the Church has lost a man that it could ill afford to lose." Bishop Lawrence Casey was equally appreciative of the role that Hallinan had played in the deliberations of the hierarchy. "It was a nice feeling to have him on deck at the bishops' meetings," he said. "He was the spearhead of the liberals, completely open and honest, and he is a grievous loss in so many ways." Aelred Tegels, O.S.B., was grateful for Hallinan's leadership with the liturgy. He made the perceptive comment that "he was not a radical in the usual sense. He loved tradition and appreciated the historical forms of liturgy. But he understood very deeply that tradition is a living thing and that it requires, not precludes, change."[19]

Many of the condolences offered by non-Catholics went well beyond the usual expressions of regret and sympathy. Bishop Fred Pierce Corson, former President of the World Methodist Council, mentioned the impression that Hallinan had made on him at the Second Vatican Council. He said: "[Hallinan] made a host of friends among the observers, and through his friendship we came to some of our deepest and most precious experiences in unity within the Church." On the day that Hallinan died, Jaroslav Pelikan, the distinguished Lutheran scholar and professor of church history at Yale University, sent a letter to the clergy of Atlanta, saying: "My admiration for Archbishop Hallinan as a man and as a Christian is exceeded only by my gratitude to that same Holy Ghost for conferring His gifts of insight and courage, modesty and integrity upon this man of God in such bounty." The Jewish community in Atlanta also valued the archbishop as a friend. The local chapter of the American Jewish Committee issued a statement, saying: "His respect for Jews and Judaism, his deep commitment to social justice and his public support for Israel endeared him to our community. . . . We thank God that he lived and worked among us."[20]

His old friend, newspaper publisher Ralph McGill, paid tribute to Hallinan in a column which sounded more like a sermon than newspaper commentary. He praised the archbishop especially for his advocacy of racial justice in the South and for his ability to allay the fears of those who instinctively resisted any suggestion of change. "He was a frail, small man, who was ill for a long time," McGill said, but he was "a giant who made many of his clerical contemporaries appear as pygmies."[21]

No bishop excels at every aspect of his office and Hallinan had little interest in the routine details of administration; once, at least, he wondered how successful he would be as a pastor in a busy parish. When he would return home to Charleston or Atlanta after an extended absence to find a pile of correspondence awaiting his attention, he would spend whole days dutifully answering letters until his desk was cleared but his heart was clearly not in this kind of work. In Charleston he was happy to leave day-to-day administration largely in the capable hands of Bernardin. When he moved to Atlanta, he inherited a chaotic administrative and financial system, complicated by the ambitious building program of his predecessor. Hallinan found it a heavy burden, especially coping with the financial problems of the diocesan high schools.

Factors beyond his control made it difficult for him to give more time to these duties even if he had wanted to do so. Six months after arriving in Atlanta, he left for the opening session of the Second Vatican Council; a year after his return he suffered the first attack of hepatitis and spent most of the next nine months in the hospital. A fund-raising campaign, delayed a year, surpassed its stated goal of two million dollars, but Hallinan failed to build the downtown Catholic Center which had been the main justification for the campaign and the apple of his eye during his first few years in Atlanta. Worried over the financial condition of the parochial schools and discouraged by bickering with architects and financiers, he abandoned his original plan and decided instead to move the chancery office to the basement of the new cathedral rectory—a far from adequate solution.

By contrast, his neighbor to the south, Archbishop Joseph Hurley, Bishop of St. Augustine, had raised a small fortune by this time and made an enormous material contribution to the future expansion of the Church in South Florida. Hurley's techniques were draconian financial quotas on his pastors and shrewd speculation in real estate.[22] Hallinan had neither the taste for the one nor talent for the other, and he breathed a sigh of relief, when Bernardin arrived in Atlanta in the spring of 1966 to resume the role in his life that he had played in Charleston.

During Hallinan's six years in Atlanta, the Catholic population increased by fifty percent (from 33,372 to 48,982), and the number of diocesan priests almost doubled (from thirty-four to sixty). Nevertheless, he started only four new parishes (including the experimental, non-territorial Community of Christ Our Brother), the same number that he had established in Charleston, where the growth of the Catholic population had not been nearly as great. The most notable change in Hallinan's diocesan priorities on coming to Atlanta was his attitude to Catholic schools. In Charleston he had continued Bishop John Russell's program of expanding the Catholic school system; but, in Atlanta, he opened only one new parish elementary school and closed two others as well as a small black high school. The total enrollment in the Catholic schools remained approximately the same over six years, but the number of students in Confraternity of Christian Doctrine classes rose steadily from 3,390 in 1962 to 8,725 in 1968. Interestingly, the number of teaching sisters continued to increase moderately during these years, but Hallinan's insistence on small classes meant that more and more lay teachers were needed (their numbers doubled between 1962 and 1968), threatening the solvency of the whole system.[23] In a report to the archdiocese in 1967, he was frankly pessimistic about the future of Catholic schools in Atlanta and he urged that more attention be given to developing an effective catechetical program for Catholic students in public schools. Hallinan's foreboding may seem justified today, but, at the time, it angered many Catholic parents in Atlanta: newcomers from the North, who were clamoring for the same kind of parochial schools that they had attended as children.[24]

One puzzling feature of Hallinan's years in Atlanta was his virtual neglect of the black apostolate. Unlike Charleston, where Bishop Emmet Walsh had established a network of black parishes and missions across the state, the Archdiocese of Atlanta had only two black parishes (both located in Atlanta itself), and there were only about 3,000 black Catholics in the whole archdiocese. Although Hallinan won praise and respect from blacks for his commitment to racial justice, he did little or nothing to promote a specific program of evangelization in the black community.

In Atlanta, more than in Charleston, some priests disliked his high visibility on public issues and his vigorous prodding of them on liturgical renewal and ecumenism. They could hardly complain about his lifestyle, however, for it remained as simple in Atlanta as it had been in Charleston or Cleveland: his idea of a good time was still a steak dinner in a local restaurant with a few friends. Every few years he appeared with a new car, but they were gifts from Archbishop Dearden, who realized how little money he had at his own disposal. Like any man, he had his personal foibles, among them a certain vanity, which made him sensitive to the reaction to his talks, although it did not prevent him from speaking unpalatable truths when moral issues (such as racial justice) were involved. It is evident too that he was not devoid of ambition. Occasionally a newspaper reporter would float the rumor that Hallinan was in line to be made a cardinal. Each time he laughed at the suggestion, but he also noted it carefully in his diary in a way that suggests that he was both flattered and pleased, and would have been even more pleased if the rumor had come true.

His temper could have gotten him into trouble, except that he kept it under tight control; outbursts of anger were rare and quickly subsided. His ususal *modus operandi* in a dispute was to take a conciliatory approach even with those who did not reciprocate his civility. Ironically, his cheerful and optimistic outlook on life was a handicap at times, because it led him to take questionable positions (on issues like ecumenism and the Vietnam war) where a little more skepticism and awareness of the hard realities involved might have been more realistic. But optimism came naturally to Hallinan, as it did for so many of his contemporaries at the time of the Second Vatican Council, and it is hard to imagine that he would ever have been comfortable, either then or later, among the prophets of gloom and doom excoriated by Pope John XXIII at the opening of the Council.

For him, as for many American prelates, the Second Vatican Council was probably the most significant educational experience in his life; but, even before the Council, there were influences at work which were broadening his intellectual horizons and softening the rigidity of his earlier years. As a young curate and as an army chaplain, there was little to set Hallinan apart from most priests of his generation (except his genial temperament): he still cultivated and advocated the intensely individualistic piety and stern morality which had so impressed him at Notre Dame during the heyday of Father John O'Hara's Catholic version of muscular Christianity. Despite his warm personal relations with non-Catholics, the sincere Protestant and the good Jew still fitted uncomfortably into his militant Counter-Reformation ecclesiology, and he probably would have agreed with the remark attributed to a French bishop at the time of the Modernist crisis: "There is only one God, and we have Him."

These attitudes began to change during the ten years that he spent in the Newman apostolate. In those years Newman clubs and Newman centers were among the liveliest places in the American Catholic Church, abuzz with talk of liturgical renewal, the social apostolate and the latest trends in European Catholic thought, and the regional and national conventions of the Newman movement regularly brought together some of the brightest and most zealous priests in the country. Ten years of this kind of stimulation left its mark on Hallinan, as did his discovery of the writings of Cardinal Newman, whom he began to read in earnest during those years. Still another influence was the scholarly work which he did in pursuit of his doctorate at Western

Reserve University. Among other things, his research forced him to read widely in American Catholic history, giving him a perspective on contemporary events which many of his episcopal colleagues lacked. When he finally received the degree in 1963 while Archbishop of Atlanta, he set a record which still stands: the first and only Catholic bishop to earn a doctorate at an American university while he was in office.

Cardinal Bernardin observed that, when Paul Hallinan went to Charleston in 1958, he was an unknown quantity. When he died in 1968, after nine-and-a-half years in two of the smallest dioceses in the United States, he was better known than most of the bishops in the country, and his reputation rested on solid achievements in a number of different areas.[25]

In Charleston, Hallinan's combination of prudence and courage was evident, for example, in the way that he tackled the problem of segregation in the Catholic schools, announcing that they would be integrated "no later but no sooner" than the public schools. He showed equal finesse in handling the anti-Catholic bigotry of the 1960 presidential campaign, defending the patriotism of Catholics without the truculence that sometimes made such apologetics counter-productive. In those pre-conciliar years, he also did pioneer work in both ecumenism and liturgical renewal, at a time when few American bishops were interested in either. One New York priest, after serving as a Navy chaplain in Charleston, returned home an enthusiastic advocate of popular participation in the (still Latin) liturgy. The local clergy told him: "It will never work," to which he replied: "I've seen it working in the diocese of Charleston."[26]

In Atlanta, Hallinan was bolder than in Charleston, but hardly reckless. He integrated the Catholic schools and Catholic hospitals without incident at a time of severe racial tension throughout the South, and he assumed a prominent and constructive role in public affairs. Moderate civil rights leaders and peaceful opponents of the Vietnam war received his support; Black Power agitators and draft-card burners did not. Under the impact of the Council, he pushed liturgical renewal far beyond the modest beginnings in Charleston, but he always claimed to base his decisions squarely on the conciliar documents themselves. The same was true of his initiatives in the area of ecumenism, which received a warm response from many Protestant leaders. A few days before his death, an official of the Methodist church told him: "Were one man chosen who has meant most to the ecumenical movement in Georgia, you would be that man."[27]

Hallinan welcomed Pope John XXIII's decision to call an ecumenical council, and he quickly allied himself with the progressive forces at the council, voting with them on such topics as revelation, ecclesiology, ecumenism and religious liberty. In the area of his own responsibility at the council—liturgy—he acknowledged his scholarly limitations, yet, thanks to his own reading and study (and the invaluable help of Frederick McManus), he was able to make a substantial contribution to the conciliar Liturgical Commission and to play a major role in the formation of the International Commission on English in the Liturgy.

One of the most gratifying aspects of the council for Hallinan was the experience of working together with other bishops, and he vigorously applauded the council's endorsement of collegiality. "Despite the pastoral sense of the past six popes," he said, "we have had a concentrated central authority and a diminished episcopacy. This is a matter of Church government, not of faith or moral conduct." He welcomed the establishment of national episcopal conferences as a "third force" capable of furnishing leadership in areas where the local bishop's authority was too circumscribed and Roman authority too remote. He had enough confidence in the faith of his fellow American Catholics not to fear that such an arrangement would threaten their bonds with the Holy See or with the rest of the Church. On the contrary, he said:

> The effective unity of American Catholics in the Church universal should be strengthened by a sharing of control. In essentials, it would certainly bind us more closely to the See of Peter, our source of unity. Loyalty to the Holy Father, and to the Church of Rome, always traditional to American Catholics, would be enhanced in this more diversified structure.[28]

Both during and after the council, Hallinan had first-hand experience of the value of national episcopal conferences through his own work on the Bishops' Commission on the Liturgical Apostolate (later renamed the Bishops' Committee on the Liturgy). As secretary and later chairman of the Committee, Hallinan played a crucial role in implementing the liturgical changes in the United States between 1963 and 1968. In those years, Cardinal Dearden said, Hallinan was often "in the middle of a firestorm," and he admired the balance which Hallinan brought to the Committee, advocating no more but no less than the principles enshrined in the Constitution on the Sacred Liturgy. "Hallinan was also a good man to have at the helm," added Dearden, "because he was a reconciler, able to pull together discordant and disparate groups, and in doing so, to get the respect of everyone—even those who disagreed with his proposals."[29]

Like Pope John XXIII, Hallinan's own spirituality was surprisingly old-fashioned. He liked to recite the rosary on long automobile trips, and he was rather shocked at a Newman convention in the early 1960's, when he first saw priests receiving Holy Communion at Mass rather than celebrating their own Masses privately. He was reticent about his piety, and he left no treatises on the spiritual life, but one sister who nursed him at St. Joseph's Infirmary said: "His real vocation was not in liturgy or ecumenism or in race relations. His vocation was to suffer and to show to his priests and people the example of a true Christian who bears his cross with dignity and joy."

Monsignor Noel Burtenshaw captured Hallinan's spirit best, perhaps, when he said: "He was never a child of the status quo: he always wanted to know if things could work better."[30] Hallinan was fortunate to become a bishop during a period of almost revolutionary changes in the Catholic Church and in American society, because it gave him the opportunity to pursue his own evolving vision of a renewed Church and a more democratic society. His death at the age of fifty-seven deprived the American Catholic Church of an articulate and progressive spokesman. Had he lived longer, he might reasonably have expected promotion to a larger see, with the possibility of becoming one of the most influential figures in the hierarchy. As it was, during his nine-and-a-half years in Charleston and Atlanta, he helped to hold American Catholics together and to pull them through a period of rapid and bewildering changes in both Church and society. In so doing, he set an example of enlightened, balanced and imaginative leadership that any churchman of that era might envy.

Abbreviations in the Notes

AAA	Archives of the Archdiocese of Atlanta
AANY	Archives of the Archdiocese of New York
ADC	Archives of the Diocese of Cleveland
ADCh	Archives of the Diocese of Charleston
ACUA	Archives of the Catholic University of America
ACUA/NCWC/NANCC	Archives of the Catholic University of America/National Catholic Welfare Conference/National Association of Newman Club Chaplains
ACUA/NCWC/NNCF	Archives of the Catholic University of America/National Catholic Welfare Conference/National Newman Club Federation
ADS	Archives of the Diocese of Savannah
AICEL	Archives of the International Commission on English in the Liturgy
AUSCC	Archives of the United States Catholic Conference
NA	National Archives of the United States of America

NOTES
Foreword

[1]Charles Stephen Dessain, *Newman's Spiritual Themes*. Dublin: Veritas Publications. 1977. p. 29.

[2]Hallinan to Ellis, Cleveland, February 5, 1955; although this was the date on the letter it was postmarked March 23, 1955.

[3]Easter pastoral letter, *Georgia Bulletin*, March 23, 1967.

[4]Baccalaureate sermon, University of Notre Dame, June 3, 1962, Vincent A. Yzermans (ed.), *Days of Hope and Promise. The Writings and Speeches of Paul J. Hallinan, Archbishop of Atlanta.* Collegeville: Liturgical Press. 1973. pp. 12-13.

[5]*Ibid.*, p. 3.

[6]David Knowles, *The Historian and Character and Other Essays.* Cambridge: At the University Press. 1963. p. 14.

Chapter 1: Painesville

[1]John Gunther, *Inside USA* (New York: Harper and Brothers, 1974), p. 441.

[2]Census Record of Lake County, in *Here Is Lake County* (Cleveland: Howard Allen, 1964), appendix.

[3]Beverly W. Bond, Jr., *The Foundations of Ohio* (Columbus: The Ohio State Archaeological and Historical Society, 1941), pp. 252-253, 358-371, Vol. I of *The History of the State of Ohio*, ed. Carl Wittke (Columbus: The Ohio Archaeological and Historical Society, 1941-1944), 6 vols.

[4]N.Church (ed.), *Painesville City Directory 1902-3* (Painesville: The Herald, 1903), p. 132.

[5]James A. Garfield, "The Northwest Territory and Western Reserve," Address Before the Historical Society of Geauga County, September 16, 1873, p. 17.

[6]Harry Graff, *Lake County History*, preface.

[7]John Struthers Stewart, *History of Northeastern Ohio* (Indianapolis: Historical Publishing Company, 1935), I, 468-469.

[8]*Painesville City Directory 1940* (Painesville: Mullin Kille Co. and Educational Supply Co., 1940), p. 7.

[9]Robert A. Diamond (ed.), *Congressional Quarterly's Guide to United States Elections* (Washington, D.C., Congressional Quarterly Inc., 1975), pp. 543-884.

[10]Painesville *Telegraph,* July 15, 1922, and *Lake County History,* p. 13.

[11]L.B. Hills, *Lake County Illustrated* (Painesville: The Herald Printing Company, 1912), pp. 66-75.

[12]*Ibid.,* p. 3.

[13]W.A. Jurgens, *A History of the Diocese of Cleveland* (Cleveland: Diocese of Cleveland, 1980), I, 539-540. Michael J. Hynes, *History of the Diocese of Cleveland* (Cleveland: Diocese of Cleveland, 1953), pp. 76-77.
Father William J. Gallena estimated that there were 200 Catholic families in the parish when he became pastor of St. Mary's, Painesville, in 1913, but the parish included a much larger area than Painesville proper. See obituary notice for Gallena, *Catholic Universe Bulletin*, December 18, 1964. In 1900 the Pastor of St. Mary's claimed to have 1200 parishioners. Painesville *Telegraph*, July 4, 1900.

There are indications that the Irish did not receive a universal welcome in nineteenth-century Painesville. A few weeks before St. Mary's Church was opened, a citizen wrote to the *Telegraph:* "Order, quiet, quaintness and snugness characterize every part of the town—unless it be the Dublin quarter, but of that even I am not sure; I may be prejudiced against foreigners. Pat has a genius for appearing ragged both in his person and his dwelling, and cares not a straw for this vain world if he can have a chance to confess his sins, get good wages and good "whiskey" and enjoy now and then a clip with his best friend with his bony fist." Painesville *Telegraph,* May 14 1857.

14Interview with Miss Agnes Lynch, first cousin of Paul J. Hallinan, Fairview Park, Ohio, December 10, 1985.

15Telephone interview with Arthur Hallinan, brother of Paul J. Hallinan, Chandler, Arizona, January 25, 1986.

16Interview with Miss Bessie Judkins, resident of Painesville, Painesville, Ohio, December 11, 1985.
Paul was baptized Paul Edward Hallinan on April 16, 1937, by Father Nicholas F. Monaghan in St. Mary's Church, Painesville, but even as a young man he called himself Paul John Hallinan, using his Confirmation name as his middle name. He listed himself that way in both his high school and college yearbook. See *The Purple and Gold* 7 (1928): 41; and *The Dome* 26 (1932): 77.

17Interview with Mrs. Clare McIvor, first cousin of Paul J. Hallinan, Fairview Park, Ohio, December 10, 1985.

18Theodore Marszal, "Pastor in the Age of Renewal: The Life and Spirituality of Paul J. Hallinan, Archbishop of Atlanta, Georgia (Ph.D. dissertation: Institute of Spirituality of the Pontifical Gregorian University, 1980), p. 7.

19Marie Brandstaetter, "The Nursery Industry in Lake County," *The Historical Society Quarterly,* Lake County, Ohio, 14 (1972): 261-263.

20Painesville *Telegraph,* June 21, 1927.

21Stewart, *Northeastern Ohio,* I, 467.

22*St. Mary's Calendar,* Painesville, Ohio, Vols. I-III (1916-1920), *passim.*

23Kenneth T. Jackson, *The Klan in the City 1915-1930* (New York: Oxford University Press, 1967), p. 164. David Chalmers, *Hooded Americanism* (Garden City: Doubleday and Company, 1965), pp. 178-179.

24Telephone interview with Monsignor Thomas Sebian, native of Painesville, LaBelle, Florida, January 23, 1986.

25Telephone interview with Sister M. Colette Link, H.M., native of Painesville, Painesville, Ohio, January 27, 1986.

26Painesville *Telegraph,* February 21, 1937.

27*The Purple and Gold* [Yearbook], 1928, p. 42; *The Latineer* [school newspaper], April 20, 1928.

28*Golden Anniversary of Cathedral Latin School 1916-1966* (Cleveland: n.p., 1966), p. 8.

29Thomas T. McAvoy, C.S.C., *Father O'Hara of Notre Dame* (Notre Dame: University of Notre Dame Press, 1967), pp. 101-102.

30Francis Wallace, *Notre Dame: Its People and Its Legends* (New York: David McKay Company, 1969), pp. 152-154.

31McAvoy, *O'Hara,* pp. 94-95.

32John F. O'Hara, C.S.C., "A Description of the System Employed in Developing the Spiritual Life of the Students of the University of Notre Dame," *Official Bulletin of the University of Notre Dame* 25 (January 1930): 11.

33John F. O'Hara, C.S.C., "Report of the Prefect of Religion to the Very Reverend Charles L. O'Donnell, C.S.C., President of the University of Notre Dame," *Official Bulletin* 25 (January 1930): 3.

[34]McAvoy, *O'Hara*, p. 97.

[35]*Official Bulletin* 24 (March 1928): frontispiece.

[36]McAvoy, *O'Hara*, p. 101, pp. 105-106.

[37]*Official Bulletin* 25 (January 1930): 14.

[38]Marszal, "Pastor in Age of Renewal," p. 5, n. 20.

[39]*Juggler* 13 (March 1932): 11.

[40]Newton outlived Hallinan and died on June 9, 1979. See the obituary notice in the *Catholic Universe Bulletin,* June 15, 1979.

[41]Interview with John Cardinal Krol, Philadelphia, October 4, 1986. Other information about Hallinan's seminary days was supplied by another classmate, Monsignor Norman Kelley of Lake Milton, Ohio. Telephone interview, February 19, 1986.

[42]Paul J. Hallinan, "Retreat Notes," Wycliffe, Ohio, 1955, in Marszal, "Pastor in Age of Renewal," p. 6, n. 26.

[43]Painesville *Telegraph,* February 21, 1937.

Chapter 2: St. Aloysius

[1]ADC, [Auxiliary Bishop and Chancellor James A.] McFadden to Hallinan, March 12, 1937.

[2]Telephone interview with the Reverend Francis G. Zwilling, St. Petersburg, Florida, January 22, 1986.

[3]William Ganson Rose, *Cleveland: The Making of a City* (Cleveland: The World Publishing Company, 1950), pp. 873-874, p. 891.

[4]*The Official Catholic Directory* (New York: P.J. Kenedy & Sons, 1937), pp. 254-256. Wellington G. Fordyce, "Immigrant Institutions in Cleveland," *The Ohio State Archaeological and Historical Society Quarterly* 47 (1938): 87-103.

[5]Rose, *Cleveland,* p. 879.

[6]Philip W. Porter, *Cleveland: Confused City on a Seesaw* (n.p.: Ohio State University Press, 1976), p. 75.

[7]Sidney Andorn, *The Cleveland Scene 1936-1946* (Cleveland: Sidney Andorn, 1946), pp. 21-25, p. 33.

[8]Lloyd Gartner, *History of the Jews of Cleveland* (n.p.: Western Reserve Historical Society and the Jewish Theological Seminary of America, 1978), pp. 267-268, p. 292.

[9]These figures and the following statistics about Glenville are based on the United States Census returns for 1910, 1920, 1930 and 1940, and the meticulous analysis of these statistics by the Cleveland demographer, Howard Whipple Green. Howard Whipple Green, *Population Characteristics by Census Tracts* (Cleveland: The Plain Dealer Publishing Co., 1931), pp. 56, 131, 145, 175, 193. Green, *Population by Census Tracts: Cleveland and Vicinity with Street Index* (Cleveland: Cleveland Health Council, 1931), p. 6, p. 9. United States Bureau of the Census, *16th Census of the United States, 1940: Population and Housing Statistics for Census Tracts: Cleveland, Ohio and Adjacent Areas* (Washington, D.C.: United States Government Printing Office, 1942), p. 5, pp. 23-24, pp. 74-75.

[10]Gartner, *Jews of Cleveland,* p. 270.

[11]Nelson J. Callahan, "The Irish in Cleveland: One Perspective," in Nelson J. Callahan and William F. Hickey, *Irish Americans and Their Communities of Cleveland,* Cleveland Ethnic Heritage Studies (n.p.: Cleveland State University, 1978), p. 166.

[12]ADC, *Status Animarum* Report of St. Aloysius Church, 1937. The priests of the parish seem to have underestimated the total population of the area. In the *Status Animarum* report of 1940,

the pastor listed 8,000 active parishioners in a population of 20,000. In fact the total population was closer to 40,000. *16th Census: Population and Housing Statistics,* p. 5.

[13]*Catholic Universe Bulletin,* March 20, 1925.

[14]The origins and organization of the Alcyon Club are chronicled in *The St. Aloysius Alcyon CYO Yearbook 1939,* a mimeographed pamphlet which was found in a scrapbook kept by Hallinan and now among the Hallinan Papers in the possession of the Reverend Theodore Marszal, Cleveland, Ohio.

[15]Interview with John and Mary Ellen Maloney, Rocky River, Ohio, December 11, 1985. Interview with Sister Katherine Harrison, C.S.J., Parma Heights, Ohio, December 10, 1985. Letter to author from Mrs. William Monreal, Eastlake, Ohio, November 8, 1985. Letter to author from Sister Hope Greener, C.S.J., Cleveland, Ohio, October 23, 1985.

[16]St. Aloysius Church, Sunday Bulletin, February 19, 1939; July 9, 1939.

[17]*Ibid.,* August 6, 1939.

[18]*Ibid.,* July 27, 1941.

[19]*Ibid.,* March 1, 1942; March 8, 1942.

[20]*Ibid.,* July 13, 1941; December 4, 1938; December 11, 1938; February 5, 1939; March 5, 1939; April 27, 1941.

[21]Andorn, *Cleveland Scene,* p. 61.

[22]Sunday Bulletin, September 3, 1939.

[23]*Ibid.,* December 14, 1941.

[24]*Ibid.,* January 4, 1942.

[25]ADC, Hallinan to McFadden, June 24, 1942. ADC, Hallinan to Schrembs, August 9, 1942. Schrembs received the personal title of Archbishop in March 1939. ADC, Schrembs to Hallinan, August 14, 1942.

[26]National Archives of the United States, United States Army, Records of the Office of the Chief of Chaplains, Record Group 247, Chaplain Reports 19A-19SC, Folder 201, Office of the Adjutant General to Hallinan, September 9, 1942, September 10, 1942.

[27]Sunday Bulletin, September 27, 1942, *The AL-O-BI,* n.d. [fall 1942].

[28]Quoted in William M. Halsey, *The Survival of American Innocence* (Notre Dame: University of Notre Dame Press, 1980), p. 61.

Chapter 3: World War II

[1]NA, War Department to Hallinan, October 18, 1942.

[2]William F. Heavey, *Down Ramp: The Story of the Army Amphibian Engineers* (Washington, D.C.: Infantry Journal Press, 1947), pp. 1-5. Brigadier General William Heavey was the commander of the Second Brigade throughout World War II.

[3]*Ibid.,* p. 48.

[4]NA, Hallinan, Monthly Report of Chaplain, Fort Ord, California, November 1942.

[5]*History of the Second Engineers Special Brigade, United States Army, World War II* (Harrisburg, Pa.: The Telegraph Press, 1946), pp. 21-23.

[6]Paul J. Hallinan, Description of Sunday Services, n.d. [February 1943], mimeographed newsletter in the Hallinan Papers in the possession of the Reverend Theodore Marszal, Cleveland, Ohio.

[7]Marszal Collection of Hallinan Papers, Paul J. Hallinan, "My War with Australia," p. 1. This is a forty-seven page essay written by Hallinan about his experiences in Australia while he was still in the Pacific.

[8]George H. Johnston, *Pacific Partner* (New York: The World Book Company, 1944), p. 133.

[9]Marszal Collection of Hallinan Papers, Hallinan, "My War with Australia," pp. 5-6, p. 23. NA, Hallinan, Monthly Report of Chaplain, Rockhampton, Queensland, Australia, April 1943, May 1943.

[10]Cleveland *Plain Dealer,* July 25, 1943.

[11]NA, Hallinan, Monthly Report of Chaplain, Rockhampton, Queensland, Australia, April 1943.
When Hallinan was in Rome for the Second Vatican Council, he asked the Bishop of Rockhampton about the fate of the chapel. He was assured that it still existed as a non-denominational chapel and that a memorial service was held there every year on the Sunday closest to the Fourth of July. One of the cathedral clergy, Father John J. Comerford, wrote to tell him that he had presided at the service in 1967. AAA, Comerford to Hallinan, July 14, 1967.

[12]Marszal Collection of Hallinan Papers, Hallinan, "War with Australia," pp. 30-31; pp. 9-10, p. 16, p. 39.

[13]*Ibid.,* pp. 17-18. AAA, Hallinan to Daly, n.d. [summer 1943].

[14]Telephone interview with Colonel Robert J. Kasper, United States Army (retired), former Executive Officer of the 542nd Boat and Shore Regiment, Mercer Island, Washington, February 18, 1986.

[15]Gerald P. Fogarty, S.J., *The Vatican and the American Hierarchy from 1870 to 1965* (Wilmington: Michael Glazier, 1985), pp. 346-353.

[16]Marszal Collection of Hallinan Papers, Hallinan, "War with Australia," pp. 14-15.

[17]*Ibid.,* p. 37.

[18]*Ibid.,* p. 32, p. 47.

[19]*Ibid.,* p. 24.

[20]Heavey, *Down Ramp,* p. 50. United States automobile manufacturers might have paid attention to Heavey's report that at Milne Bay his brigade salvaged some sunken Japanese landing craft. They found that the Japanese boats were better designed than their American counterparts and three times more fuel efficient. *Ibid.*

[21]Samuel Miller, *Victory in Papua: The United States Army in World War II* (Washington, D.C.: The Office of the Chief of Military History, 1957), pp. 56-57.

[22]Cited in David Dexter, *The New Guinea Offensive: Australia in the War of 1939-1945* (Canberra: The Australian War Memorial, 1961), Series I, VI, 21.

[23]NA, Hallinan, Monthly Report of Chaplain, Oro Bay, New Guinea, October 1943.

[24]Marszal Collection of Hallinan Papers, Paul J. Hallinan, "My War with New Guinea,", p. 2. This is a fifteen-page continuation of his earlier essay about army life in Australia.

[25]NA, Hallinan, Monthly Report of Chaplain, Finschhafen, New Guinea, December 1943. The comments were added to the report by Captain Wallace M. Mulliken on February 7, 1944.

[26]NA, Hallinan, Monthly Report of Chaplain, Finschhafen, New Guinea, February 1944. The comments were added by CWO George S. Gilbert on March 2, 1944.

[27]NA, Hallinan, Monthly Report of Chaplain, Finschhafen, New Guinea, May 1944. The comments were added by Captain Mulliken on May 5, 1944.

[28]NA, United States Army, RG 94, The Adjutant General's Office, World War II Operations Reports 1940-1948, Engineers, Engr. 542-0.3, 5-1-44 to 6-30-45, Box #19647, Headquarters 542nd Engineers Boat and Shore Regiment, Report after Action against Enemy, Biak Island, August 29, 1944. Marszal Collection, Hallinan, "War with New Guinea," pp. 6-11.

[29]*History of Second Engineers Special Brigade,* p. 95. NA, Hallinan, Monthly Report of Chaplain, Biak Island, November 1944.

[30]Heavey, *Down Ramp,* pp. 161-162.

[31]NA, Hallinan, Monthly Report of Chaplain, Tacloban, Philippine Islands, December 1944.

NA, Hallinan, Monthly Report of Chaplain, Cebu City, Philippine Islands, April 1945.

[32]NA, United States Army, Record Group 247, Records of the Office of the Chief of Chaplains, Chaplain Reports 19A-19SC, Folder 201, Benjamin C. Fowlkes, Efficiency Report of Captain Paul J. Hallinan, April 15, 1945.

[33]Telephone interview with Father Raymond O. Meier, former chaplain of the 532nd Boat and Shore Regiment, Second Engineer Special Brigade, Oil City, Pennsylvania, February 18, 1986.

[34]Manuscript Copy of Notes for Sermon at St. Aloysius Church, Cleveland, Ohio, August 5, 1945. The notes are in the possession of Father Theodore Marszal, Cleveland, Ohio.

[35]*542nd Alumni News,* July 1947, p. 2.

Chapter 4: Newman Hall

[1]ADC, Hoban to Hallinan, December 6, 1945.

[2]Telephone interview with the Reverend Monsignor Norman Kelley, Lake Milton, Ohio, February 19, 1986.

[3]Ralph Wiatrowski, *Cathedral of St. John the Evangelist* (Cleveland: Cathedral of St. John the Evangelist, 1978), pp. 14-18.

[4]Telephone interview with the Reverend Caspar A. Heimann, former assistant at St. John's Cathedral, Berea, Ohio, February 27, 1986.

[5]ADC, Hoban to Hallinan, June 25, 1946.

[6]Richard Butler, O.P., "The End of the Newman 'Club,'" *Commonweal* 82 (September 3, 1965): 629.

[7]*Needle,* June 1950, pp. 12-13. In 1945 the enrollment at the three Catholic colleges in Cleveland was: John Carroll University, 594; Notre Dame College, 220; Ursuline College, 240. The total Catholic population of the diocese was 443,000. *Official Catholic Directory,* 1946, pp. 390-394.

[8]Clarence H. Cramer, *Case Western Reserve University: A History of the University 1826-1976* (Boston: Little Brown & Company, 1976), pp. 126-130, pp. 149-150.

[9]*Needle,* October 1946, p. 1.

[10]*Ibid.,* December 1946, p. 3; May 1947, p. 1; October 1947, p. 3.

[11]*Ibid.,* October 1946, p. 1; November 1946, p. 2; December 1946, p. 6; December 1946, p. 1.

[12]*Ibid.,* March 1947, p. 1.

[13]*Ibid.,* November 1947, p. 1. One year later Hallinan replaced Monsignor Richard Walsh as diocesan director of Newman Clubs. ADC, Balmat to Hallinan, November 23, 1948.

[14]ADC, Report of the Chaplains of the Intercollegiate Newman Club of Cleveland to Hoban, June 28, 1948.

[15]*Catholic Universe Bulletin,* October 1, 1955.

[16]*Needle,* June 1950, p. 9.

[17]Interview with Mr. Eugene C. Best, former diocesan director of Cleveland Newman Clubs, Poughkeepsie, N.Y., February 25, 1986.

[18]Letter to author from Mary Lou Wurstner Rogel, Rancho Cordova, California, January 20, 1986.

[19]*Needle,* March 1949, p. 5; February 1950, p. 2; December 1949, p. 2; November 1948, p. 1; April 1949, p. 1; April 1950, p. 7.

[20]*Ibid.,* June 1950, p. 9.

[21]*Ibid.,* September 1951, p. 3.

²²Richard Butler, O.P., *God on the Secular Campus* (Garden City: Doubleday and Company, 1963), p. 74.

²³*Needle*, September 1949, pp. 3-4.

²⁴Quoted by Butler, *God on the Secular Campus*, pp. 75-76.

²⁵Interview with Miss Bernadette Williams, housemother at Newman Hall, *Georgia Bulletin*, March 19, 1968.

²⁶Telephone interview with Reverend John J. Kilcoyne, Hallinan's successor as diocesan director of Cleveland Newman Clubs, Cleveland, Ohio, February 28, 1986.

²⁷*Needle*, February 1949, p. 4.

²⁸*Catholic Universe Bulletin*, October 1, 1955. Hallinan's contention that many of the Catholic apostates lost their faith before they came to secular colleges got substantial confirmation a few years later, when the National Opinion Research Center conducted a poll involving 35,000 graduates of 135 colleges. According to this poll, 87% of the Catholic graduates of secular colleges still considered themselves to be Catholics, and Andrew Greeley made this comment about the 13% who apostatized: "There is reason to believe that those who leave their religion are pretty much inclined to do so before they come to college. The familiar Newman Club expression that 'well-instructed Catholics do not lose their faith in secular colleges' seems to be supported." Andrew M. Greeley, "Do They Lose the Faith at Secular Colleges?" *Catholic World* 195 (June 1962): 147.

²⁹*Catholic Universe Bulletin*, June 16, 1950.

³⁰*America* 83 (June 3, 1950): 263.

³¹Cleveland Newman Alumni Association, *The Newsletter*, February 1967, pp. 3-4.

³²Paul J. Hallinan, "The Influence of William James upon the Political Actions of Theodore Roosevelt" (M.A. thesis, John Carroll University, 1953), 74 pp.

³³Interview with Eugene Best. Cf. note 17.

³⁴Telephone interview with Reverend Monsignor Thomas C. Corrigan, former Newman Club chaplain at Western Reserve University, Parma, Ohio, March 10, 1986.

³⁵Telephone interview with Reverend James Reymann, former resident student at Newman Hall, Wellington, Ohio, February 27, 1986.

Chapter 5: Newman Work in Cleveland and the Nation

¹ACUA/NCWC: YD/NNCF, Box 101, Mitty to Hallinan, August 8, 1952.

²John Whitney Evans, *The Newman Movement: Roman Catholics in American Higher Education 1883-1971* (Notre Dame: University of Notre Dame Press, 1980), p. 44, p. 92, pp. 111-112.

³ACUA/NCWC:YD/NANCC, Box 101, Robert E. Tracy, The Status of the Priest in the Local Newman Club and in the National Newman Federation.

⁴ACUA/NCWC:YD/NANCC, Box 101, Committee on Policy to Schieder, December 29-30, 1952. There were four major recommendations in the memorandum:
    a. that the National Chaplain be the liaison between the Youth Division of the NCWC and the Newman Federation;
    b. that the Director of the Youth Division consult with the National Chaplain before reversing or modifying any decision made by him;
    c. that the Chaplains' Association have the right to submit three names to the Youth Director for the post of National Chaplain of the Newman Federation;
    d. that the operation of the Federation and the Chaplains' Association be left in the hands of the National Chaplain subject to the general guidelines laid down by the Youth Division of the NCWC.

[5]ACUA/NCWC:YD/NANCC, Box 101, Schieder to Hallinan, April 4, 1953.

[6]ACUA/NCWC:YD/NNCF, Box 101, Thomas A. Carlin, O.S.F.S., Report on the National Office, December 30, 1953 [*sic*].

[7]ACUA/NCWC:YD/NANCC, Box 101, Minutes of the Annual Business Meeting, Purdue University, September 4-5, 1952; ACUA/NCWC:YD/NNCF, Box 101, Report on the Newman Club from Monsignor Joseph E. Schieder and Father Thomas A. Carlin, O.S.F.S., to National Chaplain, January 1, 1953.

[8]ACUA/NCWC:YD/NNCF, Box 101, Paul J. Hallinan, Report to the National Convention of the NNCF, University of Minnesota, September 1953; Hallinan, Report on Ninety Days, September 15, 1953-December 15, 1953.

[9]*Ibid.,* Hallinan, Report on Ninety Days, December 15, 1952-March 15, 1953.

[10]*Ibid.,* Hallinan, Report on Ninety Days, March 15, 1954-June 15, 1954.

[11]*Ibid.,* Hallinan, Report to the National Executive Committee of the NNCF, December 29, 1952; Hallinan, Report to the National Executive Committee of the NNCC, April 10, 1953; Hallinan, Report on Ninety Days, December 15, 1953-March 15, 1954.

[12]There are several sample letters in the files of the Federation. ACUA/NCWC:YD/NNCF, Box 101.

[13]ACUA/NCWC:YD/NNCF, Box 101, Hallinan, Report to the National Executive Committee of the NNCF, December 29, 1952.

[14]ACUA/NCWC:YD/NNCF, Box 101, Hallinan, Report to the National Executive Committee of the NNCF, Ames, Iowa, April 10, 1953; Hallinan, Report to the national convention of the NNCF, University of Minnesota, September 1953.

[15]Paul J. Hallinan (ed.), *Newman Club Manual* (n.p.: National Newman Club Federation, 1954), 61 pp. *The Newman Club on the American Campus* (n.p.: National Association of Newman Club Chaplains, 1954), 115 pp. Robert J. Welch and Paul J. Hallinan, *The Newman Club in American Education* (Huntington, Indiana: National Association of Newman Club Chaplains, 1953), 62 pp.

[16]ACUA/NCWC:YD/NANCC, Box 101, Hallinan, Report on the Executive Meeting of the Advisory Committee of NANCC, June 12, 1953.

[17]ACUA/NCWC:YD/NANCC, Box 101, Hallinan, Report on Business Meeting of NANCC, September 1-2, 1953; ACUA/NCWC:YD/NNCF, Box 101, Hallinan, Report on Ninety Days, September 15, 1953-December 15, 1953; Hallinan, Report to the National Executive Committee of the NNCF, March 26, 1954.

[18]ACUA/NCWC:YD/NANCC, Box 101, Address by the Reverend Joseph Connerton, Newman Club Chaplain at the University of Chicago, Boulder, Colorado, December 30, 1952. Hallinan added his comments in longhand at the bottom of his copy of the speech.

[19]ACUA/NCWC:YD/NNCF, Box 101, Hallinan, Report on Ninety Days, March 15, 1953-June 15, 1953. Tracy's remarks originally appeared in the Boulder Memorandum.

[20]ACUA/NCWC:YD/NNCF, Box 101, Hallinan, Report to NNCF and NANCC, April 30, 1954.

[21] *Time* 70 (October 7, 1957): 47; *United States News and World Report* 34 (October 4, 1957): 114-116.

[22]Finis Farr, "Princeton and the Priest," *National Review* 4 (October 19, 1957): 345-347; William F. Buckley, Jr., *National Review* 5 (January 11, 1958): 41; 5 (January 25, 1958): 90; 5 (February 8, 1958): 137; Aidan M. Carr, O.F.M. Conv., "Princeton vs. Father Halton," *Homiletic and Pastoral Review* 58 (January 1958): 353-366; John Cogley, "The Princeton Affair," *Commonweal* 67 (October 18, 1957): 73; James Finn, "The Princeton Controversy," *Commonweal* 67 (January 17, 1958): 399-402.

A side controversy developed over the allegation (reported in the New York *Herald-Tribune* of September 30, 1957) that Halton had said that "Dr. Maritain does not have a very sound philosophical background." When *America* reported the remark in the October 12th issue, it left the door open for Halton to claim that he had been misquoted. Instead, he offered *America* $1,000 to prove that he said what the *Herald-Tribune* claimed he said about Maritain. *America* 98 (December 14, 1957): 355.

[23]Tracy and Hallinan to Archbishop Leo Binz, Episcopal Chairman of the Youth Division of the NCWC, August 13, 1958. The letter is among the Hallinan Papers in the possession of His Eminence, Joseph Cardinal Bernardin, Archbishop of Chicago, who graciously allowed me to use them.

[24]Tracy and Hallinan to Binz, June 25, 1958, in Hallinan Papers, *ut supra.*

[25]Hoban to Hallinan, May 31, 1958; Schexnayder to Hallinan, May 28, 1958, in Hallinan Papers, *ut supra.*

[26]Binz to Hallinan, August 5, 1958, in Hallinan Papers, *ut supra.*

[27]*Our Sunday Visitor,* June 21, 1959.

[28]Diary of Paul J. Hallinan, November 12, 1956, in the possession of Cardinal Bernardin who allowed me to use it. Hallinan started a diary on January 1, 1955, but dropped it at the end of February. He started it again in 1956 from January to April, then from July to December. Thereafter he made almost daily entries, except for long gaps in his last years, when he was seriously ill in the hospital.

[29]Diary, November 15, 1956.

[30]Diary, November 20, 1956.

[31]Diary, January 16, 1957.

[32]Diary, April 22, 1957.

[33]Diary, May 7, 1957; August 5, 1957; October 3, 1957; May 27, 1958-June 12, 1958.

[34]Diary, November 29, 1956.

[35]ADC, Hallinan to Krol, April 5, 1958.

Chapter 6: Dixie

[1]Diary, September 3, 4, 5, 1958. Telephone interview with Monsignor Norman Kelley, Lake Milton, Ohio, February 19, 1986. Telephone interview with the Reverend Richard Butler, O.P., former President of the National Newman Club Chaplains' Association, River Forest, Illinois, April 9, 1986.

[2]Interview with Mrs. Clare McIvor, cousin of Archbishop Hallinan, Fairview Park, Ohio, December 10, 1985.

[3]Diary, October 10, 1958.

[4]Diary, September 21, 1958. *Catholic Universe Bulletin,* October 24, 1958.

[5]*Catholic Universe Bulletin,* October 31, 1958.

[6]Diary, September 19, 27, 28, 29, 1958.

[7]Interview with Joseph Cardinal Bernardin, Chicago, Illinois, October 3, 1985.

[8]Diary, October 17, November 12, 1958.

[9]Diary, November 23, 24, 25, 1958. *Catholic Banner,* November 30, 1958.

[10]Diary, November 26, 1958; December 10, 1958.

[11]Ernest McPherson Lander, *A History of South Carolina 1865-1960* (Chapel Hill: University of North Carolina Press, 1960), pp. 215-225. In 1957 only Arkansas and Mississippi had a lower per capita income than South Carolina. The national average was $2,027; the highest was

Connecticut with $2,821; in South Carolina it was $1,180. *Ibid., p.* 244.

[12]Joseph J. Spengler, "Economic Trends and Prospects," in John C. McKinney and Edgar T. Thompson (eds.), *The South in Continuity and Change* (Durham: Duke University Press, 1965), pp. 118-119.

[13]Lander, *History of South Carolina,* p. 234. p. 236. Between 1945 and 1960 there were nine presidents at the four South Carolina universities (The Citadel, Clemson, University of South Carolina and Winthrop), but only two had earned doctorates. Several members of the Clemson Board of Trustees held honorary doctorates awarded by the board itself. *Ibid.*

Another complaint was the lack of academic freedom at South Carolina educational institutions. In 1958, when Donald Russell ran for governor in the Democratic primary, he boasted that, as President of the University of South Carolina, he had "promptly terminated" the contract of a professor who had publicly advocated racial integration. Earl Black, *Southern Governors and Civil Rights: Racial Segregation as a Campaign Issue in the Second Reconstruction* (Cambridge: Harvard University Press, 1976). p. 82.

[14]Lander, *History of South Carolina,* p. 213. Lewis P. Jones, *South Carolina: A Synoptic History for Laymen* (Columbia, S.C.: The Sandpaper Press, 1971), p. 250. Neal R. Peirce, *The Deep South States of America* (New York: W.W. Norton & Co., 1974), pp. 426-429. Jack Bass and Walter DeVries, *The Transformation of Southern Politics: Social Change and Political Consequence Since 1945* (New York: The New American Library, 1977), p. 249.

Mendel Rivers' solicitude for his home district was legendary. One journalist commented: "The Charleston area became one of the most elaborately fortified patches of geography in the nation—one survey toting up an Air Force base, a Navy base, a Polaris missile maintenance center, a naval shipyard and ballistic missile submarine training station, an Army depot, a naval hospital, a naval supply center and weapons station, a Marine air station, a Marine recruiting depot and training center, a Coast Guard station, a mine-warfare center, and the Sixth Naval District Headquarters. Rivers himself surmised: 'I brought 90 percent of it in.'" Marshall Frady, *Southerners: A Journalist's Odyssey* (New York: The New American Library, 1980), p. 83.

[15]David Duncan Wallace, *South Carolina: A Short History 1520-1948* (Columbia: University of South Carolina Press, 1961), p. 694. Bass and DeVries, *Transformation of Southern Politics,* p. 259. Jones, *South Carolina,* p. 251.

Dwayne E. Walls, a reporter for the Charlotte *Observer,* gave a graphic account of black migration to the north in *The Chickenbone Special,* the name given by railroad conductors to the Gulf Coast Special, the all-stops local train which carried many Carolina blacks to new homes in Washington, Baltimore and New York. Dwayne E. Walls, *The Chickenbone Special* (New York: Harcourt Brace and Jovanovich, 1971), pp. 233.

[16]V.O. Key Jr., *Southern Politics in State and Nation* (New York: Vintage Books, 1949), p. 130.

[17]The United States Supreme Court declared the white primary unconstitutional in 1944, but South Carolina Democrats continued to exclude blacks from the ballot for four more years by turning the state Democratic party into a private club. To qualify for admission, one had to take an oath to uphold white supremacy. In 1948 the primary was finally opened to blacks by Federal Judge J. Waites Waring, an eighth-generation Charlestonian, who was promptly ostracized by Charleston society for his decision. He eventually resigned from the bench and left the state. Peirce, *Deep South States,* p. 391.

The statistics on black voter-registration are estimates made in 1966. Donald R. Matthews and James W. Prothro, *Negroes and the New Southern Politics* (New York: Harcourt, Brace and World, 1966), p. 148.

[18]James F. Byrnes, *All In One Lifetime* (New York: Harper and Brothers, 1958), p. 407. A native of Charleston, Byrnes was baptized and reared as a Catholic. He left the Church in 1906, when he married a young lady in the Episcopal Church in Aiken, South Carolina. *Ibid.,* pp. 15-16.

[19]Black leaders deliberately picked Clarendon County as a test case to challenge the doctrine of "separate but equal" facilities because the evidence of discrimination was so blatant. In 1951 the

county contained 23,000 blacks and 8,000 whites. The public school population consisted of 6,531 blacks and 2,375 whites, but the county spent $395,329 for the white students and only $282,950 for the blacks. Howard Quint, *Profile in Black and White* (Westport, Ct.: Greenwood Press, 1973), p. 12.

[20]*Ibid.,* p. 21.

[21]W.D.Workman, Jr., a prominent South Carolina political journalist dubbed the 1956 legislative session the "Segregation Session." The lawmakers passed standby legislation to close all public schools and colleges rather than allow them to be integrated. They also gave sheriffs the power to transfer students from one school to another at the request of any school official, and they made it illegal for any state employee to join the NAACP. Lander, *History of South Carolina,* p. 202.

[22]Black, *Southern Governors and Civil Rights,* p. 68.

[23]Marshall Frady, *Wallace* (New York: The World Publishing Company, 1968), p. 127. Wallace denied that he had made the statement. Bass and DeVries, *Transformation of Southern Politics,* p. 57.

[24]*Ibid.,* p. 196.

[25]Black, *Southern Governors and Civil Rights,* p. 82.

[26]In the state senate there were thirty-three standing committees. "The four senators representing Dorchester, Bamberg, Berkeley and Darlington, four black-belt counties having no city larger than 10,000 held fifteen chairmanships. The five senators representing counties containing Greenville, Charleston, Spartanburg, Columbia and Anderson, the state's largest cities, swung nary a gavel." Numan V. Bartley, *The Rise of Massive Resistance: Race and Politics in the South During the 1950's* (Baton Rouge: Louisiana State University Press, 1969), pp. 18-19.

[27]Charleston *News and Courier,* September 6, 1958.

[28]John Bartlow Martin, *The Deep South Says Never* (Westport, Ct.: Negro Universities Press, 1970), p. 7.

[29]Diary, January 11, 1959.

[30]These and the following statistics are derived from *Churches and Church Membership in the United States: An Enumeration and Analysis by Counties, States and Regions* (New York: Bureau of Research and Survey: National Council of the Churches of Christ in the United States of America, 1957), Series C, Number 36, and from *The Official Catholic Directory* (New York: P.J. Kenedy & Sons, 1958), pp. 346-349.

[31]Joseph H. Fichter and George L. Maddox, "Religion in the South, Old and New," in McKinney and Thompson (eds.), *South in Continuity and Change,* p. 364.

[32]Richard C. Madden, *Catholics in South Carolina* (Lanham, Md.: University Press of America, 1985), p. 257.

[33]*Catholic Universe Bulletin,* July 22, 1960.

[34]A Charleston pastor proudly reported in 1960 that thirty-six of the eighty diocesan priests were native-born South Carolinians, and he claimed that this was the highest percentage among comparable Southern dioceses. J. Lawrence McLaughlin, "Catholic People of South Carolina," *Catholic Banner,* special edition, December 4, 1960, p. 18A.

[35]Joseph L. Bernardin, "The Church and the Negro," *Catholic Banner,* special edition, December 4, 1960, p. 21A.

[36]Columbia *Record,* April 17, 1961.

[37]Atlanta *Constitution,* February 26, 1961.

[38]The proportion of Catholic school children to the total Catholic population in the Diocese of Charleston was 1: 3.87. In the Diocese of Cleveland, it was 1: 4.45; in Philadelphia, 1: 4.5; in New York, 1: 4.8; in Chicago, 1:5. *The Official Catholic Directory,* 1958, *passim.*

[39]*Catholic Universe Bulletin,* July 22, 1960.

[40]The sisters withdrew from the hospital because of the lack of money to replace the antiquated hospital building and their own shortage of personnel. ADCh, Mother M. Liliosa Wiesner, O.S.F., to Hallinan, March 4, 1959.

There may have been other reasons too. A fund-raising drive for a new building fared poorly, partially at least because of opposition from local people to the integrated parochial school at St. Anne's Parish in Rock Hill. There was also local opposition to the labor union activities of one of the Oratorian priests, Father Maurice Shean, C.O. ADCh, Monsignor George Lewis Smith, Diocesan Director of Hospitals, to Joseph Bernardin, October 3, 1958.

The local newspaper thanked the sisters for keeping "the decaying, crowded building in operation longer than their better judgment told them was wise" and said that "the marvelous work that the Sisters of the Third Order of St. Francis have done in this area for the past twenty three years will be sorely missed." Rock Hill *Evening Herald,* June 3, 1958.

[41]ADCh, Hallinan to Mother M. Liliosa Wiesner, O.S.F., March 6, 1959, copy.

[42]ADCh, Hallinan to Mother M. Carmelita Reilley, C.S.A., January 4, 1960, copy.

[43]Diary, January 1, 1959.

Chapter 7: A Southern Bishop

[1]Diary, March 5, 1959; May 23, 1959; January 23, 1959; February 26, 1959.

[2]Charleston *News and Courier,* October 18, 1958.

[3]Charleston *News and Courier,* September 8, 1958; September 23, 1958.

In an article for *Harper's Magazine,* Waring said that Southern whites would not send their children to the same schools as blacks because the blacks suffered from a high incidence of venereal disease, poor home environment, deplorable marital habits, greater propensity to crime and retarded intellectual development. Thomas R.Waring, "The Southern Case Against Desegregation," *Harper's Magazine* 212 (January 1956): 39-45.

Ironically Waring was the nephew of Federal Judge J. Waites Waring whose decision in 1948 had demolished the white primary in South Carolina.

[4]Eugene C. Best, *The Newsletter,* Cleveland Newman Alumni Association, June 1968, p. 12.

[5]Madden, *Catholics in South Carolina,* p. 350. Diary, January 20, 1959.

[6]*Catholic Banner,* April 19, 1959; *Catholic Banner,* June 14, 1959. Diary, March 17, 1959; March 19, 1959; April 1, 1959.

[7]Charleston *News and Courier,* December 13, 1958.

[8]*Ibid.*

[9]Diary, May 31, 1959; January 6, 1960; November 25, 1960.

[10]Diary, June 1, 1959; January 3, 1960.

[11]Diary, May 25, 26, 1959; January 15, 1960; October 17, 1960.

[12]Interview with the Reverend Henry F. Tevlin, C.O., pastor of St. Mary's Church, Rock Hill, South Carolina, Charlotte, N.C., April 30, 1986.

[13]ADCh, Hallinan to the Reverend Michael A. Snider, O.P., April 25, 1961. The article appeared in the Columbia *Record* on April 17, 1961.

[14]Diary, June 20, 21, 22, 23, 1959.

[15]ADCh, Minutes of a Meeting at Catholic High School, Columbia, June 5, 1959.

[16]*Catholic Banner,* January 31, 1960.

[17]ADCh, Hallinan to Sister M. Paul Johnston, C.S.A., Superintendent of Providence Hospital, April 25, 1960, copy.

[18]ADCh, Hallinan to Mr. J.C. Long, November 4, 1959, copy.

[19]ADCh, Hallinan to Sister Maria, O.L.M., Administrator of St. Francis Hospital, Charleston, June 2, 1960, copy.

[20]ADCh, Account of Meeting of Advisory Board of Providence Hospital, Columbia, S.C., June 21, 1960. This is a handwritten summary made by Hallinan himself.

Public opinion in Columbia was so hostile to integration that the board decided that it would be prudent to make no public announcement about their decision. In the event that rumors began to circulate, they agreed to issue this statement: "In the present proposed expansion of Providence Hospital, there will be no change in the admission policy. Later on, in the further expansion of facilities, which will be some years hence, there will be a separate section for Negro patients."

Hallinan later admitted that he was stretching diocesan policy to accept this compromise. He explained: "I accepted the deferring of compliance at Providence Hospital because the new addition would be mostly central facilities, and by a fiction, it was possible to consider that no 'new beds' were added.... I think that all the board members agreed that this was an extremely liberal interpretation of diocesan policy." ADCh, Hallinan to Sister M. Paul Johnston, C.S.A., November 22, 1960, copy.

[21]ADCh, Hallinan to Sister M. Paul Johnston, C.S.A., November 22, 1960, copy.

[22]ADCh, Hallinan to Sister M. Paul Johnston,C.S.A., December 1, 1960, copy.

[23]ADCh, Monsignor George Lewis Smith to Hallinan, December 20, 1960. Blacks still had to wait several more years—until the new hospital facilities were completed—before they were admitted to the three hospitals. A civil rights group found that, as of September 1962, no black patients had yet been admitted to St. Francis Hospital in Charleston. Their report said: "Up to the present time policy has been to admit only white patients. Exceptions have been made whenever hospitalization was necessary for non-white religious in the diocese." *Survey of Discrimination in Hospitals and Health Facilities in Charleston, South Carolina, for the Year 1 October 1961 to 30 September 1962,* compiled by a subcommittee of Charleston County Residents on Request by the South Carolina Advisory Committee to the United States Commission on Civil Rights, T.C. McFall, Chairman, p. 8.

[24]ADCh, Hallinan to Father Roy F. Aiken, March 10, 1959, copy.

[25]ADCh, Hallinan to "Dear Father," May 11, 1959.

[26]*Catholic Banner,* October 11, 1959.

[27]*Catholic Banner,* November 8, 1959.

[28]ADCh, Hallinan to Cushing, April 24, 1959; Hallinan to Sheen, April 24, 1959, copies.

[29]Diary, March 11, 1960.

[30]*Catholic Banner,* May 1, 1960; May 8, 1960.

[31]Diary, April 29, April 30, May 1, 1960. Vagnozzi returned the $500 stipend which Hallinan had given him with a gracious note, saying: "It was your pleasure to give it; now it is mine to return it." Diary, May 5, 1960.

[32]ADCh, Hallinan to "Dear Father," May 21, 1960.

[33]ADCh, Hallinan, Notes on the First Meeting of the Diocesan Committee on Liturgy, Charleston, September 16, 1959. Diary, April 23, 1960.

[34]ADCh, Hallinan to "Dear Father," January 5, 1961.

[35]Columbus *Catholic Times,* cited by Madden, *Catholics in South Carolina,* p. 340.

[36]Diary, September 1, September 30, October 11, 1960, December 18, 1960.

[37]Diary, February 6, May 7, July 9, July 19, 20, 21, 26, 1960.

[38]Diary, August 4, 5, 12, 20, 21, 1960.

[39]Madden, *Catholics in South Carolina,* p. 341.

[40]Diary, January 2, 1960, December 2, 1960.

[41]ADCh, Hallinan to Father Walter J. Melfi, March 18, 1960, copy.

[42]ADCh, Hallinan to Father Theophilus McNulty, O.F.M., May 12, 1959.

[43]*Catholic Banner,* April 19, 1959.

[44]ADCh, Hallinan to "Dear Father," January 5, 1961; *Catholic Banner,* January 15, 1961.

[45]ADCh, March 7, 1962.

[46]*New York Times,* June 25, 1959; February 11, 1960.

[47]Charleston *News and Courier,* November 22, 1959.

The *News and Courier* had been one of Al Smith's staunchest supporters in 1928. Mr. Waring might have pondered an editorial which appeared in his newspaper that year at the end of the campaign. "Whether or not Governor Smith be elected, his candidacy is a permanent victory for tolerance. The nomination for President of a Roman Catholic by one of the two major parties is in itself reassertion of the constitutional abolition of religious tests for public office. The Smith nomination explodes the notion that a Roman Catholic is not to be considered for the highest office, and in future national parties will think with increasing disregard of the church affiliations of prospective candidates." *News and Courier,* November 7, 1928.

[48]*Catholic Banner,* December 6, 1959.

[49]*Catholic Banner,* December 20, 1959.

[50]The text of their statement appeared in the *New York Times* on September 8, 1960.

Among the participants were Dr. Daniel Poling, editor of *The Christian Herald,* and Dr. Glenn L. Archer, executive director of Protestants And Other Americans United For Separation of Church and State. Peale's presence gave the group added lustre, but he was also something of a loose cannon on the deck. When asked why he had not invited Dr. Reinhold Niebuhr, Vice-President of Union Theological Seminary in New York City, Peale replied: "If he were here, we would never get anything done." He also mentioned that he had no fears about Vice-President Richard Nixon's Quaker faith because "I don't know that he ever let it bother him." *New York Times,* September 8, 1961.

On September 15, Peale announced that he had "completely disassociated himself from Citizens for Religious Freedom, saying that "public agitation of religion as an issue can only be divisive." At the same time, he tried to defend the meeting of the organization on September 7 by claiming that it had been "invaded by reporters who distorted its purpose and gave a very false and distressing picture of my own relationship to the matter." Davenport *Catholic Messenger,* September 22, 1960.

[51]The text of the statement appeared in the *New York Times* on September 12, 1960.

[52]*Catholic Banner,* October 16, 1960.

[53]Columbia *State,* October 24, 1960.

Patricia Barrett compiled a sixty-five page annotated bibliography of anti-Catholic booklets, pamphlets and newsletters which circulated during the 1960 election campaign. Patricia Barrett, *Religious Liberty and the American Presidency* (New York: Herder and Herder, 1963), pp. 60-125.

[54]New York *Catholic News,* August 20, 1960, November 5, 1960.

[55]The letter was signed by Archbishop James Davis of San Juan, Bishop James McManus, C.Ss.R., of Ponce and Auxiliary Bishop Luis Aponte of Ponce. The governor was a divorced Catholic who had favored government-sponsored programs for birth control and sterilization. The bishops also objected to inadequate provisions on the island for religious instructions for Catholic children in the public schools. Berton Dulce and Edward J. Richter, *Religion and the Presidency* (New York: Macmillan, 1962), p. 201.

[56]*New York Times,* October 24, 1960.

[57]*New York Times,* October 28, 1960; New York *Catholic News,* November 5, 1960; Diary, October 25, 1960.

[58]"Archbishop Karl J. Alter Answers 19 Questions about a Catholic President," *Sign* 39 (July 1960): 11-14.

Alter was asked how a Catholic President should react, if Congress passed a bill authorizing birth control information for undeveloped countries. He replied:

"No President of the United States, whether he be a Catholic, Protestant, Jew or infidel, can nullify an act of Congress. If as a Catholic he be convinced of the immorality of a specific law, he can take a passive attitude toward its enforcement. And thereby he violates neither his conscience nor his oath of office. A Catholic in office has no obligation in conscience to attempt to obstruct the fulfillment of any law by some futile action of his own.

There is a false inference in the question, namely, that a Catholic would be obliged to follow his conscientious convictions on birth control, but that a Methodist would not need to do so, let us say, on legalized gambling, or a Quaker on the issue of war, or a Christian Scientist on a question of compulsory medical immunizations." *Ibid.,* p. 12.

[59]*Our Sunday Visitor,* October 9, 1960. The article first appeared in the *Catholic Banner* on July 17, 1960.

Neither Alter nor Hallinan would have found comprehensible the statement of United States Supreme Court Justice William J. Brennan, Jr., explaining that he had reconciled his religious and civic duties by abdicating the former in favor of the latter. Said Justice Brennan: "In my confirmation hearing ... the [congressional] committee unanimously said that it was most inappropriate to ask me whether, as a Catholic, I would follow the Constitution. But then they did ask me. And I had settled in my mind that I had an obligation under the Constitution which could not be influenced by any of my religious principles. As a Roman Catholic I might do as a private citizen what a Roman Catholic does, and that is one thing, but to the extent that it conflicts with what I think the Constitution means or requires, then my religious beliefs have to give way. And, as I say, I settled that in my mind and that took care of it." Jeffrey T. Leeds, "A Life on the Court," *New York Times Magazine,* October 5, 1986, p. 79.

Chapter 8: School Integration

[1]ADCh, Bernardin to Mr. Henry Cabirac, Jr., Executive Director of the Catholic Council on Human Relations, New Orleans, Louisiana, May 16, 1961. The Charleston synod of 1958 declared: "No person shall be refused admittance to any church or the sacraments because of race or color."

[2]*Southern School News,* October 1, 1954, p. 12.

The pastor of St. Anne's personally traveled to thirty-four motherhouses from Massachusetts to Indiana, looking unsuccessfully for sisters to staff the school. The cost of lay teachers (at a salary of fifty dollars a week) was a heavy burden on the parish. ADCh, Robert Sweeney, C.O., to Russell, December 12, 1956.

By 1960 the school was staffed by three Immaculate Heart of Mary Sisters and there were fifteen blacks in the total enrollment of ninety-six children. The financial situation was still precarious, and the pastor, Father Maurice Shean, C.O., had to drive the school bus as well as teach in the school. However, Hallinan said: "All of us are determined not to let this lone integrated school go under." ADCh, Hallinan to Archbishop William O'Brien, January 11, 1961.

[3]Diary, January 1, 1960.

[4]Charleston *News and Courier,* January 5, 1960.

[5]Hallinan to Hollings, January 5, 1960. The letter is part of the Hallinan Papers in the possession of the Reverend Theodore Marszal, Cleveland, Ohio.

[6]Hollings to Hallinan, January 6, 1960, Marszal Collection.

[7]Hallinan, Memorandum of a Conversation with Governor Ernest F. Hollings, Columbia, South Carolina, January 28, 1960, Marszal Collection.

Hollings was not exaggerating the limited scope of the governor's power. V.O. Key said that

South Carolina had a "legislative government" and quoted the common saying that "there's nothing to it [the governorship] except the honor." V.O. Key, Jr., *Southern Politics*, p. 150.

[8]Diary, March 7, 1960.

[9]Diary, March 16, 1960.

[10]Hallinan, Draft of Letter to Governor Ernest F. Hollings, n.d. [March 17, 1960], Marszal collection. Workman's book was *The Case For the South* (New York: Devin Adair, 1960), 309 pp.

[11]Diary, March 27, April 6, October 3, 1960.

[12]*Catholic Banner*, January 8, 1961.

[13]James Hennesey, S.J., *American Catholics* (New York: Oxford University Press, 1981), p. 306.

Archbishop Joseph Ritter of St. Louis ended segregation in the Catholic schools of his archdiocese in 1947 and Archbishop Patrick A. O'Boyle of Washington did the same in the District of Columbia and in Southern Maryland between 1948 and 1956. *Ibid.*, pp. 305-306.

By the end of 1960 Spring Hill College in Mobile, Alabama, St. Mary's elementary school in Houston, Texas, and a few Catholic schools in the Miami area had been integrated. *Southern School News*, May 1961, p. 4

[14]*Southern School News*, April 1962, p. 1.

Archbishop Rummel announced the decision on March 27, 1962 without mentioning the word "desegregation" and without referring to Negroes or to race. The announcement merely said that "all Catholic children may apply for admission to the Catholic schools of the Archdiocese ... according to accepted educational standards."

[15]Francis M. Wilhoit, *The Politics of Massive Resistance* (New York: George Braziller, 1973), pp. 183-187.

Three days after Archbishop Rummel's announcement ending segregation in the Catholic schools, Perez told the Citizens' Council of Greater New Orleans: "Every decent white parent should take his child out of parochial school. You know the Negro customers are not going to support the parochial schools. They will all dry up on the vine and close up. Shut their water off and you'll see them turn about face." *Southern School News*, April 1962, p. 6.

[16]*Southern School News*, December 1960, p. 13.

[17]*Southern School News*, January 1961, p. 5.

[18]Wilhoit, *Politics of Massive Resistance*, p. 191.

[19]Diary, January 3, 1961.

[20]ADCh, Hallinan, Draft of Suggested Statement on the Admission Policy of Catholic Schools, Charleston, January 4, 1961.

Earlier Hallinan had considered integrating the Catholic schools without waiting for the public schools, but Henry Tecklenburg, a layman who was a friend of both Hallinan and Hollings, pointed out to him that such a decision would hardly be fair to the public school authorities in Charleston. The Catholic schools could achieve integration relatively easily, since whites out-numbered blacks by a margin of eight to one. In the public schools of Charleston, the ratio was almost exactly reversed.

Hallinan saw the justice of Tecklenburg's objection. Hence his formula, that the Catholic schools would be integrated no later than the public schools. Interview with Henry and Esther Tecklenburg, Sullivan's Island, South Carolina, April 26, 1986.

The percentage of blacks enrolled in the Charleston public schools in 1960-1961 was actually 72%, but that hardly affected the main point of Henry Tecklenburg's argument. *Southern School News*, December 1961, p. 16.

[21]Diary, January 10, 1961.

[22]ADCh, Hallinan, Notes on a Meeting About School Integration, Savannah, Georgia, January 12, 1961.

[23]Diary, January 14, January 26, 1961.

[24]ADCh, Hyland to Hallinan, January 25, 1961.

[25]AAA, Hallinan to Hyland, February 7, 1961. ADCh, Hyland to Hallinan, February 10, 1961.

[26]Diary, February 6, February 7, February 15, 1961.

[27]Charleston *News and Courier,* February 13, 1961. Diary, February 15, 1961. Interview with Father Henry Tevlin, *ibid.*

[28]ADCh, Hallinan to "Dear Father," February 15, 1961.

[29]*Catholic Banner,* February 26, 1961.

[30]Diary, February 20, 1961.
In April 1959 Robert Tracy had been appointed auxiliary Bishop of Lafayette. In August 1961 he was named the first Bishop of Baton Rouge.

[31]Diary, February 21, 22, 23, 24, 1961.

[32]Hollings to Hallinan, February 20, 1961, Marszal Collection.

[33]Fortunately, the Citizens' Councils were never as strong in South Carolina as in some other Southern states, such as Alabama and Mississippi. Membership in South Carolina peaked in 1956, and by 1961 their influence was definitely on the wane. Neil R. McMillen, *The Citizens' Council: Organized Resistance to the Second Reconstruction 1954-1965* (Urbana: University of Illinois Press, 1971), p. 77.

[34]Ethel Surface to Hallinan, n.d.; Gordon Lewis to Hallinan, March 11, 1961; Donn Mills to Hallinan, March 2, 1961. Marszal Collection.

[35]AAA, Hughes Spalding, Sr., to Hyland, February 21, 1961.

[36]Savannah *Morning News,* February 21, 1961.

[37]Frank Campbell to Hallinan, March 4, 1961. Marszal Collection.

[38]James E. Sulton to Hallinan, March 9, 1961. Marszal Collection.

[39]Hallinan to Sulton, March 17, 1961. Marszal Collection.

[40]AAA, Hallinan to Paul Tanner, February 13, 1961.

[41]*New York Times,* February 20, 1961.

[42]*Time,* March 3, 1961. *Newsweek,* March 6, 1961.
Time criticized the bishops for not ordering immediate integration and sneered that Hallinan's position was "not later, but not now."
Hallinan was furious at the "snickering quip," and protested that the magazine had ignored most of the information which he had given to its Atlanta correspondent on February 21. "There was a news story in all this," he wrote, "but *Time* missed it completely. Ralph McGill, Atlanta editor, got it." Hallinan, letter to editor, *Time,* March 17, 1961.

[43]The pastoral was ignored in the small weekly newspapers like the Cheraw *Chronicle,* the Marion *Star* and the Georgetown *Times.* It received prominent attention, however, in the larger dailies, including the Charleston *News and Courier,* Charleston *Evening Post,* Columbia *State,* Aiken *Standard and Review,* Anderson *Independent,* Greenville *News,* Greenville *Piedmont,* Rock Hill *Evening Herald,* Florence *Morning News,* Spartanburg *Herald* and Spartanburg *Journal.*
In Georgia press coverage was less extensive, but the pastoral was mentioned in the Macon *Telegraph,* Augusta *Chronicle,* Atlanta *Constitution,* Savannah *Morning News,* Savannah *Evening News,* Valdosta *Daily Times,* and the Waycross *Journal-Herald.*
The Savannah *Evening News* published the full text of the bishops' letter and a statement by Mrs. B.J. Gaillot, Jr., a leading Catholic foe of integration in New Orleans, who said that the bishops were disobeying God's law, which demanded the retention of segregation. She invited them to come to New Orleans to debate the question with her. In the meantime, she warned them

that all "integrators" were cursed according to Holy Scripture and a decree of Pope Urban VIII. Savannah *Evening News,* February 21, 1961.

[44]Columbia *State,* February 21, 1961. Charleston *Evening Post,* February 22, 1961. Charleston *News and Courier,* February 21, 1961.

[45]Atlanta *Journal and Constitution,* February 26, 1961.

Ralph McGill knew the mood of the South as well as any contemporary, and a year later, in Spartanburg, South Carolina, the Reverend James Copeland, a Methodist minister, asked the South Carolina Methodist Conference to integrate the two Methodist colleges in the state. He said: "Most ministers of South Carolina believe as I do, and many of our laymen."

The Conference rejected his petition, and one official explained: "I am afraid that Mr. Copeland's motion is too far down the road for our people to accept [at] the present time." Florence *Morning News,* June 15, 1962.

Only one year later, however, the Methodists reversed themselves and agreed to desegregate both colleges. William Bagwell, *School Desegregation in the Carolinas: Two Case Studies: Greensboro and Greenville* (Columbia: University of South Carolina Press, 1972), p. 170.

[46]Diary, March 4, 1961. *News and Courier,* March 5, 1961.

[47]Charleston *Evening Post,* March 7, 1961.

The President of Save Our Nation was the irrepressible Mrs. Gaillot, who said that she possessed pamphlets proving that the Bible approved of segregation. She sent a supply of them to the cathedral rectory in Charleston, addressed to "Catholic parents opposed to Integration, c/o Bishop Hallinan." Diary, March 8, 1961.

Along with Leander Perez, she was excommunicated by Archbishop Rummel on April 17, 1962 for her opposition to school desegregation in New Orleans. William A. Osborne, *The Segregated Covenant* (New York: Herder and Herder, 1967), p. 85.

[48]Diary, March 6, March 8, 1961.

There was one last flareup of opposition in August 1961, shortly before the reopening of school, when some of the parents threatened to establish a segregated Marian Academy. Hallinan nipped it in the bud by writing a stiff letter to the ringleaders, threatening them with penalties just short of excommunication.

He said: "I have extended to you every kindness and every opportunity of regaining your place in the Catholic community. I have written to you courteously, spoken with you patiently, prayed for you daily.... Indeed, even now, a letter from you, or a visit from you, with the honest assurance that you will stop these demonstrations, will cause me to withdraw from the course of action outlined in this present week." ADCh, Hallinan, Form Letter to Parents, August 8, 1961.

His combination of kindness and firmness had the desired effect, and the Marian Academy never got beyond the talking stage.

[49]Charleston *News and Courier,* March 6, 1961.

[50]Charleston *News and Courier,* March 10, 1961.

[51]Diary, March 19, 1961.

[52]Charleston *Evening Post,* March 7, 1961, March 9, 1961.

[53]ADCh, Hallinan to "Dear Father," March 14, 1961.

[54]*Catholic Banner,* October 22, 1961.

[55]*A Syllabus on Racial Justice For Use in Catholic Schools* (Charleston: Diocese of Charleston, 1961), pp. 21, 30, 33, 23.

[56]*Ibid.,* pp. vii-viii. The *Southern School News* published extensive excerpts from the *Syllabus* in January 1962. *Southern School News,* January 1962, p. 15.

[57]It was left to Hallinan's successor, Bishop Francis F. Reh, to implement the pastoral letter of February 1961. In July 1963 he announced that all Catholic schools would be open to all children in September 1964. A month after Reh's announcement, however, the federal courts ordered the integration of four Charleston public schools for the following September.

Reh was now faced with the prospect that the diocese would not be able to honor Hallinan's pledge that the Catholic schools would be integrated "no later than the public schools." At the last minute, therefore, he changed his timetable and ordered the immediate integration of the twelve Catholic schools (ten white and two black) in the Greater Charleston area.

For the rest of the Catholic schools in the diocese, the deadline remained September 1964, when they were peacefully integrated. ADCh, Statement of the Diocese of Charleston Concerning the Admission Policy of Parochial and Diocesan Schools in South Carolina, n.d. [late August 1963]. *Catholic Banner,* September 1, September 8, 1963. Madden, *Catholics in South Carolina,* p. 356.

Chapter 9: The Newman Apostolate

[1]Diary, April 8, April 25, 1961; February 4, February 5, 1962.

[2]Diary, May 28, December 10, 1961; November 6-20, 1961.

[3]Hallinan to Nelson Callahan, March 18, 1960. The letter is in the possession of Father Nelson Callahan of Bay Village, Ohio, who kindly allowed me to see it.

[4]Diary, July 1, 2, 3, 30, 1961; November 5, 13, 1961.

[5]Diary, December 28, 1961; January 8, 15, 16, 1962.

[6]Diary, January 20, 21, 1962. Hallinan, "Richard Gilmour, Second Bishop of Cleveland, 1872-1891" (Ph.D. dissertation, Western Reserve University, 1963), p. 47.

[7]Diary, February 3, 1962. Interview with Cardinal Bernardin, *ibid.*

The dissertation was not Hallinan's only contribution to church history. The 140th anniversary of the Diocese of Charleston occurred in 1960, and he took note of it with a sixty-two page supplement to the *Catholic Banner.* While he did not write anything himself, he supervised every stage of the preparation from the first planning sessions to the final copy, even stopping at the printer in Fort Wayne, Indiana, on his way to a meeting in Chicago, to read the page proofs and catch a few last errors. He was extremely proud of the issue, which contained several lengthy articles on the history of the diocese by Joseph Bernardin, John Tracy Ellis, Richard Madden, and others. *Catholic Banner,* December 4, 1960.

[8]Diary, November 22, 1960.

[9]ACUA/NCWC/NNCF, Box 101, Hallinan to National Executive Committee of the National Newman Club Federation, December 24, 1960.

[10]ACUA/NCWC/NANCC, Box 101, Hallinan, Address to National Chaplains, Baton Rouge, January 23, 1961.

[11]The six units were: National Newman Club Federation, National Association of Newman Club Chaplains, John Henry Newman Honorary Society, National Newman Alumni Association, National Newman Foundation, National Newman Association of Faculty and Staff.

[12]ACUA/NCWC/NNCF, Box 101, Annual Report, 1961.

Monsignor Sigur was bubbling with optimism, when he wrote to congratulate Hallinan on his appointment as Episcopal Moderator. "I am astounded," he said, "at the current general interest across the country in the Newman Apostolate. Everywhere centers are going up, new priests are being appointed, and bishops are studying out the extension of the Apostolate for the large number of Catholic students on the campus. There are so many opportunities that the field is both heartening and challenging...." CUA/NCWC/NNCF, Box 101, Sigur to Hallinan, December 8, 1960.

[13]Diary, June 12, September 27, 1961.

In the meantime Hallinan also sampled the opinions of the chaplains at the national convention in San Francisco in August. Diary, August 28-30, 1961.

[14]ACUA/NCWC/NANCC, Box 101, Hallinan, Memorandum on Recommended Structure for the Newman Movement, September 11, 1961.

[15]Diary, October 6, 1961. ACUA/NCWC/NANCC, Box 101, Hallinan to Sigur, October 9, 1961.

Hallinan was pleased with the support that he received from Dearden. He told Sigur: "[Dearden] is very sympathetic to the Newman movement, enjoys our company and fortunately is in a position to give the movement prestige and real stature, especially in the minds of the other bishops." *Ibid.*

[16]ACUA/NCWC/NNCF, Box 101, Sigur to Hallinan, October 14, 1961; Sigur to Hallinan, December 19, 1961.

[17]ACUA/NCWC/NNCF, Box 101, Hallinan, Report on Newman Apostolate to the Bishops of the United States, Washington, D.C., November 16, 1961.

[18]ACUA/NCWC/National Newman Foundation, Box 101, Progress Report at the Annual Membership Meeting, Pittsburgh, September 1, 1962.

[19]Diary, December 7, 1961. ACUA/NCWC/NANCC, Box 101, Hallinan to Sigur and Albright, n.d. [late December 1961].

[20]Diary, January 30, 31, 1962. NCWC Press Release, April 18, 1962.

As part of the new structure, Father Albright became Coordinating Secretary of the National Newman Apostolate and Monsignor Sigur became Chaplain of the Apostolate.

[21]*National Newman News* II (October 1961): 2.

[22]ACUA/NCWC/NNCF, Box 101, Orlett to Sigur, February 2, 1962.

[23]ACUA/NCWC/NNCF, Box 101, Sigur to Orlett, February 9, 1962.

[24]ACUA/NCWC/NNCF, Box 101, Albright to Orlett, February 23, 1962.

[25]ACUA/NCWC/NNCF, Box 101, Orlett to Sigur, March 16, 1962.

[26]ACUA/NCWC/NNCF, Box 101, Form Letter from Orlett re Proposed Summit Meeting, March 17, 1962.

[27]ACUA/NCWC/NNCF, Box 101, Albright to Orlett, March 22, 1962.

[28]ACUA/NCWC/NNCF, Box 101, Hallinan to Sigur, March 22, 1962.

[29]ACUA/NCWC/NNCF, Box 101, Hallinan to Orlett, March 23, 1962.

[30]ACUA/NCWC/NNCF, Box 101, Hallinan, Memorandum on the Future of the Newman Apostolate, March 19, 1962. He sent a copy to Sigur on the same date.

In this memorandum, Hallinan identified five primary tasks for the Newman Apostolate:

1. "to reach every student of the Catholic faith on the non-Catholic campus;
2. to identify him with the Church on the campus;
3. to enroll him in a sound program of religious instruction;
4. to provide pastoral care and spiritual formation for all Catholic students;
5. to encourage and form a vigorous leadership for the Catholic lay apostolate."

[31]ACUA/NCWC/NNCF, Box 101, Sigur to Hallinan, April 18, 1962.

[32]ACUA/NCWC/NNCF, Box 101, Hallinan to Presidents of Newman Organizations, n.d. [April 1962?].

[33]ACUA/NCWC/NNCF, Box 101, Minutes of the Newman Apostolate Meeting, Ann Arbor, June 22-24, 1962.

[34]*Ibid.* The young priest was Father John Whitney Evans, the future historian of the Newman movement. Evans, *Newman Movement,* p. 281, n. 28.

[35]Evans, *Newman Movement,* p. 134.

[36]Various causes have been suggested for the demise of the Newman Apostolate. One obvious cause was the general restlessness and rebelliousness of many college students in the 1960's. Another factor was the shift away from student clubs of any kind on many campuses. The

student federation sought a remedy at first by closer cooperation with Protestant students, held a few joint conventions with them, then ceased to exist. The chaplains opened their ranks to priests and religious who were doing similar work at Catholic colleges, out of which emerged a new organization, the National Campus Ministry Association. Finally many chaplains thought that they could achieve their pastoral and liturgical objectives more effectively in the context of a campus parish organized like any other parish. Telephone interview with Charles W. Albright, C.S.P., Columbus, Ohio, May 23, 1986.

Father John Whitney Evans summarized the twilight years of the Newman movement in this way: "Even as the Newman Apostolate took its place within the structured mission of the Church in the United States, that Church, its structure, and even its missions, was undergoing the kind of changes that would eventually make the Newman Apostolate, as put together at Ann Arbor in 1962, superfluous. I do not mean to say that whatever went on at Ann Arbor marked the beginning of the end as a cause; rather more in the sense that the summit began closing the barn doors while the cattle were already taking leave." Letter to author, May 26, 1986.

[37]Even as an archbishop, Hallinan was not isolated from the climate on campus in the 1960's. After spending $325,000 to build a Newman Center at one university in his archdiocese, he asked a group of students what they thought of it. Their answer was: "It's one big fat booboo, Bishop. You should have given the money to the slums." He asked them if they knew who was the first to say: "It should have been given to the poor." Hallinan, Address to the National Newman Congress, Northern Illinois University, DeKalb, Illinois, August 31, 1967. The text is in the possession of Cardinal Bernardin.

[38]AAA, Hallinan to Krol, August 8, 1962, copy.

[39]Diary, February 15, 1962.

[40]Diary, February 16, 1962.

[41]Charleston *Evening Post*, February 21, 1962.

[42]Charleston *News and Courier*, February 22, 1962.

[43]Diary, March 8, March 9, 1962.

[44]Charleston *Evening Post*, March 28, 1962.

Chapter 10: Atlanta

[1]Atlanta *Constitution*, March 29, 1962. Diary, March 28, 1962.

[2]Vincent A. Yzermans, ed., *Days of Hope and Promise: The Writings and Speeches of Paul J. Hallinan* (Collegeville: The Liturgical Press, 1973), pp. 1-5.

[3]Atlanta *Constitution*, March 30, 1962.
Vagnozzi told him at the dinner that the Holy See had originally intended to make St. Augustine, not Atlanta, the site of the new archdiocese. Diary, March 29, 1962.

[4]Atlanta *Constitution*, April 8, 1962.

[5]Diary, April 6-9, 1962.
In his six years in Atlanta, Hyland constructed, renovated or converted to church use fifty-five buildings. His most ambitious project was the construction of three diocesan high schools at a cost of almost two million dollars. *Georgia Bulletin*, April 28, 1962.

[6]Diary, April 9, 1962.
His remarks about the South occur in the sermon which he gave at the installation of Francis F. Reh as the Bishop of Charleston, July 18, 1962. Text: AAA.

[7]Joseph J. Spengler, "Economic Trends and Prospects," in McKinney and Thompson, *South in Continuity and Change*, p. 110. Numan Bartley, *A History of Georgia*, (ed.) Kenneth Coleman (Athens: University of Georgia Press, 1977), pp. 348, 376.

[8] *Church and Church Membership in the United States* (New York: Division of Home Missions of the National Council of the Churches of Christ in the United States of America, 1957), Series C, Number 36. Earl D.C. Brewer, "Religion in Georgia," in William H. Schabacker, Russell S. Clarke, Homer C. Cooper (eds.), *Focus on the Future of Georgia* (Atlanta: Georgia Department of Education, 1970), p. 302.

[9] Bass and DeVries, *Transformation of Southern Politics*, pp. 138-139.

[10] Bartley, *History of Georgia*, p. 362; Bass and DeVries, *Transformation of Southern Politics*, p. 137; Peirce, *Deep South States*, p. 355.

[11] Bartley, *History of Georgia*, p. 361.

[12] *Ibid.,* pp. 364-365.

[13] Charles F. Floyd, *The Georgia Regional Economies: The Challenge of Growth* (Athens: University of Georgia Press, 1974), p. 7.

[14] *Ibid.,* pp. 15-16.

[15] Bartley, *History of Georgia*, pp. 341-343.

[16] Peirce, *Deep South States*, pp. 349-351.

[17] Bartley, *History of Georgia*, p. 395.
The county-unit system was an ingenious American version of the English rotten borough system. It was used exclusively in Democratic primary elections for state-wide offices. The county-unit system remained in effect in Georgia from 1917 to 1962. See Joseph L. Bernd, *Grass Roots Politics in Georgia* (Atlanta: Emory University Research Committee, 1960), p. 4.

[18] Bartley, *History of Georgia*, pp. 352-354.

[19] Ivan Allen, Jr. with Paul Hemphill, *Mayor: Notes on the Sixties* (New York: Simon and Schuster, 1971), p. 82.

[20] Interview with Ivan Allen, Jr., Atlanta, Georgia, April 28, 1986.

[21] These figures are based on the statistics contained in *The Official Catholic Directory, Church and Church Membership in the United States,* and Douglas W. Johnson, Paul R. Picard, and Bernard Quinn, *Church and Church Membership in the United States: 1971* (Washington, D.C.: Glenmary Research Center, 1974), pp. 42-50.

[22] "History of the Archdiocese," *Georgia Bulletin*, April 28, 1966.
The author of this history also claimed that "over half of the newcomers from out-of-state are Catholics."
More significant was the fact that, at least until the early 1960's, most of the people moving to Atlanta were not coming from out of state but from other areas of Georgia. A study of the Atlanta population in 1961 showed that 28% of the residents were native-born Atlantans; 56% came from other parts of Georgia; and only 16% came from outside the state. This provided a partial answer to the question why the Catholic population here never grew to the same extent that it did in Florida and Virginia, where there was a large-scale influx of Catholics from other states. Bartley, *History of Georgia*, p. 351.
Pastors also complained of the rapid turnover of people in their parishes; many of those who moved to Atlanta from out of state did not remain as permanent residents. AAA, Minutes of the Meeting of the Board of Diocesan Consultors, December 18, 1962.
There were signs that the growth of the Catholic population was already beginning to taper off in the mid-1960's. The Catholic population in the state as a whole grew at the rate of 10.5% per year from 1955 to 1965, but only grew at the rate of 2.7% from 1965 to 1968. Brewer, "Religion in Georgia," p. 286.

[23] *Georgia Bulletin,* January 31, 1963.

[24] *Georgia Bulletin,* December 7, 1967.

[25] Harold H. Martin, *Ralph McGill Reporter* (Boston: Little Brown and Company, 1973), pp. 125-126.

[26] Diary, April 9, 1962.

[27]Paul J. Hallinan, *Profile of the Archdiocese: Part One: The Mind* (Atlanta: Archdiocese of Atlanta, 1964), pp. 1-3. This was one of three small pamphlets written by Hallinan describing the resources and activities of the archdiocese.

[28]Paul J. Hallinan, *Profile of the Archdiocese: Part Two: The Heart* (Atlanta: Archdiocese of Atlanta, 1964), pp. 3-4.

[29]James J. O'Connell, O.S.B., *Catholicity in the Carolinas and Georgia: Leaves of Its History* (New York: D. and J. Sadlier Co., 1879), p. 502. Franklin M. Garratt, *Yesterday's Atlanta* (Miami: E.A. Seeman Publishing Company, 1974), pp. 13-14.

A new Immaculate Conception Church was built in 1873, a red-brick Gothic building, which is today the oldest church structure in Atlanta.

[30]Robert R. Otis, "Highlights in the Life of Father Thomas O'Reilly," *Atlanta Historical Bulletin* 8 (October 1945): 13-27. Michael Gannon, *Rebel Bishop: The Life and Era of Augustin Verot* (Milwaukee: Bruce Publishing Company, 1964), pp. 183-191.

[31]David M. Chalmers, *Hooded Americanism: The First Century of The Ku Klux Klan 1865-1965* (Garden City: Doubleday & Co., 1965), pp.70-77; Kenneth T. Jackson, *The Ku Klux Klan in the City 1915-1930* (New York: Oxford University Press, 1967), pp. 29-44; Philip N. Racine, "The Ku Klux Klan, Anti-Catholicism and the Atlanta Board of Education 1916-1927," *Georgia Historical Quarterly* 57 (1963): 63-75; John Higham, *Strangers in the Land* (New Brunswick: Rutgers University Press, 1963; New York: Atheneum, 1981), pp. 286-291. Higham says that, within the Klan, "anti-Catholicism grew to surpass every other nativist attitude." *Ibid.*, p. 291.

This outburst of anti-Catholic bigotry led a group of Georgia Catholics to form the Georgia Laymen's Association in Macon in 1916. Their stated purpose was to "bring about a friendlier feeling among Georgians irrespective of creed." Throughout the 1920's and 1930's they were busy countering anti-Catholic prejudice through advertisements in local newspapers, an active inquiry bureau (which answered every letter no matter how scurrilous), and the publication of a quarterly *Bulletin,* which eventually became the diocesan newspaper under the direction of Richard Reed, later the editor of the New York *Catholic News.* R. Donald Kiernan, "Georgia Laymen's Association," *Georgia Bulletin,* January 21, 1965.

[32]Hallinan became involved in a minor racial crisis himself, when he agreed to go to the Georgia Institute of Technology for a Newman Club Mass and breakfast. The college administrators objected to the presence of black students at the breakfast. Only when the archbishop threatened to cancel his visit, did the dean relent and allow the two black students to attend the breakfast. Diary, May 13, 1962.

[33]Diary, April 10, 11, 12, 16; May 7, 16, 21, 1962.

[34]AAA, Minutes of the Meeting of the Board of Diocesan Consultors, Atlanta, May 24, 1962.

[35]Diary, June 5, 1962.

[36]Four days later the superintendent of Atlanta's public schools announced that forty-four black high school students would be allowed to transfer to white schools in September. *Southern School News,* July 1962, p. 8.

[37]Atlanta *Constitution,* June 11, 1962.

[38]AAA, Hallinan, Pentecost Letter, June 10, 1962.

[39]In addition to the Atlanta dailies, the story appeared in the Macon *Telegraph,* Rome *News Tribune,* Savannah *Evening News,* Columbus *Enquirer,* Dalton *Daily News,* Valdosta *Daily Times* and the Waycross *Journal-Herald.*

The *New York Times* carried the story on the front page the next day with a photograph of the archbishop. *New York Times,* June 11, 1962. *Newsweek* also gave it considerable prominence (June 25, 1962), but *Time* ignored it, perhaps because Hallinan refused to give *Time* an interview over the telephone after his last unhappy experience with their correspondent. Diary, June 13, 1962.

[40]Atlanta *Constitution,* June 11, 1962. Atlanta *World,* June 14, 1962.

⁴¹Atlanta *Constitution,* June 12, 1962.

⁴²Diary, June 11, 1962. On September 4th, seventeen black children entered six white parochial schools without incident. Diary, September 4, 1962.

⁴³Diary, June 7, June 21; July 18, 1962.

As the metropolitan of the new province of Atlanta, Hallinan presumed that he would install Reh as the Bishop of Charleston. However, Cardinal Spellman had other plans. He wished to perform the ceremony, since Reh was a former New York priest. Hallinan agreed to defer to Spellman, but he was not happy about it. "The nerve!" he wrote in his diary. Diary, June 16, 1962.

When he met Spellman in Charleston on July 17th, he sized him up as someone who "thinks all bishops should agree with him." Diary, July 17, 1962.

Chapter 11: The Second Vatican Council

¹AAA,Minutes of the Meeting of the Board of Diocesan Consultors, Atlanta, May 24, December 18, 1962. Diary, June 12, 15, 19.

²Diary, August 26, September 17, September 18, 1962. AAA, Minutes of the Meeting of the Board of Diocesan Consultors, December 18, 1962.

³Diary, July 22, July 26, August 18, 1962.

⁴Diary, October 10, 1962.

The Italian bishops had drawn up an international list at the suggestion of Cardinal Giovanni Battista Montini of Milan. Xavier Rynne, *Letters From Vatican City: Vatican Council II (First Session) Background and Debates* (New York: Farrar Straus and Company, 1963), p. 86.

Of all his colleagues in the hierarchy, Hallinan found McIntyre the least attractive. "Absolutely stupid" was his verdict after one lengthy meeting. Diary, October 16, 1962. On another occasion Bishop Joseph McShea of Allentown asked him if he thought that St. Joseph's position was enhanced by being identified as a layman. "No," he replied, "but I think the layman's position is enhanced by being identified with a saint." Diary, November 18, 1962.

⁵Diary, October 11, 1962.

⁶Diary, October 12, 1962.

Finally, on October 16, Auxiliary Bishop Philip M. Hannan of Washington proposed the establishment of a press office for American reporters. Hallinan seconded the motion and it was adopted with strong support from Cardinal Joseph Ritter of St. Louis and Archbishop Karl Alter of Cincinnati. Diary, October 16, 1962.

The United States Bishops' Press Panel was not a press office in the strict sense, since the secrecy of the Council's proceedings limited the information that could be made available to the press. However, the Bishops' Press Panel provided newsmen with background information from various American priests who were experts in their fields. Hallinan was a member of the committee of the NCWC which administered the panel. Floyd Anderson (ed.), *Council Daybook Vatican II, Session I, October 11 to December 8, 1962, Session 2, September 29 to December 4, 1963* (Washington: NCWC, 1965), p. 46.

⁷Rynne, *Letters From Vatican City,* p. 85.

⁸Diary, October 13, 14, 15, 1962.

The name of Bishop Victor Reed of Oklahoma City and Tulsa had originally surfaced among the American bishops as a likely candidate for the Liturgical Commission, but Archbishop Egidio Vagnozzi—of all people—suggested Hallinan's name, since he remembered his liturgical activities in Charleston and had himself presided at the close of Hallinan's Liturgical Week in Charleston in May 1960. Interview with Monsignor Frederick McManus, Washington, D.C., August 16, 1985.

[9]McManus was largely reponsible for this development, and hence for Hallinan's election to the Liturgical Commission.

What happened was this: Father Anscar Dirks, O.P., acting on behalf of the Dutch and French bishops, asked McManus to suggest a North American bishop for the international list that their bishops were preparing for the Liturgical Commission. McManus gave him two names: those of Hallinan and Dworschak. Dirks said that the Northern European bishops would not vote for two Americans for fear that a divided vote would prevent either of them from getting elected.

Therefore, McManus told Hallinan: "In all likelihood, if the various bishops see two American names on the list you distribute, they will, if they wish to vote for only one, choose your name, even if unknown to them in preference to Bishop Dworschak, simply on the basis of archiepiscopal rank." ACUA, Hallinan Papers, Box 146, McManus to Hallinan, Rome, October 15, 1962.

[10]Diary, October 17, 1962.

[11]Diary, October 20, 1962.

[12]"Once he found himself on the commission," Bishop Tracy said, "he went to work with that drive and originality which are so characteristic of him." Robert E. Tracy, *American Bishop at the Vatican Council* (New York: McGraw Hill, 1966), p. 57.

[13]Diary, October 22, 23, 25, 1962.

[14]Anderson, *Council Daybook, Sessions 1 and 2,* p. 51.

On October 21 the American bishops decided to meet regularly during the Council and to set up twelve small study committees, one for each of the major topics to come before the Council. The members of the Committee on Liturgy were: Bishop Vincent S. Waters of Raleigh (Chairman), Leo F. Dworschak of Fargo, Charles A. Buswell of Pueblo, Victor J. Reed of Oklahoma City and Tulsa, Clarence G. Issenmann of Columbus, John J. Russell of Richmond, and Auxiliary Bishop Gerald V. McDevitt of Philadelphia. *Ibid.,* p. 61.

Hallinan was not present at the bishops' meeting on October 21 because he was called to attend the first meeting of the conciliar Liturgical Commission. Diary, October 21, 1961.

[15]Rynne, *Letters From Vatican City,* p. 119.

[16]Vincent A. Yzermans, *American Participation in the Second Vatican Council* (New York: Sheed and Ward, 1967), pp. 157, 158. The Latin text is printed in *Acta Synodalia Sacrosancti Concilii Oecumenici Vaticani II* (Vatican City: Typis Polyglottis Vaticanis, 1970), Volumen I, Periodus Prima, Pars II, p. 75.

Bishop Tracy noticed the startled look of some prelates when Hallinan mentioned the advantage of making the Mass more intelligible to non-Catholics. Tracy, *American Bishop,* pp. 47-48.

[17]Diary, October 31, November 5, 1962.

[18]Bishop Tracy succinctly described what this commission (and the others) was supposed to do: "To receive the interventions of the Council Fathers, whether spoken on the floor of St. Peter's or written: to assign them to sub-committees so that the original text of the *schema* could be reworked in the light of these interventions with a view to winning a two-thirds favorable vote for the revised text from the Fathers when it was next presented to them." Tracy, *American Bishop,* p. 36.

[19]"The original sin of the Council lay in the defective work of the Preparatory Commissions," said Archbishop Denis Hurley, O.M.I., of Durban, South Africa. Quoted in Rynne, *Letters From Vatican City,* p. 164. That criticism did not apply to the Preparatory Liturgical Commission, which performed its function with exceptional competence and thoroughness. Yzermans, *American Participation,* pp. 131-132.

Bugnini's efforts as Secretary of the Preparatory Liturgical Commission brought him more grief than praise. Not only was he dismissed as secretary, but an attempt was even made to deprive him of his post as professor of liturgy at the Pontifical Urbanian (Propaganda Fide) University. He accused Larraona of being directly responsbile for this. Rumors were circulated that he was a "progressive" and an "iconoclast." He credited Cardinals Lercaro and Bea with being his "good angels," who intervened with Pope John XXIII on his behalf. But even the pope, said Bugnini, was not able to crack the intransigence of Larraona. Bugnini called it a vindication, *"un gesto di giustizia,"* when Pope Paul VI made him Chairman of the new Consilium ad Exsequendam Constitutionem de Sacra Liturgia on January 3, 1964. Annibale Bugnini, C.M., *La Riforma Liturgica* (Rome: Edizioni Liturgiche, 1983), p. 41.

[20]ACUA, Hallinan Papers, Box 146, Hallinan, Proposal Made at Meeting of Commission on Sacred Liturgy, November 8, 1962.

[21]Diary, November 7, 1962.

They also talked about many other topics. When Cicognani praised the American hierarchy, Hallinan replied that Cardinal Spellman and Cardinal McIntyre did not represent the American bishops and he mentioned others who did, such as Archbishops Krol, Cody, Dearden and Shehan. He also put in a good word for Bernardin as *episcopabile,* but Cicognani (like Vagnozzi six months earlier) said that he was too young. The Cardinal asked about one of Hallinan's suffragan bishops, Archbishop Joseph P. Hurley of St. Augustine, and said: "I divided his diocese suddenly because he is so odd." He also revealed his admiration for President John F. Kennedy and his nostalgia for the United States, where, he said, there is "more freedom."

[22]Diary, November 8, 1962.

Hallinan had intended to present the proposal himself but was called away to his meeting with Cicognani. He asked Archbishop Grimshaw to introduce it for him, explaining: "All it is really is an attempt to break the log-jam. Apparently everybody wants to vote and this is also favored *in excelsis.*" ACUA, Hallinan Papers, Box 146, Hallinan to Grimshaw, November 8, 1962.

[23]Diary, November 9, 1962.

The thirteen members of the Liturgical Commission who signed the petition were: Archbishop Francis J. Grimshaw of Birmingham, England; Bishop Guillaume van Bekkum, S.V.D., of Ruteng, Indonesia; Bishop Franz Zauner of Linz, Austria; Bishop Carlo Rossi of Biella, Italy; Bishop Karel Calewaert of Ghent, Belgium; Bishop Henri Jenny of Cambrai, France; Bishop Otto Spülbeck of Meissen, East Germany; Auxiliary Bishop Joseph Malula of Leopoldville, the Congo; Bishop Alfred Pichler of Banjaluka, Yugoslavia; Bishop Enrique Rau of Mar del Plata, Argentina; Bishop Franciszek Jop of Opole, Poland; Bishop Albert Martin of Nicolet, Canada.

[24]ACUA, Hallinan Papers, Box 146, Hallinan to Cicognani, November 10, 1962.

[25]Diary, November 10, 11, 12, 1962.

[26]Anderson, *Council Daybook Sessions 1 and 2,* p. 75.

[27]*Ibid.,* pp. 77-78. Diary, November 16. Hallinan says that the voting took place on the 16th. The four amendments were introduced on the 16th, but the voting took place on the 17th.

Hallinan helped to expedite the passage of the Introduction through the commission by successfully suggesting that the pertinent subcommissions meet with the Theological, Juridical and Latin Subcommissions before the suggested *emendationes* were brought before the full commission. Diary, November 14, 1962.

[29]Rynne, *Letters From Vatican City,* p. 148. Diary, November 16, 1962.

[30]*Ibid.,* pp. 164-166. Diary, November 20, 21, 1962.

[31]Diary, November 20, 21, 1962.

[32]ACUA, Hallinan Papers, Box 146, Hallinan, *De Modo Procedendi,* November 19, 1962.

[33]ACUA, Hallinan Papers, Box 146, Bishops of the United States to the Presidency of the Second Vatican Council, November 22, 1962. The Latin text is dated November 26, 1962.

[34]Diary, November 23, 1962.

A few days earlier Hallinan said that Vagnozzi and Griffiths almost came to blows in the coffee bar at St. Peter's. The Delegate said contemptuously to Griffiths: "You are only an auxiliary," to which Griffiths replied: "Tell your friend Ottaviani...." Diary, November 19, 1962.

[35]Diary, November 26, 27, 1962. The number of bishops who signed appears in handwritten notes which Hallinan used for an address to the American bishops on December 3, 1962. ACUA, Hallinan Papers, Box 146.

Spellman complained that some bishops had signed the petition twice. Hallinan explained that a few bishops had sent him notes, asking him to sign their names to the petition and then had inadvertently signed the petition a second time, when it was circulated at the bishops' meeting on November 26. ACUA, Hallinan Papers, Box 146, Hallinan to Spellman, November 28, 1962.

[36]Diary, November 26,27, 1962.

[37]Anderson, *Council Daybook Sessions 1 and 2,* p. 103. Diary, November 30, 1962. In a surprising gesture, Larraona invited Bugnini to read the *relatio* at the meeting of the Liturgical Commission that afternoon.

[38]Diary, December 1, 2, 1962.

[39]Diary, December 3, 1962.

[40]ACUA, Hallinan Papers, Box 146, Hallinan, Notes for Address to United States Bishops, North American College, December 3, 1962.

[41]Diary, December 4, 1962.

[42]*Acta Synodalia,* Volumen I, Periodus Prima, Pars IV, p. 384. Diary, December 5-7, 1962.

[43]Diary, December 6, November, 11, 17,18; December 4, 1962.

[44]Tracy, *American Bishop,* p. 40.

[45]Diary, December 14, 15, 1962.

Chapter 12: Hopes and Plans

[1]Telephone interview with the Reverend Charles W. Albright, C.S.P., Columbus, Ohio, May 23, 1986.

[2]Diary, June 19, August 14, September 9, 1962. He told Ellis of his plans in August and asked: "Do you think it can be done?" ACUA, Papers of Monsignor John Tracy Ellis, Hallinan to Ellis, August 14, 1962.

[3]Diary, January 1, 9, 16, 17, February 15, March 5, 1963. ACUA, Ellis Papers, Ellis to Hallinan, March 14, 1963.

[4]ACUA, Ellis Papers, Hallinan to Ellis, February 27, 1963. Hallinan also told him: "I cannot thank you enough for all you've done. And if Gilmour ever reaches the WRU finals, and if I reach the honor of an earned degree, as distinct from an honorary one, you will be the single person most responsible for getting me thru."

[5]Hallinan, "Richard Gilmour," p. 145, p. 164, pp. 177-180, p. 313.

[6]Hallinan, "The Responsibility of Catholic Higher Education," Address to the National Catholic Educational Association, St. Louis, Missouri, April 19, 1963, *National Catholic Educational Association Bulletin* 60 (August 1963): 150.

[7]Hallinan, "Richard Gilmour," p. 318.

[8]Diary, March 10, 11, 1962.

[9]ACUA, Ellis Papers, Hallinan to Wittke, March 8, 1963, quoted in letter from Hallinan to Ellis, March 9, 1963.

[10]Diary, March 16, April 8, April 14-23, 1963.

[11]Diary, May 8-11, May 20, 21, 1963. ACUA, Ellis Papers, Hallinan to Ellis, n.d. [late May 1963].

[12]Cleveland *Plain Dealer,* June 13, 1963.

[13]Diary, June 12, 1963.

In the space of one year Hallinan actually received four doctorates. On June 3, 1962, his *alma mater,* Notre Dame University, awarded him an honorary LL.D. along with Federal Judge J. Skelly Wright, who had ordered the integration of the New Orleans public schools. The following year Duquesne University in Pittsburgh gave him a Litt.D., and two days later he received another LL.D. from Belmont Abbey College.

What mattered most to him, however, was the degree that he earned. As he told Ellis in 1962: "I still won't accept the Kenedy Directory's bestowal of a D.D.—I want my own Ph.D. the hard way. Nothing but stubborn Irish pride." ACUA, Ellis Papers, Hallinan to Ellis, n.d. [February or March 1962].

[14]Hallinan, *Georgia Bulletin,* January 4, 1963.

[15]*Georgia Bulletin,* February 28, 1963; May 9, 1963.

[16]The most scurrilous letter that he received came from the local chapter of the White Citizens' Council, addressed to Mr. P. Hallinan, Archbishop, R.C. Church:"

"We read about you people are planning to locate some colored people around in your parishes.

We have a deserving mother, Miss Sugarbelle King, who would appreciate you all's help to find a home for her little brood of fourteen, all lovely youngsters of mostly light shades.

Miss Sugarbelle receives substantial help from the Federal Government on the Bastard Relief, but of course, her quota is up now. Mr. Kennedy was able to help her a little with two of them as Emergency Disaster Flood Relief Aid, and one little boy of Jewish cast features gets $19.98 per month from Bonds for Israel, but needs exceeding means still, Miss Sugarbelle has been able to earn a little on the side, though not foolproof, that is how she got the last one. Poor thing can't read directions.

Being she would be out of her own neighborhood, we thought, however, if we could take advantage of your kind offer and locate her—well, you know a houseful of single men could be a nice place for her to live close to, and maybe she could help to clean up some, too.

We will communicate with you further, but hasten to approach you about this, because we hear the Louisiana Branch is lining up a family for you, and we feel justly that local people should be considered first.

Miss Sugarbelle will need the mortgage payments paid like the paper said, out of church money, for the present at least, though she has three growing girls coming on in a few years. We would like to express that we feel that it is very Christian of you Catholic people to help these poor people like this."

White Citizens' Council to Hallinan, February 5, 1963, Letter in the possession of the Reverend Theodore Marszal, Cleveland, Ohio.

[17]AAA, Hughes Spalding, Sr., to Hallinan, February 7, 1963.

[18]Diary, February 8, 13; March 14, 22, 1963.

[19]AAA, Hallinan, Statement of Admissions Policy of the Catholic Hospitals in the Archdiocese of Atlanta, March 28, 1963.

[20]Diary, January 13; March 27; April 2, 3, 4; December 10; January 19, 31; September 10; November 6, 1963.

[21]AUSCC, General Secretary's Files, McManus to Hallinan, April 10, 1963.

[22]AAA, Hallinan to Larraona, March 4, 1963, copy. Larraona denied the report and said: "The Commission for Sacred Liturgy has never thought of limiting in any way his participation in the work." ACUA, Hallinan Papers, Larraona to Hallinan, March 9, 1963. One wonders what Larraona made of Hallinan's double-edged compliment: "Your leadership of the work done in the First Session will not be forgotten."

[23]Diary, April 22, 25, May 2, 1963.

[24]Diary, April 29, May 1, 2, 3, 1963. ACUA, Ellis Papers, Hallinan to Ellis, May 4, 1963.

[25]Diary, May 1, 1963.

[26]ACUA, Hallinan Papers, Hallinan to Larraona, February 7, 1963, copy.

[27]ACUA, Hallinan Papers, McManus to Hallinan, June 2, 1963; McManus to Hallinan, July

14, 1963.

Neither Hallinan nor McManus was completely satisfied with the final draft of the *relatio* on Chapter Three. The Liturgical Commission made eleven major changes in the text of Chapter Three. Hallinan and McManus thought that eight of these changes were improvements, but they regarded the other three as retrogressions, decidedly inferior to the original draft of the *schema*.

The three amendments to which they objected (1) restricted the authority of episcopal conferences to make liturgical changes, (2) restored the name "Extreme Unction" for the Sacrament of the Anointing of the Sick, and (3) suppressed the recommendation that the rite of religious profession take place during Mass.

The three changes were made at the last minute by the *Subcommissio Praesidum:* the new body composed of the presidents of the other subcommissions.

[28]ACUA, Hallinan Papers, Hallinan, Transcript of Press Conference Remarks, Columbus Hotel, Rome, May 7, 1963.

[29]ACUA, Hallinan Papers, McManus to Hallinan, July 14, 1963.

McManus gave a practical example of what this change meant. The original draft allowed for the celebration of Mass at a mixed marriage. According to McManus, the only one who seemed opposed to this concession was Larraona. Nevertheless, it was cut out of the *schema* by the *Subcommissio Praesidum* without the approval of the other members of the commission. When the final vote was taken on the article dealing with mixed marriages, there was no way for them to express an opinion about a provision which had simply been stricken from the text and no longer existed.

[30]The original draft of article 41 of the *schema* limited the use of the vernacular to "the lessons, the *oratio communis* [the prayer of the faithful] and some chants."

The Liturgical Commission amended the text to permit a much greater use of the vernacular in the Mass, but it did so in a cautious, indirect way in the hope of securing the necessary two-thirds majority in the full Council. Blanket permission for the vernacular was still limited to "a suitable place ... especially in the lessons and in the *oratio communis*." However, episcopal conferences would be able to authorize the use of the vernacular for "the parts which pertain to the people," that is all the chants of the Ordinary of the Mass (*Kyrie, Gloria*, Creed, *Sanctus, Agnus Dei*) and the Proper of the Mass (*Introit*, Gradual, Offertory, Communion), whether recited or sung.

To make this palatable to the traditionalists, the Liturgical Commission added the following qualification: "Nevertheless, provision shall be made that the faithful may also be able to recite or sing together in the Latin language the parts of the Ordinary of the Mass which pertain to them." This was really a bit of eyewash, for Hallinan told the American bishops that it was "intended for international gatherings, etc." and he assured them that "the new version [of the *schema*] represents a major vernacular concession to countries like the United States where the indults prevalent elsewhere have not been received." ACUA, Hallinan Papers, Hallinan, Report on the Work of the Commission on the Sacred Liturgy for the Meeting of the Bishops of the United States, Chicago, August 6-7, 1963.

[31]ACUA, Hallinan Papers, Hallinan, Report on the Work of the Commission on the Sacred Liturgy for the Meeting of the Bishops of the United States, Chicago, August 6-7, 1963.

He told McManus that the bishops were generally pleased about the vernacular in the Mass and the sacraments, and with the idea of concelebration and the reception of Holy Communion under both species; but, he said, they were "furious" about the text on the vernacular breviary.

The newly enhanced status of episcopal conferences also led to considerable discussion among the bishops in Chicago. "In its present form," Hallinan said, "it needs a good deal of clarification, and even then, I am afraid that the infringement on the local ordinary's present freedom and autonomy will be a bitter pill for some. Whether the disarray, diversity and scandal to the faithful resulting from a checkerboard of usages (on e.g. the vernacular) will prevail, at least in this field, I do not know." AUSCC, General Secretary's Files, Hallinan to McManus, n.d. [August 1963].

[32]ACUA, Hallinan Papers, Issenmann to Hallinan, August 19, 1963; Carberry to Hallinan, August 16, 1963; Connare to Hallinan, August 13, 1963.

[33]ACUA, Hallinan Papers, Hallinan to Larraona, n.d. [September 2, 1963-?]. The letter is included among the "Animadversiones Scriptae de Sacra Liturgia" published in the *Acta Syno-*

dalia, Volumen II, Periodus Secunda, Pars V, pp. 861-862.

The text of article 19 of the *schema* as amended by the Liturgical Commission now read: "Juxta secularem traditionem ritus latini, in Officio divino lingua latina clericis servanda est, facta tamen Ordinario potestate usum versionis vernaculae ad normam art. 36 confectae concedendi, singulis pro casibus, iis clericis, quibus usus linguae latinae grave impedimentum est quominus Officium debite persolvant."

By contrast, Meyer wished to give general permission for the vernacular to all clerics who found it more beneficial to pray in their own language. His proposed *emendatio* read as follows: "Juxta secularem traditionem Occidentalis Ecclesiae [in] Officio Divino lingua latina clericis servanda est. Attamen, majoris pietatis causa, in privata recitatione liceat adhibere versionem probatam in lingua vernacula."

Hallinan quoted both texts (article 19 of the amended *schema* and Meyer's proposed *emendatio*) in his letter to Larraona. See *Acta Synodalia, ibid.* He sent copies of this letter to Cardinals Cicognani, Spellman, Meyer and Ritter, Archbishop Krol, and Father McManus.

³⁴ACUA, Hallinan Papers, Spellman to Hallinan, September 23, 1963.

Chapter 13: The Constitution on the Sacred Liturgy

¹Diary, September 13, 18, 1963.

²Diary, September 19, 26, 1963.

³Diary, September 30, 1963. ACUA, Hallinan Papers, Hallinan, Declaratio de Quinque Propositis in Capite III (De Ceteris Sacramentis et De Sacramentalibus), September 30, 1963; Hallinan, Supplement to the Report on the Work of the Commission on the Sacred Liturgy, October 4, 1963.

⁴Diary, September 30, 1963.

⁵Diary, October 1, 1963.

Up until this time McManus was the only English-speaking *peritus* on the Liturgical Commission. Diekmann, a well-known scholar and editor of *Worship,* who had served on the Preparatory Liturgical Commission, was under a cloud at the moment because of his interest in a vernacular liturgy. For that reason he had been dropped from the faculty of the summer school at the Catholic University of America in 1962 and barred from speaking there in the spring of 1963.

⁶ACUA, Hallinan Papers, Hallinan, Supplement to the Report on the Work of the Commission on the Sacred Liturgy, October 4, 1963.

⁷*Acta Synodalia,* Volumen II, Periodus Secunda, Pars II, pp. 329, 335, 338, 342, 360-361, 384, 435-436.

⁸*Ibid.,* p. 520.

⁹Anderson, *Council Daybook, Sessions 1 and 2,* p. 184.

¹⁰ACUA, Hallinan Papers, Hallinan, Report to the United States Bishops, October 11, 1963.

The Council *Daybook* mentions without further identification that "mimeographed sheets were passed among a particular national group of bishops which made suggestions on what points they should vote 'affirmative with reservations,' and which supplied them with a Latin formula to append to their 'with reservations' vote. In view of the narrow margin by which the second chapter failed to pass, its failure was attributed by some to the mimeographed sheets." Anderson, *Council Daybook, Sessions 1 and 2,* p. 184.

The Liturgical Commission decided on November 11 to reject both changes and the Fathers approved the decision in the general congregation on November 20 by a vote of 2,112 to 40. Diary, November 11, 1963. Anderson, *Council Daybook, Sessions 1 and 2,* p. 285.

¹¹*Acta Synodalia,* Volumen II, Periodus Secunda, Pars II, pp. 560-571.

¹²*Acta Synodalia,* Volumen II, Periodus Secunda, Pars II, pp. 598, 601, 610, 618, 639; *Acta*

Synodalia, Volumen II, Periodus Secunda, Pars III, pp.48-49. The vote on Chapter Three as a whole was: 1,130, *placet;* 30, *non placet;* 1,054, *placet juxta modum. Ibid.,* p. 91.
ACUA, Hallinan Papers, Hallinan, Report to the United States Bishops, October 11, 1963. Anderson, *Council Daybook, Sessions 1 and 2,* p. 194.

[13]ACUA, Hallinan Papers, Martin et al. to "Venerabiles Patres," October 19, 1963. The signatories were Bishops Franz Zauner of Linz, Austria; Carlo Rossi of Biella, Italy; Otto Spülbeck of Meissen, East Germany; Bernardo Fey Schneider of Potosi, Bolivia; William van Bekkum of Ruteng, Indonesia; Cesario D'Amato, Abbot Nullius of St. Paul's Outside the Walls, Rome; and the following *periti:* Emmanuel Bonet, Johannes Wagner, Aimé-Georges Martimort, Cypriano Vagaggini, O.S.B., Anscar Dirks, O.P., and Marie Rosaire Gagnebet, O.P.

[14]ACUA, Hallinan Papers, Hallinan, Latin Draft of Statement to the Liturgical Commission, October 23, 1963. At the bottom of the page Hallinan wrote that, instead of presenting the protest to the commission, he spoke to Martin privately. In his diary he gives October 23 as the date of his "bitter little set-to with Bishop Martin." Diary, October 23, 1963.

[15]The results were: 1,638, *placet;* 43; *non placet,* 552, *placet juxta modum. Acta Synodalia,* Volumen II, Periodus Secunda, Pars III, p. 290.

[16]*Acta Synodalia,* Volumen II, Periodus Secunda, Pars V, pp. 686, 690, 696, 767. There was yet another "final" vote on the whole *schema* on December 4 (the results: 2,147 to 4), after which Pope Paul VI promulgated it as the Constitution on the Sacred Liturgy. *Acta Synodalia,* Volumen II, Periodus Secunda, Pars VI, pp. 407-497.

[17]Yzermans, *American Participation,* p. 145. Hallinan was not at the party. He was having dinner with friends from Atlanta in a Roman restaurant when a waiter came to tell him the news of the assassination. Diary, November 22, 1963.

[18]Diary, October 10, October 18, October 25, 1963.

[19]ACUA, Hallinan Papers, Hallinan to O'Connor, November 13, 1963.

[20]Xavier Rynne, *The Second Session* (New York: Farrar, Straus and Company, 1964), pp. 158-160. Gustave Weigel, S.J., tried to take a positive view of the proceedings, but even he admitted that "it seems quite clear that the exuberance and liveliness so manifest at the beginning of last year have somewhat tapered off." Gustave Weigel, S.J., "How Is The Council Going?," *America* 109 (December 7,1963): 730.
Hallinan had his own ideas about speeding up the proceedings, as he explained to Bishop Griffiths the previous January. He favored elimination of the three-day waiting period for speakers and limitation of speeches to five minutes. He would have made it possible to petition for clôture on any section of a *schema* upon presentation of a sufficient number of names. He also wanted to eliminate the three rounds of voting on the *schemata* and to introduce multiple voting on amendments by means of I.B.M. cards. One of his other suggestions was to end all *juxta modum* votes ("hangovers from the days when 300 to 700 prelates could take their time"), which is rather ironic in view of the deft use that he made of that tactic nine months later. AANY, Hallinan to Griffiths, January 14, 1963.

[21]Diary, November 20, 1963. Rynne, *Second Session,* pp. 170-171.

[22]Diary, December 4, 1963. Anderson, *Council Daybook, Sessions 1 and 2,* p. 329. The three journalists were John Cogley of *Commonweal,* Robert Kaiser of *Time,* and Michael Novak of the Kansas City *Catholic Reporter,* Rynne, *Second Session,* p. 257.
Robert McAfee Brown, Professor of Religion at Stanford Univesity and an Official Observer at the Council, said that "anti-Catholics will have a field day" with the implications of the Communications Decree. Robert McAfee Brown, "The Vatican Council: A Protestant Assessment," *Commonweal* 79 (December 27, 1963): 397.

[23]AICEL, Council Notes of Denis E. Hurley, O.M.I., October 2, 1963, copy.
The caucus ended abruptly when Archbishop Felici reprimanded them (and others) for talking too loudly and delaying the proceedings.

[24]ACUA, Hallinan Papers, Minutes of the Meeting of the Episcopal Committee at the English College, Rome, October 17, 1963.

Present at the meeting were Archbishop Francis Grimshaw of Birmingham, England; Archbishop Hallinan of Atlanta; Archbishop Guilford Young of Hobart, Tasmania; Archbishop Michael O'Neill of Regina, Canada; Archbishop Joseph Walsh of Tuam, Ireland; Archbishop Gordon Gray of St. Andrews and Edinburg, Scotland; Archbishop Denis Hurley, O.M.I., of Durban, South Africa; Bishop Leonard Raymond of Allahabad, India; Auxiliary Bishop Owen Snedden of Wellington, New Zealand; and Auxiliary Bishop James Griffiths of New York.

Frederick McManus traced the origins of I.C.E.L. back even further to a "remote and rather indirect beginning" in October 1962, when Hallinan held an informal meeting with several bishops from English-speaking countries. However, his interest at that time was not a common English text but cooperation among English-speaking prelates on the liturgical *schema.* Frederick R. McManus, *ICEL: The First Years* (Washington, D.C.: I.C.E.L., 1981), p. 4. McManus says that Archbishop Young was present at the meeting, but Hallinan mentioned only three Englishmen, one Welshman and a Canadian. Diary, October 19, 1962.

Shortly before the end of the first session, however, there was a dinner party at the Grand Hotel, attended by four American bishops (Hallinan, Shehan, Christopher Weldon of Springfield and Michael Hyle of Wilmington) and four Britons (Grimshaw, George Beck of Salford, Edward Ellis of Nottingham and John Murphy of Cardiff), at which they discussed a common English-language Missal and Ritual. McManus, *ICEL,* p. 5. Hallinan, Diary, December 5, 1962.

In the spring of 1963 Archbishop Hurley sent Grimshaw a proposal to establish an International English Liturgical Commission with Grimshaw and Hallinan acting as a "sort of unofficial convening committee." He assured the English archbishop: "This is not passing the buck, but leaving it in the hands of the most capable and influential persons." AICEL, Hurley to Grimshaw, April 2, 1963, copy.

Grimshaw, however, was more interested in promoting his own translation of the Ritual than in a common English-language liturgy. When he failed to act on Hurley's proposal, the Archbishop of Durban resorted to his "liturgical caucus" in the *aula* to get the ball rolling. He later said of Grimshaw: "It was disastrous that he was elected chairman in 1963." AICEL, Hurley to John E. Rotelle, O.S.A., Executive Secretary of I.C.E.L., May 12, 1975.

[25]ACUA, Hallinan Papers, McManus to Hallinan, n.d. [November 1963].

[26]ACUA, Hallinan Papers, Hallinan, Memorandum on the Use of the Vernacular for the Bishops of the United States, November 10, 1963.

[27]ACUA, Hallinan Papers, McManus to Hallinan, n.d. [November 1963].

[28]ACUA, Hallinan Papers, Hallinan, Report to the United States Bishops on the Liturgical Apostolate, November 16, 1963.

[29]Diary, November 16, 1963.

[30]AUSCC, Minutes of the Forty-Fifth Annual Meeting of the Bishops of the United States, November 1963, p. 58. The votes were: (1) 130 to 5; (2) 127 to 7; (3) 126 to 6; (4) 126 to 3.

[31]ACUA, Hallinan Papers, Report on the Meeting of the American Bishops' Commission on the Liturgical Apostolate, November 30, 1963.

[32]Diary, December 4, 5, 1963.

[33]*Georgia Bulletin,* December 19, 1963. Hallinan confused the Theocrat of the Breakfast Table with his son, Wilfrid Ward, to whom he attributed the remark.

Chapter 14: A Horizontal Archbishop

[1]Diary, December 13-29, 1963.

He was in the hospital from December 29, 1963 to July 15, 1964, and again from mid-October to mid-February 1965 with a few weeks' respite over Christmas. During the first few weeks he talked to his doctors about resigning as archbishop.

His diary contains detailed entries about the course of his illness which he wrote months later with the help of hospital records.

[2]Diary, January 2-May 29, 1964.

[3]AAA, Hallinan to McManus, May 20, 1964, copy.

[4]Diary, June 4, 10, July 15, 1964.

[5]AAA, Hallinan to Dearden, January 4, 1964, copy.

[6]AAA, Hallinan to Cicognani, March 10, 1964, copy.

[7]AAA, Dearden to Hallinan, June 11, 1964; Hallinan to Dearden, June 15, 1964, copy.

[8]AAA, Hallinan to Dearden, March 31, 1964, copy; AUSCC, McManus to Hallinan, March 25, 1964, copy.

[9]Auxiliary Bishop Joseph Pernicone of New York brought up the question of the use of languages other than English. After some discussion, the bishops voted to allow the use of such versions provided that they had been approved by the appropriate territorial body and that the use of these languages did not exceed the limits set for the use of English in the United States. AUSCC, Minutes of the Bishops' Meeting on the Liturgy, Washington, D.C., April 2, 1964.

[10]*Ibid.*

[11]AUSCC, Decree of the Consilium ad Exsequendam Constitutionem de Sacra Liturgia in Minutes of the Bishops' Meeting on the Liturgy, April 2, 1964. An English translation of the decree was released by the NCWC News Service on May 16, 1964.

Approval had now been given for the use of the vernacular in the following parts of the Mass:

a. lessons, epistles, Gospels;
b. *Kyrie, Gloria, Credo, Sanctus, Agnus Dei;*
c. the Lord's Prayer;
d. the formula *Ecce Agnus Dei* and *Domine, non sum dignus* before the Communion of the faithful;
e. *Introit,* Gradual, Offertory, Communion verse;
f. the acclamation and dialogue formula in which the people participate;
g. the Prayer of the Faithful.

The Preface and Canon of the Mass remained in Latin as well as the Collect, Secret and Postcommunion prayers. Permission to recite the Divine Office in English was granted only on condition that clerics recite it "with a group of the faithful or of members of institutes dedicated to acquiring perfection who lawfully use the mother tongue."

[12]Bishop Brunini stopped to see Hallinan in the hospital on his way home from the meeting. Diary, May 5, 1964. McManus thought that Brunini and Tracy (together with Cardinal Ritter in the chair) were "the heroes of the closing minutes of the April 2 meeting of the bishops." AUSCC, McManus to Hallinan, n.d. [May 1964], copy.

[13]AUSCC, Minutes of the Bishops' Meeting on the Liturgy, Rome, October 19, 1964.

[14]AAA, Hallinan to Dearden, June 15, 1964, copy. His request to Bugnini for information about the forthcoming Instruction yielded nothing but a flat refusal couched in the most polite and cryptic language: "Proh dolor! Nihil dicere possum de quaestionibus gravibus quas ponis cum expectemus quid statuatur circa schema nostrum. Quaevis indicatio in errorem inducere posset." AUSCC, Bugnini to Hallinan, July 4, 1964.

[15]AAA, Hallinan to Dearden, June 15, 1964, copy.

[16]*Georgia Bulletin,* February 20, 1964. It is reprinted in Yzermans, *Days of Hope and Promise,* pp. 62-65.

The pastoral was so well received that he expanded it into a fourteen-page pamphlet, "How To Understand Changes in the Liturgy," which discussed the new approaches to the sacraments as well as changes in the Mass. It soon sold 20,000 copies, but he attributed the success to the introduction by Cardinal Ritter and the electric blue cover. AUSCC, Hallinan to McManus, October 2, 1964.

17AAA, Hallinan, "The Church's Liturgy: Growth and Development," National Liturgical Week, St. Louis, August 27, 1964. The text was published in John Gartner, S.S.S. (ed.), *The Challenge of the Council: Person, Parish, World: Twenty-Fifth North American Liturgical Week, St. Louis, Mo., August 24-27, 1964* (Washington, D.C.: The Liturgical Conference, 1964), pp. 94-100.

18AUSCC, Hallinan to Grimshaw, September 9, 1964, copy.

19ACUA, Hallinan Papers, Krol to Hallinan, September 22, 1964.

20ACUA, Hallinan Papers, Tracy to Hallinan, September 16, 1964.

21ACUA, Hallinan Papers, Tracy to Sherry, September 15, 1964.

22ACUA, Hallinan Papers, Cushing to Hallinan, n.d. [September 1964].

23An English translation of the Instruction was published in *Worship* 38 (November-December 1964): 588-611. McManus wrote a commentary which appeared a few months later in *Worship* 39 (April 1965): 226-237. Among other changes, this Instruction eliminated Psalm Forty-Two from the prayers at the foot of the altar, suppressed the Last Gospel and Leonine Prayers, permitted the celebration of a sung Mass with a deacon only, and instituted a new dialogue formula ("*Corpus Christi . . . Amen*") for the reception of Holy Communion by the people.

Still further revisions occurred with the publication of the new *Ordo Missae* on January 27, 1965, and the promulgation by the congregation of Rites on March 7, 1965 of the new rites for concelebration and the reception of Holy Communion under both species.

24AUSCC, Minutes of the Bishops' Meeting on the Liturgy, Rome, October 19, 1964.

25AUSCC, McManus to Hallinan, September 28, 1964; McManus to Hallinan, October 18, 1964; Minutes of the Bishops' Meeting on the Liturgy, Rome, October 19, 1964.

26AUSCC, Report of the Meeting of the Bishops' Commission on the Liturgical Apostolate, Rome, September 21, 1964; Hallinan to McManus, October 2, 1964.

27Minutes of the Forty-Sixth Annual Meeting of the Bishops of the United States, Rome, November 12, 1964.

28AUSCC, Hallinan to Dearden, January 22, 1965, copy.

29AUSCC, Dearden to Hallinan, January 26, 1965.

30*Acta Apostolicae Sedis* 56 (February 15, 1964): 97-144.

Xavier Rynne, *The Second Session: The Debates and Decrees of Vatican Council II: September 29 to December 4, 1963* (New York: Farrar Straus and Company, 1964), pp. 327-330. The author of this volume said that "mystery surrounds the release of the *Motu Proprio* on January 27." Clifford Howell, S.J., told Hallinan that he had the "inside story" about it. According to him:

"The Conciliar Liturgical Commission drew up a document, suggesting how the Constitution should be put into action and gave it to Larraona to present to the Pope as soon as the Constitution was passed. But Larraona happened at that time to be a *persona non grata* with the Pope—who was refusing to appoint Larraona's nephew to some post which Uncle wanted to get for him. Therefore, instead of handing the document to the Pope, he gave it to Felici, a curia man. He set Antonelli (another curia man) to monkey about with it, cooked up a document in which almost every paragraph started *Sancta Sede approbante,* put in that business into #9 about submitting the texts of vernacular translations to Rome, and handed it in to the Pope as proposed text for a *Motu proprio*. The Pope didn't like it much—knocked out heaps of *Sancta Sede approbante,* cut out most restrictions concerning Mass and sacraments, but seems to have overlooked the practical consequences of the insertion in #9 which was a direct contradiction of Constitution nn. 36, 54 and 101. He signed it and it came out in *Osservatore* to the dismay of the whole world. The French were very annoyed; they sent the Archbishop of Rouen (Martin) to the Pope about it. Pope was angry with the trick played on him, sacked Antonelli and sent for Bugnini (whom the curial party had ousted from the secretaryship just before the Council) and told him to redraft the *Motu proprio* to bring it in harmony with the Constitution, yet so far as possible, in a face-saving way; sent Bugnini personally to the Polyglot Press to see the new version into print; issued new version later in *A.A.S;* set up new commission under Lercaro and told it to get cracking."

AAA, Howell to Hallinan, n.d. [May 1964].

[31]ACUA, Hallinan Papers, A.G. Martimort, Note Confidentielle sur les Difficultés du Conseil Exécutif de Liturgie avec la Congrégation des Rites, June 27, 1964.

[32]AAA, Howell to Hallinan, n.d. [May 1964].

Not all English Catholics were as impatient as Howell about the pace of liturgical reform. Archbishop Grimshaw in his delightfully languid style described a recent meeting of the English bishops at which they decided to keep *Ite Missa est* and *Deo Gratias* in Latin "partly because nobody can suggest a satisfactory translation and partly for the same reason as that which has retained throughout the centuries the *Kyrie eleison* and such words as *Hosannah* and *Alleluia* and *Amen.* Being English and sharing the mentality which preserves Saxon doorways and chancel arches in churches otherwise completely rebuilt, I rather like the idea." AUSCC, Grimshaw to Hallinan, August 20, 1964.

[33]AUSCC, Hallinan to Lercaro, October 2, 1964, copy.

[34]AUSCC, Ritter to Hallinan, October 8, 1964.

[35]AUSCC, Weakland to Dearden, January 13, 1964, copy.

[36]AUSCC, Hallinan to Dearden, October 1, 1964, copy; Dearden to Hallinan, November 8, 1964.

[37]AUSCC, McManus to Hallinan, November 8, 1964.

[38]AUSCC, Minutes of the Forty-Sixth Annual Meeting of the Bishops of the United States, Rome, November 12, 1964.

[39]AUSCC, Memorandum of Bishop Victor J. Reed re The Liturgical Conference Question, November 10, 1964.

Hallinan saw no reason why the secretariat and the Liturgical Conference could not cooperate. Unlike Reed, he feared that the difficulty would come on the part of the bishops, not the Liturgical Conference. He told Dearden: "Frankly, John, I think that this rumored distrust of the Liturgical Conference men by certain bishops is grossly exaggerated and should be ignored when it does occur. It is surely unbecoming to our American body of bishops to hold in suspicion and dislike the very men who fought hard for the principles that are now part of the universal law of the Church. Men like McManus and Diekmann are sound theologians, solid liturgists, excellent priests. They have served on the preparatory Consilium and conciliar commissions and the Consilium. Yet I recall two years ago in Rome when certain bishops objected to Father McManus speaking to the bishops; one suggested the most uncivilized thing I have ever heard (that he be kept waiting outside the door while we voted whether to hear him or not!); and when he was finally introduced, the bishop said: 'Father McManus will present his side of the liturgical question' as if *Mediator Dei* and the Instruction of 1958 had never appeared." AUSCC, Hallinan to Dearden, November 22, 1964, copy.

[40]AUSCC, Minutes of the Forty-Sixth Annual Meeting of the Bishops of the United States, Rome, November 12, 1964.

Many of the bishops may have opposed the proposal because the secretariat was to be established on the premises of the Liturgical Conference in Washington. Connare himself was strongly opposed to this aspect of the plan. AUSCC, McManus to Hallinan, December 1, 1964.

[41]AUSCC, McManus to Hallinan, December 1, 1964, copy.

[42]AUSCC, Hallinan to McManus, November 22, 1964.

[43]AUSCC, Hallinan to Dearden, November 22, 1964, copy.

[44]AUSCC, Dearden to Hallinan, November 30, 1964.

Chapter 15: On the Home Front

[1]AUSCC, Hallinan, Notes for Talk at Clergy Conference, Atlanta, September 15, 1964.

[2]AUSCC, Hallinan to McManus, October 2, 1964.

[3]AUSCC,Hallinan, Priest's Guide for Liturgical Practices, Archdiocese of Atlanta, September 15, 1964.

[4]AUSCC, Hallinan, Supplement to Priest's Guide for Liturgical Practices, Archdiocese of Atlanta, February 4, 1965.
On certain issues the archbishop could be quite definite and demanding. In a directive to all his priests in September 1965, he laid down the law on a number of points, such as their availability to the people, clerical dress, vacations, expenditure of parish money and the employment of boys and girls in the rectory. One peculiar hobby-horse was his loathing for the "civil rights" shirts which were just becoming popular with the clergy as a substitute for rabat and collar. He told priests that they could wear them only in the priest-section of the rectory. AAA, Hallinan to "Dear Father," September 7, 1965.

[5]AUSCC, Hallinan to "Dear Father," March 10, 1965.

[6]AAA, Leo Croghan and Eugene Kelly to Hallinan, December 3, 1963. Hallinan to Croghan and Kelly, June 1, 1964, copy.

[7]AUSCC, Hallinan to McManus, February 19, 1964; AAA, Hallinan to McManus, January 21, 1965, copy.

[8]AUSCC, Diekmann to Hallinan, June 9, 1964.

[9]AAA, Hallinan to Bugnini, June 17, 1964, copy. AUSCC, Bugnini to Hallinan, June 22, 1964.

[10]Marszal Papers, Hallinan to Santo Pullella, April 21, 1965.

[11]AAA, Minutes of the Meeting of the Board of Consultors, Atlanta, February 5, 1964.

[12]He called his column "The Archbishop's Notebook." It first appeared in the *Georgia Bulletin* on June 27, 1963. He did not try to write a column every week, but it appeared at fairly regular intervals until March 14, 1968, two weeks before his death.

[13]*Georgia Bulletin,* January 30, 1964; April 23, 1964; May 7, 1964; July 2, 1964. The books which he recommended were: Godfrey Diekmann, *Come Let Us Worship;* Frederick McManus, *The Revival of the Liturgy;* Louis Bouyer, *Life and the Liturgy;* Augustine Cardinal Bea, *The Unity of Christians;* Daniel Callahan, *The Mind of the Catholic Layman;* and Karl Rahner, *The Christian Commitment.* "Some people," he admitted, "are name-droppers; others are book-title-droppers. Others, I suppose, just enjoy reading and talking about it." *Georgia Bulletin,* April 23, 1964.

[14]Father Joseph Ratzinger was the Professor of Fundamental Theology at the University of Bonn and personal theologian to Joseph Cardinal Frings of Cologne. In a recent lecture at the University of Bonn he had praised the "decentralization of liturgical control" and hailed the establishment of national conferences of bishops as "a fundamental step in the renewal of ecclesiology." Joseph Ratzinger, "The First Session," *Worship* 37 (August-September 1963): 534.

[15]ACUA: Ellis Papers, Hallinan to Ellis, June 29, 1964.

[16]*Georgia Bulletin,* July 9, 1964.

[17]*Georgia Bulletin,* July 9, 1964. Whatever the accuracy of the remark attributed to McIntyre, many American blacks believed that he was insensitive to their complaints about prejudice and discrimination. Benjamin Muse, *The American Negro Revolution: From Non-Violence to Black Power* (Bloomington: Indiana University Press, 1968) pp. 50, 216.

[18]Davenport *Catholic Register,* September 24, 1964. The union leaders told Hallinan privately that they were concerned about racial prejudice among white union members and feared that many of them would vote for Senator Barry Goldwater in the Presidential election in November. AUSCC, Hallinan to McManus, October 2, 1964.

[19]Allen, *Mayor,* pp. 95-96.

[20]Interview with Ivan Allen, Jr., Atlanta, April 28, 1986. The four main sponsors of the dinner were Hallinan, Rabbi Jacob Rothschild of the Atlanta Temple, Ralph McGill of the Atlanta *Constitution,* and Dr. Benjamin I. Mayes, the President of Morehouse College. *Georgia Bulletin,* February 4, 1965.

In his autobiography, Allen tells the story that King apologized to him for arriving late at the dinner:

"I forgot what time we were on," he said with a grin.
"How's that?," I said.
"Eastern Standard Time, C.S.T. or C.P.T."
"C.P.T.?"
"Colored Peoples' Time," he said. "It always takes us longer to get where we are going." Allen, *Mayor,* p. 99.

[21]AAA, Hallinan, Remarks at Civic Reception for Dr. Martin Luther King, Jr., Atlanta, Georgia, January 27, 1965.

[22]N.C.W.C. News Service, March 19, 1965.

Toolen also criticized King for "taking children out of school to demonstrate in the streets" and he contended that King was "hurting the cause of the Negro rather than helping him." On the other hand, a week earlier, Toolen had issued a strong statement when the Reverend James J. Reeb, a white Unitarian minister from Boston, had been murdered in Selma. "It is a sad and shameful thing," said Toolen, "that hatred and violence could bring about the death of this man of God and of high principles." *Ibid.*

Hallinan had long since come to recognize the constructive role of King in the civil rights movement. He told his friend, Bishop Thomas McDonough of Savannah: "I remember being almost ostracized for saying in Charleston that the day would come when whites would look back and earnestly wish that they had done business with Martin Luther King." ADS, Hallinan to McDonough, May 30, 1963.

[23]*Georgia Bulletin,* March 11, 1965.

[24]*Georgia Bulletin,* March 18, 1965.

[25]ACUA, Ellis Papers, Hallinan to Ellis, March 29, 1965.

[26]Marszal Papers, R.C. Helmholz to Hallinan, March 25, 1965.

[27]Marszal Papers, Anonymous to Hallinan, n.d. [March 1965].

[28]Marszal Papers, Anonymous to Hallinan, March 26, 1965.

[30]Marszal Papers, Name Illegible to Hallinan, March 23, 1965.

[31]Marszal Papers, Open Letter to Cardinal Spellman, March 18, 1965, copy.

[32]*Georgia Bulletin,* March 18, 1965.

Hallinan was not the only Southern bishop to praise the demonstrators in Selma. Archbishop Robert E. Lucey of San Antonio gave his explicit blessing to the participation of the Catholic clergy and religious in the demonstrations. "Fortunately, the voice of religion has been heard in Selma," said Lucey. "And Catholic sisters, God bless them, marched down the streets of Selma giving testimony to the charity of Christ in need and in truth." N.C.W.C. Press Release, March 19, 1965.

[33]ADS, Statement of the Bishops of the Province of Atlanta, June 6, 1965. The signatories were Hallinan, Vincent S. Waters of Raleigh, Ernest L. Unterkoefler of Charleston, Thomas J. McDonough of Savannah, Coleman F. Carroll of Miami and Auxiliary Bishop Charles B. McLaughlin of Raleigh.

Ralph McGill devoted a whole column to the Pentecost Statement. After recalling the long history of discrimination suffered by Catholics in the South, he said: "One of the forces for challenging the world's revolutionary changes that have come to the South in social reform has been and is the present Roman Catholic leadership of the South. With but few exceptions, its archbishops, bishops, priests and nuns have been forthright and determined in support of those things which may be done to enable the South to free itself from the more unworthy shackles of the status quo." Ralph McGill, "A Modern Pentecost," The Atlanta *Journal and Constitution,* June 6, 1965.

[34]*Georgia Bulletin,* August 5, 1965.

[35]*Georgia Bulletin,* July 29, 1965.

[36]*Georgia Bulletin,* August 26, 1965.

[37]ACUA, Ellis Papers, Hallinan to Ellis, April 13, 1965. Diary, April 14, 15, 16, 18, 25, 1965.

[38]AUSCC, Bishops' Commission on the Liturgical Apostolate, Annual Report 1965. Diary, May 3, 4, 1965.

One of the most outspoken episcopal supporters of the vernacular was Archbishop Lucey. He wrote to both Dearden and Hallinan before the May meeting asking that the entire Mass (with the exception of the Canon) be in English. He told them in his characteristically gruff way: "It might seem irreverent for one to declare that Holy Mass as offered presently by American bishops and priests is a linguistic hodgepodge of Latin, English, Greek and Hebrew, but it seems to me to be entirely appropriate to say that our present mixture of Latin and English is undignified and, I think, unworthy of a divine service. . . . I look forward to the day when in the liturgy of the West the magnificent words of consecration may either be chanted or recited aloud. There is neither logic nor charity in our effort to hide from the people of God the drama and tragedy of Calvary." AUSCC, Lucey to Dearden, April 19, 1965, copy.

At the other end of the spectrum was Cardinal Spellman. He told Dearden: "I don't know how things are in Detroit, but there continues to be considerable confusion in this area about liturgical matters." He asked Dearden how to respond to a prominent Catholic layman who had said that he was hoping that "the changes in the Mass will be discontinued and the Church will get back to what people like and which was successful for nearly two thousand years." AANY, Spellman to Dearden, May 11, 1965, copy; AANY, Fred B. Snite to Spellman, April 30, 1965.

On at least two occasions Spellman passed along to Archbishop Vagnozzi, the Apostolic Delegate, copies of letters from priests and laymen complaining about the liturgical changes. One such letter came from a prominent Chicago priest and Roman classmate of Spellman, who was disturbed that young priests were concelebrating Mass three times a week. AANY, Spellman to Vagnozzi, May 21, 1965, February 1, 1966, copies; AANY, J. Gerald Kealy to Spellman, May 18, 1965.

[39]Hallinan told John B. Mannion, Executive Secretary of the Liturgical Conference, two weeks after the bishops' meeting: "Now that a secretariat has been established with Father Frederick R. McManus as Executive Secretary, the path seems clear for a delineation of roles that will best serve the liturgical renewal in our country. The territorial body of bishops have entrusted our commission, in keeping with the instruction of September 26, 1964, with 'regulating the pastoral liturgical action of the entire nation' and 'supervising the application of the decrees of the territorial body.' "

To make the point even clearer, Hallinan explained that the Bishops' Commission had decided to publish a newsletter, which would "express the official voice of interpretation, leaving the whole area of creative liturgical discussion to the Conference. Thus it would free the news organs of the Conference for a healthy expression of opinion by clergy, religious and laity. And more importantly it would free the Liturgical Conference from the burden of interpretation, thus avoiding the hazard of two distinct sources of authority in liturgical matters. Priests appealing over their bishops to an opinion expressed in an organ of a private organization will not help the Church through this period of transition."

Hallinan did invite the Liturgical Conference to cooperate with the bishops in two important projects: the preparation of a catechesis for the reception of Holy Communion under both species and the composition of a series of model formats for the Prayer of the Faithful. AUSCC, Hallinan to Mannion, May 14, 1965, copy.

Twenty years earlier the bishops had turned down the opportunity to take over the direction of the National Liturgical Weeks, the most influential activity of the Liturgical Conference. The first two Weeks had been sponsored by the Benedictine Liturgical Conference. Then, in 1941, the Benedictine abbots in this country asked the N.C.W.C. to assume responsibility for them. However, Monsignor Michael J.Ready, the General Secretary of the N.C.W.C., replied (eleven months later) that "the matter of the request ... does not come within the ambit of the N.C.W.C." When the Benedictines dissolved their own Liturgical Conference in 1943, the present Liturgical Conference was organized to provide the National Liturgical Weeks with a sponsor. Ready to Michael Ducey, O.S.B., September 9, 1942, quoted in Paul B. Marx, O.S.B., *Virgil Michel and the Liturgical Movement* (Collegeville: The Liturgical Press, 1957), pp. 128-129.

[40]AUSCC, Hallinan to Spellman, June 12, 1965.

[41]AUSCC, Report to the International Episcopal Committee on English in the Liturgy, September 30, 1965.

The committee indicated in November 1964 that the Executive Secretary should be an English priest, but Cardinal John Heenan of Westminster argued that it would make more sense to have an American Executive Secretary, if the office were to be located in Washington. Archbishop Gordon Gray of St. Andrews and Edinburgh agreed with him. AICEL, McManus to Hallinan, February 26, 1965, copy; Gray to McManus, April 7, 1965.

In addition to the Executive Secretary, the committee also had an International Advisory Body, which had been approved by the bishops in November 1964. The members were: Father Godfrey Diekmann (U.S.A.); Father Frederick R. McManus (U.S.A.); Professor G.B. Harrison (U.S.A.); Father Harold Winstone (England); Professor H.P.R. Finberg (England); Father Percy Jones (Australia); Father Stephen Somerville (Canada); and Father John J. McGarry (Ireland). McManus, *ICEL: The First Years,* pp. 15-16.

[42]For the crisis of November 1964, see Xavier Rynne, *The Third Session: The Debates and Decrees of Vatican Council II: September 14 to November 21, 1964* (New York: Farrar, Straus and Giroux, 1965), pp. 256-263, and Fogarty, *Vatican and the American Hierarchy,* pp. 397-399. Writing a few months later in America, Father John Courtney Murray, S.J., said that it was "too facile" to blame the defeat solely on the machinations of the Roman Curia. Part of the problem, he pointed out, was that the proponents of the Declaration were themselves divided on the arguments and tactics to be used. John Courtney Murray, S.J., "This Matter of Religious Freedom," *America* 112 (January 9,1965): 40-43.

[43]*Acta Synodalia,* Volumen IV, Periodus Quarta, Pars I, pp. 327-328. The complete text is reprinted in Yzermans *American Participation,* pp. 661-662, and in Floyd Anderson (ed.), *Council Daybook, Vatican II, Session 4* (Washington, D.C.: N.C.W.C., 1966), p. 27.

It was an accident that Hallinan got to deliver his address on September 17. He was originally placed far down the list of speakers and probably would not have had an opportunity to speak at all. However, Bishop Robert Tracy happened to submit to the General Secretariat a written intervention on a technical point. The Secretariat mistook Tracy's note for a request to speak and called him to the rostrum over the public address system. He was not there but back at his hotel room writing letters home. Hallinan knew that Tracy was absent and asked permission to take his place, which the Secretariat allowed him to do. Tracy, *American Bishop at the Vatican Council,* p. 200.

[44]ACUA, Hallinan Papers, Hallinan, Written Intervention on the Pastoral Constitution *De Ecclesia in Mundo Hujus Temporis. Acta Synodalia,* Volumen IV, Periodus Quarta, Pars II, pp. 757-758. A translation of part of Hallinan's text appears in Floyd, *Council Daybook, Session 4,* pp. 128-129.

[45]ACUA, Hallinan Papers, Hallinan, Written Intervention on the Pastoral Constitution *De Ecclesia in Mundo Hujus Temporis,* October 8, 1965. *Acta Synodalia,* Volumen IV, Periodus Quarta, Pars II, pp. 754-756. An English translation of most of his text appears in Floyd, *Council Daybook, Session 4,* pp. 118-119.

[46]Yzermans, *American Participation,* pp. 483-487. *Acta Synodalia,* Volumen IV, Periodus Quarta, Pars V, pp. 351-352.

[47]ACUA, Ellis Papers, Hallinan to Ellis, December 20, 1965. AICEL, Hallinan to Sigler, November 16, 1965, copy.

[48]Hallinan, "Boldness of John and Vision of Paul," *Georgia Bulletin,* November 11, 1965.

Chapter 16: Odium Liturgicum

[1]Gerald Ellard, S.J., "Are We on the Right Track with the Laymen's Missals?," *The Church Year: Nineteenth Annual North American Liturgical Week: Cincinnati, August 18-21, 1959* (Washington: The Liturgical Conference, 1959), p. 106; Godfrey Diekmann, "Popular Participation and the History of Christian Piety," *Participation in the Mass: Twentieth Annual North American Liturgical Week: Notre Dame, August 23-26, 1960* (Washington: The Liturgical Conference, 1960), p. 63; Gary Wills, *Bare Ruined Choirs* (Garden City: Doubleday and Company, 1971), pp. 43, 58.

[2]John B. Mannion, "A Dull New Day," *Commonweal* 84 (August 19, 1966): 519.

[3]Leo T. Mahon, "What Is To Be Done?," *Commonweal* 82 (August 20, 1965): 591.

[4]Hans A. Reinhold, "No Time To Stop," *Commonweal* 82 (August 20, 1965): 585.

[5]Aelred Tegels, O.S.B., "The Present Liturgical Reform, Jesus Christ Reforms His Church:" *Twenty-Sixth Annual North American Liturgical Week: Baltimore, June 21-24, 1965; Portland, Oregon, August 16-19, 1965; Chicago, August 30-September 2, 1965* (Washington: The Liturgical Conference 1966), pp. 14-21.

[6]Thomas E. Ambrogi, S.J., "A Mass of the Future," *Experiments and Community: Twenty-Eighth Annual North American Liturgical Week: Kansas City, August 12-24, 1967* (Washington: The Liturgical Conference, 1967), pp. 43-44.

[7]AUSCC, Weakland to Hallinan, October 15, 1965; Weakland to Hallinan, February 23, 1966, copies.

[8]AUSCC, Schuler to Hallinan, February 25, 1966; Hallinan to Schuler, March 31, 1966, copy.

[9]AUSCC, Hallinan to Johannes Overath [President of the Consociatio Internationalis Musicae Sacrae], February 20, 1967; José Lopez-Calvo, S.J., to Hallinan, March 15, 1967; Hallinan to Lopez-Calvo, S.J., April 7, 1967, copy.

[10]AUSCC, Hallinan to Weakland, February 18, 1966, copy.

[11]Diary, November 29, 1966. Weakland's talk was published in *Worship* 41 (January 1967): 5-14. The editor of *Worship* described the meeting as "the beginning of effective dialogue between Church musicians and liturgists." Aelred Tegels, O.S.B., "Chronicle," *Worship* 41 (January 1967): 54. AUSCC, Hallinan to Weakland, July 18, 1967, copy.

[12]Instructio de Musica in Sacra Liturgia, March 5, 1967, *Notitiae* 3 (1967): 81-105. Hallinan, Press Release, Religious News Service, March 16, 1967. The British composer and musicologist, Anthony Milner, was considerably more restrained in his appraisal of the document. "In sum," he said, "the Instruction is generally a forward-looking document, though hampered by attempts to satisfy irreconcilable viewpoints.... Until Roman documents are written in simple, straightforward language, this Instruction is probably the best we can hope for." Anthony Milner, *Worship* 41 (June-July 1967): 322-333.

[13]AUSCC, Hallinan to Dearden, February 22, 1966, copy.

[14]AUSCC, Minutes of the Annual Meeting of the National Conference of Catholic Bishops of the United States, Washington, November 14-18, 1966. The other petitions involved such matters as permission to substitute prose translations for the metrical translations of the Sequences in the

Roman Missal, and permission to substitute the Apostles Creed for the Nicene Creed in Masses for the deaf. The bishops also tried to brighten up the funeral liturgy by requesting that the *Dies Irae* be made optional.

[15]*National Catholic Reporter,* October 26, 1966.

[16]*National Catholic Reporter,* November 2, 1966.

[17]AUSCC, Hallinan, Statement on Liturgical Change and Experimentation, Washington, November 17, 1966.

[18]*National Catholic Reporter,* December 7, 1966. Hallinan was conflating two different parables. See Luke 11:5-8; 18:1-8.

[19]AUSCC, Hallinan to Dearden, December 13, 1966, copy. The biblical allusion was to Exodus 17:8-13.

[20]*Notitiae* 2 (1966): 375.

[21]*Ibid.* Tegel's criticism appeared in *Worship* 40 (November 1966): 589-591.

[22]AUSCC, Vagnozzi to Hallinan, December 21, 1966.

[23]*Notitiae* 3 (1967): 39-40. The Declaration was dated December 29, 1966 but released on January 4, 1967.

[24]John B. Mannion, "The Pope and Mr. Dooley on Jazz Masses," *Commonweal* 85 (January 20, 1967): 417.

[25]AUSCC, Vagnozzi to Hallinan, January 26, 1967.

[26]AUSCC, Mannion to McManus, January 23,1967.

[27]"There seems to be something of a stalemate in the development of the official liturgical reform," said Aelred Tegels, O.S.B. Aelred Tegels, O.S.B., "Chronicle," *Worship* 41 (February 1967): 115.
The name "Bishops' Commission on the Liturgical Apostolate" was changed to "Bishops' Committee on the Liturgy" in order to give this group the same nomenclature as the other standing committees of the Bishops' Conference. AUSCC, Hallinan, Annual Report, Bishops' Committee on the Liturgy, 1967.

[28]Bishops' Committee on the Liturgy, Statement on Masses in Homes and on Music, February 17, 1967. *Notitiae* 3 (1967): 218-220.

[29]AUSCC, Hallinan to Lercaro, appendix, March 14, 1967, copy. Before he sent the letter, Hallinan checked with Dearden, who told him that he had no objection to the contents. AUSCC, Dearden to Hallinan, March 14, 1967.

[30]AUSCC, Minutes of the Meeting of the Bishops' Committee on the Liturgy, Washington, February 14, 1967. The other members of the committee were: William Connare of Greensburg; Victor Reed of Oklahoma City and Tulsa; Auxiliary Bishop John Dougherty of Newark; James Malone, Apostolic Administrator of Youngstown; Coadjutor Bishop John Morkovsky of Galveston-Houston; Auxiliary Bishop Warren Boudreaux of Lafayette, Louisiana; Bernard Flanagan of Worcester; Auxiliary Bishop Aloysius Wycislo of Chicago; and Leo Byrne of Wichita.

[31]AUSCC, Minutes of the Second General Meeting of the National Conference of Catholic Bishops and the United States Catholic Conference, Chicago, April 11-13, 1967.

[32]AUSCC, NCCB, Bishops' Committee on the Liturgy, Pastoral Statement on Liturgical Renewal, May 15, 1967.

[33]*National Catholic Reporter,* May 31, 1967.

[34]Richard John Neuhaus, "The Bishops' Loyal Opposition," *Commonweal* 86 (September 22, 1967): 565-567. The most controversial feature of the 1967 Liturgical Week was not liturgical experimentation but a recommendation by the Study Group on Ecumenism (endorsed by the Directors of the Liturgical Conference) for common Eucharistic celebrations and inter-commu-

nion with Protestants during the Church Unity Octave in 1968. *Worship* 41 (October 1967): 499-500.

Hallinan attended the Kansas City sessions and, at a meeting with the Board of Directors, assured them that the Liturgical Conference enjoyed the confidence of the Consilium. Diary, August 23, 1967.

[35]*America* 116 (February 25, 1967): 275. Others who made the same point were Rosemary Haughton, "Open Experiments Openly Arrived At," *Commonweal* 86 (August 25,1967): 511-513; Leo Croghan, "The Beginning of the Children's Work," *Ave Maria,* March 25, 1967, pp. 6-8; William Birmingham, "Toward An Urbanized Liturgy," *Cross Currents* 16 (Fall 1966): 385-393; Aelred Tegels, O.S.B., "Chronicle," *Worship* 41 (February 1967): 115.

[36]Some of the impatient liturgists might have had more sympathy for Hallinan and Dearden, if they had been aware of the tortuous process involved in securing approval for the English Canon. The American petition went to Rome in November 1966. The Consilium granted the request in principle on February 13 and Dearden had a copy of the decree by February 27. *Notitiae* 3 (1967): 151; AUSCC, Dearden to Hallinan, February 27, 1967.

Then it was necessary to come up with an English text that Rome would approve. There were two possibilities: either to select one of the existing translations or to wait for the I.C.E.L. translation which was almost finished. Bugnini, Hallinan and McManus all favored the latter course and Dearden accepted their recommendation. AUSCC, McManus to Dearden, March 6, 1967, copy.

At the April meeting of the hierarchy, Hallinan distributed a preliminary draft of the I.C.E.L. translation and got the bishops' approval to continue work on a final draft. AUSCC, Minutes of the Second General Meeting of the National Conference of Catholic Bishops and the United States Catholic Conference, Chicago, April 11-13, 1967. At the end of May the I.C.E.L. translators finished their revisions and sent them to Archbishop Gordon Gray of St. Andrews and Edinburg (Episcopal Chairman of I.C.E.L.). He then submitted the text to the Presidents of the various English-speaking conferences of bishops including Dearden, who in turn sent copies to all the United States bishops for their approval. The American bishops approved the text by a margin of 193 to 9, and Dearden informed the Consilium of the vote on June 28, 1967. AUSCC, Dearden to Lercaro, June 28, 1967. It was at this point that the impasse occurred.

The English-speaking Canadian bishops had the same problem as their American counterparts in getting Roman approval for the vernacular Canon. Their difficulties were compounded by the likelihood that the French Canadians would get the permission before they did, "leaving us," said Bishop Emmet Carter, "very definitely in the role of Cinderella. And since our priests have long since deserted the cinder and sackcloth mentality, we will have another outburst of unauthorized action. I feel seriously the responsibility of the Bishops to lead, not to follow." AAA, Carter to Gerald Sigler, Executive Secretary of I.C.E.L., May 4, 1967, copy.

[37]AUSCC, Hallinan to Dearden, August 14, 1967, copy.

[38]Diary, August 15, 1967. AUSCC, McManus to Hallinan, August 9, 1967. At one point Dearden feared that Rome would reject the I.C.E.L. translation in favor of one of the existing texts. In that case, he favored suspending action because it would be a serious blow to the future of I.C.E.L. AUSCC, Dearden to McManus, August 10, 1967.

[39]Diary, September 12, 1967. AUSCC, Hallinan to Connare, September 26, 1967, copy.

[40]AUSCC, Dearden to "Dear Bishop," September 13, 1967, copy. AUSCC, Draft of Press Release, September 18, 1967. The English Canon in question here was the translation of the so-called Roman Canon, Eucharistic Prayer I in the present (1974) *Sacramentary.*

[41]AUSCC, Hallinan, Annual Report of the Bishops' Committee on the Liturgy, 1967. Eight months earlier, Hallinan had rejected Bishop Connare's suggestion to give each bishop this authority.

A procedure existed for authorizing liturgical experiments, but it was practically unworkable, since each request had to be submitted to the local ordinary, then to the Bishops' Committee on the Liturgy, then to the N.C.C.B., then to the authorities of the Consilium in Rome. AUSCC, Minutes of the Annual Meeting of the National Conference of Catholic Bishops and the United

States Catholic Conference, Washington, November 14-18, 1966.

Dearden, while favoring a simplified procedure, pointed out to the President of the Liturgical Conference that the Bishops' Committee on the Liturgy had gotten very few requests for experimentation and he thought that the procedures had never really been given a fair trial. AUSCC, Dearden to Father Joseph Connolly, November 7, 1967, copy.

[42]AUSCC, Hallinan to James Malone, September 8, 1967, copy.

[43]AUSCC, Leo Byrne to Hallinan, n.d. [September 1967]; Francis Furey to Hallinan, September 13, 1967; Victor Reed to Hallinan, October 2, 1967; John Dougherty to Hallinan, September 25, 1967; Bernard Flanagan to Hallinan, September 19, 1967; James Malone to Hallinan, September 11, 1967; Warren Boudreaux to Hallinan, September 12, 1967; Aloysius Wycislo to Hallinan, September 9, 1967; William Connare to Hallinan, October 10, 1967. There is no record of a reply from the other member of the committee, Coadjutor Bishop John Morkovsky, Apostolic Administrator of Galveston-Houston.

[44]AUSCC, O'Boyle, Pastoral Letter, September 18, 1967.

[45]AUSCC, Hallinan to O'Boyle, November 8, 1967, copy.

[46]Diary, November 11, 1967.

[47]AUSCC, Hallinan to Joseph Connolly, November 8, 1967. Auxiliary Bishop John Dougherty of Newark, together with two lay members of the Board of Directors of the Liturgical Conference—William Baroody and Robert Rambusch—made peace between the Conference and O'Boyle, whereupon the Cardinal gave his permission for the Liturgical Week to be held in Washington in 1968. AUSCC, McManus to Hallinan, November 24, 1967; O'Boyle to Joseph Connolly, December 1, 1967.

[48]AUSCC, Hallinan to Thomas Connolly, November 8, 1967, copy.

[49]Diary, November 13, 14, 1967. *Georgia Bulletin,* November 23, 1967.

In addition to approving the two proposals about liturgical experimentation, the bishops turned down two other proposals: one pertaining to guidelines for Masses in small groups and the other a request that women be allowed to act as lectors and commentators.

They approved proposals to ask the Holy See for permission to: (1) authorize experimental liturgies during parish missions; (2) substitute suitable hymns for the *Introit,* Offertory and Communion prayers; (3) substitute the Psalms in the Jerusalem Bible for those in the Confraternity of Christian Doctrine version; (4) allow the repetition of the Good Friday service; (5) permit the celebration of the Easter Vigil in the early morning of Easter Sunday; (6) allow priests to confirm adult converts; (7) permit several ritual changes in the Mass, such as cleansing the sacred vessels in the sacristy rather than at the altar.

With regard to matters within their own competence, they approved: (1) the use of additional hymns at Benediction; (2) the use of vernacular texts set to music in earlier periods; (3) the use of musical instruments other than the organ at Mass. Another proposal to introduce the practice of standing while receiving Holy Communion was dropped from the agenda. AUSCC, Minutes of the Third Annual Meeting of the National Conference of Catholic Bishops and the United States Catholic Conference, Washington, November 13-19, 1967.

[50]Diary, November 23, November 27, 1967.

[51]AUSCC, Hallinan to Whalen, December 6, 1967, copy.

[52]AUSCC, Bugnini to Carter, December 19, 1967, copy.

[53]AUSCC, Hallinan to Dearden, January 19, 1968, copy.

[54]The *National Catholic Reporter* of January 7, 1968 contains both the letter from the Liturgical Conference and Hallinan's reply.

[55]AUSCC, Hallinan to Benelli, January 8, 1968, copy.

[56]Hallinan Papers in the possession of Cardinal Bernardin, Bugnini to Hallinan, January 19, 1968.

[57]AUSCC, Hallinan to Dougherty, February 1, 1968, copy.

[58]AUSCC, Hallinan to Dearden, January 31, 1968, copy.

[59]Hallinan Papers in the possession of Cardinal Bernardin, Hallinan to Bugnini, February 2, 1968, copy. Bugnini promised to relay Hallinan's request to both Cardinal Gut and the Pope. "I keenly appreciate your viewpoint and position," he told Hallinan. "The situation is indeed complex and difficult, but we go on in hope." Hallinan Papers in the possession of Cardinal Bernardin, Bugnini to Hallinan, February 8, 1968.

[60]*National Catholic Reporter,* February 28, 1968.

[61]*National Catholic Reporter,* March 6, 1968.

[62]AAA, Hallinan to "Dear Father," March 7, 1968.

[63]AUSCC, Hallinan to Aidan Kavanagh, O.S.B., July 18, 1967, copy.

[64]Two years after Hallinan's death, the Bishops' Committee on the Liturgy asked the University of Notre Dame, Woodstock College in New York City and St. John's Abbey and University in Collegeville, Minnesota, to develop programs of liturgical research. Since the Consilium had still not given permission for general liturgical experimentation, the bishops were careful to explain that they were not formally establishing experimental centers at those institutions. Bishop James W. Malone, the Chairman of the Bishops' Committee on the Liturgy, said: "It is not a question of creating research centers or endorsing the work of such centers ... but of recognizing their potential and seeking their assistance." Aelred Tegels, O.S.B., "Chronicle," *Worship* 44 (August-September 1970): 438-439.

Chapter 17: Church and Community

[1]Diary, January 1, 1966. ACUA, Ellis Papers, Hallinan to Ellis, March 20, 1966.

[2]Diary, January 25, March 25, March 9, May 4, 1966. Bernardin was consecrated in the cathedral in Charleston on April 26, 1966 by Hallinan with Ernest Unterkoefler and Francis Reh (Hallinan's two successors in Charleston) as co-consecrators.

[3]The four committees were Steering, Administration, Education, and Future Expansion and Development. AAA, Minutes of the Meeting of the Diocesan Consultors, Atlanta, July 2,1965; Hallinan to "Dear Father," January 19, 1966; Capsule History of the 1966 Lay Congress, Archdiocese of Atlanta, May 1966.

[4]*Georgia Bulletin,* May 26, 1966.

[5]AAA, Recommendations of the 1966 Lay Congress, Archdiocese of Atlanta, 1966.

[6]AAA, Final Proposals of the Sisters' Development Committee, Archdiocese of Atlanta, 1966; Report of the Young Adults' Congress, Archdiocese of Atlanta, 1966.

[7]AAA, Hallinan to "Dear Father," November 9, 1966.

[8]A few months earlier Hallinan had discussed the topic of clerical celibacy in his newspaper column, "I am not persuaded that clerical celibacy should be written off or offered as an option simply because some have asked for it,' he said. "At the present moment, many of the requests that I have heard could be summed up in the same words that married couples often use: 'It isn't easy.' But priests, as well as husbands and wives, have known this for a long time." *Georgia Bulletin,* July 28, 1966.

The *National Catholic Reporter* played up this incident as if it were the most important event of the synod. It left the impression that Hallinan himself was questioning the value of clerical celibacy in a front-page story with the misleading headline: "Hallinan Says He Wants Study of Celibacy." *National Catholic Reporter,* November 30, 1966.

[9]AAA, The Church of Christ: Decree Enacted by the First Synod of the Archdiocese of Atlanta, 1966. Diary, November 21, 22, 1966. *Georgia Bulletin,* February 16, 1967.

[10]AAA, Hallinan to Vincent P. Brennan, S.M., June 5, 1962.

[11]AA, Hallinan to "Dear Father," November 21, 1963.

[12]AAA, Hallinan to "Dear Father," January 10, 1966. Diary, January 18, 1966. Catholics were not the only ones who were slow to respond to ecumenical gestures. Father Noel Burtenshaw estimated that ninety percent of the people attending the services at the cathedral were Catholics. Diary, January 18, 1966.

[13]AAA, Archdiocesan Directory on Ecumenism, Atlanta, 1966. The Church of Christ: Decree Enacted by the First Synod of the Archdiocese of Atlanta, 1966, pp. 48-51.

[14]*Georgia Bulletin,* November 9, 1967.

[15]*Georgia Bulletin,* September 15, 1966.

[16]AAA, Hallinan, The Vatican Council and the Jews, Address delivered in the Atlanta Temple, January 7, 1966.

[17]*Georgia Bulletin,* October 3, 1963; November 9, 1967.

[18]*Georgia Bulletin,* January 21, 1965; February 10, 1966; February 3, 1966.

[19]Nolan, *Pastoral Letters of the United States Catholic Bishops,* III, 93-97.

[20]*Georgia Bulletin,* March 3, March 10, 1966.

[21]Allen, *Mayor,* p. 137.

[22]*Georgia Bulletin,* July 20, August 11, 1966.

[23]Atlanta *Constitution,* October 6, 1966. He repeated the same points in an editorial in the *Georgia Bulletin* of October 6, 1966.

[24]Atlanta *Constitution,* October 7, 1966.

[25]Los Angeles *Times,* October 7, 1966. ACUA, Ellis Papers, Hallinan to Ellis, October 26, 1966.

[26]*Georgia Bulletin,* January 12, 1967.

[27]ACUA, Ellis Papers, Hallinan to Ellis, June 5,1967.

[28]Atlanta *Constitution,* September 22, 1967. The newspaper agreed that the black complaints about overcrowding in the schools were justified and said: "Today we face a crisis in our schools almost as monumental as that one we faced and survived in 1961." Atlanta *Constitution,* September 16, 1967.

[29]*Georgia Bulletin,* February 1, 1968.

[30]AAA, Hallinan to Allen, February 1, 1968; Hallinan to Samuel Williams, February 1, 1968, copies.

[31]Daniel J. Boorstin, Brooks Mather Kelley, Ruth Frankel Boorstin, *A History of the United States* (Lexington, Mass.: Ginn and Company, 1981), pp. 673-675.

[32]Charles A. Meconis, *With Clumsy Grace: The American Catholic Left 1961-1975* (New York: The Seabury Press, 1979), pp. 8-22.

Both at the time and later, the "New York Chancery Office" was blamed for the reassignment of Father Daniel Berrigan, S.J., to Central America. *National Catholic Reporter,* December 1, 1965; Meconis, *With Clumsy Grace,* p. 13. James Hennesey,S.J., who was an assistant to the provincial of the New York Province of the Society of Jesus at the time of Berrigan's transfer, said that the Archdiocese of New York had nothing to do with it. The initiative came from the Jesuits themselves. James Hennesey, S.J., *American Catholics,* p. 374.

[33]The latter supposition seems more likely, since a Gallup Poll late in 1966 showed that Catholics were far more likely than either Protestants or Jews to support Johnson's handling of the Vietnam war. *Commonweal* 85 (November 11, 1966): 158.

[34]*Georgia Bulletin,* December 9, 1965. Even when he was most depressed about United States involvement in Vietnam, Hallinan never came close to the pacifism of some opponents of the war. In speaking of American commitment to the security of Israel at the Atlanta Press Club in June 1967, he said: "I do not want more war. I do not want war at all. But just as I require that

the United States keep herself from all forms of aggression . . . so do I defend our right and duty to keep our commitments, undergird our own defense and help, as much as we can, to keep the civilized world from being brutally absorbed by those who put power, land and warfare before justice, freedom and peace." AAA, Hallinan, The Open Church, Address Delivered at the Atlanta Press Club, June 5, 1967.

[35]*New York Times,* February 15, 1966.

[36]Bishop Leo Pursley of Fort Wayne-South Bend said: "We are *de facto* in. Whether we should have got in and whether we should get out is a question for which I can find no certain and definite answer." Bishop Alphonse J. Schladweiler of New Ulm said: "I am in full accord with the goals of the war. Communism must be contained and the aggressor from the North must be halted." Bishop George J. Rehring of Toledo said: "I find it difficult, even impossible, to form a judgment about our involvement in Vietnam." *National Catholic Reporter,* March 30, 1966.

[37]*Commonweal* 84 (April 15, 1966): 93-94.

[38]*Commonweal* 84 (July 22, 1966): 459.

[39]Paul J. Hallinan and Joseph L. Bernardin, "War and Peace: A Pastoral Letter to the Archdiocese of Atlanta," October 1966, in John Tracy Ellis (ed.), *Documents of American Catholic History,* (Wilmington: Michael Glazier, 1987), II, 696-702.

The letter expressed the thinking of both bishops, but Bernardin actually wrote it and Hallinan then made a few stylistic changes. Interview with Cardinal Bernardin, *ibid.*

With regard to conscientious objectors, the two bishops did not distinguish between those who were opposed to all wars and those who were opposed to the Vietnam war because they considered that particular conflict to be immoral. Both types of conscientious objectors could appeal to the authority of the pastoral, which quoted the relevant passage (No.79) of the Pastoral Constitution on the Church in the Modern World: "It seems right that laws make humane provisions for the case of those who (for reasons of conscience) refuse to bear arms, provided, however, that they accept some other form of service to the human community."

[40]*National Catholic Reporter,* October 19, 1966. Leo welcomed both pastoral letters for another reason: he thought that they would provide a basis for priests to express their disagreement with the war without fear of reprisals by their bishops, and he jumped to the highly improbable conclusion that "if they had come earlier, it is doubtful that we would have seen the harassment of Catholic dissenters in New York and the expulsion of Father Berrigan." It was hardly fair to Shehan, Hallinan and Bernardin to obscure the differences between them and the draft-card burners associated with the Catholic Worker.

[41]"Peace and Vietnam: Statement Issued by the National Conference of Catholic Bishops," November 18, 1966, in Nolan, *Pastoral Letters of the United States Catholic Bishops,* III, 76.

The *National Catholic Reporter* complained: "The bishops do not say why they find the American involvement justified; they do not try to say what kind of war it is, what kind of present tactics are morally dubious, what kind or degree of escalation would render the war intolerable." *National Catholic Reporter,* November 23, 1966.

[42]*Commonweal* 85 (February 17, 1967): 547-549; *National Catholic Reporter,* March 29, 1967.

A few weeks before Hallinan's talk in New York, twenty-three protestors were arrested in St. Patrick's Cathedral, when they staged a silent demonstration during the ten o'clock High Mass. *National Catholic Reporter,* February 1, 1967.

[43]On his return from his Christmas visit to the troops in Vietnam, Spellman told reporters: "Total victory means peace." *National Catholic Reporter,* January 4, 1967. Hallinan told Spellman that he intended to confine his remarks to a presentation of the teaching on war of Pope Paul VI, the Second Vatican Council, and the United States Bishops as expressed in their statement of November 1966. AAA, Hallinan to Spellman, January 27, 1967, copy.

[44]The crux of the problem for critics of the war was precisely the question of alternatives. If United States military action in Vietnam was immoral, what other means could be used to achieve a reasonable peace settlement? Father James V. Schall, S.J., argued for continued

American intervention on the grounds that "practically any alternative ... has a degree of evil connected with it." He asked: "Can the possession and use of military force to preserve the liberty of ourselves and others be in fact the lesser evil, and, therefore, in these circumstances, to be chosen?" He answered the question for himself in the affirmative. James V. Schall, S.J., "Religion and War," *Commonweal* 85 (November 18, 1966): 195.

[45]*National Catholic Reporter,* March 1, 1967.

[46]Atlanta *Constitution,* May 11, 1967; *Georgia Bulletin,* May 18, 1967.

[47]Other Catholic supporters were Monsignor Salvator Adamo, Editor of the Camden *Catholic Star Herald;* John G. Deedy, Jr., Managing Editor of *Commonweal;* Monsignor Charles Owen Rice of Pittsburgh; Monsignor John Scanlon of San Francisco; Philip Scharper, Vice-President of Sheed and Ward Publishing Company; and Father Vincent Yanitelli, S.J., Vice-President of St. Peter's College, Jersey City. *Commonweal* 87 (July 28, 1967): 471.

Bishop John Wright of Pittsburgh said that he favored Negotiation Now "as far as it goes," but he declined to endorse it because it did not insist that the Communists stop the "systematic murder" of South Vietnamese leaders. *National Catholic Reporter,* August 23, 1967. A few months earlier, in a sermon at a "Peace Mass" in his cathedral, Wright questioned whether the traditional Catholic theory of the just war could apply any longer to modern warfare. "In our day," he said, "it is more and more difficult, if not impossible, to reconcile modern war with the principles of a just war, though the theoretical possibility of doing so remains such that the Second Vatican Council did not totally exclude recourse to war in last ditch defense of actual aggression." *National Catholic Reporter,* March 29, 1967.

[48]*Georgia Bulletin,* August 24,1967.

[49]*Ibid.*

[50]*Georgia Bulletin,* September 21, 1967.

[51]*Ibid.* Three months later he still found it necessary to emphasize the distinction between his support of Negotiation Now and his rejection of the extremists in the antiwar movement. Shortly before Christimas, he wrote:

"Unless a churchman, educator, business or labor leader stays silent, he must face up to the half-truths and untruths attributed to him. Last summer, after I had signed Negotiation Now, four or five other anti-war agencies falsely stated that I supported them too. I did not. I conscientiously felt that Negotiation Now represented a reasonable position aimed at neither escalation nor withdrawal. . . . Negotiation Now is reasonable and honest, offering a new set of options, well within the framework of the official Catholic position on war.

I absolutely refused to give my name to pacifism, massive refusal to serve, campaigns to burn draft cards, spill blood, damn the President or demonstrate in other weary and messy forms of the ritual of refusal. The leaders of such antics have certain rights ... and I respect these and forgive those who in their misguided way are doing harm to our nation. I see no reasons to defend or to seek support for them. Not all sons of Adam are mature men. Some are adolescents." *Georgia Bulletin,* December 21, 1967."

[52]*Georgia Bulletin,* March 7, 1968.

Chapter 18: The Measure of the Man

[1]Interview with Cardinal Bernardin, *ibid.*

[2]Hallinan, "The Common Goal," *America* 116 (January 7, 1967): 11-14; Hallinan, "A Time to Create," *Commonweal* 87 (October 11, 1967): 47-49.

[3]Hallinan, "The Church—The Open Circle," Homily Preached at the Installation of the Most Reverend Gerard Frey, Savannah, August 10, 1967, in Yzermans, *Days of Hope and Promise,* pp. 187-190.

[4]Hallinan Papers in the possession of Cardinal Bernardin, Hallinan, "The Fork in the Road." Address Given at the National Newman Congress, Northern Illinois University, DeKalb, Illinois, August 31, 1967.

[5]In a telephone interview with the *National Catholic Reporter,* Hallinan confirmed that he had cast the one vote in Curran's favor, but he would not disclose the votes of the other trustees. *National Catholic Reporter,* April 26, 1967.

[6]Hallinan Papers in the possession of Cardinal Bernardin, Hallinan to O'Boyle, August 4, 1967, copy.

Hallinan's concern for the Catholic University of America was of long standing. In 1962, when the same rector barred Hans Küng, Godfrey Diekmann, O.S.B., John Courtney Murray, S.J., and Gustave Weigel, S.J., from speaking on the campus, Hallinan told John Tracy Ellis: "I have been following the Catholic University embarrassment closely because it pains me deeply . . . and this at a time when Vatican II is hopefully opening up the Catholic mind instead of wrapping it in disciplinary cellophane." ACUA: Ellis Papers, Hallinan to Ellis, February 27, 1963.

Apparently Hallinan (then a trustee only six months) made no protest over this incident, but he was delighted with the blistering letter which Cardinal Ritter sent to the rector, in which he told him:

"I am profoundly dismayed that the officials of a citadel of learning could fail to realize the slur on the reputations of these four eminent and orthodox priests by ruling them unacceptable 'at this time.'

Finally I believe that the spirit of the Second Vatican Council has been compromised by this decision. It is tragic that, at the very time Pope John has led the Church into an ecumenical dialogue, the Catholic University has shown unmistakable signs of fear over an exchange of views among Catholics.

I am sure you realize, dear Monsignor, that it is my interest and concern for the Catholic University that has prompted me to set forth my views in this manner. A great institution must uphold its tradition." Hallinan Papers in the possession of Cardinal Bernardin, Ritter to McDonald, February 19, 1963, copy.

[7]Donald Foust, "Parish Without Bounds," *Commonweal* 86 (August 25, 1967): 514-515.

[8]*National Catholic Reporter,* June 9,1967. ACUA, Ellis Papers, Hallinan to Ellis, July 19, 1967.

[9]Diary, January 2-9, 17, 22; February 1, 1968.

[10]Diary, February 4, 5, 1968.

[11]AAA, Bernardin, Homily for the funeral of Archbishop Paul J. Hallinan, Atlanta, April 1, 1968.

[12]AAA, Hallinan to Dearden, February 20,1968, copy.

[13]John Tracy Ellis, "Archbishop Hallinan: In Memoriam," *Thought* 43 (1968): 544; Eugene Best, "As I Remember Him," *The Newsletter,* Cleveland Newman Alumni Association, June 1968, p. 12; Theodore Marszal, "Pastor in the Age of Renewal," p. 60; AAA, Hallinan to Malone, March 18, 1968, copy.

[14]AAA, Bernardin, funeral homily for Hallinan.

[15]*Georgia Bulletin,* March 29, 1968.

[16]AAA, Hallinan, Last Will and Testament, Atlanta, July 18,1967. He also gave his personal physician, Dr. Joseph Wilber, authority to use his body for medical experimentation, and he donated his eyes to an eye-bank.

[17]*America* 118 (April 13, 1968): 469.

[18]AAA, Bernardin, funeral homily for Hallinan. In accordance with the directions in his will, the archbishop was buried in the priests' section of Arlington Cemetery in Atlanta.

[19]AAA, Healy to Bernardin, April 1, 1968; Casey to Bernardin, March 28, 1968; Aelred Tegels, O.S.B., "Chronicle," *Worship* 42 (May 1968): 309.

[20]AAA, Corson to Christopher Eckl, Managing Editor of the *Georgia Bulletin,* April 2, 1968; Pelikan to Reverend Fathers and Brethren, March 27, 1968; Statement of William B. Schwartz, Jr., Chairman of the Atlanta Chapter of the American Jewish Committee on the Death of Archbishop Hallinan, n.d. [April 2, 1968].

[21]Ralph McGill, "Death Comes for the Archbishop," *Atlanta Constitution,* March 29, 1968.

[22]Michael J. McNally, *Catholicism in South Florida 1868-1968* (Gainesville: University of Florida Press, 1982), pp. 76-84. On the other hand, Hurley displayed none of the leadership which Hallinan showed in such areas as civil rights, ecumenism and the liturgy.

[23]The statistics are taken from *The Official Catholic Directory,* 1958, 1962, 1968.

[24]AAA, Hallinan, Foreword to the Annual Report of the Secretary for Education of the Archdiocese of Atlanta, June 30, 1967.

[25]Interview with Cardinal Bernardin, *ibid.*

[26]Interview with the Reverend James Connolly, Yonkers, New York, October 16, 1986.

[27]AAA, Eugene Carroll, Director of Public Relations for the Methodist Church in Georgia, to Hallinan, March 21, 1968.

[28]Hallinan, "The Myth of the Monolith," *Continuum* 2 (1964-1965): 601-602.

[29]Interview with John Cardinal Dearden, Detroit, October 14, 1986.

[30]Interview with the Reverend Monsignor Noel Burtenshaw, former Chancellor of the Archdiocese of Atlanta, Atlanta, June 18, 1985.

Bibliographical Essay

Manuscript Sources

Archbishop Hallinan's papers and correspondence have not been well preserved. The Hallinan Papers in the archives of the Archdiocese of Atlanta are scarcely sufficient to fill a single filing cabinet. Some of his papers were dispersed at his death; others were apparently lost in a fire shortly thereafter at the Atlanta chancery office. The remaining Hallinan Papers in Atlanta consist largely of manuscript copies of his sermons and talks, memorabilia from his early years, memoranda and directives to the clergy of the archdiocese, newspaper clippings and documentation on the Atlanta synod of 1966. The Hallinan Papers in the archives of the Diocese of Charleston are more numerous and were useful for tracing his preparations for the integration of the Catholic schools and hospitals of the diocese. Neither in Atlanta nor in Charleston is there a chronological collection of Hallinan's correspondence; in both archives, his letters are scattered among various collections and filed according to topic.

Unfortunately for the historian, in Atlanta Hallinan often used the telephone rather than the pen in communicating with such friends as Frederick McManus in Washington and Joseph Bernardin in Charleston. Thus, there are many letters from McManus to Hallinan on matters pertaining to the liturgy, but relatively few replies in writing from Hallinan. Likewise, his communication with Bernardin seems to have been done almost entirely by telephone. For example, on his return to Atlanta from the Second Vatican Council on December 14, 1962, Hallinan spent an hour on the telephone with Bernardin, but all that survives of his conversation is the mention of it in his diary.

Joseph Bernardin was Hallinan's executor, and he retained possession of Hallinan's diaries and some other papers. They are now in the Cardinal's residence in Chicago, where he kindly gave me permission to use them. The diaries are especially revealing for Hallinan's views on the civil rights movement and for his reaction to events at the

Second Vatican Council. They need to be used with caution, however, for Hallinan sometimes made entries weeks after the events that he was recording and he was not always accurate about dates. Hallinan kept a diary from the beginning of 1955 until six weeks before his death. For the first few years his comments were rather brief; but, on New Year's Day of 1960, he noted how often he had "cussed out" Bishop Gilmour because *his* diary was so cryptic, and from that point on, his own entries became considerably more informative. Regrettably, these diaries are not complete: there are several gaps, due mainly to Hallinan's illness in his later years. (There are no entries for the periods: March 1—December 31, 1955; April 22—December 31, 1956; October 26, 1964—March 16, 1965; December 14, 1966—February 9, 1967; February 16—March 27, 1968.) Cardinal Bernardin also possesses numerous newspaper clippings which Hallinan made for his own use as well as some important correspondence between Hallinan and the Roman authorities with regard to the liturgy.

There are many valuable items among the Hallinan Papers in the possession of Father Theodore Marszal, the administrator of the Cathedral of St. John the Evangelist in Cleveland. This collection includes essays and poems from Hallinan's college days, parish bulletins and newsletters which he wrote as a young curate in Cleveland, and two memoirs of his experiences as a chaplain in World War II. Father Marszal also has in his possession important correspondence relating to Hallinan's role in the civil rights movement both in Charleston and in Atlanta, all of which he was most generous in sharing with me. Sister Mary Laurent Duggan, C.S.J., Chancery Administrator of the Diocese of Savannah, furnished me with copies of the correspondence between Hallinan and Bishop Thomas McDonough, which was helpful in tracing the collaboration of the two bishops on many aspects of the civil rights movement.

For Hallinan's years as a young priest, the archives of the Diocese of Cleveland were useful mainly for a few letters pertaining to his work in the Newman movement, especially his efforts to establish a Newman club at Baldwin Wallace College in Berea. Hallinan gave a rather lengthy description of his wartime service in the memoirs mentioned above. Additional information was found in the National Archives of the United States, which contain Hallinan's monthly chaplain's reports and evaluations of him by his superior officers. I am grateful to Mr. Richard Boylan of the National Archives for calling my attention to the Operations Reports of the 542 Boat and Shore Regiment of the Army engineers, which mention Hallinan's heroism in the capture of Biak Island from the Japanese.

The archives of the Catholic University of America contain a vast quantity of documents from the files of the National Catholic Welfare Conference, most of it unprocessed and only roughly catalogued. However, Box 101 of this collection contains a well-organized selection of letters, memoranda and newsletters pertaining to the National Federation of Newman Clubs and the National Association of Newman Club Chaplains during the period (1952-1954) when Hallinan was National Chaplain of the Federation and President of the Chaplains' Association. The Ellis Papers in the archives of the Catholic University of America contain numerous letters between Hallinan and Ellis for the years 1955-1968, and they were often valuable for Hallinan's candid comments on a wide variety of topics.

At Hallinan's death, Joseph Bernardin deposited in the archives of the United States Catholic Conference most of Hallinan's extensive correspondence stemming from his position on the Bishops' Commission on the Liturgical Apostolate and its successor, the Bishops' Committee on the Liturgy. This is the largest single collection of Hallinan Papers, spanning the years 1963 to 1968 and furnishing detailed information about the part that he played in implementing the liturgical changes in the United States. For Hallinan's participation in the Second Vatican Council, especially his contribution to the Commission on the Sacred Liturgy, the Paul J. Hallinan Vatican Council II Papers in the archives of the Catholic University of America are indispensable. The archives of the International Commission on English in the Liturgy also contain valuable information about Hallinan's role in the formation of that organization. The archives of the Liturgical Conference may also contain relevant material, but a spokesman for that organization said that their archives were not open to the public.

Interviews

Mr. Ivan Allen Jr., former Mayor of Atlanta, Atlanta, Georgia, April 28, 1986.

*The Reverend Charles Albright, C.S.P., former Coordinating Secretary of the Newman Apostolate, Columbus, Ohio, May 23, 1986.

Joseph Cardinal Bernardin, Archbishop of Chicago, Chicago, Illinois, October 3, 1985.

Mr. Eugene Best, former Director of the Intercollegiate Newman Clubs of Cleveland, Poughkeepsie, New York, February 25, 1986.

The Reverend William Burn, archivist of the Diocese of Charleston, Charleston, South Carolina, June 20, 1985.

The Reverend Monsignor Noel Burtenshaw, former Chancellor of the Archdiocese of Atlanta, Atlanta, Georgia, June 18, 1985.

*The Reverend Richard Butler, O.P., former National Chaplain of the National Newman Club Federation, River Forest, Illinois, April 9, 1986.

The Reverend Nelson Callahan, priest of the Diocese of Cleveland, Bay Village, Ohio, December 10, 1985.

*The Reverend Thomas A. Carlin, O.S.F.S., former Executive Secretary of the National Newman Club Federation, Wilmington, Delaware, March 10, 1986.

The Reverend James Connolly, priest of the Archdiocese of New York, Yonkers, New York, October 16, 1986.

*The Reverend Monsignor Thomas C. Corrigan, former Director of the Intercollegiate Newman Clubs of Cleveland, Parma, Ohio, March 10, 1986.

Mr. Jack Daniels, resident of Painesville, Painesville, Ohio, December 11, 1985.

John Cardinal Dearden, former Archbishop of Detroit, Detroit, Michigan, October 14, 1986.

*Mr. George Garrelts, former National Chaplain of the National Newman Club Federation, Erie, Pennsylvania, May 21, 1986.

*Mr. Arthur Hallinan, brother of Archbishop Hallinan, Chandler, Arizona, January 25, 1986.

Sister Katherine Harrison, C.S.J., former parishioner of St. Aloysius Parish, Cleveland, Parma Heights, Ohio, December 10, 1985.

*The Reverend Caspar A. Heimann, former curate at the Cathedral of St. John the Evangelist, Cleveland, Berea, Ohio, February 27, 1986.

Miss Bessie Judkins, resident of Painesville, Painesville, Ohio, December 11, 1986.

*Colonel Robert Kasper, United States Army (retired), former Commanding Officer of the 542nd Boat and Shore Regiment, United States Army Engineers, Mercer Island, Washington, February 18, 1986.

*The Reverend Monsignor Norman Kelley, classmate of Archbishop Hallinan at St. Mary Our Lady of the Lake Seminary, Cleveland, Lake Milton, Ohio, February 19, 1986.

*The Reverend John Kilcoyne, former Director of the Intercollegiate Newman Clubs of Cleveland, Cleveland, Ohio, February 28, 1986.

*The Reverend Robert Knuff, former Newman Club chaplain at Baldwin Wallace College, Euclid, Ohio, February 28, 1986.

John Cardinal Krol, Archbishop of Philadelphia, Philadelphia, Pennsylvania, October 4, 1986.

*Sister Mary Colette Link, H.M., native of Painesville, Painesville, Ohio, January 27, 1986.

Miss Agnes Lynch, first cousin of Archbishop Hallinan, Fairview Park, Ohio, December 10, 1985.

Mr. and Mrs. John Maloney, former parishioners of St. Aloysius Parish, Cleveland, Rocky River, Ohio, December 11, 1985.

Mrs. Clare McIvor, first cousin of Archbishop Hallinan, Fairview Park, Ohio, December 10, 1985.

The Reverend Monsignor Frederick R. McManus, former Executive Secretary of the Bishops' Committee on the Liturgy, Washington, D.C., August 16, 1985.

*The Reverend Raymond O. Meier, former chaplain of the 532nd Boat and Shore Regiment, United States Army Engineers, Oil City, Pennsylvania, February 18, 1986.

*The Reverend James Reymann, former member of the Newman Club of Case Institute of Technology, Cleveland, Wellington,

Ohio, February 27, 1986.

*Mr. Paul Sebian, resident of Painesville, Painesville, Ohio, January 30, 1986.

*The Reverend Monsignor Thomas Sebian, former resident of Painesville, LaBelle, Florida, January 23, 1986.

*Mr. Gerard Sherry, former editor of the *Georgia Bulletin,* Las Vegas, Nevada, June 17, 1986.

*The Reverend Monsignor Alexander Sigur, former National Chaplain of the National Newman Club Federation, Lafayette, Louisiana, June 17, 1986.

The Reverend Monsignor Louis Sterker, former administrator of the Cathedral of St. John the Baptist, Charleston, Columbia, South Carolina, April 27, 1986.

Mr. and Mrs. Henry Tecklenburg, friends of Archbishop Hallinan in Charleston, Sullivan's Island, South Carolina, April 26, 1986.

The Reverend Henry Tevlin, C.O., former Pastor of St. Mary's Church, Rock Hill, South Carolina, Charlotte, North Carolina, April 30, 1986.

*The Reverend Francis Zwilling, former curate at St. Aloysius Parish, Cleveland, St. Petersburg, Florida, January 22, 1986.

* Telephone interview

Writings of Hallinan

Neither of Hallinan's two projected books on the Second Vatican Council was ever written. Nor did he find a publisher for his 500-page doctoral dissertation, "Richard Gilmour: Second Bishop of Cleveland 1872-1891" (Ph.D. dissertation, Western Reserve University, 1963). After his death a selection of his sermons, addresses and pastoral letters was edited by Vincent A. Yzermans, *Days of Hope and Promise* (Collegeville: The Liturgical Press,1973). In addition to "The Archbishop's Notebook," his regular column in the *Georgia Bulletin,* he wrote a popular little pamphlet, *How to Understand Changes in the Liturgy* (Atlanta: Georgia Bulletin Publications, 1964). The Lenten pastoral letter of 1961 (on integration) was published in the *Interracial Review* 34 (April 1961): 103-104; his last pastoral letter in Charleston, "The Ecumenical Catholic," was published in the *Catholic Mind* 61 (December 1963): 53-57; a sermon on St. Benedict, delivered at St. Vincent's Archabbey in Latrobe, Pennsylvania, appeared in the *American Benedictine Review* 19 (March 1968): 69-72; and his last address on the liturgy, "Toward a People's Liturgy," was published in *Worship* 42 (May 1968): 258-262.

In his own field of history, he reviewed James J. Hennesey's *The First Council of the Vatican: The American Experience* in the *Catholic Historical Review* 51 (October 1965): 379-383; and he wrote a foreword to John Tracy Ellis' *Perspectives in American Catholicism* (Baltimore: Helicon, 1963). During his last few years he also contributed articles on a wide variety of subjects to many Catholic newspapers, magazines and periodicals. They are listed below in chronological order: "That New Strictly American Religion," *Information* 75 (November 1961): 24-28; "The Vocation Image," *Homiletic and Pastoral Review* 62 (April 1962): 660; "Your Job as a Christian Layman," *Maryknoll* 57 (January 1963): 25-28; "An American View," *Worship* 37 (August-September 1963): 547-550; "On Veneration of Mary," Davenport *Catholic Messenger,* October 10, 1963; "On the Index," *Magnificat* 112 (December

1963): 29-30; "Toward Our Destiny: An Interview with Gerard E. Sherry," *Sign* 43 (January 1964): 14-17; "The Ecumenical Movement in the United States of America," *Catholic Mind* 62 (January 1964): 16-21; "The Bishop as Publisher," *The Catholic Journalist* 15 (September 1964): 3-5; "The Corporal Works of Mercy," *Ave Maria* 100 (October 17, 1964): 5-8; "Mercy in the Missionary Church," *Spiritual Life* 10 (spring 1964): 12-15; "Liturgy," *Catholic Mind* 62 (December 1964): 49-54; "One World One Word," *America* 113 (April 28, 1965): 202-204; "The Informed Catholic Layman," *Catholic Mind* 63 (October 1965): 4-10; "The Myth of the Monolith," *Continuum* 2 (1964-1965): 590-605; "The Catholic Woman: Is She at Home in the Church?," *Sign* 45 (January 1966): 16-17; "God Dead but Christ Lives," *Catholic Mind* 64 (October 1966): 2-4; "The Common Goal," *America* 116 (January 7, 1967): 11-14; "A Second Mile for Peace," *Extension* 62 (August 1967): 20-21; "A Time to Create," *Commonweal* 87 (October 13,1967): 47-49; "Faith and the Human Condition," *Ave Maria* 106 (November 18, 1967): 28-30; "Archbishop Admits He Was Wrong," *Critic* 26 (April-May 1968): 30-31; "Experiments in Liturgy," *Catholic Mind* 68 (May 1968): 8-11; "Is A Bishop Eligible?," *Triumph* 3 (May 1968): 42.

Works About Hallinan

There is no full-length biography of Hallinan. However, Cardinal Bernardin provided a vivid portrait in his foreword to Yzermans' *Days of Hope and Promise.* John Tracy Ellis did the same in greater detail in his introduction to Yzermans' volume (pp. i-xxiii) and in "Archbishop Hallinan: In Memoriam," *Thought* 43 (1968): 539-572, in both instances drawing upon Hallinan's unpublished writings and his own correspondence with him. The most extensive treatment of Hallinan's life and work is to be found in Theodore Marszal, "Pastor in the Age of Renewal: The Life and Spirituality of Paul J. Hallinan, Archbishop of Atlanta, Georgia" (Ph.D. dissertation, Pontifical Gregorian University, 1980). The first two chapters of this dissertation, containing a well-documented biography of Hallinan, were published separately: Theodore Marszal, *Pastor in the Age of Renewal: The Life and Spirituality of Paul J. Hallinan, Archbishop of Atlanta, Georgia (U.S.A.)* (Rome: Pontifical Gregorian University, 1981). Also valuable are the personal recollections of the archbishop by many of those who knew him as a Newman club chaplain in Cleveland in *The Newsletter,* Cleveland Newman Alumni Association, June 1968, pp. 1-23.

Newspapers, Magazines and Periodicals

The *Catholic Banner* of Charleston and the *Georgia Bulletin* of Atlanta, the newspapers of those two sees, are indispensable for information about Hallinan's activities in each diocese. The *Catholic Universe Bulletin,* the newspaper of the Diocese of Cleveland, was useful for occasional mention of Hallinan's work in the Newman movement. In Charleston, Thomas Waring, the editor of the *News and Courier,* was an outspoken segregationist and crossed swords with Hallinan several times on civil rights issues. By contrast, in Atlanta, Ralph McGill, publisher of the *Constitution,* frequently voiced support for Hallinan's policies on integration and racial justice.

In order to sample editorial reaction to Hallinan's stand on racial issues, the following South Carolina newspapers were also consulted (at the library of the University of South Carolina in Columbia): Aiken *Standard and Review;* Anderson *Independent;* Beaufort *Gazette;* Charleston *Evening Post;* Cheraw *Chronicle;* Columbia *State;* Florence *Morning News;* Georgetown *Times;* Greenville *News;* Greenville *Piedmont;* Marion *Star;* Rock Hill *Evening Herald;* Sumter *Daily Item;* Spartanburg *Herald;* Spartanburg *Journal.*

For similar purposes, the following Georgia newspapers were consulted (at the library of the University of Georgia in Athens): Athens *Banner Herald;* Atlanta *World;* Augusta *Chronicle;* Columbus *Enquirer;* Dalton *Daily News;* Macon *Telegraph;* Rome *News Tribune;* Savannah *Morning News;* Savannah *Evening News;* Valdosta *Daily Times:* Waycross *Journal Herald.*

The Painesville *Telegraph* contains many fascinating vignettes of Paul Hallinan's home town during his boyhood years. The *Historical Society Quarterly* of Lake County was useful for information about the nursery industry in Lake County. The *Needle,* the newspaper founded by Hallinan as the voice of the Intercollegiate Newman Clubs of Cleveland, provides many glimpses of the local Newman movement in the late 1940's and early 1950's. An incomplete collection of the newspaper is available at the Hallinan Catholic Center at Case Western

Reserve University in Cleveland. *Southern School News,* the official publication of the Southern Education Reporting Service, was established by Southern newspaper editors after the Supreme Court decision of 1954 outlawing segregation in public schools. It is a convenient and reliable source of information on the progress of school desegregation during the 1950's and 1960's.

America, Commonweal, Worship, Continuum and the *National Catholic Reporter* were useful for liberal Catholic reaction to the Second Vatican Council and to the liturgical changes in the United States. *Notitiae,* the official organ of the Consilium ad Exsequendam Constitutionem de Sacra Liturgia, contains the text of several important decisions and explanations issued during the period of Hallinan's involvement with the liturgy.

Secondary Works

For information on Lake County in the early twentieth century, two recent popular histories are helpful: Harry Forest Lupold, *The Latch String Is Out: A Pioneer History of Lake County* (Mentor: Lakeland Community College Press, 1974); and *Here Is Lake County* (Cleveland: Howard Allen, 1964). Several older works are still valuable for their references to Painesville: John Struthers Stewart, *History of Northeastern Ohio* (Indianapolis: Historical Publishing Company, 1935), Vol. I; and L.B. Hills, *Lake County Illustrated* (Painesville: The Herald Printing Company, 1912). Also useful is the *Lake County History Compiled by the Workers of the Writers Program of the Works Projects Administration in the State of Ohio* (Columbus: The Ohio State Archaeological and Historical Society, 1941). On Painesville itself, it is worth comparing the brief descriptions in N. Church (ed.), *Painesville City Directory 1902-1903* (Painesville: The Herald, 1903), and *Painesville City Directory* (Painesville: Mullin Kille Company and Educational Supply Company, 1940). The origins of the Catholic Church in Lake County are mentioned in W.A. Jurgens, *A History of the Diocese of Cleveland* (Cleveland: Diocese of Cleveland, 1980), I, 539-540; and Michael J. Hynes, *History of the Diocese of Cleveland* (Cleveland: Diocese of Cleveland, 1953), pp. 76-77.

For the resurgence of bigotry in the United States in the 1920's, see John Higham, *Strangers in the Land: Patterns of American Nativism*

1860-1925 (New Brunswick: Rutgers University Press, 1955: reprint ed., New York: Atheneum, 1981), pp. 264-331. For the activities of the Ku Klux Klan, both Kenneth T. Jackson, *The Klan in the City 1915-1930* (New York: Oxford University Press, 1967) and David Chalmers, *Hooded Americanism* (Garden City: Doubleday and Company, 1965) are useful. On the history of the Western Reserve, see Beverly W. Bond, Jr., *The Foundations of Ohio* (Columbus: The Ohio State Archaeological and Historical Society, 1941), pp. 252-253, pp. 358-371, Vol. I of *The History of the State of Ohio,* ed. Carl Wittke (Columbus: The Ohio State Archaeological and Historical Society, 1941-1944), 6 vols., and Harlan Hatcher, *The Western Reserve: The Story of New Connecticut in Ohio* (Cleveland: The World Publishing Company, 1966).

For Hallinan's college years at the University of Notre Dame, see the readable popular history of that institution: Francis Wallace, *Notre Dame: Its People and Its Legends* (New York: David McKay Company, 1969). On Father John O'Hara, there is a sympathetic but not uncritical biography: Thomas T. McAvoy, C.S.C., *Father O'Hara of Notre Dame* (Notre Dame: University of Notre Dame Press,1967). O'Hara spelled out his own ideas on the spiritual formation of Catholic college students in "Report of the Prefect of Religion to the Very Reverend Charles L. O'Donnell, C.S.C., President of the University of Notre Dame" and "A Description of the System Employed in Developing the Spiritual Life of the Students of the University of Notre Dame," *Official Bulletin of the University of Notre Dame* 25 (January 1930): 3-18.

There is no adequate history of modern Cleveland, but there is an enormous amount of factual material in the lengthy chronicle of William Ganson Rose, *Cleveland: The Making of a City* (Cleveland: The World Publishing Company, 1950. Less detailed but still useful are: Philip W. Porter, *Cleveland: Confused City on a Seesaw* (n.d.: Ohio State University Press, 1976; George E. Condon, *Yesterday's Cleveland* (Miami: E.A.Seeman Publishing Company, 1976); Sidney Andorn, *The Cleveland Scene, 1936-1946* (Cleveland: Sidney Andorn, 1946); and Robert I. Kutak, *Manual of Cleveland* (Cleveland: The Weidenthal Company, 1927).

A good sociological profile of St. Aloysius Parish can be gleaned from United States Bureau of the Census, *Sixteenth Census of the United States, 1940: Population and Housing Statistics for Census*

Tracts: Cleveland, Ohio, and Adjacent Areas (Washington, D.C.: United States Government Printing Office, 1942). A local demographer, Howard Whipple Green, provided two helpful guides to population changes in the city in *Population Characteristics by Census Tracts* (Cleveland: The Plain Dealer Publishing Company, 1931), and *Population by Census Tracts: Cleveland and Vicinity with Street Index* (Cleveland: Cleveland Health Council, 1931). There is a brief history of the Catholic Church in the Glenville section of Cleveland in Robert M. Mendelken, "The Catholic Church and Glenville" (M. Div. dissertation: St. Mary Our Lady of the Lake Seminary, 1970), pp. 17-20; and Ralph Wiatrowski has sketched the history of the cathedral parish in *Cathedral of St. John the Evangelist* (Cleveland: Cathedral of St. John the Evangelist, 1978). Some indication of the ethnic composition of Cleveland can be gotten from Lloyd Gartner, *History of the Jews of Cleveland* (n.p.: Western Reserve Historical Society and the Jewish Theological Society of America, 1978); Nelson J. Callahan and William F. Hickey, *Irish Americans and Their Communities of Cleveland* (n.p.: Cleveland State University, 1978); and Wellington G. Fordyce, "Immigrant Institutions in Cleveland," *The Ohio State Archaeological and Historical Society Quarterly* 47 (1938): 87-103.

A readable, but not always accurate, account of military and naval operations in the Southwest Pacific during World War II is available in (Lieutenant General) Robert L. Eichelberger, *Jungle Road to Tokyo* (London: Odham Press Ltd., 1951). The campaigns can be followed in more detail in the official Australian and American histories: Lionel Wigmore: *The Japanese Thrust: Australia in the War of 1939-1945* (Canberra: The Australian War Memorial, 1957), series I, Vol. IV: David Dexter, *The New Guinea Offensive: Australia in the War of 1939-1945* (Canberra: The Australian War Memorial, 1961), series I, Vol. VI.; Samuel Miller, *Victory in Papua: The United States Army in World War II* (Washington, D.C.: The Office of the Chief of Military History, Department of the Army, 1957); Robert Ross Smith, *The Approach to the Philippines: The United States Army in World War II* (Washington, D.C.: The Office of the Chief of Military History, Department of the Army, 1953).

A popular history of Hallinan's brigade is *History of the Second Engineers Special Brigade, United States Army, World War II* (Harrisburg: The Telegraph Press, 1946). A more satisfactory work is (Brigadier General) William F. Heavey, *Down Ramp: The Story of the*

Army Amphibian Engineers (Washington, D.C.: Infantry Journal Press, 1947). William C. Baldwin has furnished a splendid summary in *Engineers in the New Guinea Campaign 1942-1944)* (Ft. Belvoir: United States Army Engineering Center,1985). There are good descriptions of the problems of American servicemen in wartime Australia in George T. Johnston, *Pacific Partner* (New York: The World Book Company, 1944); and an American journalist, E.J. Kahn, Jr., gave a firsthand account of his experiences in *G.I. Jungle: An American Soldier in Australia and New Guinea* (New York: Simon and Schuster, 1943).

Relatively little has been published on the history of the Newman movement. An indispensable work is John Whitney Evans, *The Newman Movement: Roman Catholics in American Higher Education 1883-1971* (Notre Dame: University of Notre Dame Press, 1980). Also useful are: Martin Winfrid Davis, S.D.S., The *Sister as Campus Minister* (Washington, D.C.: Center for Applied Research in the Apostolate, 1970); and Richard Butler, O.P., *God on the Secular Campus,* which provides an informative description of the responsibilities of a Newman Club chaplain in the 1950's and 1960's. Andrew Greeley provided reassuring statistics about the fidelity of Catholic college students in "Do They Lose the Faith at Secular Colleges?," *Catholic World* 195 (June 1962): 143-148. For the growth of Western Reserve University and other colleges in the Cleveland area, see Clarence H. Cramer, *Case Western Reserve University: A History of the University 1826-1976* (Boston: Little Brown and Company, 1976). Also of interest are two pamphlets edited by Hallinan during the time that he was National Chaplain of the National Newman Club Federation and President of the National Association of Newman Club Chaplains: *Newman Club Manual* (n.p.: National Newman Club Federation, 1954), and a collection of speeches, *The Newman Club on the American Campus* (n.p.: National Association of Newman Club Chaplains, 1954). Together with Father Robert J. Welch, Hallinan wrote a short introduction to the movement, *The Newman Club in American Education* (Huntington, Indiana: National Association of Newman Club Chaplains, 1953).

A good survey of the situation in South Carolina in the 1950's and 1960's is Neal R. Peirce, *The Deep South States of America* (New York: W.W. Norton and Company, 1974), pp. 384-434. The best general history of South Carolina is Ernest McPherson Lander, *A*

History of South Carolina, 1865-1960 (Chapel Hill: University of North Carolina Press, 1960). For a more recent popular treatment, see Lewis P. Jones, *South Carolina: A Synoptic History for Laymen* (Columbia: The Sandpaper Press, 1971). Unfortunately, David Duncan Wallace's massive and misnamed tome, *South Carolina: A Short History, 1520-1948* (Columbia: University of South Carolina Press, 1961), does not reach the period of Hallinan's years in Charleston. For economic conditions in the South at that time, see Joseph Spengler, "Economic Trends and Prospects," in John C. McKinney and Edgar T. Thompson (eds.), *The South in Continuity and Change* (Durham: Duke University Press, 1965), pp. 101-131.

A good introduction to the distinctive religious climate of the South is Joseph H. Fichter and George L. Maddox, "Religion in the South, Old and New," *ibid.,* pp. 359-383. A recent survey of Catholicism in South Carolina is Richard C. Madden, *Catholics in South Carolina* (Lanham, Maryland: University Press of America, 1985). For the 140th anniversary of the Diocese of Charleston, the *Catholic Banner* published a sixty-two page supplement with several valuable articles on the history of the diocese (*Catholic Banner,* December 4, 1960). The statistics in *The Official Catholic Directory* (New York: P.J. Kenedy and Son) may be supplemented by *Churches and Church Membership in the United States: An Enumeration and Analysis by Counties, States and Regions* (New York: Bureau of Research and Survey: National Council of the Churches of Christ in the United States of America, 1957). James F. Byrnes, *All in One Lifetime* (New York: Harper and Row, 1958) are the memoirs of one of South Carolina's most distinguished politicians (and a former Catholic).

A classic exposition of Southern politics is V.O. Key, Jr., *Southern Politics in State and Nation* (New York: Vintage Books, 1949). A more recent study of the impact of the civil rights movement on Southern politics is Jack Bass and Walter DeVries, *The Transformation of Southern Politics: Social Change and Political Consequence Since 1945* (New York: The New American Library, 1977). The most thorough study of the civil rights movement in South Carolina is Howard Quint, *Profile in Black and White* (Westport, Connecticut: Greenwood Press, 1973). For the effects of the increased numbers of black voters in the South, see Donald R. Matthews and James W. Prothro, *Negroes and the New Southern Politics* (New York: Harcourt, Brace and World, 1966). White determination to maintain segregated schools is ably described in Numan V. Bartley, *The Rise of Massive Resistance: Race and Politics in the South During the 1950's* (Baton Rouge: Louisiana State University Press, 1969); Francis M. Wilhoit, *The Politics of Massive Resistance* (New York: George Braziller, 1973); and Earl Black, *Southern Governors and Civil Rights: Racial Segregation as a Campaign Issue in the Second Reconstruction* (Cambridge: Harvard University Press, 1976).

Benjamin Muse traced the evolution of the civil rights movement in the black community in *The American Negro Revolution: From Non-Violence to Black Power* (Bloomington: Indiana University Press, 1968); and Dwayne E. Walls described the flight of poor Southern blacks to the ghettos of the North in *The Chickenbone Special* (New York: Harcourt, Brace and Jovanovich, 1971). Marshall Frady, *Southerners: A Journalist's Odyssey* (New York: The New American Library, 1980), and John Bartlow Martin, *The Deep South Says Never* (Westport, Connecticut: Negro Universities Press, 1970) furnish eye-witness accounts of contemporary Southern attitudes to race relations. Thomas Waring, editor of the Charleston *News and Courier,* presented the segregationist case to a national audience in "The Southern Case Against Desegregation," *Harper's Magazine* 212 (January 1956): 39-45. William D. Workman, Jr., presented the same case in less extreme form in *The Case for the South* (Chicago: Devin Adair Company, 1960). William Bagwell studies the successful integration of one South Carolina public school district in *School Desegregation in the Carolinas: Two Case Studies: Greensboro and Greenville* (Columbia: University of South Carolina Press, 1972). By contrast, Jack Nelson and Jack Bass give a vivid account of the bloodiest incident in the civil rights movement in South Carolina in *The Orangeburg Massacre* (New York and Cleveland: The World Publishing Company, 1970).

Marshall Frady's *Wallace* (New York: The World Publishing Company, 1968) is a popular biography of the Alabama governor. Neil R. McMillen documents the role of the White Citizens' Councils in *The Citizens' Councils: Organized Resistance to the Second Reconstruction 1945-1965* (Urbana: University of Illinois Press, 1971). William A. Osborne's *The Segregated Covenant* (New York: Herder and Herder, 1967) is an unflattering sociological survey of Catholic attitudes to racial integration in both the North and the South.

A good introduction to conditions in Georgia in the 1960's is Peirce, *Deep South States,* pp. 306-379. The best recent scholarly survey is

Numan Bartley, "History of Georgia: 1940 to the Present," in *A History of Georgia,* ed. Kenneth Coleman (Athens: University of Georgia Press, 1977), pp. 339-405. Another excellent study by the same author is *From Thurmond to Wallace: Political Tendencies in Georgia 1948-1968* (Baltimore: The Johns Hopkins University Press, 1970). For the economic development of Atlanta, see Charles F. Floyd, *The Georgia Regional Economies: The Challenge of Growth* (Athens: University of Georgia Press, 1974); Bruce Galphin, "Atlanta: A New Kind of City," *Atlanta* 7 (June 1967): 47-53; Curtis Driskell, "The Force of 'Forward Atlanta,'" *Atlanta* 4 (August 1964): 37-40; and "A Decade of Drive," The Atlanta *Journal and Constitution,* January 18, 1970. For the notorious county unit system used in Democratic primary elections in Georgia, see the excellent monograph of Joseph L. Bernd, *Grass Roots Politics in Georgia* (Atlanta: Emory University Research Committee, 1960).

For the civil rights movement in Georgia, see Bass and DeVries, *The Transformation of Southern Politics;* Matthews and Prothro, *Negroes and the New Southern Politics;* Bartley, *Rise of Massive Resistance;* Wilhoit, *Politics of Massive Resistance;* and McMillen, *The Citizens' Councils.* Also valuable are Harold H. Martin, *Ralph McGill Reporter* (Boston: Little Brown and Company, 1973); Ivan Allen, Jr., with Paul Hemphill, *Mayor: Notes on the Sixties* (New York: Simon and Schuster, 1971); and Roger Williams, "The Negro in Atlanta," *Atlanta* 6 (June 1966): 25-31. An attractive popular history of Atlanta is Franklin M. Garratt, *Yesterday's Atlanta* (Miami: E.A. Seeman Publishing Company, 1974); and still useful is *Atlanta: A City of the Modern South* (Atlanta: Board of Education of the City of Atlanta, 1942).

An informative essay on the state of religion in Georgia is Earl D.C. Brewer's "Religion in Georgia," in William H. Schabacker, Russell S. Clark, Homer C. Cooper (eds.), *Focus on the Future of Georgia* (Atlanta: Georgia Department of Education, 1970), pp. 281-302. For statistics on the Catholic Church in Georgia, see *The Official Catholic Directory, Churches and Church Membership,* 1957, and Douglas W. Johnson, Paul R. Picard, Bernard Quinn, *Churches and Church Membership in the United States: 1971* (Washington, D.C.: Glenmary Research Center, 1974). There is no adequate history of the Catholic Church in Georgia: the most detailed general work is a century old: James J. O'Connell, O.S.B., *Catholicity in the Carolinas and Georgia:*

Leaves of Its History (New York: D. and J. Sadlier Company, 1879). It may be supplemented by Robert R. Otis "Highlights of the Life of Father Thomas O'Reilly," *Atlanta Historical Bulletin* 8 (October 1945): 13-27; Michael Gannon, *Rebel Bishop: The Life and Era of Augustine Verot* (Milwaukee: The Bruce Publishing Company, 1964), pp. 183-191; Philip N. Racine, "The Ku Klux Klan, Anti-Catholicism and the Atlanta Board of Education," *Georgia Historical Quarterly* 57 (1963): 63-75; R. Donald Kiernan, "Georgia Laymen's Association," *Georgia Bulletin,* January 21, 1965; "History of the Archdiocese of Atlanta," *Georgia Bulletin,* April 28, 1966; Edward J. Cashin, "Thomas E. Watson and the Catholic Laymen's Association of Georgia" (Ph.D. dissertation: Fordham University, 1962); and three short pamphlets written by Hallinan, *The Mind of the Archdiocese, The Heart of the Archdiocese,* and *The Voice of the Archdiocese* (Atlanta: Archdiocese of Atlanta, 1964).

There is a vast literature on the Second Vatican Council. The text of the decrees as well as the written and spoken interventions of the Council Fathers is printed in *Acta Synodalia Sacrosancti Concilii Oecumenici Vaticani II* (Vatican City: Typis Polyglottis Vaticanis, 1970-1980), 23 vols. A valuable guide is Floyd Anderson (ed.), *Council Daybook, Vatican II, Session 1, October 11 to December 8, 1962; Session 2, September 29 to December 4, 1963* (Washington, D.C.: National Catholic Welfare Conference, 1965); *Council Daybook, Vatican II, Session 3, September 14 to November 21, 1964* (Washington, D.C.: National Catholic Welfare Conference, 1965); *Council Daybook, Session 4, September 14 to December 8, 1965* (Washington, D.C.: National Catholic Welfare Conference, 1966). A readable (although partisan) contemporary account of the Council is the four-volume Xavier Rynne, *Letters from Vatican City: Vatican Council II (First Session): Background and Debates* (New York: Farrar, Straus and Company, 1963); *The Second Session: The Debates and Decrees of Vatican Council II, September 29 to December 4, 1963* (New York: Farrar, Straus and Company, 1964); *The Third Session: The Debates and Decrees of Vatican Council II: September 14 to November 21, 1964* (New York: Farrar, Straus and Company, 1965); *The Fourth Session: The Debates and Decrees of Vatican Council II, September 14 to December 8, 1965* (New York: Farrar, Straus and Giroux, 1966). The role of the American bishops at the Council is carefully documented by Vincent A. Yzermans in *American Participation in the*

Second Vatican Council (New York: Sheed and Ward, 1967). Hallinan's friend, Bishop Robert E. Tracy, described his own impressions of the Council in *American Bishop at the Vatican Council* (New York: McGraw Hill, 1966); and Frederick McManus has provided a succinct account of the origins of the International Committee on English in the Liturgy in *ICEL: The First Years* (Washington, D.C.: International Committee on English in the Liturgy, 1981).

The "Chronicle" in *Worship* is a good source for tracing the progress of the liturgical changes as they occurred in the United States in the years after the Second Vatican Council. The published proceedings of the annual North American Liturgical Weeks provide valuable indications of the issues that were of interest to liturgists at the time. Especially useful are: *The Challenge of the Council: Person, Parish, World: Twenty-Fifth Annual North American Liturgical Week: St. Louis, Mo.: August 24-27, 1964* (Washington, D.C.: The Liturgical Conference, 1964); *Jesus Christ Reforms His Church: Twenty-Sixth Annual North American Liturgical Week: Baltimore, June 21-24, 1965; Portland, Oregon, August 16-19, 1965; Chicago, August 30-September 2, 1965* (Washington, D.C.: The Liturgical Conference, 1966); *Experiments and Community: Twenty-Eighth Annual North American Liturgical Week: Kansas City, August 12-24, 1967* (Washington, D.C.: The Liturgical Conference, 1967).

A popular account of Catholic radicalism in the 1960's and 1970's by one of the participants is Charles A. Meconis, *With Clumsy Grace: The American Catholic Left 1961-1975* (New York: The Seabury Press, 1979). A well-documented history of Catholicism in Hallinan's neighboring diocese to the South is Michael J. McNally, *Catholicism in South Florida 1868-1968* (Gainesville: University of Florida Press, 1982).

Index